HARRY BRELSFORD'S SMB SERIES

Microsoft Small Business Server 2008 Blueprint

Harry Brelsford and Philip Elder

SMB Nation, Inc

SMB Nation Press
12715 Miller Road NE
Suite 202
Bainbridge Island, WA 98110
206-201-2943

10 9 8 7 6 5 4 3 2

Printed in the United States of America

ISBN10: 0-9770949-9-5

ISBN13: 978-0-9770949-9-8

Cover Design: Mike Young
Editor: Vicki McCown
Interior Layout: Stephanie Martindale
Proofreader: Cyndi Moody
Indexing: Carolyn Acheson

To all the SMB consultants out there!

Contents

SECTION TWO - Extending Small Business Server 2008

SECTION FOUR - Small Business Server 2008 Advance Topics

About The Authors

This book was written by two authors: Philip Elder and Harry Brelsford.

Philip Elder

Philip has been involved with Small Business Server since the BackOffice SBS 4.x days. He has worked in the SMB market for most of his I.T career. With the advent of SBS 2003, the SMB market became the primary focus due to the SBS 2003 feature set providing the best possible value to SMBs.

In 2003, Monique and Philip Elder started MPECS Inc. with the company's primary market focus being the 5-35 seat market. Solutions provided to MPECS Inc. clients were based around Microsoft software products such as Small Business Server, Windows Server, Microsoft desktop OSs including Windows XP and Windows Vista, and Microsoft Office products. A number of different hardware manufacturers were used, though the primary server and workstation products were and still are based on Intel branded motherboards and CPUs.

In an effort to set MPECS Inc. apart from the competition, Philip challenged and passed the Microsoft Designing, Deploying and Managing a Network Solution for the Small and Medium-sized Business 70-282 exam in November 2005. With MPECS Inc. already a Microsoft Partner and the 70-282 exam successfully challenged, he successfully challenged the Microsoft Partner Microsoft Small Business Specialist online exam. With these two prerequisites accomplished along with the other needed steps, MPECS Inc. became a Microsoft Small Business Specialist company in November of 2005.

With knowledge comes responsibility. It is with that thought in mind that Monique and Philip decided that Philip should start sharing that knowledge via a blog in January of 2007.

Some of Philip's accomplishments:

- MPECS Inc. Blog started in January 2007: http://blog.mpecsinc.ca
- Initiated and leads an SMB/SBS focused sub group of the Edmonton Microsoft User Group.
- SBS 2008 article in SMB Nation's SMB PC Magazine for June/July 2008.
- SBS 2008 Blueprint co-author with Harry Brelsford published November 2008.
- Numerous SMB Nation and Microsoft online Webinar Presentations on SBS 2008.
- Numerous in-person User Group and Webinar User Group presentations.
- Challenged and passed the TS: Windows Small Business Server 2008, Configuring 71-653 Beta Exam earning the new Microsoft Certified Technology Specialist Designation in September 2008.

Harry Brelsford

Involved with SBS since June 3rd, 1997, at 9:00am Pacific (true story!), approximately half a year before its commercial release, Harry Brelsford is a longtime SBSer. His SBS accomplishments include:

- As a SBS consultant, he served a wide and diverse group of clients, including Contra Costa Cardiology, Wallace Properties, EIS Group, the Peace Corps, and CainSweet.
- Founding the SMB Nation tribe (www.smbnation.com) which is focused on SBS and the broader SMB consulting community. The tribe now has

over 22,000 members. The 2008 annual conference was held in Seattle, Washington with over 600 SBSers attending! Recent "other" events include small conferences and workshops in London, New York City, Toronto, Australia, New Zealand, India, Asia, the Caribbean region, Ireland and other locations in Europe, the US, and Canada.

- Authoring numerous books and countless articles on SBS, including the Microsoft Press Small Business Server 2000 Resource Kit.

- Serving as editor and publisher of a free bi-weekly SBS newsletter titled SMB Advisory.

- Serving the Microsoft SBS team in Redmond as a vendor, participating in setup videos, and acting as the subject matter expert for Course 2301a and the advanced SBS 2000 computer-based training (CBT) module. In the SBS 2003 time frame, Harry assisted in the online course development. In the SBS 2008 time frame, Harry wrote the 1.5 day SBS 2008 sales and marketing course.

- Harry is the publisher of the monthly SMB Partner Community magazine (SMB PC) with over 35,000 readers worldwide. This publication is focused on the channel partner.

- Delivering speeches frequently on SBS at numerous venues including the Microsoft Worldwide Partner Conference (WPC). Looking back in time, early speaking engagements included Microsoft Puerto Rico Direct Access event (Spring 2001), the Gateway/Intel/ Microsoft Solutions Tour at ITEC (Fall 2001), and MCP Magazine TechMentor and SuperConference (accounting group, Chicago 2001).

Harry works from his home office on Bainbridge Island, Washington. He holds two degrees (BSBA and MBA) and numerous industry certifications: Small Business Specialist (SBSC), MCSE, MCT, CNE-retired, CLSE, CNP. The author of 17 books on technology topics, Harry can be reached at harryb@smbnation.com.

Acknowledgements

Where, oh where to start!

We certainly would not be here today in the SBS community without the grace and goodness of the Microsoft Small Business Server marketing and development teams. Special thanks to Dean Paron, Sean Daniel and Kevin Beares.

Thanks to the wonderful group at SMB Nation including Cyndi Moody, Jennifer Hall, Patti Passinault, Sandy Bettenhausen, Marianne Poulos and other greats both past and future (who we haven't met yet!).

Thanks to the helpers on this book including Vicki McCown, Stephanie Martindale, Alan Shrater, Carolyn Acheson and Mike Young. Good on ya!

And all the rest (that's et. al. for y'all lawyers out there).

Preface

Welcome aboard the SBS 2008 boat, mate! This book is a comprehensive guide to Microsoft Windows Small Business Server 2008 from a real world, third-party perspective. Embedded herein, you'll find the following highlights as presented in the next few sections.

Methodology

Much care has been taken to develop a sample company storyline that is presented in each chapter. Over the course of the book, and we suspect several weeks of reading and practice, you'll successfully set up the SBS 2008 network for Springer Spaniels Limited (SPRINGERS), a 10+ employee fictional firm located on Bainbridge Island, Washington, USA. Fact of the matter is that, if you carefully follow each procedure, you'll be a bona fide SBSer within a short amount of time. All examples have been tested and include the implementation of third-party SBS solutions, such as virus detection. So, hang in there with us and this book, and you'll enjoy a completely satisfying SBS experience!

Real World

Part of the fun in writing a third-party book is that we can weave in real world scenarios, such as client war stories. Equally important, this book is written on the released version of SBS 2008 - plus a hands-on, in-the-field, ass-kicking, real-world experience. It's the type of computer book we've always wanted to write!

Microsoft SBS Team and Partner Insights

To balance our real-world SBS-isms, we've asked for and received tons of feedback from members of the SBS marketing and development teams at Microsoft. It's a win-win situation for all. They've commented on our works so that inaccuracies are stopped from hitting the printing press. And our insights from real-world SBS consulting, expressed herein, also help the SBS teams at Microsoft understand how we work with SBS. So back at ya!

Tips

Central to this book are our TIPS. These odd SBS factoids are sometimes stranger than fiction. We attempt to divulge these hard-learned lessons and little-known nuggets from SBS 2008 between the covers of this book. As a rule, each chapter has several TIPS.

Notes

We have instructed the wonderful page layout artist to insert Notes here and there on the pages of this book. That decision was made after looking at how readers have used Harry's previous technology books. These books have become tattered, dog-eared daily references with hand written notes in the margins. We've now institutionalized that positive behavior by adding Notes sections on several pages per chapter. Go ahead and doodle away. Treat this book as your journal on your SBS 2008 journey.

Usual Stuff

Oh yes! This is a book with a start, middle, and finish. It features SBS 2008 planning, setup, deployment, administration and troubleshooting issues. Each SBS 2008 component is explored in-depth, including:

- Core operating system matters with Windows Server 2008
- Messaging with Exchange Server 2007
- Collaboration and document management with Windows SharePoint Services
- Remote Web Workplace
- VPN
- Standard security with THIRD PARTY SOLUTIONS!
- Advanced security topics
- Database management with SQL Server 2008
- SBS consoles and wizards
- Client computer setup
- Shared Fax Service
- Internet Connectivity
- Outlook 2007 and Internet Explorer
- And more...

Texas and Canadian Accent

All authors like to think their books are unique, just as all homeowners feel their real estate is unique. While that's not true, one thing that helps make this book more unique than other technology tomes is Harry's written Texas accent and Philip's Canadian accent. Harry knew those days at summer camp in the Kerrville, Texas hill country would someday, some way yield royalties (literally!). Philip was blessed to be born in Canada and that has made this book much more international in flavor. Our shtick is to present SBS and SMB technology matters in a kind, nurturing, and sincere way that is friendly and affirming. Go ahead, thumb through a few pages now and see if Harry's twisted Texas tongue doesn't tickle you! Maybe Philip's CanadianSpeak does you right, eh?

Warning: HUMOR!

Let us try again to make one of our points from the last section. Consider this your first dose of expectation management. We've poured our heart, soul, and personality into this SBS 2008 tome. We look at the decision to include humor on a computer book as doing the greatest good for the greatest number. The feedback about our casual technical writing style has been overwhelmingly positive.

Organization

A lot of thought went in to the design of this book. We first looked at how we and other SBSers work in this business. Then we looked at how paying clients use SBS 2008. This resulted in four sequential sections:

Part 1: Small Business Server 2008 Deployment

This is the planning and setup section. It all starts here. Time to rock and roar!

Part 2: Extending Small Business Server 2008

SBS 2008 is, in many ways, here to help organizations function better. This section shows you how to connect securely to the Internet and configure Exchange Server 2007-based e-mail to take full advantage of Outlook 2007. You will configure the SBS 2008 sample network for remote connectivity with Remote Web Workplace and faxing. And, don't overlook our discussion on Windows Share-Point Services.

Part 3: Small Business Server Administration

After you've set up an SBS network, you need to manage it! This section explores the recurring administration tasks (daily, weekly, monthly, and annual) plus a long look at network monitoring.

Part 4: Small Business Server Advanced Topics

So, you want more out of SBS 2008, you got more! This section takes you to the next level with SBS 2008. It is here that you'll learn about advanced security topics and SQL Server 2008 (a premium component). You will also learn about the deployment of a second Windows Server 2008 machine – something your beloved SBS MVPs fought long and hard for!

Appendix Matter

You're pointed to some great SBS 2008 resources on Appendix A. Appendix Z, which was Philip's idea, provide configuration information you will find very interesting.

And don't let us forget to mention there is a photo section in this book showing SBS around the world!

High Standards

This book should more than meet your needs, surpass your expectations, and be held to the highest standards. There should be no free pass here in SBS-land. We offer these measurements for judging how successful this book is:

- **Save an hour, pay for the book.** We believe that if this book has saved you one or more hours of SBS tail-chasing, it's paid for itself. At this basic level, the time and money you invested in this book should yield high dividends.

- **Entertain you.** Life's too short not to have fun with SBS 2008. Kindly accept our good humor in the spirit that it was written. You might find yourself laughing while reading a computer book, an oxymoron if we've ever heard one!

- **"I didn't know that."** Granted, there are many things you will already know in this book. However, we are hopeful that just once (okay, maybe twice or even more) you'll utter "I didn't know that" while reading this SBS 2008 book.

- **Next steps!** This book picks up where other SBS resources end. That is, after surveying existing SBS resources and listening to feedback from other

SBSers, we've handcrafted a book that flies higher, further, and faster than many other SBS resources available to you.

Reader Feedback

As writers, we welcome and relish reader feedback. We need your feedback and, more important, the world needs your feedback. Your feedback on the SMB Nation Press book on SBS 2003 resulted in some big changes in this SBS 2008 book.

Drop us a note or post your feedback, hopefully positive, as "Reader Reviews" at the following online book reseller sites:

- Amazon: www.amazon.com
- Barnes and Noble: www.bn.com

So - turn the page! It's now time to start SBSing!

Harry Brelsford and Philip Elder

PS - As SBSers, we live by referrals. If you like what you've read in this book, please tell friends, family, and, of course, fellow SBSers! Thanks!

SECTION ONE

Small Business Server 2008 Deployment

Chapter 1
Welcome to Small Business Server 2008

Chapter 2
Small Business Server Design and Planning

Chapter 3
Small Business Server Installation

Chapter 4
Introduction to the SBS Consoles

Chapter 5
SBS 2008 Deployment

Small Business Server 2008 Photo Essay

CHAPTER 1

Welcome to Small Business Server 2008

Howdy and welcome to Microsoft Windows Small Business Server 2008, better known as *SBS*. SBS, now in its FIFTH major revision and over a decade old, solidifies Microsoft's position in the small and medium business (SMB) space. In past editions of the SBS books, written by this book's coauthor Harry Brelsford, the point was made that Microsoft was starting to "get there" technically with earlier SBS versions and beginning to understand the SMB space. With SBS 2008, such historical talk is exactly that: legacy chatter. It's time to look forward, and not only appreciate the product maturity, but also appreciate its positioning into two versions (standard and premium) with pricing that best meets the needs of different types of small businesses.

With the SBS 2008 release, it's safe to say SMBs who fit the fewer than 75 client access license (CAL) profile, are overdue to implement this solution! It's NOW time to go forth and implement SBS 2008 without the hesitations you justifiably had with the younger SBS versions such as SBS 4.x.

SBS clearly represents Microsoft's strongest commitment to the smaller seat count SMB market, which, as you will see later in the chapter, represents the largest computing market when measured by sheer number of businesses. With a single Microsoft networking product such as SBS, it is possible to "right-size" a small business networking solution, and all with one reasonably priced and powerful personal computer known as a *server*.

A properly set up SBS network can improve the way you run your business (or the way your clients run their businesses if you're an SBS/SMB consultant), help lower computing costs, provide a business disaster recovery option, and, perhaps most important, make it easier for you, the technology consultant or SBS administrator, and your users to use and enjoy computers.

Defining SBS

Exactly what is SBS? Actually, there is more than one answer to that question. We like to think of defining SBS as akin to being a tax attorney: everyone's situation is different and tax codes can be interpreted differently by different people. Note, this section speaks towards both the standard and premium editions of SBS. Specific SBS constituencies, further described below, include:

- Cost-effective, cost-efficient crowd
- Larger-than-life image crowd
- SBS feature creatures
- SBS Zen crowd
- The Big B crowd: Small BUSINESS Server
- Converters and others

TIP: Before you delve deeper into this book, there is no better time to expand on our comment in passing (above), about the standard and premium editions of SBS. The premium edition most closely resembles the long-ago predecessor SBS 2000 release in both price and bundled features and applications. It includes everything! The standard edition is much cheaper compared to the premium edition, which includes a second Windows Server 2008 Standard Edition and SQL Server 2008 licenses. Table 1-1 below defines all the SBS 2008 components, and the premium edition is discussed much more in Section Four of this book.

Cost-Effective, Cost-Efficient Crowd

SBS provides a cheap, robust, reliable, and easy-to-manage small business networking solution. The small business crowd wants to work with business applications, send and receive e-mail, print, and make sure the data is backed up and protected from viruses. Properly deployed, SBS scores high marks in these respects. SBS offers a cost-effective way of bundling *full version* Microsoft Server applications and the Windows Server 2008 operating system. Here the emphasis is on bang-for-buck, and SBS is viewed as the best Microsoft stock keeping unit (SKU) value for small business.

Larger-Than-Life Image Crowd

Presenting a larger-than-life image is the goal of some SBS clients who use SBS to look more impressive and bigger than their small business size warrants. With a high-speed Internet connection and SBS, these businesses look and act as if they are much larger entities. More than once, customers who've conducted business with these small businesses, thinking they're engaging in transactions with a larger firm, are surprised to learn it's been just three buddies, a pizza, and an SBS network all along. And get out your digital camera, for when these customers visit such an SBS site, a photograph of the look on their faces when they discover the firm that appeared to be a big-time organization is just an incredibly efficient small business, is priceless.

Another take on the larger-than-life crowd is keeping up with the Joneses. SBS is sexy and allows you to use and show off the latest Microsoft Server products. You too can be part of the hip, happenin' SBS crowd on your block.

SBS Feature Creatures

Many view SBS as a set of mini-Microsoft Servers or "mini-me" (to quote from the popular Austin Powers movie) and like to fully exploit SBS applications, such as Microsoft Exchange 2008 and SQL Server 2008 Standard Edition For Small Business (SQL Server). This group, the SBS feature creatures, are going to be most interested in Table 1-1, which is divided, as much as possible, into the server-side (the powerful computer that typically resides in a closet or workroom in a small business), hosted (in the "cloud"), and the client-side (user workstations) components. Almost to a fault, this group is sometimes more interested in SBS as a technology rather than as a device for running a more sophisticated and efficient business. That is a dangerous and ominous warning sign to beware of, as any college business professor will tell you. Anytime you start to get more excited about the technology instead of your core business, then please set the book down and take a slight break. While the SBS technology is cool, it's still a business tool.

Each SBS component is discussed further in later chapters in this book, so don't worry if you don't understand, much less master, each one right now. Such comfort levels and expertise will be developed over the next several hundred pages and in your career as a SBSer. For example, each server component is defined in great detail in its own chapter. Take Microsoft Exchange Server 2007. You'll learn much more about this e-mail messaging solution in Chapter 7.

Table 1-1
SBS Components at a Glance

Component	Description	Server, Hosted, or Client Component
Windows Server 2008 x64	Microsoft's 64-bit network operating system. An operating system controls the basic functions of a computer, including security, storage, printing, user management, remote communications, and so on. Supports built-in virtualization via Hyper-V, Active Directory, Terminal Services, Group Policy for homogeneous Windows Server 2008 networks, full Internet Protocol support (IPv6), disk quotas, advanced security such as encrypted file system (EFS) and BitLocker Drive Encryption (Premium), Network Access Protection (NAP), Integrated Identity and Access (IDA) solution, and Read-Only Domain Controller. Windows Server 2008 is necessarily discussed across many chapters in this book. Your greatest interaction with Windows Server 2008 will be during the initial setup and configuration of the SBS network.	Server

Component	Description	Server, Hosted, or Client Component
Microsoft Exchange Server 2007	64-bit e-mail messaging application used for communication and collaboration. It also supports Outlook Web Access (OWA). Improvements include security, increased storage, and stronger search capabilities (especially in Outlook Web Access). Discussed in Chapter 7.	Server
Windows SharePoint Services 3.0	An intranet Web-based portal and basic document management program discussed in Chapter 8. Here is the Microsoft explanation: *Microsoft Windows SharePoint Services 3.0 is a versatile technology that organizations and business units of all sizes can use to increase the efficiency of business processes and improve team productivity. Share internal documents, coordinate calendars, manage issues, and participate in discussions while you're on the road. Windows SharePoint Services gives people access to information they need.*	Server
Microsoft SQL Server 2008 Standard Edition	Powerful database application offered in premium edition of SBS 2008. Provides line-of-business application support. Discussed in Chapter 15.	Server

Notes:

Component	Description	Server, Hosted, or Client Component
Securty: Windows Live OneCare for Server Microsoft Forefront Security for Exchange Server	Windows Live OneCare for Server (OneCare) helps protect, maintain, and manage your server. Working quietly in the background on your computer, OneCare helps protect against viruses, spyware, hackers, and other unwanted intruders. (In late November 2008, Microsoft removed OneCare from SBS 2008) Microsoft Forefront Security for Exchange Server (Forefront) helps protect e-mail from viruses, worms, and spam. Forefront incorporates multiple antivirus engines for layered protection against the latest e-mail-based threats. Kindly note these security solutions are 120-day trial versions. For permanent use, you must purchase and license these products separately. Also note that the SBS 2008 product has elevated the third-party security conversation (that we will have across this book).	Server

Notes:

Component	Description	Server, Hosted, or Client Component
Microsoft Internet Information Server 7.0	In reality—SBSers have limited interaction with IIS 7.0 but here is the Microsoft description nonetheless. (Note, that you should avoid hosting your Web pages directly on the SBS 2008 server machine.) Internet Information Services 7.0 (IIS 7.0), is a Web server and security-enhanced, easy-to-manage platform for developing and reliably hosting Web applications and services. A major enhancement to the Windows Web platform, IIS 7.0 includes a componentized architecture for greater flexibility and control. IIS 7.0 also provides simplified management, powerful diagnostic and troubleshooting capabilities that save time, and comprehensive extensibility. *Internet Information Server IIS 7.0, together with the .NET Framework 3.0, provides a comprehensive platform for building applications that connect users and data, enabling them to visualize, share, and act on information. Additionally, IIS 7.0 plays a central role in unifying Microsoft's Web platform technologies—ASP.NET, Windows Communication Foundation Web services, and Windows SharePoint Services.*	Server
Shared Fax Service	A powerful faxing application discussed in Chapter 10.	Server

Notes:

Component	Description	Server, Hosted, or Client Component
Consoles	GUI-based management consoles are powerful, yet friendly interfaces to run administrative wizards. The SBS Console provides a central location to accomplish tasks; the SBS Console (Advanced Mode) gives you access to specific server components like DNS and DHCP; and the SBS Native Tools MMC found under All Programs. Windows Small Business Server gives us a deep dive into each server component's MMC. The SBS 2008 consoles are discussed all across the book and specifically in Chapter 4.	Server
Microsoft Management Console 3.0 (MMC)	Provides the framework for creating management consoles to perform task management. The SBS consoles are based on the MMC. Discussed in Chapter 4.	Server
Server-Based Wizards	Includes the Connect to the Internet, Set up your Internet address, Add a trusted certificate, and the Fix My Network wizards among others. Wizards are discussed across the book.	Server
Reports and Monitoring	Server 2008 Event Logs. Provides real-time monitoring of critical performance variables. Has the ability to generate alerts and e-mail them. Discussed in Chapter 13. Server Status Reports. A tool that can be configured to send reports on system operations and third-party applications via e-mail. Discussed in Chapter 13. Reliability Monitor. Provides a view of critical events, performance counters, and services. Discussed in Chapter 13.	Server

Component	Description	Server, Hosted, or Client Component
Microsoft Connector for POP3 Mailboxes	Created with great pride by the SBS development team, to allow small businesses to use existing POP3 e-mail services with Exchange Server 2007. ISP POP3 accounts are mapped to internal e-mail accounts, and now delivered via SMTP so they can be filtered like regular incoming e-mail! Discussed in Chapter 7.	Server
Windows Terminal Services	Terminal Services is a multi-session solution in Windows Server 2008 that facilitates remote management of the SBS server by the technology consultant. New support for remote workers in the SBS 2008 setup would be on the secondWindows 2008 Server . Terminal Services in Application Server Mode, being delivered via the Remote Web Workplace is also an option. Similar to remote control applications such as RDP, PCAnywhere, or VNC. Discussed in Chapters 9 and 11.	Server
Windows Server Update Services	Microsoft Windows Server Update Services (WSUS) enables management and deployment of the latest Microsoft product updates to computers running the Windows operating system. It offers automatic system checks for new software updates and makes it easier for you or your IT consultant to monitor and distribute updates. This is discussed in several chapters across the book.	
Online Guide	Robust online help for SBS administrators.	Server
Remote Web Workplace	An SSL-secured Internet-facing Web site, that gives the user access to Outlook Anywhere, the CompanyWeb SharePoint site, Remote Desktop access, Terminal Services Desktop, Applications access, and more. We cover the Remote Web Workplace and other mobility approaches in Chapters 9 and 11.	Server

Component	Description	Server, Hosted, or Client Component
Office Live Small Business	SBS 2008 integrates with Office Live Small Business to provide everything needed to take, promote, and manage a business on the Internet. Customers can create a professional Web presence without the hassle or expense of setting up a complicated infrastructure or hiring technical staff to maintain it. Office Live Small Business is a hosted service for customers with an Internet connection. (Note this is a 120-day trial version and must be purchased and licensed separately for permanent use.)	Hosted
Internet Explorer 7.x (IE)	Internet browser for navigating both the Internet and SharePoint intranets. Discussed across the book (for example, client computers on the SBS network are now added via IE) and in Chapter 11.	Client/ Server
Default Page Internet	Connects IE to the CompanyWeb as the default Web site. Discussed in Chapters 7 and 10.	Client/ Server
Desktop Workstation Operating Systems Supported	Windows XP Pro Service Pack 2 (or higher) Windows Vista Business, Premium, Ultimate Windows Mobile 5.0 or higher	Client

SBS Zen Crowd

Meanwhile, continuing with our broad definition of SBS, there is another group of SBSers who view SBS as a state of mind and a lifestyle. While SBS is a full member of the Windows Server 2008 computing family, these folks view SBS as special, unique, and their life calling. As you might say in Texas, these folks "GET IT" when it comes to SBS. For them, unique SBS tools, such as the consoles, are what life is all about. We have observed one positive development over the 11+

year life of SBS: these SBSers have matured, gotten married, and many are starting families. They have put family first ahead of SBS—that is a good thing!

The Big B Crowd: Small BUSINESS Server

Another view on defining SBS is looking at it from a business perspective—that is, how does SBS support the mission of the business to be efficient and successful? The SBS wheel in Figure 1-1 addresses this point of view.

Figure 1-1
  The SBS wheel allows you to analyze SBS, using an analytical framework for gaining perspective on core SBS applications.

The left side of the wheel predominately speaks toward server-side components, such as Windows Server 2008, Exchange Server 2007, and the like. The lower portion of the wheel speaks to the management function via the consoles. The right side of the wheel speaks to the client-side applications, such as Microsoft Outlook 2007 (which must be licensed separately in the SBS 2008 timeframe, but is pervasive in the SBS community).

The mention of "business" in the world of SBS continues in a moment in the Finder, Minder, Grinder section on core business operations.

Converters

Finally, as part of the goal to define and segment the SBS customer population, consider the following. There are these candidates for SBS:

- Linux Lovers
- Peer-to-peer upgraders
- Windows Server standaloners
- The soon-to-be newly networked
- Novell NetWare Converters
- The I want to get secure access from the Interneters

Linux Lovers

So shareware's not your bag, at least when it comes to running a bona fide business operation. And the Linux user experience is just a tad too much on the bit twiddler side, eh? No hard feelings. Welcome back to SBS.

Just a bit of context for you. Step back to the SBS 2000 time frame. Ever since the Microsoft FUSION conference (now known as the Worldwide Partner Conference) in Anaheim, California, in July 2001, and forward, the Microsoft SBS team has gone to great lengths (at times) to compare SBS to Linux. Turns out, according to extensive Microsoft studies conducted in 2003 and beyond, the argument that Linux is free is very misleading. When you consider the total cost of ownership of a computer network (labor, hardware, training, and software, including the operating system), the operating system represents a very small fraction of the overall cost! The major cost involved is the labor to set things up and subsequently to maintain them.

Peer-To-Peer Upgraders

As you may or may not know, peer-to-peer networks are workstations that have been cabled together into a quick-and-dirty network. This is a significant SBS customer group, because two factors are driving the upgrade decision: pain and gain. Peer-to-peer networks traditionally suffer from poor performance and difficulty sharing resources (that's the pain part), and many small businesses can easily see that a true client/server network such as an SBS based one, can deliver simplicity in sharing networked resources (that's, of course, the gain part).

Windows Servers (NT, 2000, 2003, 2008)

Standaloners are considered the low-hanging fruit in the small business space. Those firms running Windows NT-based networks are more than overdue to upgrade to SBS. A big part of the Microsoft message and efforts with SBS 2008, centers on moving folks on NT-based (plus 2000-based, 2003-based, and even 2008-based) systems up to SBS 2008. The performance gains alone justify the conversion.

Soon-To-Be Newly Networked

These are the last frontiers in networking left today. According to D&H (a major SBS distributor in the USA and Canada), there are 5 million small businesses in the USA with multiple computers but NO NETWORK!

Networking consultants, acting as explorers, seek out this type of SBS customer with a vengeance. Why? Because we can put our stamp on their successful network, and it is likely this type of client hasn't yet had a negative networking experience (or negative experience with their network consultant). Great SBS customers, if you can find them.

Novell NetWare Converters

This is perhaps historically one of the touchiest and most difficult SBS customer group to work with for several reasons. We know, we know, you're saying that NetWare is dead. Not so quick, my friend! Why are so many small businesses running good old NetWare 3 even to this day? Granted, NetWare isn't the dominant force it once was, but it's a huge source of billable hours for us—converting Net-Ware to SBS. NetWare sites are prime to go to SBS 2008, in order to enjoy broad industry support for LOB applications.

The I want to get secure access from the Interneters

No matter what the current network configuration this particular group has at the time, they are looking for a network setup that will give them secure access to their data, desktops, and resources. They are a prime candidate for SBS, due to the Remote Web Workplace (RWW) Internet Web site feature.

Finder, Minder, Grinder

With respect to how SBS supports core business operations, let us take a moment to speak about the three major functions of nearly any small business: finder, minder, and grinder.

> **TIP:** The book *SMB 2.0 Consulting Best Practices*, written by Harry, is dedicated to viewing the SMB space and SBS specifically from the finder, minder, grinder perspectives. So we'll only touch on the business stuff here and encourage you to follow-up with that other text, which is more of a "pocket MBA" for SBSers!

Finder

A finder is a rainmaker: the person who markets and "gets" or develops business for the firm. In many firms, it is the owner, CEO, or president; in others, it is a salesperson. Whoever has this important responsibility can directly benefit from SBS in many ways.

At a minimum, a salesman in the early 21st century can benefit from using Internet e-mail, a feature supported by SBS with the Microsoft Exchange Server 2007. A finder can benefit from the Outlook e-mail client most often used with Exchange Server 2007 in other ways as well. Outlook provides contact management and scheduling capabilities in addition to serving as an e-mail client. Outlook is discussed in Chapter 7. You will learn basic Outlook functionality, such as e-mail and using Company contacts, under Public Folders in SBS 2008. You will even learn how to run Outlook over the Internet, via Outlook Web Access. This allows you to check your SBS-based e-mail from a late-model Web browser from any Internet-connected PC in the world! Saying you are disconnected while vacationing in the Australian Outback is no longer an excuse with Outlook and Exchange Server 2007-based technologies.

What's really been said in this finder section, is that SBS can offer you a competitive advantage over your competition!

Minder

There's one law of business that we've never seen broken: For every finder, there is at least one minder. Minders serve as office managers, administrators, COOs, and all-around bean counters. Bless 'em, because we need 'em. SBS was designed with minders in mind (please don't *mind* the pun!). Typically, when we've deployed SBS from a minder's perspective, it has been to implement a piece of industry-specific line of business (LOB) software. You will see in Figure 1-1 that LOB applications are listed on the server side. There is one class of LOB applications however, that belong on the user side: CRM or Customer Relationship Management. There are numerous CRM solutions including Microsoft's Dynamics CRM solution that can use SBS Premium edition's SQL Server 2008 databases for its engine. CRM and its abilities to track all aspects of the customer relationship is very much a "minder" tool. CRM solutions are often integrated with accounting applications and the overall solution, a minder's dream, is called an *Enterprise Resource Program* (ERP). These CRM/Accounting solutions can actually be found in industry specific form Again, a "minder's" dream come true!

The minder at such a customer site benefits unknowingly from SBS, because SQL Server is included as part of the SBS Premium edition bundle. All the minder knows is that his LOB makes his job easier and he is more productive.

Also falling into the minder category with SBS, is the whole business planning cycle plus, cultural and organizational reengineering. Here's what we mean. When SBS is introduced into an organization like a small business, it often upsets the apple cart in a good way. Managers start thinking, "We're gonna do things differently around here, and we need a fresh business plan." And the collaboration of Outlook and Windows SharePoint Services, will improve communication and improve organization outcomes, etc. There's a management revolution inside each box of SBS! To some extent we make this point again in the Grinder section that follows next.

Grinder

Grinders are the worker bees. These are the people who are typically task-oriented and look at the SBS infrastructure as a support system that makes them more productive. Grinders benefit from SBS in two distinct ways.

First, LOB applications that run on top of SBS Premium edition's SQL Server, allow the staff to turn data into important information. Simply stated, this is how much of the work that is accomplished by the company, can be measured and quantified. Bottom line—grinders trust that SBS allows them to better do their work. Such has not always been the case with worker bees, known for coining such pithy phrases as "The #@%$!&* computer network is not working again!" in the early days of computer networking (and during the first two releases of SBS in the late 1990s—OUCH!).

Second, basic communication applications, such as Exchange with Outlook e-mail, contacts, and scheduling, have allowed grinders to improve the quality of their work, which translated into greater productivity for the firm. Many times SBS is introduced into business environments that have no prior network or e-mail service, often fundamentally changing how people do their work and, in its own way, reengineering workflow. The improvement in e-mail communications is but one example. Throughout this book, many more business workflow improvements are presented hither and yon.

SBS Philosophy 101

It is difficult to overlook the sheer numbers of small businesses that could benefit from an SBS-type networking solution. Such was the idea behind SBS. Microsoft has made SBS a cornerstone of its push into the relatively virgin small business space. The numbers speak for themselves when it comes to measuring the number of small businesses. Although you can easily say that there are only 1,000 companies in the Fortune 1000 list, conversely you might be surprised to know that there are over 22 million small businesses in the United States, according to the U.S. Small Business Administration. Can't you just see the marketing wheels at Microsoft turning, and the marketing staff dreaming of an SBS installation at every small business? You betcha.

In this section, we'll present SBS philosophy from three views: that of the small business, the SBS consultant, and Microsoft.

The Small Business

Understanding that small businesses are fundamentally different from larger enterprises, the SBS product literally sells itself when positioned by SBS consultants as a tool to help small business run better, with less effort, and, ultimately, with more ease. You could say that SBS is nothing more than a return to the original LAN paradigm that both Apple Computer and Novell rode in the 1980s. This LAN paradigm, with a few modifications to accommodate SBS, is anchored by these key tenets:

- **Sharing:** The major justification for implementing SBS in the small business, is the ability to share information. Sharing information, such as cost accounting data at the construction company, allows staff to work together with less redundancy (multiple entries are eliminated). Owners get better information about their operations. Staff works together as a team.

- **Security:** Like the enterprise, small businesses demand that reasonable levels of security be provided to protect sensitive information from competition and from loss or casualty. SBS provides all of the Windows Server 2008-based security goodness (and you'd better believe there are a lot of security features) in both SBS editions, plus the security afforded by third-party security-independent software vendors (ISVs) who actively support SBS.

- **Cost Effectiveness:** Relatively speaking, SBS is cheap. The standard version of SBS, a very popular option, can be purchased for about a 40 percent or more discount, versus the prices of the individual components (e.g., Exchange Server 2007). Tack on a few $800 USD very capable workstations and another $1,000 to $3,000 USD for necessities (cabling, third-party security protection solutions, switches, wireless cards, etc.) and you're up and running on a pauper's payroll, not that of the prince! Note that you might need a mid-range server when you look closely at your situation. Such a server runs $1,750 USD standalone as of this writing.

TIP: When amortized, for accounting purposes, over the typical five-year holding period seen in many small businesses (versus the more aggressive three-year holding period typically seen at the enterprise level), SBS is really cost-effective. After the basic installation, allowance for training (say, a one-time $500 USD per user outlay) and technology consulting fees, an SBS network easily costs less than $500 USD per user per year. THIS IS $1.38 USD PER USER, PER DAY, FRIEND! (Yes, we are shouting for emphasis.) That's less than our subscriptions to the *USA Today* and *Wall Street Journal* newspapers! That's less than your first cappuccino!

If you've ever worked at the enterprise level, you'd be viewed as kooky if you told someone you had lowered your annual IT costs per user to less than $500 (more likely it would be over $5,000 USD per user, per year). Microsoftie Eric Ligman documented this philosophy in his infamous Web site: www. lessthancoffee.com.

- **Efficiency:** After a firm goes through an initial period of negative productivity (measured in hours) while everyone is learning the new SBS network and its powers, company-wide productivity quickly soars to a level exceeding pre-SBS days. One example of this is the use of broadcast e-mails instead of making lots of telephone calls.

- **Better Work, New Work:** This includes fewer mistakes because of better communications, such as e-mail with staff, vendors, and customers; better scheduling with Exchange-based calendaring, etc.; and new work, such as winning new contracts because your work is of higher quality (proposals with accurate financial information derived from staff, and so on). In fact, as an SBS site starts using more and more SBS features, we've seen these small businesses dramatically increase their business. Small businesses, enlightened by the powers of SBS, have also been known to enter into new business areas, knowing they have the network infrastructure to back up promises. Need more convincing? A small construction company we worked with, confident that SBS-based e-mail and remote communications solutions wouldn't fail them, took on work in other cities.

- **Bottom Line:** How does SBS sum up? Properly implemented, SBS can help small businesses enjoy higher-quality work and get more work finished faster, with the same resources:

  Land - Office space is used more efficiently, as older office machines, file cabinets, and the like are eliminated. Heck, with the Remote Web Workplace feature we'll explain in Chapter 9, the whole darn office space can nearly be eliminated and everyone sent to Starbucks coffee shops to use Wi-Fi to do their business! It is true that SBS has been architected to support the remote or mobile worker, and it does a damn good job at it.

Labor - Existing staff works more efficiently, allowing owners to squeeze out more productivity. It's like have a 40-day month when you introduce SBS into a small business, and they leverage out a 20 percent or greater productivity gain.

Fear not that SBS will result in staff downsizing. We've worked with a variety of SBS sites and have never seen a layoff or firing related to SBS. In fact, the opposite tends to occur. Small businesses get excited very quickly with SBS when they understand it and see it working. In short order, additional (and unplanned) work requests roll in. For example, several of our small business clients who barely used the Internet prior to the SBS installation called back and asked for Web home page development assistance. If we cannot do this work, we typically refer an intern from the local college to these clients, allowing them to save on Web page development costs and giving a starving college kid the chance to earn some money. And guess what! More often than not, the college intern becomes a full-time employee, actually increasing headcount at the client site as a result of the SBS implementation.

Capital - Not to understate the initial capital investment in getting an SBS network up and running, but, after that outlay is made, the general consensus is that SBS delivers a positive return on investment (ROI), by increasing the firm's productivity and mitigating additional large capital outlays for the foreseeable future. One example of this is the reduced wear and tear on photocopiers. A client of ours who has aggressively exploited SBS features now stores documents electronically and faxes directly to vendors. By doing so, this customer found it could forego the purchase of a new, expensive photocopier.

SBS Consultant

To paraphrase from Harry's *SMB 2.0 Consulting Best Practices* book, SBS is a "consulting practice in a box." It's a structured setup with an assured positive outcome; it's wizards and consoles that are used at each site; and it's about making every customer implementation exactly the same, to contribute to consulting success. SBS is a consultant's dream, and we'll leave it there as the aforementioned tome uses over 600 pages to express these sentiments (and has been updated to discuss managed services).

Microsoft

So what does Microsoft think? Well, Microsoft extends this SBS paradigm specifically by adding these design goals:

- **Ease of Use/Simplicity:** The idea was to make everything easy, easy, easy. And when compared to the old command-line interface of NetWare 3.x (which a surprisingly high number of small businesses are still running, having foregone the opportunity to upgrade to NetWare 4.x, 5.x and beyond), you could say that SBS is easier to manage and use. For example, Dawn, who works at an athletic club we assisted some years ago, mastered NetWare in the first part of her career. When Dawn was confronted with the decision to upgrade, we loaned her a training machine that had SBS installed. One week later, Dawn was confident in the SBS setup's abilities given her own experience, and had even confirmed that her narrow market vertical applications would run on SBS. Not surprisingly, Dawn and her firm became another SBS success story.

  If it is usability you are measuring, clearly SBS wins when compared to other NOSs such as open source-based Linux solutions and NetWare. With its superior graphical user interface (GUI), SBS encourages even those on-site power users unaccustomed to managing a network server to feel comfortable using the Start button, menus, consoles, wizards, and so on. Score one for SBS for high usability.

- **Making Decisions for the Customer:** In the context of having an automated setup and implementation process ("just add water"), SBS (in Microsoft's view) reduces the research, engineering, and guesswork that goes into making the networking decision. Microsoft correctly asserts that users do not have to decide whether the SBS machine should be a domain controller (it should, because it controls the operations of the network), and whether to install Active Directory. Active Directory is the directory services database used to store user and computer account information, and in fact it is automatically installed as part of the SBS deployment process.

- **Designed for Success:** This point speaks to the SBS consoles we've previously discussed. The idea is that SBS administrators should enjoy a "simple, stupid" networking management experience and not really have to plan what they intend to do. Adding a user is a click away in the consoles. Simple.

TIP: Here again, we must interject a few clarifying comments regarding the pro-Microsoft comments. For new users, Open Sourcers, and NetWare administrators coming over to SBS (such as Dawn), we've found the SBS cool tools—such as the management console and wizards—are great and really aid the SBS learning process. So on that count, Microsoft is correct with its ease of use, automatic decision making, and successful design assertions. But for old-school Windows Server gurus with headstrong ways of doing things, the SBS consoles are sometimes more of an enemy. These Windows Server gurus begrudgingly use the SBS Server Management console (interestingly, the native tools are exposed in the Server Management console, removing the need to drop down and use the Administrative Tools folder). We'll say it now and most assuredly say it again: Do everything from the SBS consoles (and its wizards).

Microsoft has another view of SBS with its Go To Market (GTM) methodology (visit www.microsoft.com/partner) and, as of press time, was refining its sales and marketing message. Please click through to this site to stay on track with current messaging.

Deciding Whether SBS Is for You

Early in your decision-making process to either install a new network or upgrade the existing network at your business, you need to decide whether SBS is for you. SBS has several practical limitations you should be aware of.

TIP: In consulting, we call this frank assessment "expectation management." You should manage your expectations up-front about what SBS can and can't do (especially the "can't do" part). That way, later on, you won't suffer severe disappointments.

Client Access License Limit

Only 75 Client Access Licenses (CALs) can be utilized on SBS 2008. These CALs can be either user or device CALs, and each has its benefits.

Here is a good example on what type of CALs you should be purchasing for an SBS setup: If an employee has multiple devices (Windows mobile device, laptop, desktop) then they should have an SBS 2008 User CAL.

In the case where an employee shares their machine with two other work shifts in a manufacturing environment, you would look at SBS 2008 Device CALs. Visit the Licensing page and the Licensing FAQ page at Microsoft for complete answers.

> **TIP:** For those of you who've been around SBS for a while, you will be delighted to know that SBS CALs are now much easier to obtain. This is accomplished via the Licensing link in the Server Management console. Heck, you can even purchase your SBS CALs online, directly from the SBS server machine over the Internet. Not only are these easier to obtain, but we can now get them in quantities of ONE! No more need to purchase that expensive SBS 5 CAL pack when you need to add just ONE user or device!

Four Walls

Please promise here and now that you'll take to heart the following point as you evaluate whether SBS is for you: four walls. In its heart of hearts, SBS was designed to serve as the server on a local area network within the four walls or confines of a bona fide small business. It's not designed to act as a branch office solution connecting multiple offices. It's certainly not designed to act as a departmental server for an enterprise. You get the point. Used outside of four contiguous walls, SBS becomes a defrocked, fallen IT solution.

Not that folks haven't tried to take SBS above and beyond what it's designed for. We've seen it firsthand and "fired" two clients who wanted us, as SBS consultants, to take SBS into the no-can-do zone! If your needs are that of a branch office or departmental server, please DO NOT USE SBS. Use the new and amazing Essential Business Server product from Microsoft. We'll be happy, and you'll be much happier!

One more point on the four walls matter. In the SBS 2008 release, Microsoft has committed itself to better supporting the mobile worker. The super-cool Remote Web Workplace portal is back, in an improved format. In addition, Terminal Services in Application Sharing Mode can be published via the Remote Web Workplace to support mobile workers even further!

TIP: One way the Remote Web Workplace can facilitate the mobile worker is by having a dedicated remote desktop machine for laptop users. How is that you say? Well, think about professionals such as lawyers, accountants, or health-care professionals that work with very sensitive data on an ongoing basis. Having a dedicated desktop machine or virtual machine available for them to connect to 24/7 enables the firm to keep sensitive data inside the four walls, even while the mobile worker is moving about! If the mobile worker has their laptop stolen, all they need to do is pick up a replacement laptop and cellular wireless card, and they are back in business. No business critical data is lost.

With the advent of inexpensive high speed cellular data networks, high speed connections in most hotels, and WiMAX urban wireless networks, this setup becomes all the more practical for the small business mobile worker.

More on Remote Web Workplace and other mobility approaches in Chapter 9.

Something we will not go into much in this book, but will endeavor to discuss in a future book, is hosted SBS scenarios such as that supported by The Planet and other ISVs. Hosted SBS implementations are challenging the "four walls" paradigm we are discussing here.

One Business, Two Businesses, Three Businesses, Four

A popular implementation of SBS is in a shared-office space scenario, where tenants rent executive suites or sublet space. SBS can support multiple Internet domain names, allowing each tenant to have an appropriate Internet identity. In fact, some executive suites implement SBS and then recoup their costs by charging tenants a monthly "networking" fee. This form of SBS implementation—supporting multiple business entities—might not be apparent at first blush, but is possible.

Single Domain, No Workgroups

SBS is limited to a single domain and must be the root of the Active Domain forest. (A domain is an administrative unit in a Windows Server 2008 environment.) This limitation is a hindrance if your organization is part of a larger enterprise that has other Windows Server 2008 machines, and typically uses Active Directory's implicit two-way "trust relationships" to interact with other domains. Don't forget this SBS rule: SBS trusts no one!

> **TIP:** A quick Active Directory primer for you: First, contrary to the rumors circulating in late 1999 and early 2000, domains are still with us in Windows 2000 and 2008. In fact, there are two domains: the traditional NT-like NetBIOS domain name typically associated with the internal network domain, and the Internet domain (ye olde dot-com) type. A forest is a collection of trees and a tree is a collection of domains. Whew!

Workgroups are not really allowed in the SBS networking model, because SBS must act as something called a *domain controller* (*DC*). A DC is the central security authority for the network. It is responsible for logging you on, auditing usage if so configured, and whatnot. Workgroups do not use such a robust security model, and interestingly, many small businesses upgrading to SBS have been using peer-to-peer networks built on the workgroup model. This change from workgroups to domains is often startling to the small business and requires extra care and planning. Why? For one reason, domains by their nature are a much more centralized management approach; workgroups are decentralized. So people who were comfortable with the workgroup-sharing model are often put off by the heavy-handed centralized management domain view. Be careful here, especially if you are working with peace-loving hippies from the 1960s!

Real SKUs

Don't let the name "small" in the SBS title fool you. The components of SBS 2008 are the "real" Microsoft Servers products or stock keeping units (SKUs). This is "really" Windows Server 2008 standard edition, and it's the "real" Exchange Server 2007 product. SBS detractors in the past have tried to paint SBS as having "lite" versions of Microsoft Server SKUs. Some from the enterprise space sneered that SBS was really "baby BackOffice." Not true, buddy boys. SBS is the real McCoy, and you can go forth with confidence in your small business infrastructure implementations.

Cost/Benefit Analysis

Another SBS consideration is cost. SBS 2008 Standard is only $90 USD more than Windows Server 2003 Standard! Witness the math:

- Windows Small Business Server 2008 Standard is $1,089 USD. The price also includes 5-pack of Small Business Server 2008 Standard CAL Suite (User or Device, selection is made after purchase). Visit http://www.microsoft.com/windowsserver/essential/sbs/pricing.mspx to learn more.

- Windows Server 2008 Standard is $999 USD. Includes 5 CALs (User or Device, selection is made after purchase). Visit http://www.microsoft.com/windowsserver2008/en/us/pricing.aspx to learn more.

In plain speaking terms—that's only ninety bucks, folks! You get so much more with SBS 2008, we struggle to think of a reason to have the standalone Windows Server 2008 Standard edition in any small business!

The SBS 2008 Premium edition can be purchased for $1,899 USD. It would appear to be nearly double the price of SBS Standard edition but consider the following:

- SBS 2008 Premium edition comes with a second edition of Windows server 2008 Standard (valued at $999 USD).

- SBS 2008 Premium edition comes with SQL Server 2008, which we consider to be priceless! The actual cost is either $6,000 per processor or $885 per server and $162 per additional CAL. (Note: All pricing quoted is as of publication date. Up to date pricing can be found at http://www.microsoft.com/sqlserver/2008/en/us/pricing.aspx.)

We want to emphasize this bargain pricing discussion, because long-time SBSers are complaining that the price of SBS 2008 (either edition) appears to have increased compared to SBS 2003. That is a simplistic argument that needs rebutting. First—under any circumstances—SBS 2008 is a great value (wouldn't you agree?). Second—there is new math involved here. The price of CALs actually dropped, and for the average SBSer and their clients, the price is the same or slightly less under the most common purchasing and deployment algorithms.

Please perform your own fact-finding investigation at the above-referenced product sites to prove it for yourself!

> **TIP:** If we put SBS 2003 Premium side by side with SBS 2008 Premium, the breakeven price point for SBS 2008 is about 13 users. That is, the cost for SBS 2008 is a little higher up front for offices with 5 to 12 users. Once the office passes the 13 user mark, they are saving money!

The net-net or bottom line on pricing is this simple rule of thumb: SBS 2008 results in a savings of 30 to 40 percent (depending on your CAL configuration), compared to the full Microsoft Server products—PLUS there is much integration engineering in these suites that is PRICELESS!

So as we summarize the "goodness of fit" SBS discussion presented in this section, consider the following. Not honoring these limitations might cause you to make a bad decision concerning your firm's computer network. The key point is to make sure that SBS is the right fit for your organization. And if SBS doesn't fit, PLEASE DON'T USE IT! Use Essential Business Server or other Microsoft Servers products.

Business Reasons for SBS

Ultimately, it's a dollars-and-cents decision. How does SBS contribute to the bottom line? Does SBS have a favorable ROI?

It has been our experience in working with SBS and small businesses, that the business software application typically drives the SBS decision (although there are exceptions that we'll mention in a moment). Other business reasons for migrating to SBS include cost-effectiveness. This has previously been highlighted in the prior section on Cost/Benefit Analysis. Basically, in a nutshell, we're talking apples are cheaper by the dozen or bundled applications are cheaper than the standalone prices for the individual components.

Believe it or not, politics will sometimes have a role in selecting SBS. In a case of "eating your own dog food," as Microsoft likes to say, we implemented SBS for a very senior Microsoft executive who had just purchased a 100-room oceanfront lodge outside of Seattle as an investment and Microsoft getaway. This executive was more familiar with the Microsoft consumer software than his division managed

(Office), and new to SBS. Upon the closing of this real estate transaction, it became apparent that the existing NetWare network would have to be tossed. Enter SBS, and a major win politically for the SBS development and marketing teams with a most senior Microsoft executive. He knew what SBS was from that day forward!

Finally, more and more SBS purchases are being swayed by the increasing catalog of SBS-specific applications and managed services solutions entering the market. Want proof and guidance? Simply look over the event sponsor list for any SMB Nation conference at www.smbnation.com to see who is who in the ISV zoo!

Microsoft SBS Design Goals

There is no argument that Microsoft's primary SBS design goals were to serve a well-defined small business market. That said, something we've learned and heard from other SMB consultants, is that serving the small business customer is dramatically different from serving the enterprise. Because of this observation, we'd like to spend a few pages presenting these differences and defining the small business market. Such discussions are bound to make you more successful in your SBS implementations as either a consultant or business person. In fact, if you are a small business person seeking to set up and use SBS, discover whether you don't see a little of yourself in these forthcoming sections. We make many comments that pertain specifically to SBS consultants, and these opinions are our own. But we can confirm we have been party to Microsoft Confidential documents that largely affirm thoughts presented in this chapter surrounding the SBS five Ps (a marketing term for pricing, placement, product, packaging, and promotion).

Defining the SBS Market: The Small Business Model

Now that we've installed several dozen SBS networks, we can wax poetically as SBS elder statesmen, about the small business firm. Small businesses are very different from the enterprise in three areas:

- Attitude
- Affluence
- Expertise

Attitude

Small businesses are more concerned with delivering goods and services than focusing on the technology being implemented, and rightly so. In fact, many small business people have a hostile attitude toward computers, viewing them as a drain on time and financial resources. Remember, these are the firms that complain long and loud when you purchase an unplanned network adapter card for $40!

Such antagonistic attitudes can be overt, such as criticizing your efforts, or more covert, like not sending staff (including the owner) to basic computer training. Don't forget that the real measure of success of the SBS network one year hence, will be a function of training. Are the users using the SBS network? Have they taken advantage of many of the SBS features, such as the Remote Web Workplace and the Windows SharePoint Services? If not, the significant investment of time and money in implementing the SBS network will be viewed unfavorably.

Even when you find and help a technology-friendly small business, you can't help but see that the owner and manager really should leave the SBS networking to you, the SBS consultant. His energies are best allocated toward running the business, not running an SBS network.

We have a client, Marc, who is the owner of a small, middleman distribution firm. Marc is from a decent technical background, that includes knowing his firm's technical products and building and flying model airplanes! It's been our observation that Marc has been successful because he's moved himself into executive management, and has become less focused on technology. One of the critical success factors in Marc's transformation from butcher, baker, and candlestick maker to president and CEO, was his shift from *doing* the work to *managing* the work. It's arguably as difficult a shift as any small business founder will ever have to make, and Marc is no exception. The point is this: When we arrived as Marc's SBS consultant, we inherited a large case of boundary definition and expectation management, because Marc wanted to participate in the SBS administration, troubleshooting, and whatnot. But better business senses prevailed, and Marc reluctantly did the things that presidents and CEOs do: go out and get the business.

This next point is a case of "fear not." Many times the negative attitude that is demonstrated by small businesses toward technology, such as SBS, is based on fear. We all get defensive when confronted with the unknown and small business people fear that SBS might make them look stupid. As an SBS consultant, you need to wear their moccasins for a moment and be a buddy and a mentor.

We have found that a fear-based negative attitude toward SBS by the small business person is really a cry for more information. In the absence of sufficient information about SBS, small business people manufacture their own information.

What's our recommendation? Overcommunicate with the small business person about SBS. Have an Internet-facing SBS lab that can be used for demonstrations. Once he or she is educated, expectations are kept in line, and you can chalk up another SBS victory. In fact, we've taken to communicating to our clients in writing—either via e-mail, fax, or mailed letter—every time we perform SBS-related work at their site. What's cool about this method is that, months later, when both you and the SBS customer have forgotten something technically related, you can easily go back to your files and look up the facts (and, here again, prevent SBS misinformation).

Be sure to keep your own attitude in check. We can directly trace our SBS failures more times than not, to having brought an enterprise "know-it-all" arrogance to the small business person. In many cases, the small business person has a perceived negative notion about arrogant computer people. Don't validate that perception. Remember that you're typically serving as both a technical consultant and a business consultant. At the small business level, you wear multiple hats. It's hard to do, and few MCSE-types really do it well. But a few random acts of kindness go a long way with the SBS clientele (even though your enterprise experience frowns on such openness).

What's our solution to this alleged attitude problem from the SBS consultant side? We now have more communicators on our consulting staff than we did in the past. Yes, there is still a role for tech heads who are appreciated for their expertise, but we've enjoyed great success with the SBS product line by taking liberal arts majors, training them on SBS, and having them score wins with our SBS clients. So, leave that big league Microsoft Servers attitude outside the door when working with SBS!

Affluence

One of the earliest lessons learned with SBS, was that the small business isn't the enterprise. And remember, that the small business truly watches the dollars closer than the enterprise ever will. Remember the example at the top of this section regarding $40 network adapter cards? The enterprise-level Windows Server 2008 site probably has a half-dozen network adapter cards stacked in the server room ready for use. An enterprise-level Windows Server 2008 administrator wouldn't think twice about getting another network adapter card from the pile. But that cavalier attitude pales against the dollar-conscious small business owner who disapproves so greatly of unnecessary SBS-related expenditures that we've witnessed:

- A small firm struggles with an older network adapter card for hours instead of buying a new card for $20 USD or less.

- A small firm didn't hook up an HP laser printer directly to the network (via the built-in HP JetDirect card) because it didn't want to run to the store to purchase another CAT 5e patch cable. (Instead, this high-priced printer was attached to the SBS server via a USB cable, which limits the location of the printer.)

Expertise

One of the great consulting opportunities today in the world of Windows Server 2008 is SBS. When performing SBS engagements, we've found that we are a large fish in a small pond. That's opposite of the typical enterprise-level Windows Server 2008 engagement at the Boeings of the world, where even as a know-it-all, you're really nothing more than a cog in a huge networking machine. So we guess you could say that rank has its privileges. Working with small businesses and helping them implement SBS can be tremendously rewarding.

The expertise coin has another side, however. As the SBS guru, you will be relied upon in more—and often unexpected—ways than you might be at the enterprise level. Here is what we mean: When working with Windows Server 2008 at the enterprise level, you likely benefit from having someone on staff in storage that can walk through a series of steps to solve a storage related problem (often while you're messaging back and forth via Messenger). But at the small business level with SBS, this may not be the case. Here you are interacting directly with paralegals, bookkeepers, cashiers, clerks, and owners—not necessarily in that order! Not only do these people often lack the technical aptitude to assist your SBS troubleshooting efforts, but they usually become intimidated and nervous when working with you, the SBS guru.

When you're the guru, you do the work when called. Haughty enterprise-level folks coming down to SBS will learn quickly that there is no staff to delegate to— except you!

Defining the SBS Market: The Small Business Model

While the *SMB 2.0 Consulting Best Practices* book dwells on market definition in some depth, let us share the following at-a-glance statistics for you about small businesses.

- There are 26.8 million "businesses" as defined by the U.S. Small Business Administration (SBA, 2006).

- Under the SBA's definition of "small business," you will find the following breakdown: There are 16,000 businesses with 500 employees or more. There are 100,000 businesses with over 100 employees. This would suggest the bulk of businesses (say 21.9 million) have fewer than 100 employees. And let's assume that all of these firms with fewer than 100 employees don't allocate a computer to each employee because of the nature of the firm's work (e.g., construction). Thus many 100-employee firms might only have 25 to 50 computers, placing it well within SBS licensing limits. This is a huge SBS marketplace opportunity for you.

- Small businesses contribute 39% of the US Gross Domestic Product.

- Small businesses create two out of three new jobs.

- More than half of technological innovations come from small businesses.

- An older IDC study (late 1990s) reported that 74% of small businesses have one or more PCs. This number should be adjusted upward now.

- The same study reported that 30% of small businesses are networked. Again, this number is out of date and should be adjusted upward.

Microsoft's old SBS partner page (www.microsoft.com/partner/sbs) offers the following interesting statistics for consumption:

- 4.1 million small businesses in the United States have more than one personal computer with no network installed, providing a strong market opportunity for Small Business Server as a first and primary server. More recently D&H Distributors reports 5 million businesses in the USA with multiple PCs, but no server machine!

- Microsoft Small Business Server sales are rapidly growing over 30% per year.

- Nearly 1.65 million servers are expected to ship into the worldwide small business market per year for the next few years.

Just between you and us, you need to engage in a little expectation management here. Based on a collection of conversations around Microsoft, we believe that much of the growth in SBS is from overseas in international markets. The USA isn't driving SBS; rather, it's hanging on to the tail and being wagged along. Hats off to the Aussies and others for banner years with the SBS product. Have a pint on us, mates!

SBS Architecture

SBS is essentially a trimmed-to-fit version of the Microsoft Servers family. SBS can be viewed as a complex wheel, as shown in Figure 1-2.

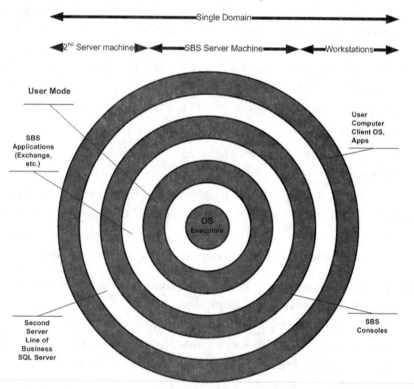

Figure 1-2
   SBS architecture presented from an easy-to-understand "wheel" perspective.

Let's look at the SBS architecture model by starting with a discussion of a single domain (in a tree in an Active Directory forest, but more on that in a moment) and ending at the Windows Server 2008 operating system kernel. As you read the next few pages, note that it's to your benefit to refer to Table 1-1, which not only lists the SBS components, but makes a distinction between server-side, hosted, and client-side components.

Root of Forest and a Single Domain

SBS must be the root of an Active Directory forest, which effectively prevents SBS from being another server (say a branch server) in an enterprise-level Active Directory domain infrastructure. In other words, practically speaking, you would say that SBS operates in a single-domain environment. As mentioned earlier, the SBS architectural model does not provide for multiple domains or explicit Windows Server 2008-like trust relationships. An Active Directory forest is a grouping of domains. A domain is an administrative or logical grouping of computers that participate in a common security model. This domain model manages the user accounts and security. Such security includes providing logon authentication for valid user accounts.

Single Server in Standard and Second Server in Premium

Only one computer on an SBS network can act as the root domain controller (DC). Out of the SBS 2008 Standard edition box, the SBS architectural model is to have one server, with the SBS machine acting as a root DC, per network. SBS Premium edition allows you to have a second server that can be a DC, run SQL Server 2008 Standard, or run Server Core with the Hyper-V role installed. It is possible to have even more servers on the SBS network acting as domain controllers or member servers.

A second DC on the SBS network will host a replica of the SBS Active Directory database. In this case, the second server could verify a user's logon credentials and, believe it or not, early market research showed this as an important customer need with SBS.

As previously discussed earlier in the chapter, a second server machine is also ripe for hosting LOB applications. Having that standalone Windows Server 2008 license with the opportunity to install and configure SQL2008 for the company's LOB application, makes it possible to run a robust server platform to drive it all.

If the LOB application does not require too much horsepower, then you can take advantage of the Windows Server 2008 1+1 virtualization licensing for our second server setup. The server would have Windows Server 2008 Server Core installed with the full version running as a Virtual Machine. Our LOB applications would then be installed on the VM. You then have the opportunity to utilize the server hardware for other company needs, such as hosted Windows Vista desktops accessed via the Remote Web Workplace.

End-User Workstations

Assuming you have the full licensing allowed for SBS (75 CALs), you know by now that up to 75 concurrent login sessions on to the SBS network at any time are supported. These sessions could be local on the LAN or from a mobile worker outside the office. SBS natively provides full support for three Microsoft operating systems: Windows Vista (Business, Ultimate, and Enterprise), Windows XP Professional SP 2 (not Home edition), and Windows Mobile 6 or later. Windows Mobile 5 is supported, but the age of the operating system means some advanced features such as automatic configuration are not available.

SBS provides extremely limited support for other clients, including Windows 2000 Professional, Windows NT Workstation, Windows For Workgroups, Windows 3.x, MS-DOS clients, Macintosh (with some network configuration), UNIX workstations, and LAN Manager Clients 2.2c. SBS does not offer support for OS/2 clients but will facilitate Apple Macintosh. We are not sure about iPODs and MP3 players, but we know that the new iPhone 3G does come with Exchange Active-Sync, and it does work rather well (big grin).

For a fully compliant SBS network, all SBS end-user workstations should be configured on the SBS domain using the http://ss-sbs/connect wizard. The wizard will set the necessary permission levels for the users that will use them.

User Applications

This area typically includes Microsoft Office, a suite of applications including Microsoft Word for word processing, Microsoft Excel for spreadsheets, Microsoft Outlook for e-mail communication and time management, Microsoft PowerPoint for presentations, plus several other applications. Other user applications include narrow vertical-market software, such as WESTMATE by Westlaw if you are an attorney, Timeslips if you're a professional who bills for your time, or QuickBooks if you are the bookkeeper in a small company. You get the picture. Trust us—there are THOUSANDS of business software application examples.

Server-Based Business Applications

Next in the SBS architecture in Figure 1-2, is server-based business applications, such as Microsoft Dynamics CRM and Financials—two applications that use SBS's SQL Server as their engine. To reiterate, it is this layer of the SBS architectural model that is so important. Powerful business applications, typically server-based, will drive the purchase decision to implement an SBS-based solution. Every industry has its own narrow vertical-market application that the small business seeks to implement. It is critical to assess that the SBS architecture will faithfully support such an application.

SBS Ecosystem

SBS 2008 only solidifies the place history for the SBS product family. From a modest start over 11 years ago as SBS 4.0, today SBS 2008 is what we would call a major political party, not a fringe candidate. As such, the SBS conversation changes micro-economics to macro-economics. By this we mean, you can look at the "attach" to the SBS network. One such attach is the super cool Microsoft Response Point (RP) telephone system (www.microsoft.com/responsepoint), which can act as a standalone telephone solution for small businesses, but really rocks with its SBS integration points. Further discussion is beyond the scope of this SBS 2008 book, but please visit Telephonation (www.telephonation.com) to learn more about RP!

Windows SBS Consoles

Yes, we said "Consoles"! There are three of them now. The Windows SBS Consoles represent the server-based graphical user interface (GUI), from which the vast majority of your SBS management and monitoring duties will be performed.

The Windows SBS Consoles come in three flavors:

- The standard Windows SBS Console with all of the required SBS wizards, monitoring features and more. This is the one that opens automatically when you log onto the server.

- The Windows SBS Console (Advanced Mode) which adds links to some key server service snap-ins such as DNS and DHCP.

- Windows SBS Native Tools Management Console that gives us most of the needed server service snap-ins to manage things directly.

Typically, we will be using the standard Windows SBS Console for most of our SBS management needs. We will discuss all the SBS Consoles in detail in Chapter 4.

Microsoft Server Applications

SBS includes several traditional Microsoft Server applications, such as Microsoft Exchange Server 2007 SP1 and SQL Server 2008 Standard Edition (SBS Premium edition), which are listed in Table 1-1. As previously mentioned, some trimming, mainly licensing, has occurred when the SBS application suite is compared to the full Microsoft Servers products. Each of these applications is discussed in this book, often in a chapter dedicated specifically to that topic.

Windows Server 2008

Windows Server 2008 can be cleanly divided between user mode and kernel mode. Figure 1-2 reflects this division. Note that this area is of keen interest to folks wanting to know more about virtualization. Virtualization provides great hardware independence and overall portability and flexibility previously witnessed by SBSers! Virtualization is discussed across this book.

User Mode

This is where services and applications run in protected memory (Ring 3) environmental space. To make a long story short, that means an individual application or service cannot explicitly crash the operating system. Each application enjoys its own protected memory space.

Kernel Mode

This contains the Windows Server 2008 executive, hardware abstraction layer (HAL) and third-party device drivers. More advanced discussion regarding user and kernel modes can be found in Microsoft's TechNet library (www.microsoft.com/TechNet). Further discussion here is beyond the scope of this book.

Bringing It All Together

A lot of great information about SBS 2008 has been presented here to kick off your SBS experience. Granted, if you are new to SBS, you have much to digest and perhaps a good night's sleep is needed before jumping into Chapter 2, where you meet the Springer Spaniels Limited methodology (the fictional company for which you will create an SBS network as you work through this book).

But allow us one last opportunity to shed light and impart knowledge on the SBS experience. This viewpoint, while oriented more towards technology consultants who implement SBS solutions, speaks towards an underlying foundational issue about why SBS is here (and why we're here using it). So here goes.

Our clients (and perhaps yours too) are business people who first and foremost care about running their businesses profitably, so that they can accumulate wealth in the long run. This is standard Economics 101 stuff from college. At the far upper left of Figure 1-3, the business person asks a simple enough question: "How can I run my business better?" This is a question we encounter early and often with our SBS clients, as we help them work through the decision to implement SBS. Such discussions usually lead to the business person understanding that more and better information is needed. Take the example of an account report he hasn't been able to receive before. Granted, this need for better information may not manifest itself as a better account report. It might well be another type of business report he hasn't been able to compile prior to the introduction of a network such as SBS or, equally likely, a report that can be compiled faster (the information was always available but took too long to obtain). Now let us throw a quick twist at you. In order to get the superior accounting information in our example, the business must upgrade its accounting package (e.g., Dynamics) to the latest version that runs best on Windows Server 2008, the underlying operating system in SBS 2008.

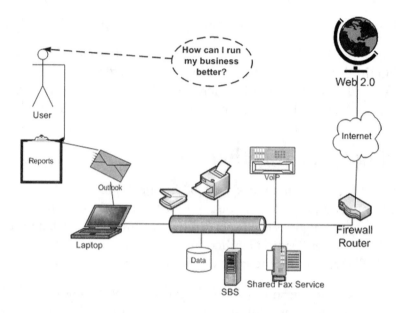

Figure 1-3
The business purposes of an SBS network: running the business better!

In the fictional example above, all the business person knows or cares about is (and perhaps you have a real-world situation in your life that you can relate to this), that the report is obtained by running the accounting client application on his workstation. That's it. Anything between the workstation through the network wall jack in the wall, to the machine running SBS, and even out to the Internet are of little concern. This is where the SBS technology consultant kicks in. We (you, us, and all the other SBSers out there), know that the workstation has to be connected to the network via cabling, and cabling is typically connected to a switch in order to manage the network media. Also connected to the switch is the machine running SBS, and the all-important accounting application (e.g., Great Plains). This last point is something that will perk up the business person's attention as you mention accounting applications again.

Well, in order for Dynamics to run in our example, it needs SQL Server 2008 as its database engine, which is provided as part of the SBS 2008 Premium edition. And yes, once asked, the business person agrees that he needs internal and Internet e-mail capabilities, such as those provided by Exchange Server 2007 SP1 in SBS 2008. And heck, if we're going to be connected to the Internet for e-mail, we better facilitate Web browsing (with Internet Explorer) and insure security with third-party firewall protection. Oh yeah, before we forget, the business person also sees value in other SBS features, such as the ability to work remotely via a secure VPN session (via RRAS), and the ability to work remotely (using the Remote Web Workplace to connect to a remote desktop PC, Virtual Desktop, or a Terminal Server in Desktop or Application services mode). Lastly, the business person responds favorably when you mention you can perform some of your network consulting duties remotely, using Terminal Services and third-party managed services tools, Whew! That's a long list of SBS success factors.

But understand what exactly has occurred here over the past few paragraphs. We've brought it ALL TOGETHER from the point a business person expressed a desire to run his business better, down to the nitty gritty details of SBS 2008. So as you can see, SBS really can help someone run his or her business better!

Competitive Analysis

No SBSer should blindly accept the awesome virtues of SBS 2008 without doing the necessary homework. By this we mean, it's a healthy exercise to look at what competes with SBS 2008. By observing the competition, you can of course, affirm the decision you've made to purchase and install SBS 2008. You'll eliminate any doubts you've had and answer any lingering questions. There are a number of competitors to SBS, near as we can tell:

* **Windows Server 2008 (and prior editions).** Good old bare-bones Windows Server 2008 in a standalone fashion, is a competitor for SBS 2008. Add in Microsoft Exchange Server 2007 SP1, Windows SharePoint Services on the primary server, and then a second server with Windows Server 2008 Standard and SQL 2008 Server and we have a somewhat similar setup to SBS. Microsoft refers to this method of setting up your network infrastructure as "The Stack". That is: You are essentially stacking one component upon the other to build a solution. This may be all you need, especially if you're using an e-mail client based POP3 mail account for your e-mail needs and some central file and print sharing. God bless you if this is the case. Understand though, that you're missing out on so many other features of SBS by selecting this alternative.

* **Windows Vista, and XP Pro Peer-to-Peer.** This is the "micro" solution recommended for two-person offices (up to 5 people). Give the devil his due: Windows Vista and XP peer-to-peer are competitors of SBS.

TIP: Another take on this: When you are as large as Microsoft, you're gonna compete with yourself. Remember this as you consider SBS as a consulting platform (for the consultant reading this book). Your biggest competitor is Microsoft!

* **Novell Open Workgroup Suite - Small Business Edition.** This was upgraded to Novell Open Workgroup Suite Small Business Edition in August 2006. You can learn more about this 64-bit competitor here: http://www.novell.com/products/openworkgroupsuite/smallbiz/. It is one of the closest, bona fide competitors to SBS 2008 on the market. It darn near matches, feature for feature, the components in SBS 2008 (including consoles, wizards, and even remote management). Figure 1-4 is a case of making our jobs easier as writers. Observe the comparison with SBS 2008.

Figure 1-4

Carefully study this figure and periodically check for updates at http://www.novell.com/products/openworkgroupsuite/smallbiz/compare.html so that you can understand what is "out there" in the SMB world .

Oh, and did we mention that NSBS is based on the open source operating system, which, while robust, is considered more difficult to work with and, more importantly, doesn't have the "mind share" or positive political support in our cozy SBS crowd? The point we're trying to make here is that business application developers, all things being equal, will typically develop their releases for a Windows Server 2008-based solution (such as our beloved SBS 2008) before a Novell open source-based solution.

* **IBM Lotus Foundations Start.** IBM, the technology company that is reinventing itself from hardware to services, acquired Toronto-based NetIntegration's NITIX line of self-managing servers, which compete directly with SBS, and rebranded them as Lotus Foundations Start. You can learn more about this competitor here (http://www-306.ibm.com/software/lotus/products/foundations/start/). You will see this product has e-mail and collaboration, backup and recovery, office productivity tools, security, interoperatability, and ease of management.

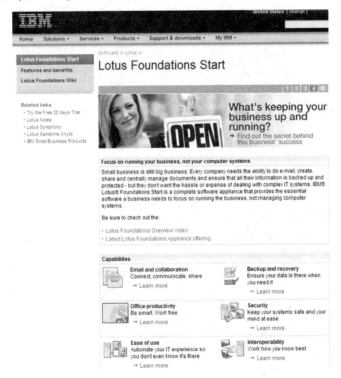

Figure 1-5
A first look at IBM Lotus Foundations Start.

* **SME Server.** When the authors were researching SBS 2008 competitors, we discovered SME Server. This server is truly Linux community-based, and it is so fringe, that the headquarters address is a house in Loveland, Colorado, and there is NO CONTACT TELEPHONE number. While this is kinda cool (Loveland is near to Boulder, Colorado, where you can show your kids real live hippies. Still, it is worrisome to consider entrusting your business operations to such an infrastructure—in our humble opinion). Learn much more at http://wiki.contribs.org/Main_Page. Yes—that is the not-for-profit domain extension you just read and that speaks towards the SME Server paradigm!

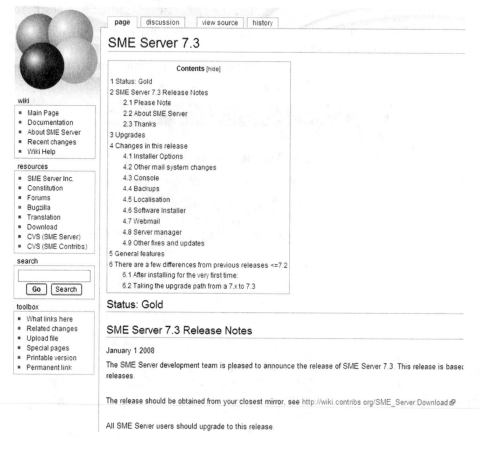

Figure 1-6
SME Server explained.

SBS 2008 Product Pre-Launch, Launch, and Availability

A very special moment in SBS history occurred when SBS 2008 was pre-launched in Houston on July 8, 2008, at the Microsoft Worldwide Partner Conference! It was at that moment that all the words in this book truly started to come to life. We say "pre-launch" because the actual event was a small, early evening "Happy Hour" attended by a couple hundred SBSers. While modest in size, this pre-launch allowed folks to appreciate that SBS 2008 was only five months away from purchase.

The SMB Nation 2008 fall conference held a sanctioned launch event in early October 2008, which was within a month (plus or minus a few days) of SBS 2008 availability. This event was significant in that SBSers celebrated the Release To Manufacturing (RTM) of the GOLD CODE for SBS 2008!

If you are reading this book, perhaps you attended the November 12, 2008, availability events. This was the day this book was released, and you could purchase SBS 2008. This launch event was a global webinar.

Now, go forward, create the Springer Spaniels Limited sample network over a few weeks to a month, and then call yourself a true SBSer! Photos from the SBS 2008 launch events are included in the photo section of this book.

The Future of SBS

There are three angles to this discussion. First is the SBS product itself. Microsoft, and more importantly, the marketplace, have given every indication that SBS is here to stay. SBS has crossed some significant financial thresholds inside Microsoft, so that it positively contributes to the bottom line of the mother ship.

SBS 2008 will undoubtedly be followed by future SBS upgrades, each one providing more functionality and stability. While we all hope SBS 2008 has a long life, it's a fact of life that future upgrades will occur.

And because SBS 2008 is a full member of the Windows Server family, it's here to stay! Past versions of SBS weren't much more than a black sheep distant cousin to the full Windows Server family, and didn't enjoy overwhelming respect! That changed with SBS 2003, when SBS became legitimate. Moving forward, SBS 2008 clearly has a seat at the Windows Server family dinner table.

The second dimension addresses the hosting market. While the authors believe SBS is here to stay, it may not be as you know it. Times are changing and perhaps the next SBS release will be off-premise with a hosted model. Within a few years, we predict we will meet you in the CLOUD!

Finally—what your future with SBS is merits discussion. Ideally, if you have a growing business, SBS is merely a stepping stone to implementing Essential Business Server and other full Microsoft Server products. This path is certainly in alignment with Microsoft's view. If you can use SBS as an incubator to help you expand your business, Microsoft will be more than happy to upgrade you to Essential Business Server and then the full Microsoft Servers products at a future date!

Summary

This chapter fulfilled several roles and met some very important goals.

- The first part introduced you to SBS with a brief introduction of each component and described SBS's capability to deliver a single-server comprehensive networking solution that is relatively simple for the small business to implement and maintain.
- A key tenet to SBS—business application support—was emphasized. The second part of the chapter defined the small business market for SBS and provided an in-depth look at SBS's underlying architecture. The future of SBS was discussed in closing.
- The chapter also provided you, in passing, with an overview of where this book is headed and how it is organized. Several topics were briefly described in Chapter 1 and cross-referenced to future chapters where the topic area or feature will be covered in more depth.

You are now ready to proceed to Chapter 2. And before you know it, a short time will have passed, and you will be a competent SBS professional. Or, as we say in the trade, an SBSer!

Chapter 2

Small Business Server Design and Planning

Welcome to Chapter 2, where you will proceed with specific planning tasks, all of which increasingly work forward to the actual hands-on activity of implementing SBS 2008. You are also introduced to Springer Spaniels Limited, the blessed sample company in this book.

Planning is considered an upstream function in a technology project. It tends to be less hands-on and more general than the actual setup and maintenance tasks that follow, these last two task areas being known as a downstream function. While it is easy to consider planning as an intuitive process that doesn't require much of a time commitment from the SBSer or businessperson, such an assumption is a fallacy. Indeed, planning is typically considered to be the best use of time in a technology implementation. In fact, you really can't escape planning. You can perform it upstream at the start of the technology implementation in an orderly and well-behaved way, or you can perform it downstream—the hard way—when you find your self-installing SBS multiple times at one business, realizing with each passing installation that you'd like to change the way you did things. Ouch!

Springer Spaniels Limited

First off, let's take a moment to meet Springer Spaniels Limited (SPRINGERS), the company for which you'll implement a complete and successful SBS-based networking solution throughout the remainder of this book. You will often hear us refer to the SPRINGERS methodology when we walk you through steps in a setup sequence. Understand that the context of our references to the SPRINGERS methodology is this: While there are numerous ways SBS can be implemented (for example, partition sizes can vary after the minimum requirements are met, company names and Internet domain names will most certainly vary, etc.), by following the SPRINGERS methodology, you will find the experience very educational, consistent, and even fun! In fact, we have designed this methodology so this book can be used in the educational sector as a curriculum in vocational technical colleges and even high school programs.

There are some very important reasons to work with an imaginary company the first pass through this book. It has been our experience with SBS (and life in general), that you know much more after you've done something once. It's another way of saying that hindsight is 20/20, a well-accepted old saw.

Such is the case with SBS. Typically, you set up SBS based on some assumptions that are made early in the planning process. Such assumptions might include the domain name you create, and so on. But, fast-forward the process, perhaps a few weeks. More than once an SBS administrator has commented to us that, now that she knows what SBS really is, she would have set it up differently. Those observations about getting it right are analogous to creating the chart of accounts when installing accounting software. You make some early decisions that you have to live with the rest of your life.

Now back to SPRINGERS. By using this company for the remainder of the book, you have the chance to learn SBS, warts and all, before installing it for real. This method also allows you to avoid the scenario mentioned previously, wherein weeks after your "real" SBS install, you might lament that you would have done a few things differently if you had the chance to do it over again. With SPRINGERS, we're providing you that chance at a very low cost.

By completing the activities in the remaining chapters, you will learn what works for you and what doesn't. When you go to install SBS for real, with live company data, you will have your feet on much more solid ground. That will result in a successful SBS install for you and your organization.

SPRINGERS, for these purposes, is a small company with 10 users and 30 employees. Please note that not every employee uses a computer. (Many clean kennels and so forth.) The company breeds, raises, and shows prize-winning Springer Spaniels. SPRINGERS is headquartered on Bainbridge Island, Washington, on a converted apple orchard. (The SPRINGERS operations and prize Springer Spaniel named "Astro" can be seen in the photo section in the middle of the book.) SPRINGERS has six departments in addition to the executive offices, as shown in Figure 2-1.

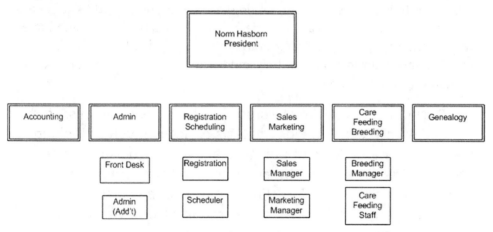

Figure 2-1
   Springer Spaniels Limited (SPRINGERS) organizational chart.

As you will see, SPRINGERS benefits from SBS in many ways, including its robust built-in Internet connectivity. How? Since canine breeders everywhere are worried about genetic variety in breeding (that is, they want to avoid inbreeding), the Internet is used to find suitable breeding partners. We are not talking about anonymous Internet dating sites full of lonely Springer Spaniels looking for love in all the wrong places. Rather, SPRINGERS intends to search sophisticated and legitimate breeding databases around the world. (If you are not aware, the Springer Spaniel breed is well respected for its diversity in breeding, which is a kind way of saying the breed hasn't been ruined by inbreeding.)

SPRINGERS also benefits from other easy-to-use SBS features, such as the Server Management console that will be featured in detail in Chapter 4. As the chapters pass in this book, we will divulge more details of SPRINGERS as needed. Periodically, you will enter SPRINGERS information into SBS to complete exercises if you are following this book chapter, and verse. It's the well-planned SPRINGERS methodology that is the foundation and backbone of this book.

Not surprisingly, we do want to tip our hat of acknowledgement to those of you who may not follow the exact steps of the SPRINGERS methodology, as you may be using this book as a quick primer to sharpen your SBS 2008 skills before building your own server (or the server of a client if you are a consultant). Right on! In addition, for those of you who are not dog lovers and find it hard to get excited about Springer Spaniels, we can appreciate that too. This book isn't a monument to dogs or the Springer Spaniel breed; rather the dogs and SPRINGERS serve as a convenient metaphor for telling a story and teaching you SBS 2008. So no e-mail from non-dog lovers please!

> **TIP:** Now is a great time to start your own *needs analysis* for your SBS project. A needs analysis typically involves looking at the ebbs and flows of business activity in your firm, often for the first time. Start by creating your own organizational chart similar to Figure 2-1. From that, you may discover that your company and SBS users are organized in ways that might not have been apparent. We have found that, early in the SBS planning process, many people use the SBS computer project as an opportunity to reorganize their businesses. In fact, an SBS consultant is often a management consultant as well.

SBS Project Management

You should never undertake an SBS project without sufficient planning. In fact, we typically spend a day or more with an SBS client doing nothing more than planning for the new SBS network. We can't emphasize enough how important planning is with an SBS implementation. These upfront hours are certainly some of the best you spend.

An SBS project can be divided into five phases. These phases, which will be described in detail, follow:

1. <u>Planning Phase:</u> The logical and physical design of the SBS network occurs here, as well as some early expectation management to avoid future disappointments.

2. <u>Server Installation Phase:</u> The SBS server (or servers in the case of SBS 2008 Premium) OS is installed, wizards are run, components are configured, and updates are done.

3. <u>Workstation Installation Phase:</u> The workstations are installed and configured.

4. <u>Follow-up Phase:</u> Over the course of several weeks, new SBS features are introduced. This mirrors the layout of this book as later chapters present additional SBS features as well as general troubleshooting, user support, and network optimization.

5. <u>Celebration Phase:</u> Projects create stress, and an SBS installation is no different. Phase Five is an opportunity to not only release some tension but also solicit feedback from SBS network stakeholders. This phase applies to both in-house SBS installations as well as those SBSers serving as consultants.

Planning Phase

For anyone considering SBS, the earliest planning exercises involve identifying and communicating why you want to implement SBS in your organization. That can be accomplished by answering the following questions. You will note that appropriate responses from SPRINGERS have been entered.

Early Planning Questions

We've got a secret for you about planning. To be honest, planning is very much about asking questions about the firm's existing and future situation with respect to technology, and then actively listening to the responses given. It's harder than it looks. You might well find it easy to ask a lot of questions, but are the questions appropriate or effective? Do you have good listening skills and incorporate the client's feedback into your planning process?

Here are some sample planning questions to get things going:

Q   List the three reasons you plan to use SBS.

A   *(1)To centralize our network security setup. (2) To centralize our e-mail setup internally. (3) To use the Companyweb SharePoint site to collaborate and share internally as well as with contacts via the Internet.*

Q   What is the time frame for implementing SBS?

A   *We intend to set up, install, troubleshoot, and train everyone on the network over a 10-week period starting in four weeks when the new computer equipment arrives. (And after you have finished reading this book!)*

Q   How have you arranged for training for the new SBS network?

A   *The SBS consultant will train those responsible for network administration. The SBS administrators will show the users how to log on to the network internally as well as via the Remote Web Workplace, share resources on the Companyweb site, and organize their data. These users will also attend three half-day training sessions on the following topics: Secure network access via the Remote Web Workplace, Windows Vista and Office 2007, and Exchange Outlook Web Access.*

Q   What roadblocks or problems can you identify today, that might make the SBS project more difficult to complete?

A   *First and foremost would be staff turnover. If our accountant leaves, not only would we have lost the individual we've identified as the SBS administrator, but we will have also lost our Great Plains Dynamics talent. To combat this potential problem, we plan to have the receptionist assist with the SBS setup and administration, so she can act as a backup SBS administrator in an emergency. A second possible problem is the bank financing for our computer equipment purchase. We anticipate that the lending process will take only two weeks and the equipment will arrive roughly two weeks later. With the SBS deployment being a critical path item, any bank financing to pay for the work would delay the start of the SBS installation.*

Existing Network Layout

Early on in the planning process, it is incumbent on SBS consultants and small business owners alike to know exactly what they have when it comes to computer hardware and software. This baseline measurement allows you to determine what must be ordered, replaced, repaired, and so on. This information is typically gathered by inventorying the network and presenting your findings in a spreadsheet table or a network diagram. Our preference has been to use a network diagram because its graphical benefits facilitate ease of understanding.

These network diagrams are usually drawn by hand or with a network diagramming software application such as Microsoft's Visio, resulting in a schematic or drawing of your existing network. More information on Visio is available at www.microsoft.com. Visio can be purchased for under $500 USD retail or, for Microsoft Partners, as part of the Microsoft Action Pack ($299 USD as of this writing). Such a drawing might look similar to the drawing created for SPRINGERS in Figure 2-2.

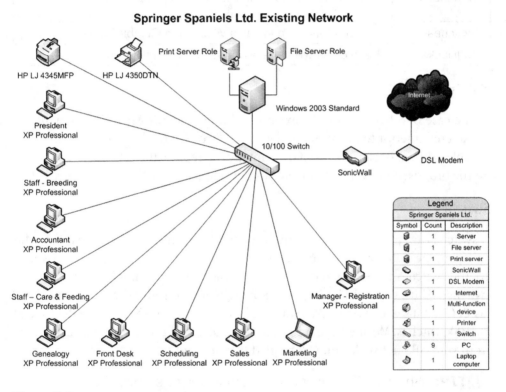

Figure 2-2
Existing network for SPRINGERS.

Check Existing Infrastructure

Assuming a network diagram has been created, you need to gather a little more information for SBS planning purposes. Take a tour of your existing physical site and make notes regarding the following items: cabling, switches, and wall jacks. Table 2-1 shows the existing infrastructure information for SPRINGERS.

Table 2-1
Existing Infrastructure

Item	Condition/Notes
Cabling	Need to implement Category (CAT) 5e or CAT 6 1000BASE-T, Ethernet cabling at site. Existing CAT 5 cabling will not work for Gigabit speeds.
Termination	Cabling will terminate to a 24-port CAT 6 patch panel in the server closet.
Switches	Will purchase and install a WebSmart Gigabit Switch.
Wall jacks	Each office will have two RJ45 CAT 6 wall jacks.

Cabling

In the case of SPRINGERS, the existing cabling media is early CAT 5, which is considered inferior to the more modern CAT 5e or CAT 6 Ethernet 1000BASE-T-capable cabling. Because SPRINGERS intends to replace the cabling, it is so noted on the proposed network layout later in the chapter.

Switches

A switch is a central gathering point for network cabling. Many people today who are using the Category 5 cabling described previously were opting for high-speed 10/100 switches to replace older, slower 10/100 hubs or multiple smaller 10/100 switches. Thus, when designing your SBS network, consider the more expensive, faster Gigabit switches with WebSmart style management features over dual speed 10/100 switches. With an eye on the future and getting the best long-term value from your SBS network, you will be glad that you did.

> **TIP:** Why the Gigabit switch? Most servers come with multiple network adapters installed along with the ability to team them up for various purposes. A network adapter team can be set for Adaptive Fault Tolerance where one network card will take over if the other in the pair fails. Or, where higher data throughput is required for the server, the team can be set to Adaptive Load Balance all network traffic across the team.

This in effect doubles the server's network throughput. Most workstations and laptops today take advantage of Gigabit network adapters as well. In fact, you will note in Table 2-2 that Gigabit switches will be purchased and installed.

Wall Jacks

When planning an SBS project, you will probably discover that you will need to increase the number of wall jacks at your site. This typically occurs for two reasons. The first is that additional networked workstations will be added as part of the SBS implementation. This is very common. More often than not, when a new network is installed, so are additional workstations. These additional workstations are most likely purchased for new hires, suggesting company growth is a driving factor in implementing a new SBS network. Or, the additional workstations might be for existing employees--formerly reluctant players--now stepping up to the table to join the networked world.

Here is what we mean. At a property management firm one of the authors served, the commission-based real estate agents must contribute financially to join the SBS network. That is, they have to buy a node on the network. Prior to introducing SBS, the old network was based on a NetWare server, something that didn't thrill many of the agents. Thus, several agents went without network connectivity in the past. Enter SBS, and these do-withouts became more excited about networking, especially with SBS's Internet connectivity. Thus, existing standalone computers were added to the network when the SBS network was up and running.

Another cause for ordering additional wall jacks is the pervasive use of network-connected printers. A popular setup is the Hewlett Packard (HP) laser printers or Multi Function Printers connected directly to the network. These network printers are typically connected directly to the network using one of the wall jacks. Many firms use the SBS network project as an opportunity to upgrade their existing printers or add more printers, so it is very common when planning an SBS network to order additional network wall jacks.

TIP: Attaching printers to the network in no way affects your user count with respect to SBS licensing. Some of you from the old NetWare days might recall that network devices, such as printers and Shiva LanRover modems, could and would consume one or more of your network logon licenses. Such is not the case with SBS. You can have as many network printers as you'd like. Your user limit in SBS is ultimately determined by counting how many users are actually logged on to the SBS network at any one time when user-based CALs are implemented.

Assuming you're going wired, it's a given that you probably need to order wall jacks for your SBS network, so be sure to over-engineer the number of wall jacks ordered. We like to order up to 25 percent more wall jacks than we anticipate needing. These extra wall jacks are typically placed in the conference room where training occurs or temporary employees work. In our experience you can never have enough wall jacks. Plus, it is cheaper to install them all at once rather than have the cabling specialist make return visits.

When you are assessing the need for wall jacks in each office and user location, it is a good idea to consider adding one extra wall jack per user in that office. This extra expense puts you in the position to install a VOIP product such as Microsoft's Response Point phone system solution.

List of SBS Stakeholders

Another important SBS planning item is to create your list of SBS stakeholders. Stakeholders include yourself, any consultants, service providers, and so on who have a role on the SBS project. And because everyone today has multiple telephone numbers (work, work-private, work-fax, home, cellular, pager, and so on), we highly recommend that you add each stakeholder's telephone numbers and e-mail addresses to your SBS stakeholders list.

Notes:

Table 2-2
SBS Stakeholders

Name	Role	Contact Information
Tom Jagger	SBS Consultant	SBS Staffing, Inc. 123 Main Street Redmond, WA 98000 W: 425-555-1212 Fax: 425-123-1234 Home: 206-222-2222 Cellular: 206-333-3333 Pager: 206-123-0987 Ski Condo: 503-200-1999 tomj@sbsrus.com
Jane Unionski	Cabling Specialist	Unionski Cabling Box 3333 Unionski, WA 98111 W: 222-333-4455 Cellular: 222-444-3344 Pager: 222-123-4567 union@cablespec.com
Bob Easter	Manager, SPRINGERS	Springer Spaniels Limited 3456 Beach Front Road Bainbridge Island, WA 98110 W: 206-555-1356 Fax: 206-555-1599 Home: 206-555-1234 bobe@springersltd.com
Roni Vipauli	Lender, SBS	Small Business Savings 123 Small Business Blvd. Small Town, WA 99882 W: 425-111-8888 Fax: 425-SBS-LEND roni@smallbusinesssavings.com
Ted Rockwell	Sales Associate	Overnight Warehouse PO Box 8855 Acorn, WA 98234 1-800-111-0000, ext. 334 ted@sales.overnight.now.com

TIP: The users contained in Table 2-2 will be among the first names entered into the company contact list in Microsoft Outlook 2007.

User List

Next in the general planning process under the SPRINGERS methodology would be creating a user list for your SBS network, those people you intend to allow to use the SBS network. It's not as easy as it sounds. First, you have to typically think through who needs SBS network access, as not all users do. Once it is decided who will be allowed on the network, you need to take extra care to spell each user's name correctly on the network and have an initial password to use. Each user's name at SPRINGERS (10 users plus one test account) is shown below. These names will be entered into the SBS network in Chapter 5.

First:	Norm
Last:	Hasborn
User Name:	NormHasborn
Password:	Sunny days!
E-mail:	NormH@springersltd.com
Job Title:	President
Office:	Executive
User Template:	Standard User with administration links
Computer Name:	SS-President

First:	Barry
Last:	McKechnie
User Name:	BarryMcKechnie
Password:	Numbers fun?
E-mail:	BarryM@springersltd.com
Job Title:	Accountant
Office:	Accounting
User Template:	Standard User
Computer Name:	SS-Accounting

First:	Melinda
Last:	Overlaking
User Name:	MelindaOverlaking
Password:	Working the desk.
E-mail:	MelindaO@springersltd.com
Job Title:	Front Desk Reception
Office:	Administration
User Template:	Standard User
Computer Name:	SS-OfficeAdmin

First:	Linda
Last:	Briggs
User Name:	LindaBriggs
Password:	Summer is here!
E-mail:	LindaB@springsltd.com
Job Title:	Manager, Registration
Office:	Registration and Scheduling
User Template:	Standard User
Computer Name:	SS-Registration

First:	Bob
Last:	Bountiful
User Name:	BobBountiful
Password:	Lots of dogs!
E-mail:	BobB@springersltd.com
Job Title:	Breeding Manager
Office:	Care, Feeding, Breeding
User Template:	Standard User
Computer Name:	SS-Breeding

First:	Tom
Last:	Benkert
User Name:	TomBenkert
Password:	Time for fun.
E-mail:	TomB@springersltd.com
Job Title:	Scheduler
Office:	Registration and Scheduling
User Template:	Standard User
Computer Name:	SS-Schedules

First:	Norm
Last:	Hasborn Jr.
User Name:	NormHasbornJR
Password:	Managing numbers.
E-mail:	NormHJr@springersltd.com
Job Title:	Sales Manager
Office:	Sales and Marketing
User Template:	Standard User
Computer Name:	SS-Sales

First:	David
Last:	Halberson
User Name:	DaveHalberson

Password: Making them count.
E-mail: DavidH@springersltd.com
Job Title: Marketing Manager
Office: Marketing
User Template: Standard User
Computer Name: SS-Marketing

First: Elvis
Last: Haskins
User Name: ElvisHaskins
Password: Platinum101 rocks!
E-mail: ElvisH@springersltd.com
Job Title: Researcher
Office: Genealogy
User Template: Standard User
Computer Name: SS-Genealogy

First: Bob
Last: Easter
User Name: BobEaster
Password: Lots to eat!
E-mail: BobE@springersltd.com
Job Title: Dog Trainer and Manager
Office: Care, Feeding, and Breeding
User Template: Standard user with
                         administration links
Computer Name: SS-FeedingCare

First: Bob
Last: McKenzie
User Name: BobMcKenzie
Password: Back bacon eh!
E-mail: BobMcK@springersltd.com
Job Title: SBS Domain Test Profile
                         Account.
Office: None. Test account only.
User Template: Standard user
Computer Name: SS-RemoteDesktp

Security

Not surprisingly, small organizations have many of the same computer network security needs as larger enterprises. The owner of a small business typically has confidential information that should not be widely distributed.

Security is a recurring theme in this book, as different SBS components are discussed, such as the Companyweb SharePoint site and Microsoft SQL Server. But, for your initial SBS planning purposes the first security issue to address is membership in the Domain Administrator group. Keep in mind that SBS 2008 disables the built-in 500 domain administrator account out of the box.

Whether using the SBS setup procedure or the SBS Answer File to perform the initial SBS OS install, we need to fill out a username and password that SBS will use as the default domain administrator account. The username and password picked should be someone such as a historical person or favorite character out of a book along with a strong *passphrase* to make sure things are nice and tight.

> **Tip:** With the advent of even more Internet-facing services such as the SBS Remote Web Workplace, Outlook Web Access, Windows Mobile devices, and more, it is important to foster a culture of passphrase security. Setting and enforcing a complex password strategy with a minimum character count of 10 is just not enough anymore.

Administrators are the functional equivalent of Admins and Supervisors in NetWare or the super user account in a UNIX environment. Thus, it behooves you to select carefully who should have "full control" as an administrator over your SBS network. Typically, this membership group is limited to the day-to-day SBS administrator, and perhaps the SBS consultant you've retained. A dedicated user account that has the Administrator Role could be created and used for the SBS consultant as well.

Project Schedule

The next step is to create an SBS project schedule. Because of the nature of SBS projects--working with small organizations--it is not necessary to use Microsoft Project to create complex Gantt/Pert/CPM charts. These high-end project-scheduling applications are better left for putting pipelines across Alaska.

However, we do recommend that you create a simple calendar-based schedule for your SBS project. Microsoft Outlook has a calendar that works fine. The project schedule for SPRINGERS is shown in Figure 2-3.

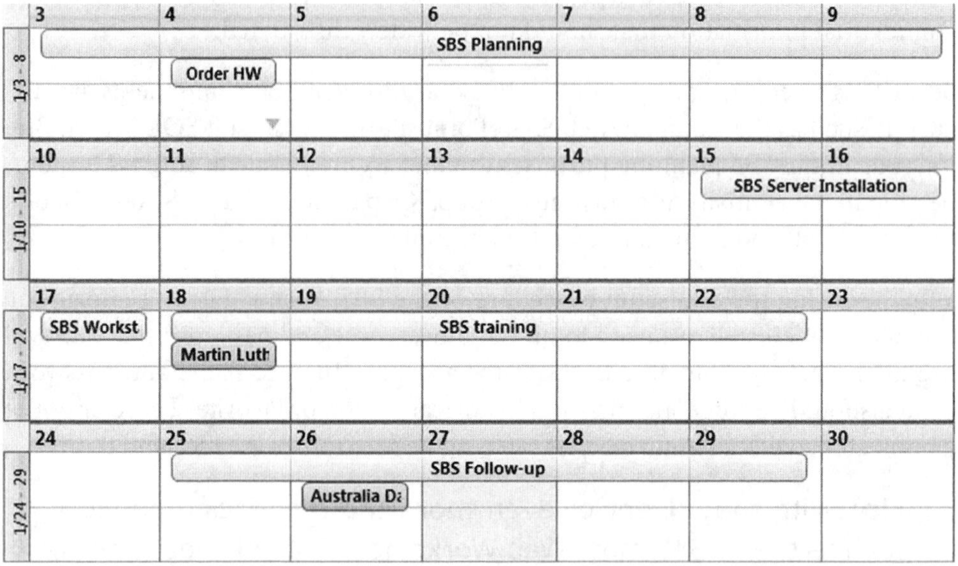

3	4	5	6	7	8	9
			SBS Planning			
	Order HW					

10	11	12	13	14	15	16
						SBS Server Installation

17	18	19	20	21	22	23
SBS Workst			SBS training			
	Martin Luth					

24	25	26	27	28	29	30
			SBS Follow-up			
		Australia Dɛ				

Figure 2-3
SBS project schedule for SPRINGERS.

> **TIP:** For more complex scheduling, consider using other scheduling programs. These range from Calendar Creator (The Learning Company), which creates more detailed calendars than Microsoft Outlook, to Microsoft Project. Microsoft Project can be used for complex projects that track durations, resources, and predecessor/successor relationships.

Addressing Hardware, Software, and Services List and Budget Needs

You must now create the hardware, software, and services lists for your SBS network as the next planning step in the SPRINGERS methodology. The list shown Table 2-3 is the desired outcome. Regarding the hardware area, a new server and new hub are being purchased by SPRINGERS. With respect to software, SBS, sufficient user licenses, and additional software are being purchased by SPRINGERS.

Several types of services will be required, including additional telephone lines for the new Internet connection and new wiring, because a new star topology based on the Ethernet standard has been selected. A *star topology* occurs when each workstation and the server is connected to the hub in a "spoke and hub" configuration similar to a bicycle tire. You will also see that, by adding an additional column in Table 2-3 for costs, the list not only serves as your purchase specifications, but also your budget. Note that we describe hardware, software, services, and budgets in much more detail later in the chapter.

Table 2-3
Hardware, Software, and Services List for SPRINGERS

Item	Description	Cost
Hardware	Intel Xeon X3360 Quad Core series Server for SMB/SBS, USB Hard Disks for backup, 8GB RAM, 640GB RAID 0+1 Array, HP 4345MFP Laser Printer, 1500VA UPS backup power with power filtering.	$3.500
Software	SBS 2008.	$3,500
Services	SBS consultant, wiring with wall jacks, telephone line hookup, Internet service.	$5,500

Proposed Network Layout

The next step is to create a drawing of the proposed network. The proposed network for SPRINGERS, shown in Figure 2-4, graphically depicts many of the items discussed previously in the section "Addressing Hardware, Software, and Services List and Budget Needs." The old NetWare server will be "retired."

Notes:

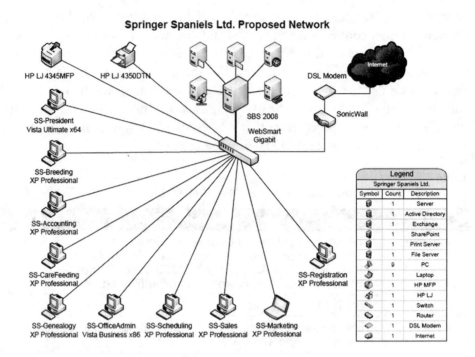

Figure 2-4
  Proposed SBS network for SPRINGERS.

Final Planning Activities

Three items remain as part of the SBS planning process: ordering, walk-through, and documentation.

Ordering

A "critical path" item in your SBS project is the need to order your hardware, software, and services. Why? Under even the best of conditions, it can take 10 or more business days to receive your new server machine. Services such as scheduling your SBS consultant and ordering additional telephone lines can take even longer (especially when the telephone company is involved).

> **TIP:** Here is an interesting comment from a customer viewpoint. If you use an SBS consultant, consider having him attend the calls placed when you are ordering ("you" being

the business person in this case). Typically we sit in a confer- ence room with our SBS customer on "order day." The vendors are placed on the speakerphone, allowing for all parties to speak up and clarify anything. We have found that, by clarify- ing purchase specifications on order day, we save the client significantly more than our hourly consulting fees. Consider it another win for our SBS customer.

Walk-Through

Now that you are near the end of the planning phase, we highly recommend that you once again walk the floors of the site that will house the new SBS network. By taking a fresh look at the site where the SBS network will be installed, you might notice a few things you initially missed. Items that have caught our eye on this final walk-through include:

- Server placement: Where will the actual server reside? Is it near power outlets? Have you coordinated the extra telephone lines such as the fax and/or DSL line to terminate at or near the SBS server machine?

- Server placement: Does the room where the server will reside have a good dead bolt? If the server won't be housed in a room, has consideration been given to a proper server cabinet that can be locked?

- Network cable termination: Will the patch panel where all of the new cabling will terminate be close enough to run short patch cables to the new Gigabit switch?

- Workstation accessibility: Can you easily reach each workstation on the network? Is there enough room between the desks and walls to allow the cabling specialist to install wall jacks?

- Building access: Do your service providers have access codes and keys to perform after-hours work on the SBS project? Believe it when we say you can count on some unexpected late-evening visits from members of the SBS team!

Documentation and Loose Ends!

It is essential that you take a few moments to gather the letters, e-mails, bids, drawings, yellow sticky notes, and the like, to organize these in an SBS project notebook. The SBS project documentation serves several purposes.

First, if you should leave the organization, you properly share your SBS knowledge with your SBS successors via the SBS project notebook. In effect, people who follow you don't have to start from the beginning. You, of course, would appreciate the same courtesy.

Second, because of the demands a small organization places on its staff, it's unlikely that you will remember the finer points of your SBS installation several months hence. The SBS project notebook will provide an excellent resource you can refer to if the need should arise.

> **TIP:** As you'll see in later chapters, SBS 2008 is "self-documenting," if you simply click a link on the completion page of each wizard and save the configuration information as a file. We don't want to tell you much more just yet, but the SBS development team made it real easy to create your network notebook with SBS 2008.

Loose ends run the whole spectrum of SBS computing. You name it, and we have probably seen it. Some doozies in this category include:

- Sufficient quantity of telephone cable. Lesson learned: Do you have enough telephone cabling to hook up the modems?
- Length of telephone cable. Lesson learned: Are the telephone cables long enough?
- Environmental controls. Lesson learned: Do you need a fan to help keep the server cool (because the work area is too warm)? Or, in the event there is more than one server in the room, do you need a portable standalone air conditioner with the appropriate venting in place?

Another loose end to consider while planning your SBS network is training. One of the keys to success with an SBS network is to over-train your users! It's a theme worth repeating (and we do so several times in this book!). Training can take several forms, all of which are discussed in Chapter 11.

> **TIP:** Note the SBS project planning phase is typically 10 to 15 hours of consulting work if you are planning on doing it "right." If you are undertaking your SBS project without a consultant, budget for one to two days of your own planning time at the minimum.

Server Installation Phase

The big day arrives. Sitting on a pallet in your workspace, are a bunch of large boxes that hold the new server, monitor, and additional networking accessories (Gigabit switch, modems, UPS, and so on).

The server installation phase includes:

- Unpacking and physically building the server.
- Physically installing the network accessories, such as the UPS, modems, and Gigabit switch.
- Reseating installed adapter cards that might have come loose during shipping.
- Installing the SBS OS with or without the SBS Answer File.
- Installing server hardware drivers and manufacturer's hardware management utilities.
- Performing several post-server installation tasks, such as running the Getting Started Tasks wizards, moving data folders, sharing folders, mapping drives, installing printers, and verifying security. This also includes completing SBS Task List items (such as adding SBS licenses) and running SBS wizards from the SBS default console.
- Configuring BackOffice applications. Typically Microsoft SQL Server must be configured for use. By itself, with no configuration out of the box, Microsoft SQL Server isn't especially useful. It is also common to configure Microsoft Exchange above and beyond its basic configuration, to accommodate public folders such as shared calendars, contacts, tasks, etc. This step may also include running wizards from the SBS consoles.
- Installing applications such as Microsoft Dynamics Customer Relationship Management, Great Plains Dynamics (accounting software), and others.

It is important to have a server installation worksheet similar to Table 2-4.

Notes:

Table 2-4

Server Installation Worksheet for SPRINGERS

Item	Description	Completed
Server Name	SS-SBS	
Internal Domain Name	SPRINGERSLTD	
External Internet Domain Name	https://remote.springersltd.com	
Initial SBS Registration Name	Bob Easter	
Organization	Springer Spaniels Limited	
Installation Codes	Small Business Server (use from product ID sticker on disc packaging)	
Area Code	206	
Address	3456 Beach Front Road	
City	Bainbridge Island	
State/Province	WA	
Zip	98110	
Country	United States of America	
Business Telephone	206-555-1356	
Business Fax	206-555-1599	
Domain Admin Username	JonathanPaul	
Domain Admin Password	L0ts and lots of fun!	
RAID Array Configuration (4x 320GB RAID 0+1, 1x 320GB Hot Spare)	SBS operating system and applications partition is 75GB. Swap partition is 25GB; the balance of 540GB will be the data partition. If you have only a single hard disk or mirrored drives (but not RAID 5), you may continue for the purposes of learning SBS 2008 via the SPRINGERS methodology. However, you'll want to consider RAID 5 or mirrored drives in the real world.	
Time Zone	Pacific	

Item	Description	Completed
Printers	Install new HP 4345MFP printer on network with HP4345MFP share name.	
Registry	No known Registry modifications needed in SBS.	
Folders	Create additional folders on Data partition: **Company** (this is the general company data folder). Access Based Enumeration will enable us to hide folders, such as "Accounting" from users with no access permissions.	
Shares	Create the **Company** share on the company folder giving all domain users read/write permissions.	
Internal IP Addressing	Use the default 192.168.40.2 IP address for the server NIC or Team, and the 255.255.255.0 Subnet Mask. The Gateway will be 192.168.40.1, which points to the third-party firewall or router. A customized IP setup is preferable for the SBSer and SBS consultant. Using the Answer File setup technique, you would set the server IP to 192.168.40.254 and leave the router where it is at 192.168.40.1.	
External IP Addressing	Use the following for the router (these are provided as a sample only—your values will be different): IP: 207.202.238.215 Subnet Mask: 255.255.255.0 Default Gateway: 207.202.238.1 Primary DNS: 209.20.130.35 Secondary DNS: 209.20.130.33	

Item	Description	Completed
Misc.	Windows Server 2008 operating system to be installed on C:\, SBS components (Exchange, etc.) to be installed on C:\, Will approve all licensing questions with "Yes."	

Regarding partitions: SBS requires that the partition containing the operating system (typically the C: drive) be formatted as NTFS to operate correctly. NTFS (NT file system) is the Windows NT Server partition scheme that allows advanced security and file management.

TIP: When it comes to configuring RAID arrays for a server setup, keep the following in mind:

- RAID 0+1 Stripe + Mirror (4 drives minimum) provides the best performance but has a higher disk cost. Example: 4x 500GB RAID 0+1 = 1TB of storage. We gain 50 percent read performance over RAID 5 due to the stripe, but lose 50 percent of our capacity to the striped drives being mirrored.

- RAID 1 Mirror provides reasonable performance with a slightly higher disk cost: 2x 500GB RAID 1 = 500GB of storage. If we configure two RAID 1 Mirror sets for our OS and swap partition on one, the second mirror array is for the data. Performance for disk reads is close to a standalone hard drive with disk writes being slower due to the need to make changes on both hard drives in the array.

- RAID 5 (3 drives minimum) utilizes the equivalent of one drive for parity data to provide protection against a single disk failure. Performance is so-so, due to the need to write parity information across all of the disks as the data is changed. Example: 4x 500GB RAID 5 = 1.5TB of storage.

- RAID 6 (4 drives minimum) utilizes the equivalent of two drives for parity data, to provide protection against two disks failing. Performance is so-so, due to the need to write parity information across all of the disks twice as the data is changed. Example: 4x 500GB RAID 5 = 1TB of storage.

Workstation Installation Phase

The workstation installation phase is really the work that occurs in Chapter 5, when you will connect a workstation to the SBS 2008 network. That said, there are a few key steps in the workstation installation stage worth listing:

- Physically unpack and connect all of the workstation components.
- Reseat the existing adapter cards that might have come loose during shipping.
- Complete installation of client operating system if necessary.

Complete the Add User/Setup Computer wizards to create the configuration information for the workstation to join the SBS network. Then at the workstation, launch the IE Web browser and point to the http://Connect to launch the over-the-wire process for joining a workstation to the SBS network. Bye-bye Magic Disk from earlier SBS releases. Very nice touch!

- Perform basic SBS client component tests, answer limited-user questions, and so on.
- Enable and demonstrate access to network files from client PCs.
- Enable and demonstrate network printing from client PCs.
- Enable and demonstrate basic internal e-mail via Outlook and Microsoft Exchange.
- Set a date to return to fully configure Outlook (shared calendar, shared contact list).
- Propose a date for network (logon, printing, saving) and Outlook training.

The middle steps involve testing the setup. These are key steps in the success of attaching and using an SBS workstation. Too often we have observed homegrown

SBS networks where the connectivity wasn't fully tested. In effect, the SBS network never did completely work. In fact, at one site, the users jokingly called it an SBS *notwork*! Unfortunately, those SBS networks that forego workstation testing usually discover such things later, rather than sooner.

And, it shouldn't be lost on you that training is mentioned as the last step of the workstation installation phase. Again, training is important.

Follow-Up Phase

As far as this book is concerned, the follow-up phase encompasses the balance of the SBS installation and administration experience. Why? It is the follow-up phase where additional SBS functions, such as faxing, and applications, such as SQL Server, are introduced. There are important reasons for staging the introduction of many SBS features as separate, discrete tasks contained within a phase separate from server and workstation setup.

It has been our experience with organizations implementing SBS, that the mere introduction of a computer network is enough to start with. The users need to become familiar with the basic Windows networking environment that is the foundation of SBS. In fact, for many users, being able to log on, save a file, and print are enough features to start out with.

Even network-experienced and computer-savvy organizations cannot absorb too many features too early. For example, e-mail is a great early candidate to introduce on the SBS network. But we have often found that even the best users aren't ready to tackle SQL Server and its strengths too early, so this speaks to delaying the heavy stuff for a while on your SBS networks.

Lastly, there is the Christmas-morning emotional response. Given a pile of wrapped toys, a child will eagerly attack, opening each and every gift until, several hours later, the child is over-stimulated and sobbing in a corner. Such is the case with many SBS sites. Users want to do everything *right now* on the first day the network is available. But by the end of the day, the same users are bewildered, frustrated, and, worst of all, have negative feelings toward the new SBS network. You, the SBS administrator, don't want and can't tolerate such an early defeat. Be smart. Stage the rollout of SBS features over time.

Celebration Phase

Yee-haw! Call it an opportunity to get a free lunch, but one of the most successful things we have accomplished as SBS consultants is to have an end-of-project pizza lunch for all SBS users. Understand that there really is a method to this madness. Not only can we solicit user feedback that might not readily reveal itself during day-to-day SBS network use, but we can offer the opportunity to provide additional meaningful services that our SBS customer might not have initially considered. Five additional services, beyond core out-of-the-box SBS functionality, have proven popular with customers:

- Windows SharePoint Services (WSS) customization (your CompanyWeb) – You can achieve the highest and best use of your SBS system by using the powers of WSS! Consider using it as a basic document management package, a place for the company's faxes to be received into, or as a vehicle for sharing data with company contacts via the Internet.

- Public folders – Many users, when they become addicted to e-mail, want additional help implementing public folders (shared resources) in Microsoft Exchange.

- Microsoft Outlook customization – When users start to use the contact list in Microsoft Outlook, the follow-up requests to create custom forms can be expected.

- SQL Server tables – The really hard-core SBS sites (using the premium version) know that SQL Server can handle their most demanding database challenges, but few of these SBS sites actually know how to execute SQL queries and so on.

- Web page development – Last, but certainly not least, the discussion over the pizza lunch inevitably turns to Web pages and electronic commerce.

SBS Expectation Management and Perception

Avoiding disappointments is perhaps job one for an SBS administrator and certainly an SBS consultant. Recall that, in Chapter 1, we set the framework for understanding what SBS actually is. Disappointment can be avoided early, for example, by understanding that you will need to purchase an additional license setup for the built-in virus scanning application because SBS includes a 120-day trial version out of the box.

TIP: Something to consider before you get too far along is the assured outcome of the SBS 2008 original equipment manufacturer (OEM) stock-keeping unit (SKU). Here, HP will just about completely install SBS on one of its SMB server machines (e.g., the ML 350 model used in this book as an example). When you start up, you'll complete a mini-setup process that constitutes the personalization of your server machine and accepting the license agreement. We'll discuss the OEM SKU more in the setup chapter, but what's important to understand here is that the SBS 2008 OEM SKU is a rapid setup methodology with an assured outcome (and a positive outcome at that).

Scope of Work

If you are using a consultant, a scope of work should be defined, largely based on much of the planning work accomplished previously. The scope of work is typically delivered as a detailed proposal that describes how the work will be accomplished. Likewise, the engagement letter, which refers to the proposal for scope items, is a contract between a consulting firm and the client. An engagement letter typically covers items such as terms and conditions of payment, how disputes will be resolved, and so on.

TIP: Here is an additional thought for SBS consultants about the scope of work and engagement letters: Many SBS consultants ask how they can get paid for their planning efforts if they haven't yet created a scope of work or gotten the client to sign the engagement letter.

Here you should contract with the client for 10+ hours of your consulting time to assist with planning. Perhaps this consulting time could be evidenced with an engagement letter separate from the SBS project engagement letter you intend to present later. It has been our experience that if the customer is not interested in paying you for 10+ hours of your planning time, that potential client isn't very serious about having a successful SBS installation. Also, if the SBS client is cautious about the planning phase, explain that the scope of work you create with 10+ hours of planning time can be easily converted into a request for proposals (RFP) that could be distributed to other consulting firms and resellers.

The thought here is that you can get 10+ hours into your SBS project with this prospective client, and either one (or both) of you might decide you don't care to work together anymore. This approach provides an out for all involved.

The scope of work would likely contain the following items:

- A detailed proposal
- A schedule
- A budget
- A project task list or checklist

Over-Communicate

Another theme to this book is that of over-communicating before, during, and after your SBS project. It is very easy to do. You can do it in person via periodic SBS network meetings, pizza lunches, and the like. You might consider sending out an SBS project update e-mail, such as presented in Figure 2-5.

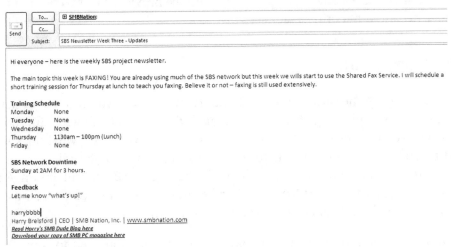

Figure 2-5
SBS e-newsletter.

Selecting SBS Service Providers

Another planning issue is that of selecting the service providers for products and services for your SBS network. There are several types of SBS service providers:

- SBS consultants
- Hardware and software resellers
- Wiring and cabling contractors
- Telco
- Internet service providers (ISP)

First, a comment regarding service providers: In general, the very best way to retain a service provider is via referral of a mutually respected third party, typically a friend at another organization who has used a service provider that did a good job. Acquiring or avoiding a service via this avenue is greatly recommended. In fact, as an SBS consultant, one of our key motivators to perform at the highest level, is the prospect of getting referrals from our existing SBS client base!

Now here is a bit of advice they didn't teach you in the Microsoft Certified System Engineer (MCSE) program or the Harvard Business School, for that matter: Avoid retaining a service provider based on an advertisement in the media, telephone book, and other outlandish promotional venues. Under these circumstances, it is very difficult to ascertain the quality of a service provider's work, communications style, and other critical factors.

SBS Consultants

Of course, one of the earliest and most important decisions you will make relates to whether you will engage the services of an SBS consultant. We wrote this book so that you could indeed implement an SBS network on your own with both study and practice (the two key tenets to this book). But many of you might want to extend the SBS best practices in this book by having an SBS consultant on your team for all or part of the SBS project. Furthermore, many of you are reading this book with the thought of becoming an SBS consultant.

Assume that you indeed plan to use an SBS consultant. You need to consider a few things up front. First, many Windows NT Server gurus have bestowed the title of SBS consultant on themselves because the shoe appears to fit. Such is not the case for reasons we presented in Chapter 1, that underscore how different SBS is from Big BackOffice and Windows 2008 Server in the enterprise. So what's our advice to you, the SBS customer? Avoid being the early training grounds for tomorrow's SBS guru (unless you're getting a significant discount on the billing rate being charged by the greenhorn SBS consultant, a point we surface in the next paragraph).

However, SBS gurus are in relatively short supply right now, so what should you do if all you have to select from are SBS newbies? At a minimum, negotiate a training rate that is significantly less (perhaps 50 percent) than the consultant's normal fees. That recognizes that your SBS installation will indeed be a learning exercise you can at least afford. We also recommend that, armed with this book, you work side-by-side with the SBS consultant to make it right!

Those consultants who are SBS gurus tend to be nichers. Like a medical specialist, true SBS gurus basically live and breathe SBS all day long. You'll potentially pay extra for this level of expertise (perhaps a 50 percent premium over the bill rates of a general practitioner), but it's typically considered to be well worth it.

TIP: SBS consulting is something Harry covers in much more detail in his *SMB Consulting Best Practices* book. However, if you're looking for an SBS consultant, be sure to check Microsoft's SBS page at http://www.microsoft.com/smallbusiness/hub.mspx, where there is a tool to find a Microsoft Small Business Specialist. A Microsoft Small Business Specialist company has passed a Microsoft certified exam that focuses on SBS and/or the SMB market.

Looking to establish yourself as an SBS guru? Then check out the *Microsoft – Small Business Specialist Primer* book to be prepared for exams 70-282 and 70-631. Also, learn more at https://www.smbizspecialist.com. Good luck!

Hardware and Software Resellers

To be brutally honest, when purchasing for SBS networks, we've found the very best hardware and software buys on the Internet and via 800 numbers. Our short list of select vendors we have used via this approach include the following:

Hardware

- HP/Compaq. (www.hp.com)
- Dell (www.dell.com)
- Intel (www.intel.com)

Software

- D&H (www.dandh.com)
- Synnex (www.synnex.com)

We have advised clients to be cautious about using resellers to perform the installation work, because these organizations, often storefront retail establishments, typically lack SBS-specific expertise.

TIP: Hardware and software resellers can be a good source of free consulting as long as you keep in mind that you get what you pay for. For example, if you call a major manufacturer to order your server, the sales consultant can serve as a reality check regarding the number of processors, amount of RAM, and hard disk storage to order. That second opinion is of value and can be obtained for free. But, in the end, only those who have firsthand experience installing and supporting SBS networks should be the ones to consult about your SBS setup. Look for the Microsoft Small Business Specialist logo!

The online help system via the Server Management console in SBS 2008 also speaks to hardware requirements.

Another avenue of gleaning knowledge would be via your local Microsoft User Group. Even better, if there is a Small Business Specialist-focused group in your neighborhood, join them, because the pool of knowledge in the group would be awesome!

Ultimately, once you, the SBS consultant, have a number of installs under your belt, you will begin to know what hardware and software combinations will best meet a prospective client's needs.

Wiring and Cabling Contractors

Here again, getting a reference is a great way to locate a competent wiring and cabling service provider. You might check with the property management firm that manages your office space. They most likely use one or two such firms when building out office space.

> **TIP:** Be sure to have the wiring and cabling contractor test and certify his work (network cabling, wall jacks, and so on). Faulty network cabling can wreak havoc on an SBS network, and you should have some type of recourse against the contractor. A cabling and wiring certification provides the documentation with diagrams produced by *professional-quality* cabling equipment.

> One of the author's SBS gigs, at a mortgage brokerage, suffered from faulty wiring. After trying to troubleshoot the software, server, other hardware, and so on, the wiring was finally discovered to be the culprit. So, beware. Bad cabling happens.

Telco

Here our options are limited for giving advice. You might not have the ability to select from multiple telephone companies (telco) that can provide you with the additional lines needed for your Internet connection, faxing, and remote access. However, many areas now have local telco competition, so choice is increasingly becoming available.

> **TIP:** Whenever working with a telco on any matter related to your SBS network, be sure to allow plenty of lead-time for the delivery of the services you request. Due to a booming demand for telephone lines, backlogs in filling service orders can be measured in weeks in many locations.

Internet Service Providers

Aside from using an ISP referral that you deem trustworthy, you have great flexibility in working with any old ISP you might stumble across. The Connect to the Internet wizard and the Internet Address Management wizard (Set up your Internet address) in SBS 2008, are open to working with existing ISP accounts, large ISPs, small ISPs, even your dog's ISP (just a little Springer Spaniel humor there). The wizards are discussed across this book. In the planning phase of the SPRINGERS methodology, it behooves you to be a prudent purchaser of ISP services. Shop around and look for ISPs that best meet your technological needs and budget. For example, you might well find an ISP that is hurricane- and earthquake-proof (having backup batteries on-site that will run for weeks and other features), but such an ISP might be very expensive to do business with.

Advanced Planning Issues

This part of the chapter presents more details on software and hardware issues surrounding your SBS project. We offer a few comments with respect to SBS budgeting and the purchasing process.

Software

SBS ships in a variety of configurations. It's important that you check the SBS 2008 product SKUs at the SBS page at Microsoft (www.microsoft.com/sbs), as these SKUs occasionally change to reflect market conditions (e.g., a competitive upgrade SKU being introduced), changes in pricing, or a new build (e.g., a service pack is slipstreamed into a SKU). You want to pick the right SKU for the right job. For many people, that'll be the OEM SKU for SBS 2008, as they'll be upgrading a server machine at the same time that SBS 2008 is being installed. For others, it'll be the Open Value Agreement with a three-year, spread-payment option SKU of SBS 2008, which provides a total of three years of Microsoft's Software Assurance along with the ability to spread the costs across thirty-six monthly payments.

> **TIP:** We're not trying to cop out here and shorten our typing in this chapter by not going into painful detail on product SKUs, part numbers, and a review of the legal agreement. When one of the authors wrote previous books, in which several pages

were dedicated to pricing, licensing, SKUs, and the such, the information would be out-of-date just six months after publication as Microsoft invariably made significant changes in the product category. Ergo, we're not kidding when we say visit Microsoft's SBS Web page at www.microsoft.com/sbs for the very latest. No book could stay current in this area!

There's even an SBS 2008 SKU that is, in effect, a time-bombed trial version. This evaluation SKU is typically given away at Microsoft events such as TS2 (www.ts2seminars.com). It allows you to run SBS 2008 for a certain amount of time, say 120 days, before you must purchase and install the "real" SBS SKU. The good news is that the evaluation SKU can be upgraded in-place, and you don't need to FDISK or perform a complete reinstall to apply the "real" SBS SKU.

Don't forget part of your SBS 2008 software purchasing process involves securing sufficient client access licenses (CALs) for the client machines that will connect to the SBS 2008 network beyond the default five CALs in the typical SBS SKU. We are delighted to report that we were engaged by Microsoft to write *Course 5499 – Growing Your Business with Windows Small Business Server 2008 and Essential Business Server 2008*. This course does a DEEP DIVE on CALs and other licensing topics (such as solution pathways) that are WAY BEYOND THE SCOPE OF THIS BOOK! Please attend this course as you are able.

Other Software

It is not uncommon to purchase other software to run on the server machine running SBS. We have found that SBS customers typically purchase:

- Third-party backup applications, such as StorageCraft or Acronis. Popular online backup solutions from vendors such as Zenith Infosystem, Divinsa, and others could be considered.

- Virus detection applications, such as Trend Micro's solution, if ForeFront Security and Windows Live OneCare Server are not for you.

- A version of Microsoft Office, accounting applications, or other business applications if needed.

A few of these application areas will be discussed later in the book. The key point is that SBS is rarely purchased and installed in a software vacuum. There is typically a support cast of other software applications running on the SBS machine to provide an organization with a complete computing solution.

> **TIP:** Don't forget that no software discussion is complete without considering what to deploy on the client computers. As of this writing in mid 2008, the choice is clear with respect to workstation operation systems: Windows Vista. Throw on the latest Microsoft Office 2007 software family and you've got a rootin', tootin', wild workstation ready for some serious business!

Hardware

With respect to hardware, you name it, and it has probably been run on an SBS network. Why? Because smaller organizations often have lots of legacy equipment that they want to continue using on their SBS network. And, small businesses aren't known for overspending.

Microsoft has a set of recommended hardware specifications for the server and client workstations on an SBS network. These specifications can be found at—you guessed it—www.microsoft.com/sbs. Here again, we've elected not to list the specifics found on Microsoft's Web page because its SBS hardware specifications are periodically updated to reflect real-world improvements, cost reductions in storage and memory, and good old-fashioned customer feedback.

> **TIP:** So a few real-world tidbits to share: First, as of mid 2008, for a workstation we would recommend 3GB of RAM memory, 250GB or higher of hard disk space, and a Core 2 Duo (say in the 2.33GHz range with a 1066MHz front-side bus). Our words will fall on deaf ears a year after the book is written, of course, as memory and disks drop in price and processors become more powerful! For the SBS configuration, a Xeon X3220 2.4GHz-based server with 6GB of RAM and at least a 500GB RAID 1 mirrored drive set would be a good start for 5-10 seats.

SBS Cheapskate, Beware!

Don't poor-boy that SBS hardware purchase. We've seen people scrimp several ways with SBS-related hardware, none of it acceptable. Here are some examples.

First, small businesspeople have attempted to recycle older monitors from retired workstations so they didn't have to purchase a new monitor with the new server (a cost savings of perhaps $150). The problem is that older monitors can't provide the screen resolution you need to work with the Server Management console. In fact, if you can't create at least a 1024x768 screen resolution on the server during the setup of SBS 2008, you'll have a hard time continuing on with the install.

Second, we've observed small businesses that wanted to use the SBS server machine as a workstation for one of its users. At a land development company, the president (the heir to a well-known Pacific Northwest retail empire) ran Microsoft Word, Outlook, and other applications right on the SBS server machine. The security implications as well as the performance of the SBS box were not acceptable. Several months later, the president purchased a workstation, allowing the SBS server machine to do what it does best: act as a dedicated server. Needless to say, both the president and we were much happier from that point forward in our SBS relationship.

> **TIP:** Better yet, leave the hassles of the cheapskate world behind and buy an honest-to-goodness name-brand server, such as those from an Intel-authorized reseller or HP, to run SBS and avoid many of the problems described above.

Hardware Necessities

It goes without saying that you should purchase at least a pair of good name brand USB hard disk drives to back up your valuable data. SBS 2008 will not support tape backup out of the box (you'll learn about backup improvements later in this book). Other necessities include an uninterruptible power supply (UPS) to protect your system from power anomalies and properly shut it down in a power outage. UPS devices from American Power Corporation (APC) ship with a free copy of a software management application called PowerChute that helps manage your server shutdowns. Make sure that the APC you order for your server is a server-grade UPS! The PowerChute Business Edition software that comes with a server-grade UPS has the ability to run scripts. Those scripts can be used to initiate shutdowns on other servers connected to the UPS. A server grade UPS will also have more runtime versus a similarly sized consumer-grade UPS.

Windows Server Catalog

One of the final hardware issues to be discussed is hardware compatibility. The good news is that SBS 2008 is much less finicky about the hardware you select for use on the server machine compared to prior releases. Here is what we mean. If the hardware runs and is supported on Windows Server 2008, it'll work with SBS 2008! Hardware devices that have been tested for Windows Server 2008 are listed in the Windows Server Catalog at http://www.windowsservercatalog.com/. This list should be honored under all circumstances. In addition, it's a sure bet that noncompliant hardware won't have the cute Windows seal of approval on its retail box!

SBS Budgeting

As the corner is turned on Chapter 2 with its focus on planning, don't forget to keep an eye on the financial farm, that is the SBS budget. We have seen many a good SBS project fail not for technical reasons, but because business basics, such as creating and adhering to a budget, were ignored.

> **TIP:** When budgeting for your network, be sure to consider the following budget tip: If you're eyeing a more powerful server than you planned on purchasing and are concerned about its cost, perhaps the more powerful one isn't as expensive as it first appears. For example, let's say a server with more processors, RAM, and storage would cost you an additional $1,500. Now, assuming you recover your costs or depreciate the server over three years, that incremental amount ($1,500) adds up to an extra $500 per year, or roughly $1.50 per day in aggregate for the entire company. So ask yourself this: For an extra $1.50 per day, shouldn't I purchase the server I really want? In all likelihood, you will probably enjoy more than $1.50 per day in increased network performance,

as measured by your staff's ability to get more work accomplished. Think about it!

Summary

You've now completed two chapters of SBS definition, needs analysis, and planning, and you know what? By our accounts, this likely took two or more days of reading, given you have other demands on your time. That is exactly the amount of time we budget for working with SBS customers when performing the same tasks.

In this chapter, we:

- Introduced Springer Spaniels Limited, including the company background, staff/users, and more, and discussed SBS project management, including several different phases such as planning and training.
- You reviewed the existing network and site and specified the new network.
- The phases ending with the celebration phase before you moved on to read about SBS expectation management, perception, and other consulting topics.
- We talked about stakeholders such as the ISP and telco, who are part of the deployment mix.
- We barely discuss pricing and licensing (that is quickly beyond the scope of this book).
- Discussed advanced planning features, including software and hardware.
- Touched on SBS budgeting.

Forward to Chapter 3, mates!

CHAPTER 3

Small Business Server Installation

The time has come to actually install SBS!

The argument could be made that installing SBS is easy. What with a DVD-based installation, a couple of reboots, and answering some basic installation questions via wizards, you might think it is duck soup. However, such an oversimplification of the SBS installation task is incorrect. You have already invested significant time defining what SBS is, performing a needs analysis, and planning in the prior chapters.

TIP: As you might have guessed from the last chapter, you will implement SBS 2008 based on the SPRINGERS methodology. That is how this chapter is constructed, after many hours of editorial design. By way of a disclaimer, let us say that your specific SBS implementation may vary slightly, based on machine types, components installed, and so on. Furthermore, after we walk you through the step-by-step installation process under the broad jurisdiction of the SPRINGERS methodology, we then present some advanced setup topics in the second part of the chapter. If you are an advanced SBSer who is interested in these advanced topics, you may look at those now before you start the setup process or, preferably, follow the setup process under the SPRINGERS methodology.

Then read the advanced setup topics, taking into account the advanced knowledge that will be imparted for your future real-world SBS setups.

We assume that you are using a new server machine for SBS. If you are using an old server machine that will be redeployed as an SBS server, many of these steps, such as unpacking the server, do not apply. Also, take note that SBS 2008 is 64 bit only. What this means is, you must verify that your existing hardware is Intel EMT64 or AMDx64 before going ahead with the installation. Not to worry, though. Most hardware since the P4 Hyper-Threading Technology (HTT) days are 64-bit capable.

Ditto for same-server-machine SBS upgrade scenarios. In the case of SPRING-ERS, the firm has purchased the following hardware and software shown in Table 3-1. The following table is used to verify that everything ordered was indeed received.

Table 3-1
SPRINGERS hardware and software

Item	Description
Server	Intel Xeon X3360 Quad Core series Server for SMB/SBS, Intel S3210SHLX Server Board, 8GB RAM, Intel SRCSASRB PCI-E RAID Controller, 640GB RAID 0+1 Array, internal DVD-ROM drive, 19" LCD Monitor
Modem	US Robotics 56K External USB
Network Adapter Cards	Intel Dual Gigabit with Adaptive Fault Tolerance-enabled post-wizard configuration steps.
Printer	HP Color LaserJet 4345MFP with internal JetDirect Card.
Other Hardware/Software	APC 1500VA Smart-UPS with PowerChute Business Edition management software.
Software	Microsoft Windows Small Business Server (SBS) 2008 Standard (comes with 5CALs), additional 5 User client access licenses (CALs), StorageCraft's ShadowProtect SBS Edition.

Item	Description
Miscellaneous	Modem cable, extra CAT6 patch cables, telephone cable, power strip/power tree with a minimum 3000 Joule surge rating.

TIP: Just a quick note on whether to pick User or Device CALs for your SBS setup. The rule of thumb is actually quite simple:

- Companies with users like the following: 1 User with 3 devices: Workstation PC, Laptop, Windows Mobile Device should be covered by User CALs.

- Companies that have two or three work shifts, with 3 users on 1 workstation: John, Jane, and Jorge should be covered by Device CALs.

In organizations where there are more devices than users, you should license via User CALs. Where there are more users than devices, you should license via Device CALs.

All of this required hardware adheres to the Windows Server 2008 hardware compatibility list (HCL) discussed in Chapter 2, now known as Windows Server Catalog at http://www.windowsservercatalog.com. If you are an SBS consultant who regularly installs SBS for different clients, you are encouraged to monitor this site regularly and look for changes to either the HCL or System Requirements.

Also, your server system component manufacturer will have a reseller support program, such as the Intel Channel Partner Program (www.intel.com/reseller), where up-to-date information on hardware compatibility as well as driver Windows Hardware Quality Labs (WHQL) certification can be found.

If you are a business person or otherwise a non-SBS consultant installing SBS as a one-time discrete event, a typical situation for a single server system at a single location, just initially verifying the hardware you intend to use for the SBS installation is sufficient.

Note that you should acquire the most current Windows Server 2008 drivers you will need for the SBS installation if necessary. One example of this is to make sure you have an up-to-date SCSI or RAID driver set, which may be needed if your SCSI or RAID controller isn't supported natively by the underlying Windows Server 2008 operating system.

The opportunity to install the SCSI/RAID controller driver will be presented once the Windows Preinstallation Environment has finished booting from the DVD. A really cool new feature we can utilize when there is a need to install drivers is the on-the-fly user of a USB flash drive! That means you can plug that puppy in when the time comes to install a driver without the need for a floppy drive!

If you have a RAID-based system, such as what we're listing above in Table 3-1 as part of our SPRINGERS methodology, you would need to perform the computer manufacturer's steps to prepare the hard disks in the RAID array for use by the operating system. In the case of our server, this is accomplished by selecting CTRL-G (depending on the RAID controller brand) when instructed by the computer during the character-based server's POST. This process will vary by manufacturer and computer model, so kindly use your very best judgment and consult the documentation that accompanied your computer.

In our case, once we are into the RAID controller's BIOS, we will set up two RAID 1 mirrored arrays as our first step. Once that is completed and the RAID controller has accepted the array configuration, we will choose the RAID 0+1 option to give us our performance-boosting RAID stripe.

Preinstallation Tasks

You need to perform several tasks before the actual setup process commences. To be blunt, failing to perform these tasks will certainly result in failure. Better to know this now than later.

Unpack and Connect

Assuming that your infrastructure, such as cabling, is in place and the server you have ordered has arrived, it's time to unpack the server and its components from the shipping boxes. If you haven't built a computer from boxes before, it's actually quite simple. Many name brand servers have color-coded guides so that you know which port the keyboard and mouse attach to. If you are still unsure of yourself, don't hesitate to hire a computer consultant to help you attach all of the necessary components and peripherals to the server. In fact, consider hiring a competent high school or college student who is both computer literate and seeking a few extra dollars. Again, putting together the computer from boxes is quite simple.

Figure 3-1
Springer Spaniel's new SBS Server.

After setting up the server, make sure the following items are properly attached to the server box:

- A monitor or screen (be sure to attach the monitor to a power source). In the case of SPRINGERS, this is a 19-inch LCD monitor.

- A keyboard. Watch out for the lack of a PS/2 port on newer entry-level servers! A USB keyboard may be required.

- A mouse. Again, make sure the mouse has the correct type of connector for the server it will be plugged into.

- A power cable. In the case of redundant power supplies, an A/C Y cable may be supplied with the redundant power supply. Just in case, make sure to have a couple of extra power cables on hand.

- Other external devices that connect directly to the server, such as the USB hard drives to be used for backup purposes, can be set aside for now.

- A set of network cables. The server may plug directly into the Gigabit switch, if it is nearby, or into a set of wall jacks (this connects your server to the network).

- UPS. Make sure to connect your server power cable(s) to the UPS. Do not connect the UPS's USB cable to the server right now. The SBS setup routine can actually trip up the UPS, causing it to step into battery mode. If that happens, the setup process will fail.

If you are interested in developing expertise as a hardware technician to supplement your SBS consulting practice or skills as an SBS administrator, you might also consider studying for and taking the A+ certification exam. The A+ certification is oriented towards computer maintenance from a technician point of view. It is a well-regarded designation created and managed by the Computer Technology Industry Association. For more information on the A+ certification, see www.comptia.com.

Another option is to look into Microsoft's new certification structure, as there are a number of hardware and software configuration-focused certifications coming down the pipe. Check Microsoft's site www.microsoft.com/learning/ for more information.

TIP: Assuming the power is off and unplugged from the computer and external devices, and you are wearing a grounding strip on your wrist to discharge any built-up static electricity (before you touch an electronic component), take a moment to open the SBS machine and reseat all of the adapter cards. It has been our experience that a new server shipped across the country from Hillsboro, OR, can arrive with loosened cards, cables, and even memory chips! That's not to be critical of our friends at Intel, but a fact of life when shipping. Such loose cards have wreaked havoc with some of our early SBS installs when the internal network adapter card couldn't be detected during setup because it had become partially dislodged from its slot. Also, for you SBS consultants, be aware that even a trip across town with a couple of bumps in the road can cause a problem.

Another experience we have had when working with new computers is that the SATA cables located inside the server machine (used to connect hard drives or hot swap backplanes to the motherboard or RAID controller) can come loose. If you need to reattach a SATA cable, be especially cautious not to bend the cable head while seating it in the hard drive or RAID hardware.

After you've completed the check on the system, plug in the power to the server and peripheral devices to proceed with the setup. Please do not forget to verify (sorry to mention this again and again, doing so will save you a lot of time and trouble) that you have sufficient power protection through surge protection power strips and uninterruptible power supplies.

Check the Network

Have the patch cables been run from the patch panel to the Gigabit switch in a tidy manner? Are both ends of the patch panel properly seated in their respective jacks? Perhaps this was a task you assigned to the cabling specialist who installed the cabling at your site. If it hasn't been done, do that now and it will not hurt to verify that things are as they should be.

To verify the fitness of your network, you must perform the "green light" test. After everything has been plugged in properly to the network, including the Gigabit switch, do the following:

1. Turn on the Gigabit switch.

2. Power up the UPS the server is connected to. The network adapters in the server should light up.

3. Observe whether the corresponding light on the Gigabit switch turns on. (This typically illuminates as the color green).

4. Observe whether the network adapter card connection light on the back of the server illuminates. (Again, typically green).

5. If you see green lights at both the Gigabit switch network adapter connections, you're green lighted!

Perform Server Quick Tests

So you've put the server together and connected it to the network. Now is the time to turn on the server to verify the server board and RAID controller BIOS information once the system has been powered up. (This is called POST and is a term used in the technology community). This quick-and-dirty test is important for several reasons. It will check:

- **Video card** – If you see no information displayed on the LCD monitor, it is possible that the video card has failed. Such was the case during an SBS class that Harry once taught. Not only was the computer unusable for the SBS class, but valuable time was wasted trying to determine exactly what the problem was. At first and second blush, it wasn't entirely clear that the video card had failed, as this type of problem can disguise itself.

- **Component attachment** – An incorrectly connected cooling fan power cable can cause problems with the server board. A poorly connected power cable to the hot swap enclosure may cause intermittent hard drive "failure." Or, a stick of memory may not be seated properly. These are exactly the type of issues that you want to catch immediately, before you try to install SBS.

TIP: Most server manufacturers will ship a CD or DVD that contains all of the necessary utilities for updating the various components installed in the server *prior* to installing SBS. These disks tend to be bootable and require that at least one of the network cards be connected to a live Internet connection.

One thing to keep in mind when it comes to the prepackaged updates: The BIOS and firmware updates may be one or two steps behind current, due to the extra development needs of packaging everything up to be accessible to the update utilities.

So, we tend to take advantage of either a simple bootable USB flash drive with all of the necessary updates on it, or, on more advanced server configurations, Intel's Extensible Firmware Interface that provides a Linux style shell from which we execute the updates located on a USB flash drive.

- **BIOS operation** – There is simply no better test to make sure the computer's all-important BIOS is functional than to turn on the machine and hit the F2 key (or whichever key is necessary for your particular configuration) and enter the server board's BIOS environment. You can then key your way through the various BIOS screens to view component information or settings. Common BIOS manufacturers are American Megatrends and Phoenix. All tend to have helpful and relevant navigation and settings change tips specific to whichever BIOS screen you happen to find yourself on.

TIP: It is very common for BIOS manufacturers to release upgrades after the original production BIOS has been shipped to market. These upgrades typically consist of bug fixes and performance and stability improvements, as well as updates to handle new CPU features or versions and the like. So consider downloading the BIOS upgrade and prepare to install or flash the BIOS.

Be extremely careful about applying a BIOS upgrade to your server. If you've applied the incorrect BIOS version to your server, the server can be rendered inoperable or become unreliable. While this can be stressful, most server board manufacturers now provide a way out via a set of jumpers on the motherboard and a separate flash method for recovery. See the BIOS release notes at your BIOS manufacturer's home page. One more thing: Make sure your UPS is *fully* charged before upgrading the BIOS ... just in case a loss of A/C power happens.

If you are at all uncomfortable with this, consider hiring a qualified technician or consultant to research and implement a BIOS upgrade for your server.

- **Operating system status** – The significant change between the SBS 2003 days and now, is the fact that system manufacturers will not preinstall the SBS OS on the server. This is primarily because the entire SBS 2008 setup requires only a few interventions by the SBS OS installer. Among those interventions, though, are things like inputting your domain name, administrator's name and password, etc.

TIP: Note that in the SBS 2000 time frame (admittedly a long time ago), we recommended running the Windows 2000 Readiness Analyzer Tool. We've searched high and low in the SBS 2008 time frame and haven't found a similar tool to recommend for you to run. Perhaps your guide for "readiness" should be the Windows Server 2008 logo on your components. This signifies the component has been tested to work with Windows Server 2008. And don't forget to check the Windows Server Catalog at http://www.windowsservercatalog.com.

One of the final aspects of working with new hardware is called the "burn-in." We use a product by PassMark Software (www.passmark.com) called ***BurnIn-Test Professional Edition***. Once we have the SBS OS installed, all of the requisite drivers and system manufacturer's monitoring and utilities installed, we run this program. A burn-in is typically run for 72 hours straight. We make sure that we set the memory, processors, and disk subsystems to be stressed at or near 100% load for that duration. If anything is going to fail on a server setup, it will more than likely do it during that 72-hour stint.

As a testament to the fact that it works, we just finished a large SBS install for a client that required a hardware refresh for the existing SBS server, which was then being bumped into Windows Server 2008, as well as two new 1U high-performance servers. One of the 1U servers was for SBS 2003, while the other was for Windows Server 2008 Standard x64 Edition with the Hyper-V role installed. While punishing the new 1U SBS server during its burn-in, the front panel light had begun to blink on-off, on-off repeatedly around Day 2. The light remained green, which meant that the problem was not critical, but should be addressed. Since we were dealing with the base OS install of SBS 2003 with no monitoring utilities installed yet, we needed to reboot into the BIOS to read the event logs. Sure enough, one of the memory sticks had failed. In this case, once we had the lid off, we were fortunate that a little LED indicated which slot the memory stick was in. So, we exchanged that stick with a stick in another slot to verify and, sure enough, the new slot the defective stick was in had its trouble light on. Off to RMA the problematic memory stick we went!

That little utility and some time on the bench just saved our client several billable hours!

Another great little utility that can come in handy when we need to quickly assess a system's components right down to their serial numbers and configuration codes is a product by Lavalys (www.lavalys.com) called "Everest." It is the most amazing system-auditing tool we have come across to date. As of this writing, it comes in two flavors:

- Everest Ultimate Edition is the ultimate in system auditing and performance benchmarks for things like CPU or disk subsystems. This edition is great for the small IT shop or the geek in us.

- Everest Corporate Edition has all of the required auditing features with none of the benchmarking capabilities. It does, however, have the ability to automate system audits with the audit data ending up in an Access or SQL database for extensible reporting.

Backup Data

With SPRINGERS, you are installing SBS on an Intel-branded server as part of our sample company setup. The company's data initially resides on the old Windows 2003 server but is also scattered across the company's workstations—until this afternoon, when we will do one final backup image of the server to a USB hard drive using our ShadowProtect IT Edition software. The data will then be transferred to the new SBS server via ShadowProtect again when we are close to going live. That being said, data backup precautions are nothing out of the ordinary. Before we take that old server offline, the last backup image taken from it will be verified.

But let's trade places for a moment and present a different scenario: the reuse of an existing server machine. This assumes you are like many small businesses and hope to reuse your existing server for SBS. So one of the first things you are confronted with is major data backup issues. That is, how do you transfer data, via a single machine, from your previous operating system (such as Windows Server 2000 or 2003) to SBS?

With a tool like StorageCraft's ShadowProtect, the above same hardware scenario is made relatively easy. In fact, the image-based backup, when utilizing the IT Edition of the product, can be used to move that already installed Windows Server OS onto a completely different hardware configuration!

TIP: For the SBS guru, or SBS consultant: Take a good look at the StorageCraft ShadowProtect product we use. It can be a life saver in the event of a hardware or hard drive failure. When utilized to its fullest potential, this product enhances the confidence of any SBSer providing disaster recovery services to their clients.

In the spirit of fairness, we encourage you to also look at Acronis and its similar offerings in this exact area. Other related storage vendors include eFolder, Backup Assist, and numerous other online vendors, such as Vembu and Divinsa. Be a smart customer and research this area.

Read the Release Notes

Take our advice and open the SBS_ReleaseNotes.rdf that can be found on the SBS 2008 DVD-ROM in the docs folder.

- This provides the following link to Microsoft's online SBS 2008 documentation on the TechNet Web site: http://go.microsoft.com/fwlink/?LinkID=91366. As of this writing, the online documentation was already in its third version.

- It also provides a number of relatively up-to-date lists of installation caveats.

Besides the SBS_ReleaseNotes.rtf file, a pair of Compiled HTML Help Files called SBS_Help.chm and SBS_MigrationCHM.chm can be found there.

- SBS_Help.chm contains links to various SBS 2008 online technical libraries and support resources. It also covers the daily management of SBS, users, groups, computers, devices, and more. Some basic troubleshooting tips can be found in the last section of the help file.

- SBS_MigrationCHM.chm contains links to various SBS 2008 online technical libraries related to the various migration scenarios you may come across. Two migration scenarios are covered: SBS 2003 to SBS 2008 and SBS 2008 to SBS 2008. The help file ends with some Migration wizard topics.

SBS Site Review

Humor us and quickly walk around the site where the SBS 2008 network will be installed and make sure that there is no existing DHCP Server (either another server machine or a router-type device). Suffering from fatigue, we didn't do this at one of our first SBS installations several years ago, and sure enough, it came home to bite us bad. It turns out, as this story goes, the client site (a law firm) was a sublease from a former dot-com enterprise gone dot-bomb. Upon moving in, the law firm used much of the technology equipment, including the DSL router, from the former tenant. It turned out the DSL router, which no one had the password to, was acting as a DHCP server and issuing internal 10.x.x.x network IP addresses to workstations. When installing the SBS server machine, we found this condition violated one of the cardinal laws in SBS land: SBS must be the one and only DHCP server on the network.

So the outcome of all this was that the SBS server didn't complete its setup. We had to manually add the DHCP Server service and configure the default scope, add the Windows Internet Naming Service (WINS), and also re-run the SBS Setup wizard in order for the licensing manager to work properly. (Initially the licensing manager wasn't accounting for logged off workstations, causing it to reach its limit of ten workstations very quickly.) The lesson learned, even though this was actually with the SBS 2000 release, was that more planning would have prevented this foolish error. Our embarrassment is clearly your gain.

One other point on telco or other supplied equipment by an ISP: Make sure to verify that the modem does not have some sort of router integrated into it. These days, many telco DSL modems we have come across *do* have a router or even a wireless access point built in. Keep in mind that these items may present a problem when it comes time to publish Internet-facing SBS features.

SBS Installation Overview

Allow us to take a moment to outline the SBS installation process for you as five major phases. Understanding this setup blueprint is important because, if your setup fails somewhere along the line, you can quickly assess at what stage your setup failed. That failure assessment is extremely beneficial in troubleshooting any setup problems you might be having. Your understanding of the setup process will also help you communicate with your SBS consultant (a.k.a. SBS guru) or Microsoft support.

TIP: These setup steps assume you have purchased SBS as a standalone retail software package, either as part of your TechNet Plus Subscription or via the Microsoft Action Pack Subscription for Microsoft Partners (one of the prerequisites to the Microsoft Small Business Specialist program, by the way). These are not the same steps undertaken by the preinstalled (or OEM) version of SBS. The SBS OEM preinstallation approach is discussed later in the chapter.

The first thing we need to keep in mind is that there are two methods for installing the SBS OS: with the SBS Answer File and without the SBS Answer File. Both methods involve booting into the Windows Preinstallation Environment (WinPE) and running through some of the initial setup questions such as language, locale, OS partition setup, and the like.

From there, the amount of time and input required to continue the SBS setup routine is significantly different as shown in Figure 3-2:

1. **Without the Answer File:** You will need to manually enter any required information such as the company name, domain name, new domain administrator name, administrator's password, and more in between certain server reboots. The information inputs happen at different stages of the setup, so you would need to be near the server while this process runs in order to avoid any unnecessary delays. This method would be fine for the business owner or in a one-time install situation.

2. **With the Answer File:** Once the initial steps in the WinPE environment have been completed, the server install will continue on its own by inputting the required information at the same points as above, but automatically. This method would be the preferred method for installing the OS for SBS consultants.

Notes:

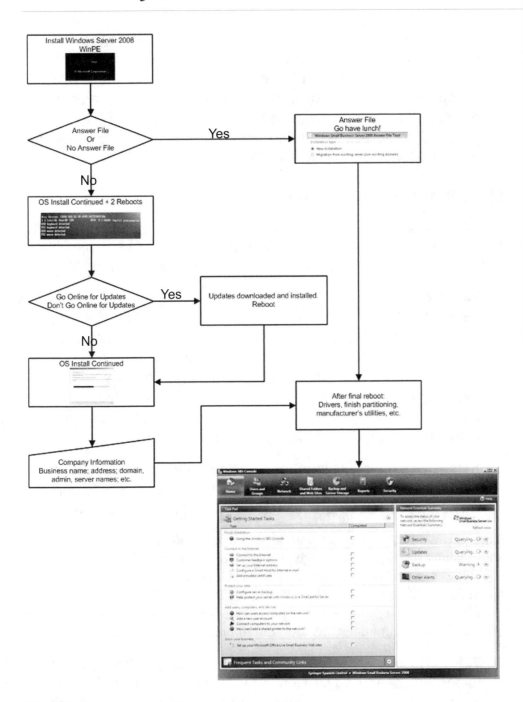

Figure 3-2

SBS installation overview.

TIP: To the SBS consultant and the SBS guru: Using the SBS Answer File will be one of the best ways to get your installs consistent across many different client setups. For those SBS consultants that are growing into needing an employee technician or two, or already have them, the SBS Answer File can give you some peace of mind knowing that your installs will be consistent across the board.

SBS OS WinPE Setup (Phase 1)

This phase consists of inserting the first SBS DVD (Premium will have an SBS DVD, Windows Server 2008 Standard x86 and x64 DVDs, and a SQL 2008 DVD) and booting the server into the Windows Preinstallation Environment (WinPE).

TIP: Take note that in SBS Premium we have the choice between a 32 bit (x86) or a 64 bit (x64, AMD64, EMT64) version of Windows Server 2008 to install on our second box. With SBS 2008, we do not have this luxury. SBS 2008 must be installed on a 64 bit capable server system. A few years ago, this may have presented a bit of a problem where legacy 32 bit hardware was more common, but most, if not all servers, within the last couple of years are 64 bit enabled.

In fact, as we discuss in other published works, the need for a hardware refresh might be one of the strongest reasons to purchase the SBS 2008 product! That's called a demand driver.

Once into WinPE, you must answer questions regarding the locale in which you are installing the OS, the language preferred for communication purposes, and your time zone. Create a partition of at least 60GB for the SBS OS to reside on. For our SPRINGERS setup, we will be setting a 75GB partition for the OS to install to leave lots of room for just about anything! Extensive file copying and expanding occurs at this stage from the SBS disc. The computer reboots once.

TIP: Also note that Windows Server 2008, acting as the underlying operating system in SBS, utilizes the same recovery console accessed by selecting the F8 key early in the boot phase of Windows Server 2008. (A text message at the bottom of the screen will advise you to hit F8.)

SBS Answer File Install (Phase 2)

Once you have set the required settings in the WinPE environment and the server is on its way into the setup routine, go have a coffee, eat lunch, or even head on home for the evening! When you come back to the server you will be greeted by the green checkmark of a successful install found in Figure 3-3!

SBS Installation and First Input Round (Phase 3)

Once the server has run its course through the expansion of the SBS files and the beginnings of putting things together, you will be asked some questions. After a couple of reboots, you will see **Preparing your desktop...** until the install routine is ready for some input.

Initially, the input required will be a question about whether to search the Internet for any needed OS updates. It would be a good idea to answer "yes" to this question, unless there is an update that is known to cause the OS to hiccup.

After the setup routine downloads the updates and continues to run for a while, you will eventually be prompted for the following information that was presented to you in Chapter 2:

1. Company information, such as the business name and address. (For example, Springer Spaniels Limited on #456 Beach Road.)
2. Server name and the domain name. (SS-SBS and SpringersLtd, respectively, and discussed more later.)
3. A name, logon name, and password for the domain admin account.
4. One last chance before final committal: A summary screen with the above settings will show up before the install routine continues. This is your very last chance before needing to start from scratch if a mistake was made.

After you provide the information in Steps 1 through 4 above, Active Directory and its required services, such as DNS, are installed and configured in the Windows Configuration stage. Additional Windows Server 2008 services, such as DHCP and Terminal Services Gateway, are installed as well.

The server will continue to run through its install routine with the requisite reboots until finished. You will be greeted with the Successful Installation green checkmark screen shown in Figure 3-3.

Figure 3-3
The Windows Small Business Server 2008 Successful Install screen.

TIP: Regarding the SBS installation process, actual installation time varies greatly. It can take anywhere from 30 minutes to a couple of hours depending on the amount of RAM your server has (4GB is slower than 8GB), speed of your CPU(s), your RAID subsystem setup, and CPU clock and front side bus speeds. The biggest factor by far in the speed of your install will be your server's RAM. For example, we were doing an SBS install on a dual Xeon E5440 series server with 4GB and a single Xeon 3070 with 8GB (our Springer's box) and the single Xeon with 8GB was a *lot* faster!

SBS Hardware Configuration, Driver Installs, and Utilities (Phase 4)

Once we have a viable server install, there will be a lot of things competing for your attention. For now, we are going to ignore them as we need to get the rest of our partitions set up, and our OS swap file moved over to a dedicated partition which requires a reboot. Note that our server board chipset drivers are installed, RAID and manufacturer's utilities are installed, and any other required software installation and configurations completed prior to running the SBS wizards.

> **TIP:** Why install your drivers and utilities before running the SBS wizards? Microsoft has done a great job of providing a broad base of drivers during the initial WinPE installation routine. Even then, we make sure to have the latest Windows Server 2008 x 64 RAID controller driver on hand to load before setting the OS partition. The same is true when we are getting ready to do the wizard-based steps on the SBS box. We make sure to download the latest drivers for our server board's chipset, the hot swap baseboard controller, RAID controller management software, and more.

SBS Getting Started Tasks List (Phase 5)

On the Successful Installation screen shown above in Figure 3-3 is the **Start using the server** button. When we click the button we are greeted with the new SBS Console and the Getting Started Tasks list.

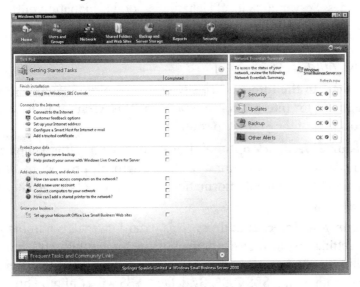

Figure 3-4
The new SBS Console and the Getting Started Tasks List.

TIP: The Getting Started Tasks list in SBS 2008 is much different from the SBS 2003 To Do List. The new Home Task Pad is divided into two categories: The Getting Started Tasks and the Frequent Tasks and Community Links. The Getting Started Tasks run the requisite SBS wizards to complete the configuration of your SBS server and the Frequent Tasks and Community Links have links to wizards such as the **Add a new user account**, **Add a new group**, or **Add a new report** that would be used during daily SBS management. Also on this task pad are links to online resources such as the Microsoft Small Business Center, Windows Small Business Server Community, and the Windows Small Business Server TechCenter. We will complete much of the SBS 2008 Getting Started Tasks in Chapter 4.

The Getting Started Tasks are grouped into five categories:

Finish Installation

1. **Using the Windows SBS Console.** This link brings up the Windows Small Business Server 2008 local Help file. A good explanation of the SBS Consoles and its features are pointed out.

Connect to the Internet

1. **Connect to the Internet.** This wizard configures SBS 2008 to work with the router for Internet communication. This wizard is unique in that it is also a part of the SBS setup routine.

2. **Customer feedback options.** This is not a wizard. It is a choice you need to make just as you do for any other Microsoft product to allow certain nonidentifying bits of information on the usage of the product to be sent to Microsoft.

3. **Set up your Internet address.** This wizard gives us a number of options for setting up our Internet domain name for use with SBS. It includes the ability to obtain an Internet domain name and have that domain managed from within SBS 2008. By default, SBS will configure https://remote. mysbsdomain.com to gain access to the Remote Web Workplace and other Internet facing services.

4. **Configure a Smart Host for Internet e-mail.** This is a new wizard for SBS 2008 to make forwarding outgoing e-mail to your ISP's e-mail servers a breeze. No more digging about in Exchange to find the particular places we needed to set up a Smart Host.

5. **Add a trusted certificate.** This wizard enables us to create a Certificate Request to use with our SSL certificate provider to obtain and subsequently install the SSL certificate into SBS.

TIP: New to SBS 2008 is how the self-issued SBS certificate is handled. We now have a zipped folder that we need to bring home via USB flash drive to run a utility to install the certificate on the PC. There are a number of security implications here too: E-mailing that zipped folder across the Internet is not a good practice, nor is posting it to a Web site. With the advent of very inexpensive third-party SSL certificates, there really should be no need to run with the self-issued SBS SSL certificate anymore.

Both authors typically use a third-party SSL certificate with SBS 2008.

Protect Your Data

1. **Configure Server backup.** Our SBS 2008 backup is no longer based on NTBackup! We now need to have a couple of external USB 2.0 hard disks, each with at least 75% of the total storage capacity of the SBS box. From there we run the wizard to initially set up our backups and manage our backup drives. Not to worry, SBS 2008 knows which drive is plugged in even when we swap them out midday.

2. **Help protect your server with Windows Live OneCare for Server.** Out of the box, SBS comes with a 120-day trial version of Windows Live OneCare for Server. We run the wizard to configure and get the most recent updates. Windows Live OneCare for Server in trial mode at least gives us some protection for our server if a decision has not been made on what security product to run with, or the security product is not going to be installed right away.

TIP: When it comes to the new SBS 2008 backups, it is important to note that the backups themselves are encrypted. Not only that, you can take one of the SBS USB backup drives and plug it into another computer and the first question the operating system will ask is **This disk is not formatted. Do you want to format now?**

Add Users, Computers, and Devices

1. **How can users access computers on the network?** This link brings up the SBS local Help file to fill you in on the various aspects of managing users' access to network resources.

2. **Add a new user account.** We use this wizard to add users and assign them permissions on the SBS network. Out of the box, SBS 2008 has three User Roles from which to choose: Standard User, Standard User with Administration Links, and Network Administrator. The second option is much like the Power User was for SBS 2003. They can perform some minor management tasks on the SBS box.

3. **Connect computers to your network.** This link brings up a note about the need for SBS to make changes to the workstation or laptop when these are added to the SBS domain. It also points out that we must add our SBS users before we are to set up any workstations for them. From there, we are given two options for configuring those workstations: http://connect or the Connect Computer program can be placed on a USB flash drive to be run on the workstation.

4. **How can I add a shared printer to the network?** This SBS Help link gives us information on sharing a printer via a Windows Vista or XP workstation as well as when the printer is plugged into the network directly.

Grow Your Business

1. **Set up your Microsoft Office Live Small Business Web sites.** This wizard will take you through the steps for creating an online presence that can be managed and updated from within the SBS network.

Microsoft created the Getting Started Tasks with the idea that you would complete each step in order (according to members of the SBS development team who shared this public information with us directly over the years). We agree with

Microsoft on this point, that the SBS Getting Started Tasks should be completed in order, because it's part of the SBS methodology for being successful (Harry spends hundreds of pages addressing this topic in his *SMB Consulting Best Practices* book). Understand that nothing prevents you from either following the Getting Started Tasks step-by-step or using an ad-hoc To Do List approach. As with the execution of any task on a computer, always think before acting and use your best judgment.

> **TIP:** You can return to the Getting Started Tasks at any time, not just the first time you log on to the SBS computer. This is accomplished by clicking the **Home** tab and the **Getting Started Tasks** at the bottom of the **Task Pad** if it is not already showing.

Final Configuration and Testing

This phase resolves loose ends, including attaching and making operational the uninterruptible power supply (UPS) we discussed in Chapter 2. You will need to verify via the Network Essentials Summary on the right-hand side of the SBS Console that everything is checking out okay. Note that the backup will reflect an exclamation mark until the first scheduled backup runs.

This would be a good time to click on the **Updates** status under the **Network Essentials Summary** and click through to the **Updates** section. Take note of any updates waiting to be approved for installation into the SBS OS and its components. Once approved, you can run the following command to force the server to check for updates:

- wuauclt /resetauthorization /detectnow [Enter]

> **TIP:** The above-mentioned program is the Windows Automatic Update Client (WUAUCLT). A good idea would be to copy the above command into a batch file, name it something like "WSUSDetect.bat," and place it in your admin folder either on SharePoint or on a company folder share. Whenever you add a new workstation or server to the SBS network, you could then run the batch file to speed up the new client's update detection after adding the client to the SBS domain.

Ready, Set, Go

Make sure you're familiar and armed with the numerous SBS setup sheets from Chapter 2. If this is your first pass through the book, these sheets, which reflect setup information for SPRINGERS, have been completed for you. If this is your second pass through the book, and you're installing SBS for real, gather blank setup sheets from our Web site at www.smbnation.com. Much of the information on the setup sheets will be called for in the next section.
You are now ready to install SBS 2008.

TIP: Let's take a deep breath at this point to reflect and meditate for a moment on exactly what is going on here.

The planning and installation presented to date, and the forthcoming setup steps, are based on the viewpoint of SPRINGERS. Why? Because this book has been written with the idea in mind that, if you invest some of your limited time and you follow each step in this book, you will begin your journey to becoming a bona fide SBSer with a functional network for SPRINGERS. That is the underlying paradigm to how we wrote this book, and as you might imagine, we jealously guard our SPRINGERS methodology for quality assurances purposes.

Now, granted, your situation may be dramatically different if you install more than one SBS network (particularly if you are an SBS consultant). For example, one client site may use an SCSI-based disk system with an add-in SCSI controller on an older P4 workstation computer as the server machine. Another site may use an onboard SATA RAID controller with a single Xeon CPU. And yet another site may use a high performance SAS RAID setup with hot swap capabilities and a dual Quad Core. Variations in SBS hardware implementations will exist, depending on your client's unique situation.

Another area of variation is data migration. You may or may not have data to migrate from another machine, such as an old server, or from a series of shares across all workstations on a peer-to-peer network setup, or even on the box on which the SBS OS is to be installed. Talk about an area where things can vary on a case-by-case basis, that area would be in data (some data is comma separate value, some is text, some uses XML, etc.)

So what's the bottom line? Stick with us and follow this methodology exactly and you'll have a functional SBS network for SPRINGERS after completing this book. (We are assuming it would take you about a month to complete the book from start to finish in a thoughtful manner.) But in the very next breath, we are not tough old Angus bulls as we first appear. If you are reading this book for pleasure and do not care to follow SPRINGERS chapter and verse, God be with you—still, it's likely you'll derive great value from these pages. But, let us get back to the SPRINGERS methodology. As an example, we have a printer installed on the SBS network later in the chapter, but you might not have a printer in the real world of SBS implementations. While it's unlikely you won't have a printer, SBS can be implemented without incident in the absence of a printer. Heck, you can even install the Shared Fax Service without a modem attached!

Vary from this specific methodology and you're on your own. (Sorry, mate!) Thanks!

The first step assumes that you have a server machine that has the BIOS boot order set to boot from the DVD drive *before* the hard drive/RAID controller setup. You may want to verify that setting prior to attempting the SBS OS setup. Some server BIOSs have the ability to make a one-time boot device choice too, which may work well for the SBS OS install.

To make things simple, we are going to run through the setup routine once for both Answer File and No Answer File based setup routines. Essentially, we will point out to you, if you are using the Answer File, when you can head out for lunch or home if it is the end of the day.

TIP: If you look back at Table 2-4 you will see that the server has an IP address of 192.168.40.2 and the router has an IP address of 192.168.40.1. During the SBS OS install there is a search routine in place to find a router.

As a rule, we set up our client IP subnet at 192.168.40.0/24. Why? Because using 192.168.0.0/24 through 192.168.5.0/24 may cause a problem for users who go home and connect to the SBS network via VPN.

For instance, let's say our SPRINGERS SBS network was on the 192.168.1.0/24 subnet. Now Bob Easter has a consumer router at home that hands out an IP address to his home computer: 192.168.1.100. Bob needs to grab some files from the company-shared folder. So, he connects via VPN, but he can't seem to get to the folder at all! A support call will be the next step.

The reason for this is that both the SBS network and the home network are on the same subnet. So, when Bob's computer at IP address 192.168.1.100 asks for the file, SBS looks around the *internal* SBS network for that IP address! Of course, SBS may find that IP address assigned to a workstation on the network, but it will not be Bob's home computer so things stall.

SBS Setup

Ladies and gentlemen, it's time to rock and roll, SBS 2008 style!

1. A very important first step is to set up your router/NAT device. You will need a workstation or laptop to plug into the device to set it up. Follow your device's instructions on how to set up the internal IP address as 192.168.40.1. You will also need to port forward 25, 443, 987, and 1723 if you are going to allow VPN in to the SBS IP address of 192.168.40.2. If you are using an Answer File, then port forward to the IP address you set in the file.

2. Power up the server.

3. Insert the Microsoft Windows Small Business Server 2008 DVD in the DVD-ROM. If you see the **Press any key to boot from CD or DVD** message, press a key to initiate the SBS setup routine.

TIP: Note that if this is the first time you are installing any OS on the server, you will see the **Windows is loading files...** with a progress bar underneath without the above **Press any key to boot from CD or DVD** message. There is a quick OS detection routine that runs when the SBS OS DVD first spools up that will jump right into the setup routine if no OS is detected. The progress bar lets us know that the Windows Preinstallation Environment (WinPE) is being loaded up to provide us with a limited Windows environment to work through our initial setup steps. Gone are the days where we needed to run through a text-based setup environment!

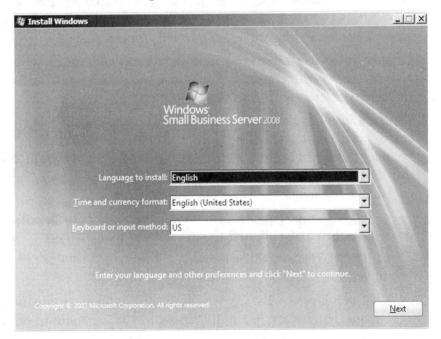

Figure 3-5
The initial Install Windows setup screen.

4. At the initial **Install Windows** page shown in Figure 3-5, verify that the **Language to Install, Time and currency format**, and the **Keyboard or input method** settings are correct then click **Next**. In our case:

    a. Language to install: **English**

    b. Time and currency format: **English (United States)**

    c. Keyboard or input method: **US**

5. Click **Install Now**. We also see a couple of links:

    a. **What to know before installing Windows**

        • This link brings up a Windows Help and Support window with install notes, system requirements, and some known install issues we may run into.

    b. **Repair your computer**.

        • This link takes us into the system recovery routine. We will delve into SBS Recovery in our forthcoming *Advanced SBS 2008 Blueprint* book (due mid-2009), as this book you are reading now is an introductory text.

6. Observe the **Please wait** page. Once we have clicked through the **Install Now** button, we will receive a **Please wait** message while the WinPE environment gets set up for the next steps.

7. **Type your product key for activation** page appears. Type in your product key now in the **Product key** field and note that the dashes will automatically be added (shown in Figure 3-6). Depending on whether you are installing the OEM version, the Open Licensing version, or a Retail version, the label containing Product Key is located in different places.

    a. **OEM:** Located on the Certificate of Authenticity that needs to be attached to the physical server box.

    b. **Retail:** The key will be located on a sticker inside of the product box.

    c. **Open License:** The key will be located on the back of Disc 1. It may be necessary with this version of SBS to obtain the product key via the Microsoft Volume Licensing Services (MVLS) Portal at https://licensing.microsoft.com/eLicense/L1033/Default.asp. A Live ID and the Agreement details will be required to set up prior to obtaining any keys from this site.

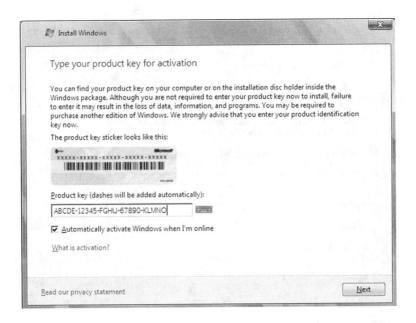

Figure 3-6
Type your Product Key for activation. No key puts SBS into trial mode that can run as long as 240 days!

TIP: At this point, we also have the option to uncheck the **Automatically activate Windows when I'm online** option. This will place the SBS 2008 OS into trial mode. The trial period will be 240 days from the date of the OS install. One of the neat new features that we inherit from the Windows Server 2008 family is the ability to input a Product Key at anytime during the trial version. So, we do not need to worry about a need to rebuild or migrate an SBS 2008 domain we may have setup in trial mode. Keep in mind that while the SBS OS can run up to 240 days without a key, some of the SBS server components may run for fewer days (some of the online components are 180-day time bombed).

8. Next you will see the **Please read the license terms** page. Once you have read through the End User Licensing Agreement shown in Figure 3-7 and agree with it, click the **I accept the license terms** checkbox, click **Next**, and you are on your way to the next step.

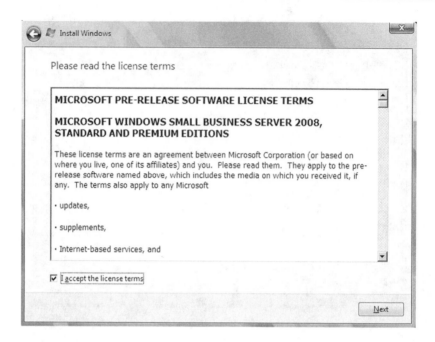

Figure 3-7
The End User Licensing Agreement.

TIP: You have read the End User Licensing Agreement (EULA) right? It contains all of the necessary information you need to know when it comes to the how, what, when, and where you can set up and use the SBS 2008 operating system.

Another important bit of information you will find in the EULA is the virtualization rights for the particular edition of SBS you have. Those rights will vary depending on whether you have an OEM, Retail, Upgrade, or Open License version of the product.

9. The **What type of installation do you want?** page is displayed. Click on **Custom (advanced)** which is the only option you can choose at this point.

TIP: Configuring partitions for an SBS setup can be quite a challenge if you are a new SBS consultant or a first-time SBS installer. Microsoft recommends a minimum of 60GB for the operating system partition. In the case of the Springer Spaniel's SBS box, we will be configuring our partitions like so:

- 75GB for the system partition (OS)

- 25GB for the Swap File (improves performance by keeping the swap file contiguous).

- Balance to server and user data.

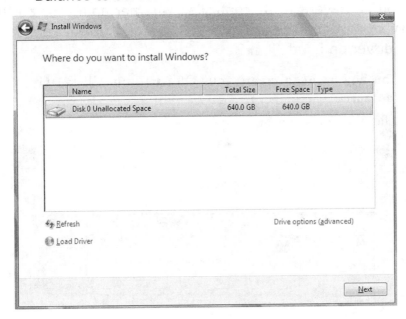

Figure 3-8
The RAID 0+1 array is ready for our system partition.

10. Next you will see the **Where do you want to install Windows?** page. You are now presented with your hard drive or RAID array setup in the form of unallocated space, as shown in Figure 3-8, or spaces if there are multiple drives, as in Figure 3-4. You have two options here (we assume you are loading a driver):

   a. Click on **New** and create the 75GB array *or*

   b. Click on **Load Driver** to load your RAID controller driver. You can plug your USB flash drive in with the driver, browse to it, and load it.

TIP: A very significant improvement in the Windows Server install routine is the ability to plug a USB flash drive into the server computer on-the-fly. The only method Server 2003 allowed for was to load that driver via a floppy drive. Be advised that having the USB flash drive plugged into the server before powering it up, or on a reboot, can throw your server's BIOS drive boot order out of whack.

If you do have a RAID controller, whether add-in or on the server board, make sure to have the most current version of the driver on hand.

11. You now want to create your OS partition. Click **Drive options (advanced)**.

12. Click the **New** star icon.

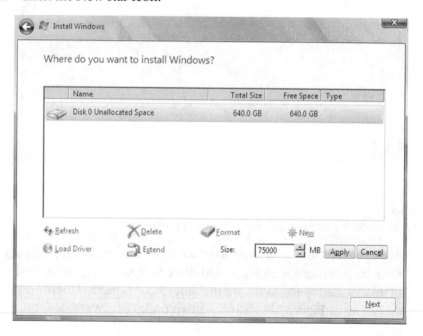

Figure 3-9
Setting up the 75GB partition to which the SBS OS will be installed.

13. Set the size to **75000** and click the **Apply** button. Make sure your highlight is on the newly created partition, which will format out to about 73.2GB.

14. Click **Next**. The **Installing Windows** page appears. The Copy files and Expanding files routine will run through until a reboot is required. This will take several minutes (up to 30 minutes by our count) for the entire setup to complete.

    For those who are using an **SBS Answer File**, now is the time to take a break, move on to other things, or head home for the evening.

15. The server will cycle through the setup routine and reboot again. You will see the **Preparing your desktop...** for a period of time depending on the speed of your server.

16. The **Continue installation** page is displayed. We have completed the first phase of the SBS 2008 install routine! Note the install timing mentioned. That timing will vary greatly depending on the configuration of your server. Click **Next**.

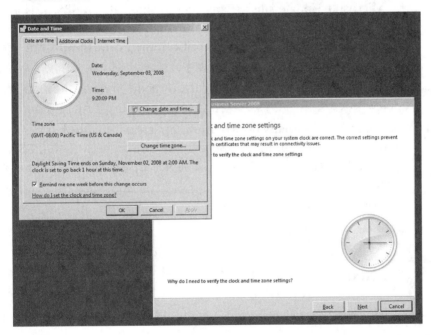

Figure 3-10
Verifying our date, time, time zone, and more.

17. View the **Verify the clock and time zone settings** page. Click the **Open Date and Time to verify the clock and time zone settings** link (as shown in Figure 3-10).

TIP: You will be presented with a popup that has three tabs: **Date and Time**, **Additional Clocks**, **Internet Time**. Date and Time are pretty straightforward. The Additional Clocks setting is Windows' ability to display up to three clocks. This feature may be important for those companies that have offices on different continents. The Internet Time setting is the setting that tells Windows where on the Internet to check for the correct time. Traditionally this is set to time.windows.com. It is important to note that having the correct time setup is key to a good Windows security setup.

18. Once the clock and time zone settings are configured, click **Next**.

19. Next is the **Get important updates** page. You are given the option to poll the Microsoft Update site for any relevant updates to SBS. It is a good idea to click the **Go online and get the most recent installation updates (recommended)** link. If timing is critical, then click the **Do not get the most recent installation updates** link.

20. If you chose to go online and update, a reboot may happen during the update process.

21. The important **Company information** appears. Fill out the business name, address, city, state, zip, and country. In the case of the SPRINGERS methodology, this was first presented in Chapter 2 (see Table 2-4) and is given to you again here.

    Name: Springer Spaniels Limited

    Address: 3456 Beach Front Road

    City, State, Zip, Country: Bainbridge Island, WA 98110, USA

    Click **Next**.

Notes:

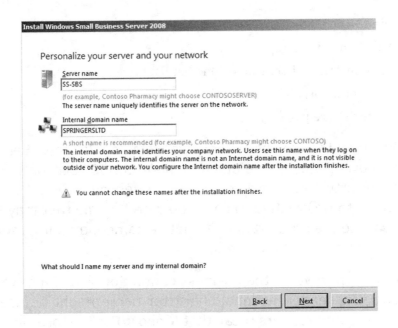

Figure 3-11
Personalize your server and your network by naming both.

22. You are now greeted by the **Personalize your server and your network** page. Choose your server name, in our case **SS-SBS**, and your **Internal domain name,** which is **SpringersLtd** for us. Note the absence of the top level domain .local. Click **Next**.

TIP: Take careful note of the name of the server and the name of the internal domain. The settings chosen remain for the life of the server and the SBS domain.

For us, a naming convention we follow for our client setups tends to be two initials indicating the company name. SS = Springer Spaniels. SS-SBS represents Springer Spaniel's Small Business Server.

23. The **Add a network administrator account** page is displayed. Enter the first and last name for the domain admin account along with the user name. Set the password following the guidelines in the window. The information you will enter is the Jonathan Paul entry in Table 2-2 in Chapter 2 and presented here.

First Name: Jonathan

Last Name: Paul

Administrator's User Name: JonathanPaul

Password: L0ts and lots of fun!

(note this is a passphrase)

TIP: Out of the box, both Windows Vista and Windows Server 2008 now disable the default administrator 500 account. This is a security best practice recommended by Microsoft. So, we need to be creative to come up with a name that may be relevant to the organization but not be someone's name, such as that of one of the owners.

With the approval of the business contact or owner, a historical person, leader, fictional character name might be used. Perhaps some readers recall that Kinko's/FedEx stores in the US had network names after movie stars. The concept is similar here.

24. The **Install security services** page appears. Leaving the checkmarks beside **Windows Live OneCare for Server** and **Microsoft Forefront Security for Exchange Server** installs a 120-day trial version of each product. For the sake of the SPRINGERS methodology, we will be leaving these checked. Click the **Next** button.

Notes:

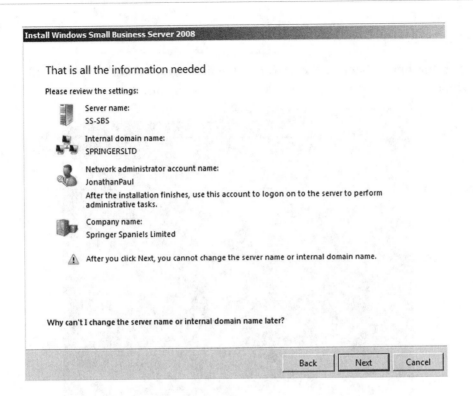

Figure 3-12
After this step, there is no turning back!

25. Finally you see the **That is all the information needed** page. Last chance shown in Figure 3-12! If you need to make any changes to the shown information, or fix a typo, this is the time to hit that **Back** button! Click the **Next** button to let the SBS setup go off on its own. You have now completed the core SBS 2008 setup procedure.

Now it is time to go have a coffee, move on to other things, or head out for the day. Depending on your system configuration, the continuation of the setup process can take anywhere from 30 to 120 minutes or more. As always, your mileage will vary!

So assuming otherwise that all went well, let us be the first to say congratulations! You have now completed the full installation of your SBS server machine using the SPRINGERS methodology. Now, more configuration items await you.

The Getting Started Tasks List Lives!

Upon the final reboot of the server, you will be greeted with Figure 3-13: The Windows Small Business Server 2008 is successfully installed!

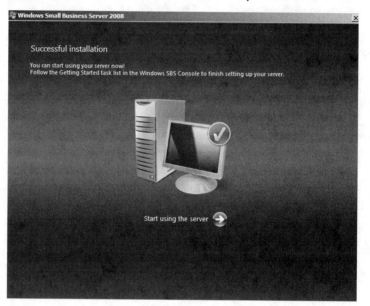

Figure 3-13
Windows Small Business Server is now successfully installed!

Note that if there were any installation problems, instead of a **green checkmark**, you will see an **Exclamation Mark** encased in a yellow triangle—a warning that indicates noncritical issues were encountered during the installation process. There will be two options to click through on:

1. View installation issues
2. How do I get help with installation issues?

We will address a few possible issues that may occur during the SBS setup later in this chapter. One place to keep an eye on, though, is the SBS Team's blog: http://blogs.technet.com/sbs/ where anything and everything related to SBS can be found.

When you click through the **Start using the server** button, you will be presented with the new SBS Console shown in Figure 3-14.

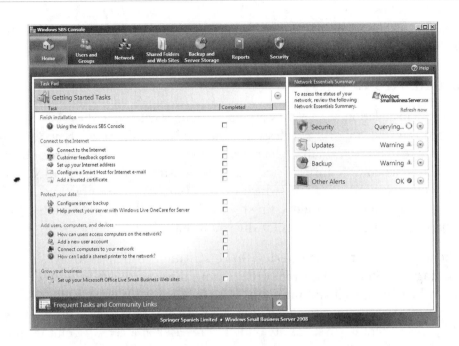

Figure 3-14
The new SBS Console and the Getting Started Tasks List.

In Chapter 5 we pick up the SBS deployment process using the SPRINGERS methodology. You will also complete the Getting Started Tasks List and learn more about the various SBS 2008 Server Management consoles. Yes, we did say *consoles*! In SBS 2008 we now have three separate consoles for the SBS administrator versus the one SBS 2003 Console with the wizards section and the Advanced section with many of the server component MMCs.

OEM Setup Scenario

With the advent of Windows Vista and the new WIM (Windows Imaging) file format, the methodology for setting up the base OS image has changed dramatically. Windows Server 2008 and now SBS 2008 also share in the WIM file format setup for bulk OS installations.

For small SBS consultancies, WIM gives you the ability to set up your client's new SBS box via DVD, bootable USB flash drive, network using a bootable WinPE USB flash drive, and even Windows Deployment Services Server if you go so far as to set up WDS on your own shop's network.

Given the new OEM structures and their complexity, besides not fitting into the SPRINGERS methodology, we will not get into the OEM.

Unsupported Devices

Every SBS installation has a right way and a wrong way to do it, the easy way and the hard way, the "follow the rules way" and the "break the rules" way. Surprisingly, you're likely to try, suffer, cheer, celebrate, and curse all approaches during your tenure as an SBS guru. So far, we've demonstrated only the SPRINGERS methodology for installing SBS (which we believe to be a "best practices" methodology). Now, and we are addressing the most advanced guru SBSers among us, let's break the rules and understand why you would do so.

Without question, one of the greatest SBS installation challenges today is that of managing your library of current drivers from third-party vendors. By that we mean, when you install and maintain SBS, you have the latest drivers from the vendors of the components attached to your system. This is extremely important because operating systems are built and released at a certain point in time. Although the periodic release of service packs allows the operating system to refresh its library of drivers, in no way can an operating system hope to ship with the latest and most current drivers from all of the third-party vendors. It's a common and daunting challenge that confronts system engineers everywhere.

What's the bottom line? If you have unusual or new drivers, you need to install them prior to setting up your partition SBS will install to.

Upgrading to SBS

New to SBS 2008 is the fact that there is no in-place upgrade. The SBS 2008 OS is 64bit only. Therefore, any existing SBS 2003 servers needing SBS 2008 to be installed on existing hardware will require a migration process. SBS 2003 is a 32bit operating system so no in-place upgrade can happen to a 64bit operating system. The two are completely incompatible with each other.

Another upgrade scenario is in the case of an existing Windows Server 2008 Standard server domain. You will not be able to insert the SBS DVD on the existing server and run an upgrade routine.

Any existing Windows domain will require some form of the SBS migration process to be used in order to move into an SBS domain setup. The migration process is quite in-depth and at this point beyond the scope of this book. We will however, address SBS migrations in our SBS 2008 Advanced Blueprint book.

Troubleshooting Setup Errors

In your career as an SBS professional, you will possibly have occasion to troubleshoot setup errors. These errors come out of left field, but the Readme.htm document contained on Small Business Server 2008 Setup DVD discusses a surprisingly large number of setup errors and the suggested resolution steps. (We discuss this document early in this chapter.) Hats off to the SBS development team for shipping this timely resource!

You may also want to consult the SBS resources listed in Appendix A to stay current with SBS 2008 setup issues. Heck, don't hesitate to throw in your own two cents at the discussion group and news list (listserv) mentioned.

Keep an eye on the Official SBS Blog for details on setup related issues, as this blog will be one of the first places you will see error-related posts: http://blogs.technet. com/sbs/

> **TIP:** And don't forget that a book is outdated the day we type its final words. The technology world changes quickly and you'll want to visit the Microsoft TechNet page to stay current with all the latest and updated knowledge related to SBS 2008. So no flames, masking as reader replies on Amazon. com, saying that our book doesn't discuss some future issue you encounter in the Year 2010 with SBS 2008. Big Grin!

Summary

As you reach the end of the SBS server machine setup and installation discussion, remember to go forward keeping a healthy perspective. Often we witness SBS professionals spending hours troubleshooting some setup- or installation-related problem. In many cases, that is not a good use of time. Remember that it often takes fewer than three hours to do a complete SBS server machine reinstall.

Believe us, we've done plenty of fresh SBS installs and come out hours ahead. Just a thought!

In this chapter, the following topics, tasks and discussion area were presented:

- Learned about the historical context surrounding the SBS product and installations.
- Reviewed the environment in which you will install SBS 2008, which included the site, technology components, and methodology.
- Completed preinstallation tasks.
- Discussed the SBS installation process in a five-phase approach, including the WinPE setup, SBS answer file installation, first input round, hardware configuration, driver installs, and utilities and ending with a successful installation seeing the Getting Started tasks list.
- Went through the actual SBS setup process and made observations on how the SBS 2008 setup approach varies from the SBS 2003 approach.
- Followed a brief discussion of advanced setup issues.

Chapter 4

Introduction to the SBS Consoles

Congratulations to you, good friends! You are well on your way to a completed, functional, and optimally performing SBS 2008 network.

Next, we are going to introduce you to the new Windows SBS Consoles. From there you will dive right into the post OS install steps that are a prerequisite to running the new SBS Getting Started Tasks.

Those prerequisites require you to install all of the necessary Windows Server 2008 x64 drivers, your RAID Management Console, Intel Server Management based on Microsoft's System Center Essentials product, and other hardware specific tasks.

Don't worry—we won't bore you with the nitty-gritty details since your hardware configurations or system manufacturers may be a lot different from ours. Suffice it to say, that the next step after we get the **Successful installation** message screen is to click on the **Start using the server** blue button, so you can have a look at the new Windows SBS Console.

Meet the Windows SBS Consoles

From the very moment you first log into the new SPRINGERS SBS box and click the **Start using the server** blue button, you can see that SBS 2008 has a completely new console. In fact, there are three new consoles!

- **Windows SBS Console**: The new standard SBS console in which most SBS-related tasks will be accomplished. You have already used the Shared Folders and Web Sites tab in this console to create the Company shared folder.

- **Windows SBS Console (Advanced Mode)**: Contains the entire standard SBS console management features with some extra links to access a number of specific Server Management Consoles.

- **Windows SBS Native Tools Management Console**: A number of key server management snap-ins, such as Active Directory Users and Computers, Update Services, Microsoft Exchange, and others gathered into one spot. You have already tailored this Management Console with some additional snap-ins for ease of access to various server components.

As you have already seen, when you are starting the various SBS consoles, you will get the User Account Control prompt just as you would in Windows Vista. This behavior is by design. It makes you pause to verify what you are about to do and identifies whether something or someone else may be acting on your behalf in the background.

> **TIP:** Have a look at Microsoft Knowledgebase article 922708: *How to Use User Account Control (UAC) in Windows Vista* for a little more detailed information on UAC. http://support.microsoft.com/kb/922708.

> It is very important to know the reasons why the UAC may pop up and what to do about those reasons. For the SBSer or SBS Consultant, this is especially true since that knowledge needs to be transferred to the client's users in the form of routine security training. It can be gut-wrenching listening to an SBS consultant whose client has lost control of their SBS installation! Believe us, it does happen!

Windows SBS Console

A very significant amount of management time over the life of the SBS box will be spent in the standard Windows SBS Console. Once the basic server configuration steps have been completed, you will be into the Windows SBS Console to configure your now installed SBS OS. Once you have your SBS Getting Started Tasks completed and SBS is in production, you will be using the Windows SBS Console for most of the basic server status checking and management needs.

The Windows SBS Console is set up in such a way as to make most SBS management tasks available in just a few clicks after opening it. Figure 4-1 shows us a screenshot of the newly opened Windows SBS Console.

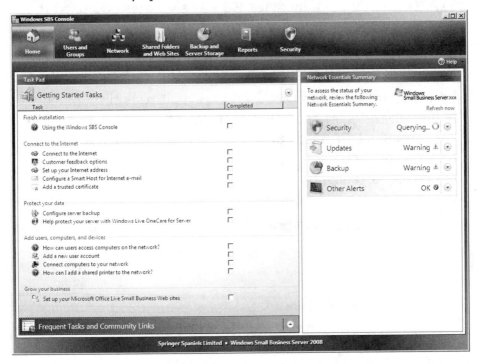

Figure 4-1
*The new Windows SBS Console right after clicking **Start using the server** button.*

Across the top of the console, you have a series of **Tabs** that group specific configuration and management tasks together.

SBS Home Page

On the Home Page, you will find the Getting Started Tasks used to complete the setup of the server, Frequent Tasks and Community Links containing quick access to frequent SBS management tasks and Web site links, and the Network Essentials Summary giving you an at-a-glance view of server and network health.

Getting Started Tasks

The Getting Started Tasks contain the various SBS wizards you are required to use to get SBS configured for the SPRINGERS production environment.

> **TIP:** Once you have installed SBS a few times and used the SBS wizards to configure the server, it is possible to start digging into the various underlying server components to see just what configuration changes the SBS wizards accomplish.
>
> Each wizard has a log that it creates as it runs through configuration tasks. Those logs can be found in **C:\Program Files\ Windows Small Business Server\Logs**. Have a look at them, as they can tell you a lot about how things are put together. The big payoff to knowing the logs comes down the road when you need to troubleshoot problems with the server.

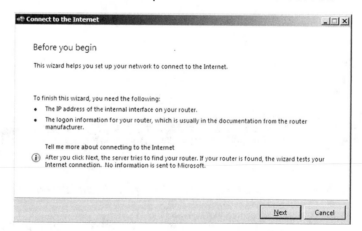

Figure 4-2
Each SBS wizard begins with an explanation of what task it will accomplish.

It is important to run the various Getting Started wizards in the order they are presented in the Tasks List. We will run through them with you in Chapter 5. Some components configured by the **Configure a Smart Host for Internet e-mail** wizard may not work if the **Connect to the Internet** wizard was not run first, for example.

Network Essentials Summary

The Network Essentials Summary section of the Home pages gives you an at-a-glance view of four key network health statistics. The **Security** component gives an overview of server and workstation virus, malware, spyware, and other security-related statistics. The **Updates** component gives an overview status for Windows server and Windows workstation updates. The **Backup** component indicates whether the backups are successful or not, or whether any servers on the network do not have their backups set up to run yet. **Other Alerts** monitor Windows servers and Windows workstation logs for critical errors.

> **TIP:** For the SBS guru or SBS consultant: The Network Essentials Summary and the SBS Reports all provide the foundation for your Managed Services structuring. Having the ability to receive reports daily via e-mail gives you an opportunity to charge your client a monthly service fee for the monitoring. You could even go further to incorporate remote patch management into that monthly fee.

Frequent Tasks and Community Links

The final piece of the Home Page puzzle is the **Frequent Tasks and Community Links** shown in Figure 4-3. To get to them, click the link at the bottom of the Getting Started Tasks list and the two will swap places.

Notes:

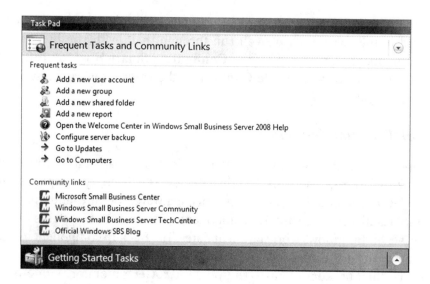

Figure 4-3
The Frequent Tasks and Community Links section.

In this section, you have the ability to get to the most common server management wizards with ease. You are also provided some links to SBS-specific Web sites and the official SBS blog. Once you have completed the Getting Started Tasks, you can leave the Frequent Tasks and Community Links up. Then, every time you log on to the server, most of the regular SBS maintenance tasks will be one click away.

Users and Groups Tab

Figure 4-4 shows the Users Tab under the Users and Groups tab. This tab gives you the ability to manage user accounts, the user roles that are used to define a user's permissions on the SBS network, and any E-mail and Security Groups.

Notes:

Users Tab

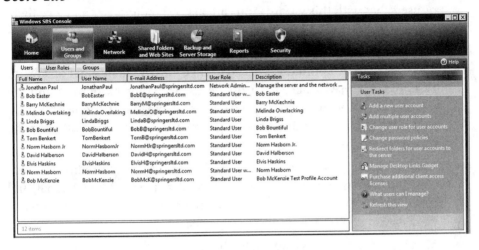

Figure 4-4
Users and Groups showing the Users Tab.

The **Users Tab** gives you a list of users on the SBS domain, access to user management wizards, and access to make changes to various aspects of the SBS user account settings on the network.

> **TIP:** A useful user wizard found here is the **Add multiple user accounts** wizard. When there is a need to add more than a couple of users at one time, this is the wizard to use. Such would be the case when needing to add all of the SPRINGERS users at once after you finished. When we are looking at inputting the new SPRINGERS users, you will have the option to run this wizard instead.

When you first see the Users Tab, you will have the list of SBS domain users and the user management tasks list to the right. The management tasks are comprised of:

- **Add a new user account**: You run this wizard to add users one at a time. This wizard is also included in the Getting Started Tasks list. A User Role, which is a permissions template, will be used when creating the user account.

- **Add multiple user accounts**: This wizard allows you to add multiple users using only one User Role at a time.

- **Change user role for user accounts**: You can change the User Role a user, or users, has with this wizard. You can take a standard user and give them the **Network Administrator** or **Standard User with administration links** user role.

- **Change password policies**: You can change the default number of days for password expiry, whether a password needs to be complex, or the minimum number of characters needed in a password. Note that changing these settings in a production SBS domain will force all users on the SBS domain to reset their passwords the next time they log on.

- **Redirect folders for user accounts to the server**: You can redirect a user's **Desktop**, **Documents** (**My Documents** on Windows XP Professional) and **Start Menu** to the server for redundancy and the ability to sign into any workstation and have a similar user profile setup.

- **Manage Desktop Links Gadget**: Enable or disable the various links, manage which users can or cannot have access to the Gadget and which Web site or Administration links are on it, and customize the title for each section on it.

- **Purchase additional client access licenses**: This link takes you to Microsoft's Web site that starts with a licensing overview.

- **What users can I manage?**: This brings up the Windows SBS Console Help.

- **Refresh this view**: This link can be found throughout the Windows SBS Console tab groups. You click this link to refresh your current view. This is especially helpful if you have made any changes to the server configuration and need to see the changes right away.

When you click on one of the users, things change. A new user-specific Tasks list will appear and essentially push down the original global User Tasks list.

Shown in Figure 4-5, the user-specific tasks make tasks such as resetting the user's password to removing them from the network a straightforward deal.

Notes:

Figure 4-5
After clicking on a user in the user list, you will see the user-specific tasks list.

- **Edit user account properties**: You can verify or change a user's properties via this link. Properties include the user's name and e-mail address, his Exchange mailbox quota size, what computers he can connect to via the Remote Web Workplace, as well as select the default computer he can connect to. Default SBS folder quotas can be changed (our Company shared folder falls out of this scope), security and e-mail distribution group membership, whether the user can access the Remote Web Workplace, the internal CompanyWeb SharePoint site, and Outlook Web Access.

- **Remove user account**: This wizard will remove the user account from the SBS domain. You have the option to retain the user's mailbox and shared folders if need be.

- **Reset user account password**: If a user loses or forgets her password after being away for a period of time, this is the wizard to use.

- **Change group membership**: A user may change positions, or have certain network privileges added or removed, thus requiring the use of this wizard.

- **Disable user account**: Click on the user's account then click on this link to disable it. The user will no longer be able to log on to the SBS domain or use network resources. Note that if the user was currently logged onto the SBS domain, the account would not be disabled until after he logged off.

- **Add a new user role based on this user account's properties**: When you add a new user to the SBS network, you choose the user's permission structure via a template. The User Role is that template. When customizing a user for certain tasks and SBS domain permissions, you can then click on this wizard to create a User Role with the same setup! From there, you can add new users to the SBS domain utilizing the new User Role, or you can run the **Change user role for user accounts** wizard to change any existing user accounts with the new User Role.

- **Print the Getting Started page for this user account**: The **Getting Started** page gives a set of instructions to the user on how to join a computer to the SBS domain using the http://connect wizard, some information on SBS features, and explains the **Windows Small Business Server Desktop Links** gadget and how to add it to the Vista Sidebar.

User Roles Tab

The next tab in order is **User Roles**. A user role is a permissions template that is used when creating a single user via the **Add a new user account** wizard or when adding multiple users via the **Add multiple user accounts** wizard. Figure 4-6 shows the **Standard User** role highlighted and the tasks that can be performed on it.

User roles provide a quick and simple way to manage users' SBS access permissions. They also provide a quick way to change multiple users' access permissions via the **Change user role for user accounts** wizard under the users tab discussed earlier in the chapter.

Out of the box, SBS has three user roles:

- **Standard User**: Has access to shared folders, printers, faxes, e-mail, Remote Web Workplace, Windows SharePoint Services, and the Internet.
- **Standard User with administration links**: Has Standard User permissions and can also view the administration links from Remote Web Workplace and the desktop gadget links.
- **Network Administrator**: Has unrestricted system access.

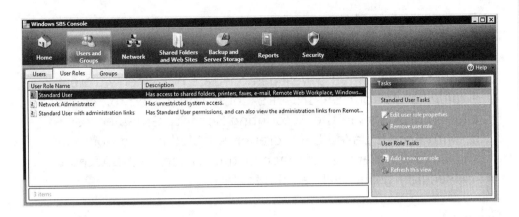

Figure 4-6
User Roles tab in the Windows SBS Console.

To see exactly what permissions the user role will apply, click on it then click on **Edit user role properties**. You can also double click on the item to bring up its properties. The user role permissions are:

- **General**: Indicates the **Role name** and the **Description**.

- **Remote Access**: Allows or denies access to the **Remote Web Workplace** and the PPTP-based **VPN** connection if configured.

- **E-mail**: Enforces a **quota** size on the user's mailbox. The default out of the box is 2GB.

- **Folders**: Enforces a **quota** on the default SBS folder shares. You can enable **folder redirection** for the user's folders and also set a **quota** on the amount of data allowed to be redirected to the server.

- **Groups**: The e-mail distribution group and security group membership that will be set for the user or users.

- **Web Sites**: Sets whether the **Remote Web Place**, **Internal Web site**, and/or **Outlook Web Access** permissions will be enabled or disabled for the user or users.

TIP: For the SBSer or SBS consultant, User Roles present an opportunity to customize and streamline user permissions management where the client site has a number of different departments.

For instance, in the case where there are two or three dedicated users in Accounting, a user role can be created to give accounting users specific permissions to the various SBS resources. In Chapter 5 we'll demonstrate this when we create a folder under our SPRINGERS Company shared folder that allows only users in the Accounting Security Group access to it. With Access Based Enumeration enabled on the Company shared folder that means that only those users in the Accounting security group will see the folder!

Groups Tab

Next, you will find the **Groups** tab. A list of the default SBS e-mail and security groups is shown in Figure 4-7.

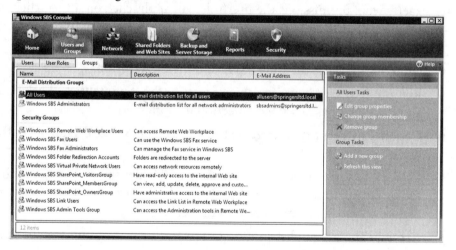

Figure 4-7
E-mail and Security Groups in the Groups tab.

You will be greeted with the E-mail Distribution Groups, of which there are two out of the box, and a list of the default SBS Security Groups.

The e-mail distribution groups are:

- **All Users**: E-mail distribution group for all e-mail-enabled SBS users. Send an e-mail in Outlook Web Access or Outlook with All Users in the TO field, and everyone with an e-mail address will receive a copy.

- **Windows SBS Administrators**: E-mail distribution list for anyone with administrator rights on the SBS network.

The security groups are:

- **Windows SBS Remote Web Workplace Users**: Users in this group can access the Remote Web Workplace from the Internet.
- **Windows SBS Fax Users**: Users can fax out and receive faxes via the SBS fax service.
- **Windows SBS Fax Administrators**: Users can manage the fax service.
- **Windows SBS Folder Redirection Accounts**: Users in this group will have their folders redirected to the server.
- **Windows SBS Virtual Private Network Users**: Users will be able to VPN into the SBS server for access to their data.
- **Windows SBS SharePoint_Visitors Group**: Users in this group will have "read only" permissions to the CompanyWeb SharePoint site.
- **Windows SBS SharePoint_MembersGroup**: Users will be able to make content contributions, that is read and write content on the CompanyWeb SharePoint site. They are also able to edit and change existing content.
- **Windows SBS SharePoint_OwnersGroup**: Users have full administrative permissions for the CompanyWeb SharePoint site.
- **Windows SBS Link Users**: The Link List will show up for users in this group.
- **Windows SBS Admin Tools Group**: Access to the SBS Administration tools will be available in the Remote Web Workplace for users in this group.

The default security groups cover all of the basics for an out-of-the-box SBS setup. Double click on one of them to bring up the group's properties. A list of the group's user membership will be the first thing you see. Click on the E-mail link and if the group is e-mail-enabled the e-mail address will be shown. There are options to allow the group to receive e-mail from outside the SBS domain as well as archive any e-mails to the group in a document library.

Network Tab

The **Network Tab** is where you will find the **Computers Tab, Devices Tab**, and **Connectivity Tab**. You will be able to manage all aspects of most physical devices connected to your SBS network including computers, networked printers, your SBS fax modem or modems, and more. Anything related to your SBS Internet connection will be found on the Connectivity tab.

Computers Tab

Figure 4-8 gives you a quick at-a-glance view of each server and workstation's status on the SBS domain.

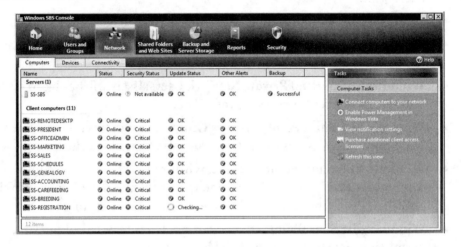

Figure 4-8
The Computers Tab shows us what the SBS network will look like once workstations are added.

Note that in this case, you are seeing that our newly added SPRINGERS workstations are claiming a **Critical Security Status**. The critical status will show for any new workstations added to the SBS domain that do not have any AntiVirus protection installed and updated.

The default **Computer Tasks** also shown are as follows:

- **Connect computers to your network**. When you click on this link you will be presented with instructions on the need to add your SBS Users prior to running the Connect Computer program either via the http://connect-computer Web page or portable media such as a USB flash drive.

- The **Enable Power Management in Windows Vista** link will do just that. If enabled, all Windows Vista-based workstations will power themselves down after one hour of idle time. The gotcha to that, of course, is the user is no longer able to establish a remote desktop connection with their work-station via the Remote Web Workplace. By default, Windows Vista power management on the SBS 2008 domain is disabled via Group Policy.

- The **View notification settings** link brings up a list of monitored SBS ser-vices, Performance Counters, and Event Log error items that can cause an e-mail to be sent to a designated e-mail address. Figure 4-9 shows some of the Event Log errors that can fire an e-mail if the event happens.

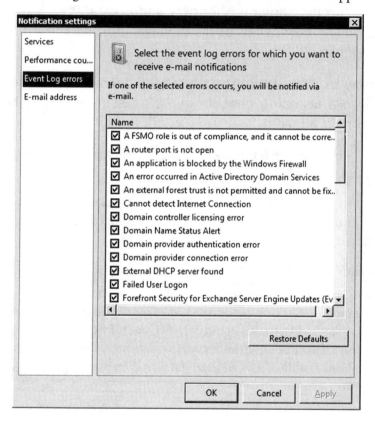

Figure 4-9
Select the event log errors for which you want to receive e-mail notifications.

- When you click the **Purchase additional client access licenses** link, you will have Internet Explorer open up to a Microsoft Licensing Web page. New to SBS 2008, is the ability to buy User or Device CALs in single packs. Also new is the ability to buy Standard CALs for SBS 2008 Standard or Premium CALs in those cases where SBS 2008 Premium is installed.

TIP: If SBS 2008 Premium is installed at a location where there are 30 users, but only five users are utilizing the SQL 2008 installation via a Line of Business application, then your CAL purchase would consist of the SBS 2008 Premium license that comes with five Premium CALs and an additional 25 SBS Standard CALs.

You can combine any number of Standard and Premium CALs based on the number of users that are utilizing the Premium components.

Also new to SBS 2008: You no longer need to input the CAL keys into a licensing console in SBS. Essentially, the honor system now applies!

- Click on the **Refresh this view** link to refresh the page before the default automatic refresh time.

Now, just as you could in the previous SBS Console tabs, you can also click on either a server or workstation in the Computers list, to bring up Tasks specific to the item clicked on.

When you click on a server, such as SBS, you get the following specific task:

- A link to **View server properties**. When you click on this link, you can see a big picture overview of the SBS server hardware configuration, as well as the OS service pack level in the default **General** view shown in Figure 4-10. You can also check out the server's update status including what updates have been installed, as well as updates that are waiting to be installed.

Notes:

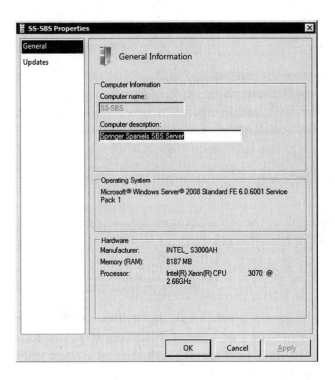

Figure 4-10
A big picture view of the SPRINGERS SBS server hardware configuration.

Move down to one of the client computers and click on it, and you get a number of specific tasks to do:

- Much like the **View computer properties** for your SBS server, you can view the various workstation properties by clicking on this link. Not only do you get the big-picture view of the workstation's hardware in the **General** section, you also get the **User Access** section to assign user access permissions as well as whether users can access the workstation via the Remote Web Workplace. The **Updates** section gives you a list of both the installed updates and any updates that are missing from the workstation.

- We inherit the **Offer Remote Assistance** link from SBS 2003. For SBS consultants, this link is a boon to providing remote management services! You can connect to users' desktops while they are logged on to the workstation and work with them on resolving a problem—all while working with the same screen! You click on the computer name prior to clicking this link, and away you go.

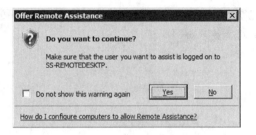

Figure 4-11
A user needs to be logged on to the workstation before a Remote Assistance Session.

- The next link in the series is **Connect to a computer by using Terminal Services**. When you click on this link after clicking on the computer you want to connect to, you will be able to connect to it via Remote Desktop Protocol. Keep in mind that you can connect only to a workstation on the SBS domain that is currently turned on.

- The final link in the list of Tasks is the **Remove SS-WorkstationName** link. When you click on this, you are able to remove the selected workstation from the SBS domain. You will be asked if you are sure you want to remove the workstation—just in case.

Note that in the case of both servers and workstations, some available Tasks will show up only if a status column shows a warning or critical error:

- When you click on a Server and there was a problem with the backup, you will see a **Go to backup** link in the server's tasks.

- If there is a problem with a computer's Security status and you click on it, you will see a **Go to security** link in the system's specific tasks.

- Any system with an Updates problem will have a **Go to updates** link available when you click on it.

- If a system shows a problem in the Other Alerts column, then a **View Computer Alerts** link will show up when you click on that server or workstation.

Devices Tab

The **Devices Tab** gives us an overview of any device connected either directly to the SBS server or that resides on the SBS domain. If you have a fax modem installed, you will see it here along with any printers connected to the server or shared on the network.

The list of Device Tasks are as follows:

- We find the **Add a shared printer to the network** link that is also shared with the **SBS Getting Started Tasks**. Click on this link to get an overview along with some instructions on connecting a shared printer to the SBS network. We will cover this subject in detail in "Chapter 10: Fax and Print."

- If there is already a shared printer somewhere on the SBS domain and you have allowed File and Print Sharing through the Windows Firewall on your workstations and/or servers, then use the **List a shared printer in this console** link to show it in the Printers section.

TIP: As we will point out in Chapter 10 on faxing and printing in an SBS 2008 domain, the workstation setup scripts in SBS 2008 no longer configure any printers connected to the server. Nor do any shared printers automatically get shared out to all the workstations on the SBS domain. Manual intervention is required to make this happen.

- The next link in the Tasks list is the **How do I add a new fax device?** This help item gives you a brief overview of how to install a fax device onto the server. Note that any USB fax device will initiate the **New Hardware Found** wizard, so you should have the necessary driver disk handy.

- You can see two different links in the next spot. If the fax service has not been installed yet, or it is stopped, you will see the **Start the Fax service** link. After connecting a modem to the SBS server you can initiate the fax service configuration by clicking on this link. Once you have the fax service link installed and configured, you will find a **Stop the fax service** link. Click this particular link and you will stop the ability for SBS to send and receive faxes.

- If the fax service is configured, then you will see the **Configure the fax service** link next. By clicking on it, you can make any necessary modifications to the fax service information or delivery options set when the original fax setup wizard was run.

- The **Configure the Windows SBS Fax Administrators group** link opens a window where you can manage the users that will be allowed to administer the SBS Fax Service. You can also designate an e-mail address for this group if there is a need.

- The **Configure the Windows SBS Fax Users group** link shown in Figure 4-12 brings up a management window so you can see who has permission to use the Windows SBS Fax Service. You can add and remove users from within this window too. You can also designate an e-mail address for this group if there is a need.

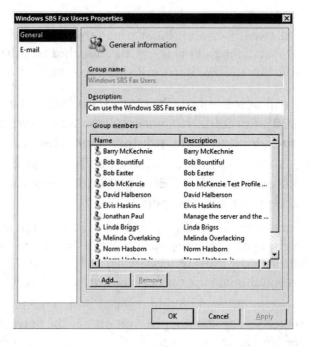

Figure 4-12
The Windows SBS Fax Users Properties page allows you to manage SBS Fax users.

- As always, the **Refresh this view** link will force the page to refresh manually.

Now, if you actually have a fax modem installed and configured, you can click on it to bring up an **Edit properties of 56K Faxmodem** link that allows you to change properties specific to the fax services and the modem.

Click on a printer listed under **Printers** and you will get the following **Printer Tasks**:

- Click on the **Printer Jobs** link and the printer's queue list window where you can manage print jobs pops up.
- Click on the **Printer Properties** link and you will get the printer's properties window with the General, Sharing, Ports, Advanced, Color Manage-

ment, Security, Device Settings, and About tabs. The number of available tabs in this window will depend on the printer model and software drivers installed.

- The final link in the task list is to **Remove Printer**, to remove a shared printer from the SBS network.

Connectivity Tab

On the Connectivity Tab, you must close everything necessary for the SBS server's Internet connectivity to occur. Most of the tasks listed in the **Connectivity Tasks** can also be found on the **Getting Started Tasks** list in the Windows SBS Console Home page.

The list of Connectivity Tasks shown in Figure 4-13 are as follows:

- When clicked, the **Connect to the Internet** link starts the Connect to the Internet Wizard. You may need to rerun this wizard if the wizard was not successful during the SBS OS setup or if you change your router.

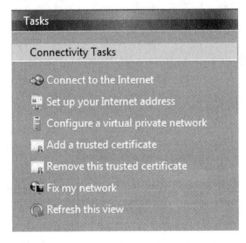

Figure 4-13
Your Connectivity Tasks list.

- The **Set up your Internet address** link starts the wizard and allows you to configure your SBS server with an e-mail domain and an Internet URL address, register a new Internet domain, and configure that domain to be used to with your SBS setup. It also allows you to manage those settings once they are in place.

- The next link is the **Configure a virtual private network** task. If your SBS users require a VPN connection, you can run this wizard. Once the wizard completes, a VPN connection can be established with the server. Make sure your router has port 1723 forwarded to the server and that you verify which users will be permitted to access the server via the VPN.

- When you click on the **Add a trusted certificate** link you will run the wizard that enables you to request and subsequently install a third-party trusted certificate. If a third-party trusted certificate is already installed, you will be given the option to either renew or replace that certificate.

- Click on the **Remove this trusted certificate** link, which shows up only if you have a third-party trusted certificate installed, and you can remove that certificate and replace it with the original SBS self-issued certificate.

- When clicked, the **Fix My Network** link on runs the wizard that will troubleshoot a number of different potential network issues and attempt to fix them. This is the first wizard to turn to if there are network-related problems. It will look into things like DNS and DHCP settings to make sure they are correct.

- If you click on the **Refresh this view** link, it will force a refresh of the view.

The list of items in the Connectivity List gives you an at-a-glance view of each item's status or how it is configured. If you need a quick answer to how many of the key SBS services are set up, this is the place to find it.

When you click on each item in the Connectivity Items List itself, you will get the specific task option to click on its properties. In order of appearance, the properties of each item is as follows:

- The **Internet connection** link shows the current status of the Internet connection and will indicate the status of the router device if SBS is managing it. If SBS is not managing the router, a **Manage router** button can be clicked to bring up a browser so you can log on to the router's management page. If SBS manages the router, you will be able to see the **Port Mappings** if you click on this option.

- The properties for the **Internet Domain Name** will show you the current domain name that has been set up either by you or if you choose to set up a domain name and have it managed by the SBS server. Your current Remote Web Workplace URL will show by default. In the case of the SPRINGERS methodology, that URL is **remote.springersltd.com**.

- The **Certificate** item will tell you if you have a third-party trusted certificate installed or are using the SBS self-issued one. When you click on the **Certificate** item in the list, you will be given two specific task options:

  1. Click on the **View certificate properties** link and you will be presented with the actual SBS self-issued certificate or the third-party certificate you imported using the above **Add a trusted certificate** wizard.

  2. The second item is a help link that will explain **How do I import an existing trusted certificate**. This can be important if you end up needing to reinstall your SBS server and have the earlier requested third-party certificate on hand.

- The **Server firewall** status is either on or off. By default, the Windows Firewall is on. Click on **Server firewall** and then its **View firewall properties** link and you will see some information on the built-in firewall. Click on the **Advanced** section and you will be able to click on a **Manage rules** button and a **Manage router** button as shown in Figure 4-14.

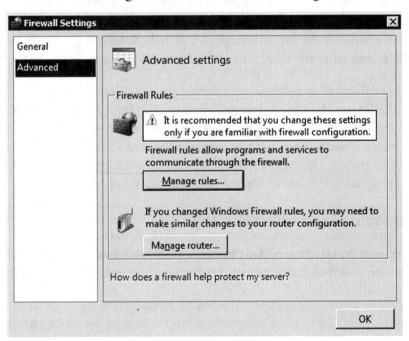

Figure 4-14
Customizing the Windows Firewall settings must be done with great care.

- The **VPN connection** status will tell you if a VPN connection will be allowed in or not. Click on it and then on the **View virtual private network properties** link, and you will be presented with a list of users that may connect to the server via a VPN connection. By default, only the domain admin account is permitted to VPN into the server. Click the **Modify** button to add or remove any existing user's permissions to use the VPN.

- The **POP3 Connector** status is either **On** or **Off**. Click on it, then on its **View POP3 Connector properties** link, and you will be presented with the **POP3 Mailboxes** window where you can manage the POP3 settings. Add a user's POP3 ISP mailbox retrieval or remove a user or users from the list. The **Scheduling** link in the window allows you to set the retrieval frequency for the POP3 Connector. Once you have added users' mailboxes to the POP3 Connector, you can set the frequency level to as often as every five minutes.

TIP: Keep in mind that many ISPs have a policy in place that permits a frequency of 15 minutes or more only. Make sure to contact the e-mail domain's hosting provider to verify if they will allow for a five-minute retrieval interval. If that call is not placed, a phone call from the provider very well may happen.

- The **Smart Host for Internet e-mail** has a status of either **Configured** or **Not Configured**. No matter what the status, when you click on it and then its **View outbound Internet e-mail properties** link, you will be greeted with the **Configure Internet Mail Wizard**. The wizard will allow you to set up a Smart Host or remove one that was already set up.

Shared Folders and Web Sites Tab

We move now to the **Shared Folders and Web Sites** tab in the Windows SBS Console. You will find management tasks to do with folder sharing and the SBS Web sites under this tab.

Notes

Shared Folders Tab

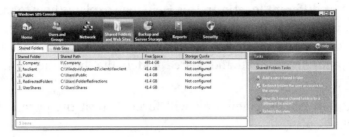

Figure 4-15
The default Shared Folders are shown along with the SPRINGERS Company shared folder you will create and share in Chapter 5.

When you first click on the tab, you will be greeted with the Shared Folders tab as shown in Figure 4-15. The general tasks in this tab are the following:

- Click on the **Add a new shared folder** link, and you will run through the **Provision a Shared Folder Wizard**. Using this wizard, you can create a folder, set its NTFS permissions, set permissions for access via the network, apply a quota to the folder, apply a file screen so that users cannot store their MP3s on the share, and publish the folder to a DFS namespace.

- When clicked, The **Redirect folders for user accounts to the server** link will bring up the **Folder Redirection Properties** window. There you can set whether a user's Desktop, Documents, and Start Menu are redirected to the server. Click on the **User Accounts** link and you can select or deselect users that will have this happen.

TIP: Folder Redirection can be a huge benefit to a company that has a lot of mobile workers. While out of the office, they work on their documents and data; then when they come back to the office and plug in, the changes they made will be synchronized to the server.

Essentially, most data that gets redirected to the server becomes part of the server's backup routine. You can even go so far as to encrypt the local folder location on the user's laptop so as to protect that data even further.

We say "most" data because you will not be able to redirect certain types of databases or live data type files.

- The next link in the Tasks list is the Help item **How do I move shared folders to a different location?** This Help item explains how to move a share that you create, such as the SPRINGERS Company shared folder created in Chapter 5, to a different partition or hard drive. Note that this method is not for SBS-created and shared folders that have their own wizard to move them!

- The **Refresh this view** link will force refresh the page if the link is clicked on.

By default, SBS creates the following shares out of the box:

- The **faxclient** share that contains the server-based fax software to install on a workstation. The fax client installs on the workstation as a printer so faxing from within Microsoft Word or any other Windows application is as simple as clicking the **Print** icon in that application.

- The **Public** folder share is a general folder share that is created during the SBS setup. This share will be removed as it is not needed.

- The **RedirectedFolders** share is the root folder for a user's redirected folders such as Documents (My Documents on Windows XP Professional), the user's desktop, and Start Menu.

- The **UserShares** share contains each user profile's dedicated folder. In the case of the SPRINGERS methodology, you will find a folder created there for each of the SPRINGERS users.

TIP: When it comes to folder security, Access-Based Enumeration gives us a definite advantage. What is Access-Based Enumeration? When enabled on a shared folder, users with permissions to use a folder in that share will see it. If a user does not have permission to access a folder in the share, the user will not see it.

Notes

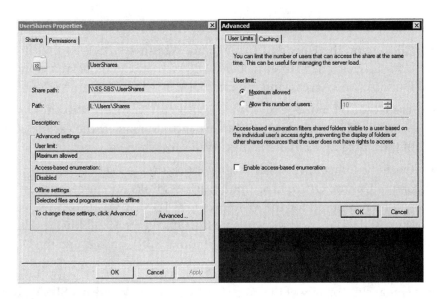

Figure 4-16
Default SBS shares do not have Access-Based Enumeration enabled.

This can be handy for important accounting or project-related folders for example. The old adage, "Out of sight, out of mind" applies here!

All of the shared folders listed have the same specific tasks that come up when you click on them:

- Click on the **Browse this folder** link and a Windows Explorer window will pop up with the contents of the folder.

- The **Stop sharing this folder** link, when you click on it, will do just that: remove the folder share.

- When you click on the **Change folder permissions** link, you will be able to change the default **Share Permissions**. Note that the Everyone group has full control by default.

Web Sites Tab

When you click on the **Web Sites** tab, you will be greeted with a list of the **Windows SBS Web sites** as well as the **Office Live Small Business Web sites** along with their status.

The general **Web Sites Tasks** contain the following:

- Clicking on the **How do I manage my Windows SBS Web sites** link will bring up Help on the three included SBS Web sites: Remote Web Workplace, Outlook Web Access, and the Internal Web site (CompanyWeb site).

- The **How do I manage my Office Live Small Business Web sites** link will bring up a Help window that explains how to manage the various aspects of the Office Live Small Business Web sites when you click on it.

- Once the Office Live Small Business Web sites are set up, when you click on the **Update Office Live Small Business links on your server** link, you will be prompted for the Windows Live ID that was used to set up the sites. The wizard will then update the Office Live Small Business links in the Remote Web Workplace, the Windows SBS Console, and the Desktop Links Gadget.

Whenever you click on any of the Web sites listed in the **Windows SBS Web sites** list, you will receive the following specific tasks as shown in Figure 4-17:

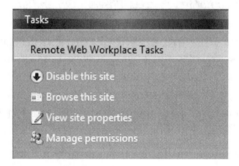

Figure 4-17
Click on one of the SBS Web sites to see its specific tasks.

- When you click on the **Disable this site** link while one of the Windows SBS Web sites is selected, you will disable that particular site. An **Enable this site** link will appear if the site was already disabled when you clicked on it.

- The second link is **Browse this site** that will open a Web browser with the site you have selected.

- Click on the **View site properties** link and you will see general information about the site along with the ability to enable or disable the site, permissions for users and groups that may access the site, and **Advanced** settings with a button to open the **IIS** Manager. The Remote Web Workplace has the ability to customize the Home page links, set who can see which links, and allow you to customize the site background and display your company logo.

Click on the Business Web site in the **Office Live Small Business Web sites** and you will get a **Browse this site** link that will open a Web browser when clicked. The **Business Applications Web site** does not have any specific tasks associated with it.

Backup and Server Storage Tab

Two very critical areas for any server setup are the backup settings and the server's storage status. A proper backup setup and regular testing of those backups, to provide reliable data recovery are mission critical for any business.

TIP: How do we structure our backups? Depending on the industry, you may be okay with two USB hard drives for your backup rotations. Have them changed out once every two weeks to keep the company's backups relatively fresh.

For industries that require some form of data compliance structures, you may need to keep a third, fourth, or even fifth USB hard drive in cold storage for those "just in case" times.

For the SBS Consultant: Because the backups are encrypted on the USB hard drive, you could very well set things up so that you do the backup rotations for your clients. Keep in mind the amount of travel time as well as the time to do the physical rotation and bill a monthly fee accordingly. A fringe benefit to having this setup is the inevitable questions you will be asked by users, thus transitioning you into billable time! On top of that, add a test recovery once per quarter and build that fee into your monthly client invoice or bill quarterly for it as you choose!

Have a good look at Figure 4-18 and you will see there are a lot of different tasks for you to manage the server backup configuration and the backups themselves.

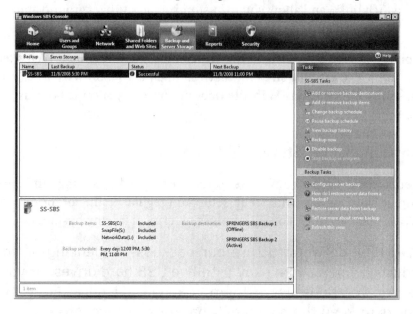

Figure 4-18
After clicking on the server backup, you will see a bunch of backup tasks.

Backup Tab

The **Backup Tasks** list are as follows:

- Click on the **Configure server backup** link to make changes to the scheduled backup. You can make changes to the backup destination list, the drives you are backing up, and the backup schedule.

- When you click on the **How do I restore server data from a backup?** link, the Help topic will come up that explains how to recover files and/or folders from the backup.

- The next link is the **Restore server data from backup** wizard. When you click on this link, the Windows Server Backup console will come up and you will be able to recover files and folders, Exchange and SharePoint data, and whole volumes.

- And finally, when you click on the **Refresh this view** link, you will force a refresh of the page.

When you click on the SS-SBS backup item, a window near the bottom gives you a good overview of the current backup configuration. It lists the drives being backed up, the backup schedule, and all of the backup destinations and their labels.

You also get the following specific tasks as shown in Figure 4-19:

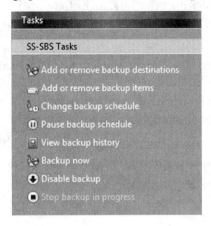

Figure 4-19
Clicking on the SS-SBS backup allows you to manage all aspects of the backup setup.

- When there is a need to make changes to the USB hard drives for backups, click on the **Add or remove backup destinations** link to do so. The window that pops up will have a current list of USB hard drives that SBS uses for backups. Click the **Add or remove drives** button to make changes.

- Click on the **Add or remove backup items** link, and you can remove drives that are being backed up, except the C: SBS drive, or add drives to be backed up.

- When clicked on, the **Change backup schedule** will bring up a window with the current backup schedule in it. You can then add or remove backup times as needed.

- If you need to make changes to the backup setup and a backup is about to start, then the **Pause backup schedule** link is the one to click. You will be prompted to confirm your choice then you will notice that the link will change to say **Resume backup schedule**. Click on the **Resume backup schedule** link to do just that.

- When you click on the **View backup history** link, a list of all of the backups taken by the SBS Backup will come up. An overview of backup status, which drives are being backed up, and the current USB hard drive destination will also be present in the window.

- Click on the **Backup now** link to initiate an immediate backup of the server. You will be prompted to make sure that you really want the backup to run.

- If the SBS backup is no longer needed, you can disable it by clicking on the **Disable backup** link. Note that if you do not have a third-party backup in place, your SBS server is then vulnerable to losing data and possibly everything, if the hardware crashes.

- If you need to make changes to the backup setup while a backup is running, click on the **Stop backup in progress** link. Note that this link is grayed out when the backup service is at idle.

Server Storage Tab

The **Server Storage Tab** gives an overview of your server's storage status. You will see each drive's current data usage, free space, and its size. Click on any of the drive items in the list and the status window at the bottom will give you an overview of what types of data the drive contains in its used space and the amount of free space left on it too.

There are no specific tasks presented to you when you click on any of the drives listed.

The **Storage Tasks** list is a series of links to wizards that move critical server data from one drive to another. To simplify things since the wizards all do the same thing we will consolidate them into one bullet:

- Click on any **Move *Service/Folder* Data** link and you will run a wizard that enables you to move the specific data folders to another drive. In the SPRINGERS methodology the Users' Shared Data, Users' Redirected Documents Data, and the Windows Update Repository Data will be moved to the SS-SBS L: drive.

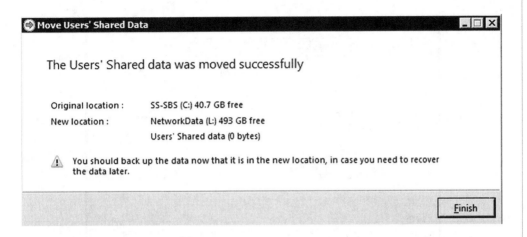

Figure 4-20
*Once you have run a Move Data wizard, you should see a "moved successfully"
message.*

- Click on the **Tell me more about managing storage of server data** link,
  a Help topic on managing data on the server. There are three Web links
  for you to click through to the TechNet Library for further reading on the
  Server Backup, Folder Redirection, and the Move Data Folder Wizards.

- Click on the **Refresh this view** link to refresh the page to catch any status
  changes immediately.

Reports Tab

The SBS Reports have been changed greatly from SBS 2003. The new report setup
allows for a lot of flexibility when it comes to what is being reported and to whom
those reports are being sent.

For a deep dive into SBS 2008 monitoring, check out Chapter 13 on SBS Reporting.

The two default reports SBS creates out of the box are the **Summary Network
Report** and the **Detailed Network Report**. Both reports can be set up to e-
mail to one or more users on the SBS network or to the SBS Consultant if the
client chooses to have her SBS network proactively monitored. Figure 4-21
shows the Summary Network Report e-mail that gives an overview of the SBS
network status.

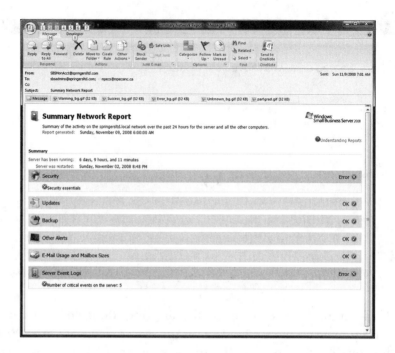

Figure 4-21
The Summary Network Report e-mail.

The only available **Network Report Tasks** task besides the **Refresh this view** link is the **Add a new report** link.

- Click on the **Add a new report link**, and you will be able to name your new report, configure content such as Security, Backup, or other reports, set the users or outside e-mail address destination(s) for the report, and set whether the report will be daily or weekly and the time the report would be generated.

When you click on either the **Summary Network Report** or **Detailed Network Report**, or any other reports that you have created, the most recent version will show in the status window under the reports list.

Whichever report you click on will have the following **Summary Network Report Tasks** associated with it as shown in Figure 4-22:

- A **View report properties** link that will bring up the report's properties when you click on it. You can make changes to the content, e-mail options, schedule, and view the archived versions of the report.

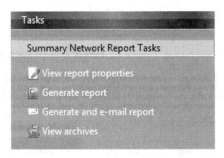

Figure 4-22
Each report has the same specific tasks to accomplish when you click on it.

- Click on the **Generate report** link to create a new version of the selected report. You may need to do this if changes were made on the server or a problem occurred or was resolved, for example.

- When you click on the **Generate and e-mail report** link, you will be able to create a new version of the report and e-mail it to selected recipients. You would want to do this to let the folks in charge know that a problem was resolved or to place a copy of the report in your own Inbox.

- The **View archives** link will bring up a list of previous versions of the selected report. You can have a look at any report throughout the history of the SBS server.

Security Tab

The security of your SPRINGERS SBS network is mission-critical. Being aware of the status of the various mechanisms in place to protect your SBS network is essential to the network's longevity and your data's integrity. Almost all aspects of your SBS network's security can be seen at a glance when you click on the **Security Tab**.

The SBS Console is set up in such a way that third-party security vendors can hook into it. By that we mean that if you install a third party's SBS 2008-compliant security product, there will be status reports and tasks available for that product in the SBS Console!

TIP: One of the most important security aspects is physical security, i.e., is the server and its critical infrastructure locked up? A dedicated room, a good steel door, and an appropriate deadbolt are absolutely required. A further tightening up of the physical security would be to install a server cabinet that can be locked and is heavy enough to make it difficult to carry things away. The server cabinet would suffice in the case where the office space does not allow for a dedicated server room or closet.

Remember: Physical access to the drives makes getting at the data stored on the hard drives very easy. Even encrypted data is in danger if the thieves have enough computer power at their hands and the right tools.

Security Tab

After clicking on the Security Tab, you will be greeted with a list of the **Security Essentials** that indicate the status of the many different SBS server and client computer security components. Those components include Forefront Security for Exchange Server, Windows Live OneCare for Server, the Windows Firewall, Exchange Server 2007 Spam protection, Windows Defender on Windows Vista and if installed, on Windows XP Professional workstations.

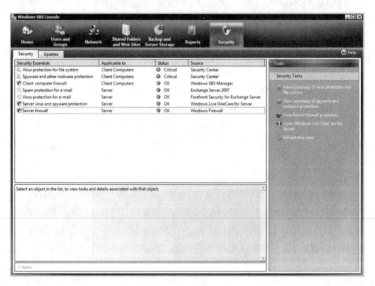

Figure 4-23
As soon as the Security page comes will see all Security services' at-a-glance status.

None of the items in the list have any specific tasks associated with them at the time of this writing.

The **Security Tasks** are as follows:

- When you click on the **View summary of virus protection for file system** link, you will see a summary AntiVirus report for every workstation in the SBS domain. The AntiVirus product and manufacturer installed on the workstation should be identified in the list. An example is Windows Live OneCare.

- Click on the **View summary of spyware and malware protection** link, and you will see a summary AntiSpyware report for every workstation in the SBS domain. The AntiSpyware product and manufacturer installed on the workstation should be identified in the list. An example is Windows Defender.

- Click on the **View Server Firewall properties** link and the Firewall Settings window will pop up. A general description of the firewall greets you. Click on the **Advanced** link, and you can manage the server's firewall rules by clicking on the **Manage rules** button. Figure 4-14 earlier in this chapter has a screenshot of this window. Be very careful about making any modifications to the default rules, as key services that communicate with the server may be restricted by doing so, causing the server to seemingly go offline. You will also find a **Manage router** button to bring up a Web browser and the router's management console.

- The next link in the Tasks list is the **Open Windows Live OneCare for Server** link. Click on this link and you will be greeted with the Windows Live OneCare for Server status window shown in Figure 4-24.

Notes

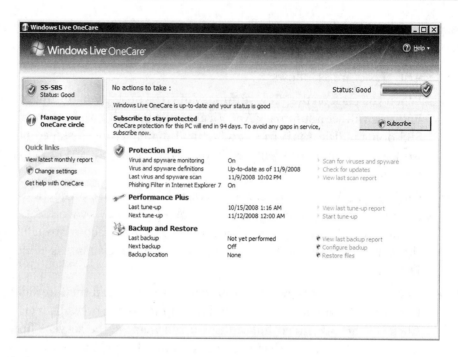

Figure 4-24
Windows Live OneCare for Server window showing a complete at-a-glance status view.

- We conclude the list with the **Refresh this view** link giving you an immediate refresh of the list item's status.

Updates Tab

When you click on the **Updates Tab** under **Security**, you will see a quick overview of any updates that are pending approval or have errors associated with them, optional updates awaiting deployment and whether there are any updates in progress.

> **TIP:** Knowing the update status of your servers and workstations on the SBS network is very critical to keeping the network secure. Around the time of this book's finishing touches, Microsoft released an out-of-band update in MS08-67. Normally Microsoft releases updates every second Tuesday of the month.

See http://www.microsoft.com/technet/security/Bulletin/ MS08-67.mspx for more information on the vulnerability.

But, in this case the vulnerability being patched was so severe that it warranted the out-of-band release. Now, one thing to keep in mind when it comes to patching: A server or workstation's most vulnerable time is actually the time between the patch's being released and the servers and workstations being patched. Why? Because people out there will download the newly released patch to reverse-engineer it so that they can figure out what the vulnerability was. They will then write some sort of exploit code and embed that in a virus-delivery package.

In the case of MS08-67, the exploits showed up in the wild within **days** of the patch's release!

The **Update Tasks** are as follows:

- When you click on the **Change the software update settings** link, you will be able change the update approval level for the server or client, specify how and when updates will be applied to both server and client machines, and manage which computers will be monitored by Windows Server Update Services for update status.

TIP: For the SBS consultant who may work with Apple Macintosh or Linux-based clients, the ability to now exclude any machine registered in Active Directory on the SBS domain from having its updates managed by Windows Server Update Services is especially refreshing. Client purchase a new iMac? Once you have set it up on the SBS domain, you will be able to make sure that the iMac stays out of the update management setup with a few clicks of a mouse. Figure 4-25 shows you a list of included computers. Any excluded systems would be in the column to the left of the included computers list.

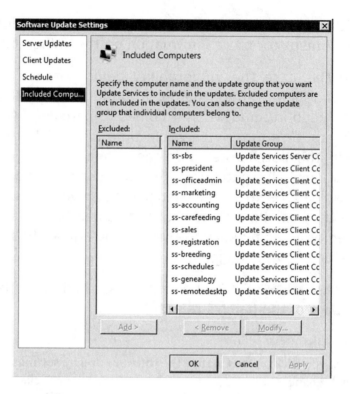

Figure 4-25
A list of the SPRINGERS SBS Update settings including all workstations.

- Click on the **Synchronize now** link to force Windows Server Update Services to synchronize the update catalog against the Microsoft Updates Web site. You will be prompted to click **OK** by a **Software Updates** pop-up window. If any new updates were available, you will see them in the updates items list.

- The last link in this list is the **Refresh this view**. Click on it and the SBS Console will query Windows Server Update Services for any status changes.

If there are updates awaiting approval, you can click on one to read through the information on that particular update in the status window under the items list:

- You will see if the update requires a reboot which is a very important consideration for servers during work/production hours.

- You will also see if the update can be removed once it has been installed. This status is a critical consideration when getting ready to deploy the update. If the update cannot be uninstalled, and it causes the server to choke, then one of the only options left to get things back is to restore from the server backup.

- A link to the dedicated Web page for the update will be present so that you can click through and do more research on the update.

- The product scope will indicate to which operating system or application the update will apply at the bottom of the list.

- Finally, a detailed description of the update will be found on the right side of the status window.

Windows SBS Console (Advanced Mode)

The Windows SBS Console (Advanced Mode) adds tasks to access the specific server service snap-ins, such as Active Directory Users and Computers, DNS snap-in, DHCP snap-in, and Certificates snap-in.

The following additions can be found under the various tabs in this SBS Console:

- **Users and Groups Tab → Users tab**
  - o Click on the **Open Active Directory Users and Computers snap-in** (ADUC) link under **User Tasks,** and it will open to the default SBSUsers OU. Using ADUC allows you to fine-tune a user's Active Directory properties, move Active Directory objects such as computers from one Organization Unit to another, and more.

- **Network Tab → Devices tab**
  - o Click on the **Uninstall the Fax Service** link, and you will be prompted to confirm that you want to uninstall the fax service. The prompt also warns you that a server restart may be required.
  - o Click on the **Repair the Fax Service** link, and you will be prompted to confirm that you want to run a repair against the fax service. Note that if you run this wizard your SBS fax settings will be reset. Indeed, after running this wizard, right click on your fax modem and click on the **Edit properties of 56K Faxmodem** (your model name). Figure 4-26 shows the SPRINGERS SBS Fax Modem. You will need to run the **Configure the fax service** wizard to reconfigure your fax service.

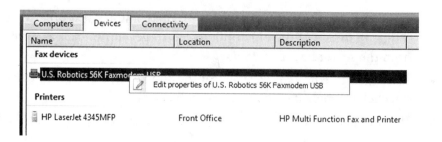

Figure 4-26
The SPRINGERS U.S. Robotics 56K Faxmodem USB right click menu.

- **Network Tab → Connectivity tab**
  - When you click on the **Remove this trusted certificate** link, you can remove the third-party trusted certificate you would have installed during the **Getting Started Tasks**. The wizard will replace the trusted certificate with the original SBS self-issued certificate that was created when the server was installed and configured. This item will not appear in the SBS Console (Advanced Mode) if you did not install a third-party trusted certificate.

  - Click on the **Stop DHCP** link to stop the DHCP server service. You may need to do this in the case of a migration or configuration change on the server.

  - When you click on the **Manage DNS** link, the DNS Manager snap-in will pop up. You can make changes to SBS's actual DNS server setup in this snap-in.

  - The **Manage DHCP** link will bring up the DHCP snap-in when you click on it. You can make changes to the DHCP scope, delete leases for computers that are no longer around, create a DHCP reservation for a new printer, or modify the Scope Options.

  - Click on the **Manage certificates** link to bring up the Certificates (Local Computer) snap-in. Your third-party trusted certificate will be found under the **Personal → Certificates** folder. You may need to export the third-party certificate with its key for a security appliance providing your firewall services or even for Internet Security and Acceleration Server if you have SBS 2003 R2 Premium Software Assurance.

Windows SBS Native Tools Management Console

Out of the box, the SBS Native Tools Management Console is a custom Microsoft Management Console consisting of a number of server component snapins installed:

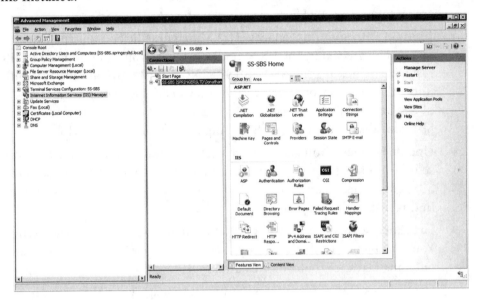

Figure 4-27
The Windows SBS Native Tools Management Console after our Chapter 5 tweaks and showing the IIS snap-in.

- **Active Directory Users and Computers:** You will use this snap-in to customize your SBS Active Directory setup. Some Line of Business applications will require a domain user account. You would create that account directly in this snap-in as the user account will not need any of the SBS specific permissions.

- **Computer Management (Local):** This snap-in gives you detailed control over services and management features installed on the SBS server. You can manage things like **Scheduled Tasks**, the **Event Viewer** and its new abilities, and server shares; **Disk Management** for managing your hard disks and partitions; manage server services such as **DHCP, DNS, Internet Information Services (IIS)**; and more.

- **Microsoft Exchange:** You will be able to manage the **Server Roles** and **Server Features** of your SBS Exchange server with this snap-in. Need to augment the Recipient Policies to add another e-mail domain? This is the snap-in you would use to do that.

- **Terminal Services Configuration: SS-SBS:** You will use this snap-in to create a new Terminal Services Connection on the SS-SBS server.

- **Internet Information Services (IIS) Manager:** Click on this snap-in and you will be greeted by the IIS **Start Page**, where you will find links to IIS resources. Click on the **SS-SBS (SPRINGERSLTD\JonathanPaul)** link under the **Connections** column and you will be able to manage all aspects of IIS. Be careful about making changes to IIS at this level as many of the SBS wizards and the overall SBS configurations are tied into IIS!

- **Update Services:** You can manage the Windows Server Update Services setup from this snap-in. Again, be careful about making changes, as the SBS setup is tied in quite tightly. We do, however, customize a few settings in this snap-in in Chapter 5.

- **Fax (Local):** This snap-in allows you to manage the SBS fax services setup. You can change the devices being used for faxing or where incoming and outgoing faxes are routed, for example.

- **Certificates (Local Computer):** You can manage your SBS domain and third-party trusted certificates with this snap-in. Some of the things you can do are to import and export certificates or add or remove an Intermediate Certification Authority certificate.

- **DHCP:** You can make changes to the DHCP scope, delete leases for computers that are no longer around, create a DHCP reservation for a new printer, or modify the Scope Options, for example.

- **DNS:** You can manage the various SBS Forward Lookup Zones and Reverse Lookup Zones, add a DNS A Record for a new network resource, or remove DNS records that no longer apply. Anything to do with your SBS DNS setup will be accomplished in this snap-in.

Summary

Before you can drive an automobile, it is reasonable to assume you can read, understand and interpret the dashboard. Imagine not be able to understand a speedometer or odometer. If you couldn't understand a fuel gauge, you might run out of gas. So consider this chapter as your introductions to the consoles in SBS (akin to dashboards). You are now ready to drive your server (starting in the next chapter).

In this chapter, a host of topics were presented:

- We have gone through the Windows SBS Console and all of its SBS management capabilities.
- We looked at the subtle tweaks that the SBS Team introduced into the Windows SBS Console (Advanced Mode).
- We then gave you a big picture view of the various server service and feature snap-ins contained in the Windows SBS Native Tools Console.

One last thought. You were introduced to many new terms, as presented in the consoles, used in SBS. So you might consider yourself to have taken the first step to learning a new language.

Chapter 5

SBS 2008 Deployment

In construction management, it is a well-known fact that extra time must be spent building the foundation of an office building. Close your eyes and imagine this building full of small businesses running SBS 2008, and you've got yourself in the right frame of mind!

But back to the importance of a perfectly shored-up foundation. When a physical building foundation is even just a quarter-inch off, the rest of the construction project becomes more burdensome. Framers have to adjust measurements, windows don't fit snugly, air drafts invade the building, and roof leaks occur.

This construction problem is analogous to the completion and ongoing use of your SBS 2008 network. Call it a case of "measure twice and cut once," but we feel strongly that extra time spent up front—such as what we discuss in the first five chapters of this book—will result in tight-fitting Windows (the Microsoft kind!).

So away we go into the deployment steps that occur after the core SBS 2008 setup.

Post OS Install Configuration Steps

Now, it is very important to make sure that the hardware and underlying Windows Server 2008 x64 operating system are properly tuned into each other using the newest available drivers to provide the greatest possible server stability.

If you are installing SBS 2008 into a VM, you will need to install your particular Virtual Server's integration components drivers before moving ahead with any of the post OS install configuration changes.

We will now cover some of the post driver and management software install and configuration steps, such as finishing off the partitioning setup, configuring your new Windows SBS Native Tools Console, and other necessary tasks. While going through the configuration process, hang on before running any OS updates via the Windows Update feature until later in the process.

We will introduce and give an overview of the various SBS consoles after the above configuration steps. This way you will already be somewhat familiar making with them.

> **TIP:** For the SBSer and SBS consultant, one of the new business possibilities is the ability to have your remote client, say halfway around the world, pick up an agreed-upon manufacturer's server hardware box and for you to send them the SBS DVD, a USB flash drive with the appropriately setup Answer File, and a small document that explains how to run through the initial setup steps. Hand-holding in the form of a phone call could also be a part of the setup routine.
>
> Once your remote client has run through the steps, including the temporary port forward of the Terminal Services port 3389 to the new SBS 2008 install, you can log in with the admin credentials specified in the Answer File and *change* that default password since anyone could have access to that USB key. Then, away you go with your post install setup steps and right into the wizards! Pretty neat, eh?

Now, given the above, we have a couple more options with regards to continuing the SBS post OS install steps and subsequently running the wizards when the client is a lot more local to you, the SBSer or SBS consultant:

1. You can continue to run the post OS install steps and the wizards in your shop before delivering the newly configured SBS box. As long as the router device you are using in your shop is at the same IP as the one at your client's site, the SBS box will be location unaware.

2. Pack up the server and anything else that needs to go to the client site and head out. Finish the post OS install steps and the SBS wizards after unpacking the box and setting it in its final location.

Keep in mind, that if Option #2 above is chosen, you very well may have the business owner watching over your shoulder all the while you are working your way through the required steps!

TIP: Let us take a moment to reiterate a key point to our time together in this SBS tome. As you work through this and other chapters, understand that this book is based on the SPRINGERS methodology (the sample SBS client based on Bainbridge Island, Washington).

The idea is that you spend the time upfront with this book creating a successful SBS network for a sample company, following every keystroke in every chapter. It is paramount you try to follow through with each example and task. At the end of the book, you're a bona fide SBSer as far as we're concerned. We also understand that your real-world SBS experience will be slightly different from ours. You'll work on different equipment under different conditions. In fact, Microsoft reports that the majority of SBS sales are international, so you're likely setting up SBS in a country other than the US of A.

More important, where possible, we try to compare and contrast different SBS features and functions, but sometimes we'll bypass some esoteric alternative path to accomplish a task in the spirit of maintaining the purity of our SPRINGERS methodology. All we can say is that some excellent advanced resources that explore every conceivable SBS feature and function, starting with the online help system, exist for your academic researching pleasure. Thanks in advanced for your understanding (and no flames on Amazon, please, as we've taken this moment to manage your expectations). Long live SPRINGERS!

All right! On to business. We have a bunch of tweaks, adjustments, configuration changes, and setup adjustments that we need to take care of!

GUI Customizations

There are some things that will be taken for granted throughout the instruction steps we will guide you through. The most significant of these is the customizations to the SBS OS GUI that we make right after we finish the driver and hardware manufacturer's utility installs.

Windows Explorer

Right away, out of the box, Windows Explorer needs a little tweaking so that there is a lot more at-a-glance information available to you.

1. Open **Windows Explorer**. Hit the **Start** key and type **Windows Explorer** [Enter] or hold the **Start** key and press the **E** at the same time.

2. Click **Tools** then **Folder Options**.

3. Click the **View** tab.

Notes

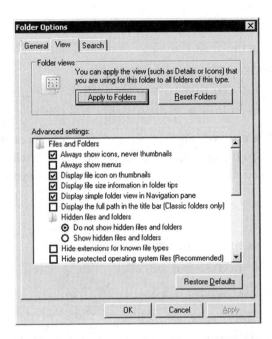

Figure 5-1
Windows Explorer custom settings.

4. Select **Hidden files and folders**: Set the radio button to **Show hidden files and folders**. Some settings are shown in Figure 5-1.

5. Uncheck **Hide extensions for known file types**.

You can optionally uncheck **Hide protected operating system files (Recommended)**. The only time this will be needed is when there is a need to touch a specific OS file. The other option is to enable the **Use checkboxes to select items** which you may or may not like. This setting is purely a personal preference.

Click **Apply** and **OK**.

Note that these customizations can be carried into your desktop OS too!

Desktop Toolbar

If you work like the authors do, then there will be a number of key shortcuts on the desktop. Well, when there are a number of windows open and you need to get to one of those shortcuts, you must either minimize everything (**Start+M**) or place a toolbar on the Task Bar that gives you quick access to desktop icons:

1. Right click on the **Task Bar** and uncheck **Lock the Task Bar**.

2. Right click on the **Task Bar** again and mouse up to **Toolbars**.

3. Click on **Desktop**. You also have the option to repeat the process to add an Internet Explorer **Address Bar** to the **Task Bar** that gives you quick access to the Internet by typing an URL and hitting [Enter].

You will now notice a new toolbar that you can click on to gain access to anything on the server's desktop quickly. This is especially handy if the windows that are presently open need to be in the background of the new window you will be opening.

Start Menu

The next thing to do is to customize the Start Menu a little.

1. Right click on the **Task Bar** and click on **Properties**.

2. Click on the **Start Menu** tab.

3. Click the **Customize** button. Figure 5-2 shows what you will first see.

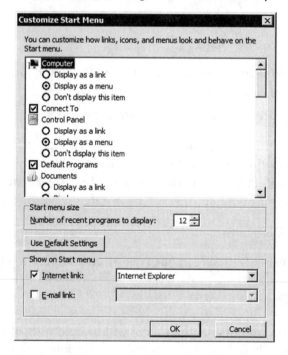

Figure 5-2
The beginning of the Start Menu customizing list.

4. Choose **Display as a menu** for the following: **Computer, Control Panel,** and **Documents.**

5. Check the following (or confirm already checked): **Default Programs, Enable context menus and dragging and dropping, Favorites Menu, Network, Help, Highlight newly installed programs, Network, Open submenus when I pause on them with the mouse point, Printers, Run Command, Search communications, Search favorites and history, Search programs,** and **Sort all Programs menu by name.**

6. Select **Search Files**: Click the **Search entire index** radio button.

7. Uncheck **Use Large Icons**. Of course, if sight demands it, this setting can be left alone.

8. Change the **Number of recent programs to display** to **12**. This setting is arbitrary. You can play with the setting to discover where you are comfortable.

9. Enable the **Internet link** for **Internet Explorer.**

10. Click **OK.**

11. Click **Apply.**

The Notification Area tab gives you the ability to manage what happens to the icons that sit in the System Tray. Check out the next section on how to make changes in it.

Click **OK** when you are done customizing your Start Menu.

Notification Area

Keep an eye on the icons in the System Tray, which is the area at the bottom right of your screen that may or may not have a clock in it. The icons reside in an area that is called the "Notification Area." If you right click on the Windows **Task Bar** and left click on **Properties,** you will find the **Notification Area** tab.

Why keep an eye on it? Because, some of the critical icons you need to see, such as the Updates Available icon, may be hidden. If you find critical icons are hidden that should not be, then get them to remain in view all of the time:

1. Right click on the Windows **Task Bar** and left click on **Properties.**

2. Click on the **Notification Area** tab.

3. You can uncheck **Hide inactive icons** to disable the feature or click the **Customize** button to select individual icons.

4. Key icons to keep in view are:

   - Safely Remove Hardware
   - Windows Updates
   - Task Manager CPU graph (hidden while minimized setting).
   - Windows Live OneCare.

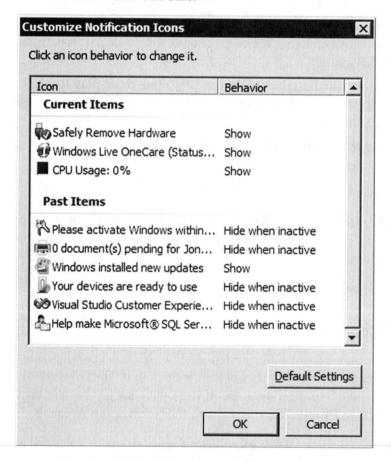

Figure 5-3
Some of the currently active icons set to show all of the time.

5. Click **OK** once you have chosen them.

6. Click **Apply** and **OK**.

Internet Explorer

There are a few settings tweaks to get Internet Explorer to behave a little differently in response to pop-ups and to enable the inline AutoComplete feature, which makes typing a breeze in IE and the Run dialogue box.

1. Open **Internet Explorer**. If needed, right click on the title bar and select **Menu Bar.**

2. Click on **Tools** then **Internet Options**.

3. Add **http://CompanyWeb** under **res://iesetup.dll/HardAdmin.htm** in the Home Page window. This gives you quick access to the CompanyWeb SharePoint site. The setting is shown in Figure 5-4.

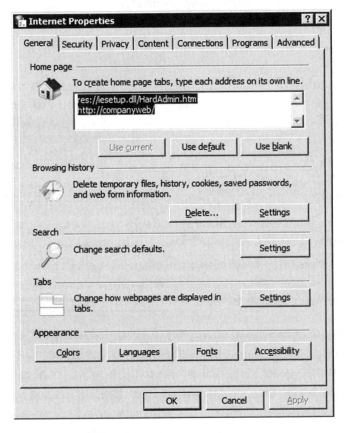

Figure 5-4
Having an extra tab open up the CompanyWeb site in Internet Explorer at start-up.

4. Click the **Settings** button for **Tabs**.

5. Check **Open home page for new tabs instead of a blank page**.

6. Click the **Always open pop-ups in a new tab** radio button.

7. Click **OK**.

8. Click the **Advanced** tab.

9. Scroll down and check **Use inline AutoComplete** and **Use most recent order when switching tabs with Ctrl+Tab**.

10. Click **OK**.

Now that you have finished tweaking the SBS OS GUI, it is time to move into some additional post OS install configuration steps.

Partitioning

There are a number of different methodologies when it comes to partitioning your available hard drive or RAID array space. Based on our experience, we have settled on the following formula for configuring our partitioning scheme in order of placement on the RAID array:

1. **C:** is the first partition we create during the initial WinPE-based SBS setup steps. In our SPRINGERS methodology, that partition is 75GB. Keep in mind that the minimum partition size for the OS must be 60GB.

2. **S:** is the partition we will create at 24GB after the OS partition. It is here that we will move our SBS OS Swap File in one of the following steps.

3. **L:** is the partition in which we will create the default Company folder and share for the SPRINGERS data, as well as move some of the relevant server services data, to later in the chapter.

TIP: Why do we set up the Swap File in its own partition after the OS partition? Think of it this way: In a large five-drawer filing cabinet, you have all of your files in no real particular order. You have one large set of files that are spread across the five drawers in whatever spot happened to be available. Now, let's say your client shows up and wants you to pull out all of the files to have a look. How much time would it take to gather them up across all of those drawers? A lot! The same is true for the Swap File. Giving it a dedicated space in which to reside can make a significant impact on the performance of your SBS box ... just like finding all of those files nicely ordered in one drawer!

Now, onto our partitioning setup:

1. Click on the **Start Button, All Programs, Windows Small Business Server,** and click on **Windows SBS Native Tools Management** shown in Figure 5-5.

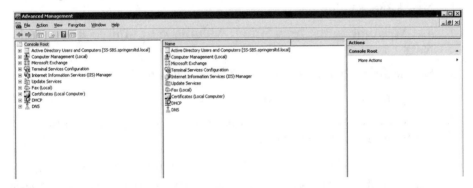

Figure 5-5
The new Windows SBS Native Tools Management gives you direct access to the various server component Microsoft Management Consoles.

TIP: If you are not already familiar with the incredible search capabilities built into Windows Vista, and now Windows Server 2008, this is as good a time as any to get a glimpse: Instead of the above Step 1, do the following:

1. Click on the **Start Button** *or* hit the **Windows Symbol key** (some keyboards will have the word **Start** on them) on your keyboard.

2. Start typing **SBS Native.**

3. Hit [Enter].

4. Select **Continue** if the **User Account Control** dialog box appears.

In the above steps you have a mouse movement and a few key strokes and you are into the Windows SBS Native Console! How neat is that? Try a few other key server management console names or others that come to mind such as DNS, DHCP, or Update.

2. Expand **Computer Management (Local)** → **Storage** → and click on **Disk Management**.

3. Right click in the **Unallocated** space to the right **SS-SBS (C:)** and click on **New Simple Volume**.

4. The **Welcome to the New Simple Volume Wizard** page appears. Click **Next**.

5. Set the **Simple volume size in MB** to **25000** and click **Next**.

6. Assign the drive letter **S:** and click **Next**.

7. Leave the File system and Allocation unit size at the defaults, but change the **Volume Label** to: **SwapFile**.

8. Click on the **Perform a quick format** radio button and click **Next**.

9. The **Completing the New Simple Volume Wizard** page appears. A summary will be shown of the settings about to be applied. Click **Finish**.

10. Repeat the above steps for the balance of the unallocated space, but leave the volume size setting with the balance of the RAID array (Step 5), assign the drive letter **L:**, and label the partition **NetworkData**.

You should now see the partition setup as shown in Figure 5-6. Note that, depending on your situation above, you might need to initialize the disk if you attempt the above procedure on a separate disk. Initialize this disk by right clicking the **Disk1** icon (as an example) and select **Initialize Disk**.

Notes

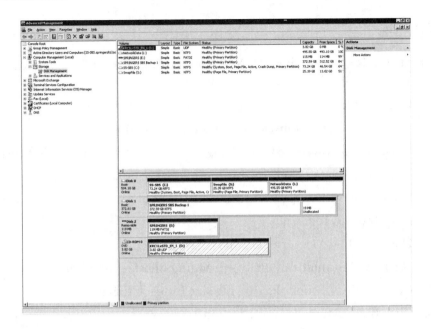

Figure 5-6
SPRINGERS SBS partitioning scheme including a couple of USB flash drives, the SPRINGERS USB backup drive, and the SBS DVD.

You can now close the Windows SBS Native Tools Management console. Say "**No**" to the request to save your settings for now.

TIP: Assigning the drive letter to the subsequent partitions is a pretty arbitrary thing. We set the letters up high because our clients have tended towards inheriting their network mapped drives from way back when. With SBS 2008, drive lettering is not so important anymore as far as the backup USB external hard drive, because the new backup system does not assign a drive letter which is also shown in Figure 5-6.

In some cases where we have the Intel Remote Management Module 2 (RMM2) installed on our SBS Intel dual Xeon configurations, four drive letters will be taken up by the Remote Management Module 2 setup. We manually assign them to the following drive letters: W:, X:, Y:, and Z:. This keeps them out of the way for our daily SBS operations.

Swap File

Your next task is to place the SPRINGERS SBS swap file onto the dedicated S: partition. To do this:

1. Click on **Start**.
2. Right click on **Computer** then click on **Properties**.
3. Click on **Advanced system settings** under Tasks near the top left corner.
4. When you see the User Access Control dialog box, click **Continue**.
5. Under Performance, click the **Settings** button.
6. Click the **Advanced** tab.
7. Under Virtual Memory, click the **Change** button.
8. Uncheck **Automatically manage paging file size for all drives**.
9. Click on the **C:** under **Paging file size for each drive**.
10. Click the **Custom size** radio button.
11. Set both the Initial and Maximum size to **400**. Any smaller than 400MB and Windows will warn you that there would be no room for a dump file.
12. Click the **Set** button.
13. Click on the **S:** under **Paging file size for each drive**.
14. Click the **Custom size** radio button.
15. Type the initial size of **12280**.
16. Type the Maximum size of **24576**, based on our server configuration with 8GB of RAM.
17. Click the **Set** button.
18. Click **OK, OK, OK**.
19. Click the **Restart Now** button when the request to restart to apply the settings dialogue pops up.

When the server comes back up and you have logged in, repeat the above steps **1** through **7** to bring up the Virtual Memory properties shown in Figure 5-7.

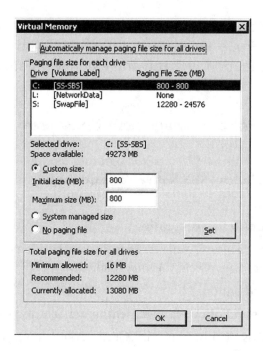

Figure 5-7
SPRINGERS SBS swap file settings showing the new swap file settings.

Windows SBS Native Tools Management Console

Okay, the server partitions are set up and the swap file is moved over. You now need to tweak the Windows SBS Native Tools Management Console to bring things up to speed for your regular SBS management needs.

TIP: The first time you open the Windows SBS Native Tools Management console, there is something missing! Can you guess what it is?

In our good old SBS 2003 Console, we had the two sections: Standard Management with all of the SBS wizards and Advanced Management with the native tools management consoles. The second console available under the Advanced Management section was the Group Policy Management Console (GPMC)!

The GPMC is the console you will use the most to configure any needed Group Policy customizations for things such as software distribution, startup and logon scripts, security settings, desktop restrictions, and so on.

Add the Group Policy Management Console

To add the GPMC:

1. Open the **Windows SBS Native Tools Console**.

2. Click on **File**.

3. Click on **Add/Remove Snap-in…**

4. Scroll down the list of Available Snap-ins and click on **Group Policy Management** (*not Group Policy Management Editor*).

5. Click the **Add** button.

6. Click on **Group Policy Management** under Selected snap-ins.

7. Click the **Move Up** button until Group Policy Management resides just below **Active Directory Users and Computers**.

8. Click **OK** (not before adding the below-mentioned consoles, though!).

9. Click **File** then **Save**. Your Windows SBS Native Tools Console will look like Figure 5-8.

10. You will now add the **Share and Storage Management** and the **File Server Resource Manager** (needed in the next step) consoles too, as there will be a need to use those consoles throughout the service life of SBS. For continuity, both of the consoles can be placed just below the **Computer Management (Local)** console. Use the just completed procedure to make these additions.

Notes

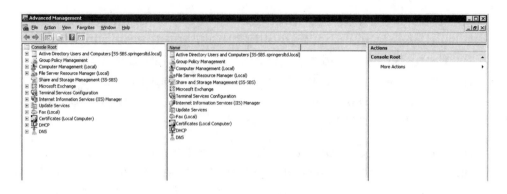

Figure 5-8
Additional management consoles added to Windows SBS Native Tools Management.

Don't go and close that console because you are going to need it for the next steps!

TIP: Something to keep in mind when you have customized your Windows SBS Native Tools Management console is to save the console to preserve those changes. And, much like MMC 2.0, when you build a custom MMC setup, every time you close the console it will ask you if you want to save your changes. If you say **Yes**, then the way the console looks when you close it will be the way it will look when you subsequently open it. If you say **No**, then the console will open up and look the same as it did the last time it was opened.

Quota Templates

For the SBSer and SBS consultant, there are going to be a lot of different ways to put things together to bring about an SBS-based network solution. Perhaps one of the key areas—when it comes to how the users will interact with the system—is where they store their data.

There will be two principle places to store the user's data: On a folder share or series of folder shares, in the SharePoint CompanyWeb site, or a combination of both.

TIP: What type of data should go in which location? Well, if we have a small photography company that runs three to five cameras every day that produce a couple of Gigabytes on a busy day, a folder share would probably be the best location for them. They could then publish a small subset of photos that have been converted to a compressed format, such as PNG to a SharePoint site dedicated to their clients to look at and download from.

A law firm would probably stand to benefit from having all of their documentation on the CompanyWeb site. The documentation would be quickly accessible using Windows Vista's built-in search feature or the CompanyWeb's built-in search. The data would also be accessible from the Intranet and the Internet.

Your SBS install has a few Quota Templates out of the box for shares we would create after the OS install. A quota is a limit that can be set on the amount of data a user can place in a network folder share. The out-of-the-box quotas are actually quite small, as they range in size from 100MB to 500MB.

TIP: Once you get into the Windows SBS Console and have a look at the user properties there, you will see that SBS does indeed have a quota setup, although, the SBS-based quotas are not reflected in the Windows Server 2008 quota templates. For now, however, we will continue on with our SPRINGERS SBS setup.

In this day and age, with storage so inexpensive, you can put together 7.5 Terabytes of RAID 5 storage in an entry-level server! In fact, Seagate has just released a 1.5TB 3.5" half height Barracuda hard drive! So, to have a user's quota limit on our soon-to-be-created Company folder share at less than 1GB does not fit with our SPRINGERS network needs—nor for most small to medium-sized offices, for that matter.

We have 10 SPRINGERS users with various roles in the company. Given the nature of the business of SPRINGERS (dog breeding), it is reasonable to say that no user should need more than 5GB of storage space. If a user comes close to the 5GB limit, an e-mail will be sent to both the administrator's account and the user notifying them of that fact. A follow-up can then be initiated to see whether the user's quota should be increased or some files removed.

To start with, in your now customized Windows SBS Native Tools console, you are going to create a 5GB Soft Quota:

1. Click on **File Server Resource Manager (Local)**.

2. Double click on **Quota Management** in the middle pane.

3. Double click on **Quota Templates** in the middle pane.

4. Right click on **Quota Templates** in the left column or anywhere under the list of quota templates and click on **Create Quota Template**. Complete the following fields.

   a. Template Name: **5GB Soft Quota**.

   b. Label (optional): **5GB soft limit on user data**.

   c. Space Limit: **5GB**.

5. Choose the **Soft quota: Allow users to exceed limit (use for monitoring)** radio button.

6. Click the **Add** button under Notification thresholds.

7. Leave the default of **85%** for the usage percentage.

8. Tick both options on the **E-mail Message** tab: **Send e-mail message to the following administrator** and **Send e-mail to the user who exceeded the threshold**. For the SBSer or SBS consultant, you can add your own e-mail address here too.

9. Click the **Event Log** tab and tick **Send warning to event log**.

10. Click **OK**.

11. Click **OK**.

Using the above steps, create a 10GB Hard Limit as well. We may need to use it in the future for certain users. The created quotas are shown in Figure 5-9.

Notes

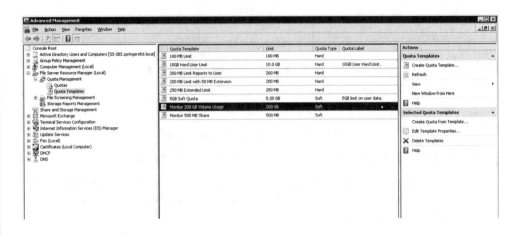

Figure 5-9
SPRINGERS SBS newly created 5GB quota and preexisting quotas.

DHCP IPv4 Properties

There are some settings that we will need to change in the DHCP manager to reduce the possibility of a support call later on in the SPRINGERS SBS lifecycle. Out of the box, DHCP is not set to update the DNS services with any IP changes unless the client requests it.

We want DHCP to update the DNS service all of the time, since we have key services such as Remote Desktop used for connecting to a workstation via the Remote Web Workplace (RWW) depending on the workstation being at the IP address listed in DNS.

In your Windows SBS Native Tools Management console:

1. Click on **Computer Management (Local)** in the Advanced Management MMC (it is already open at this point).
2. Double click **Services and Applications** in the middle column.
3. Double click the servers **FQDN: SS-SBS.SpringersLTD.Local** in the middle column.
4. Double click on **IPv4** in the middle column.
5. Right click **IPv4** in the left column and click on **Properties**.
6. On the **General** tab: tick both **Automatically update statistics every 10 minutes** and **Show the BOOTP table folder**.

7. Select the **DNS Tab**: tick the **Enable DNS dynamic updates according to the settings below:**

    a. **Always dynamically update DNS A and PTR records** radio button.

    b. **Discard A and PTR records when lease is deleted.**

    c. **Dynamically update DNS A and PTR records for DHCP clients that do not request updates (...).** Figure 5-10 shows the correct settings.

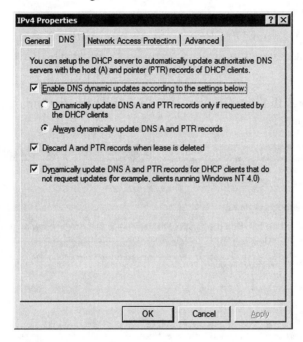

Figure 5-10
DHCP IPv4 Properties for DNS updates.

8. Select the **Network Access Protection Tab**: We will leave the defaults for now. We will address Network Access Protection in our *Advanced SBS 2008 Blueprint* book.

9. Select the **Advanced Tab**: Click the **Credentials** button.

    a. **User name:** JonathanPaul.

    b. **Domain:** SPRINGERSLTD.

    c. **Password** and **Confirm password**: L0ts and lots of fun!

10. Click **OK**.

11. **Apply** then **OK**. Apply may not light up.

> **TIP:** Now that you have set the JonathanPaul credentials to allow for the DNS dynamic updates, you should get into the habit of changing that password for the **Credentials** button whenever the domain admin account's password changes.

DNS Settings

Now that you have your DHCP set to make sure that DNS is updated when any IP address changes occur, you need to make a couple of settings changes in the DNS service too.

Figure 5-11 shows the settings you need to make sure that the A records in DNS are the correct ones.

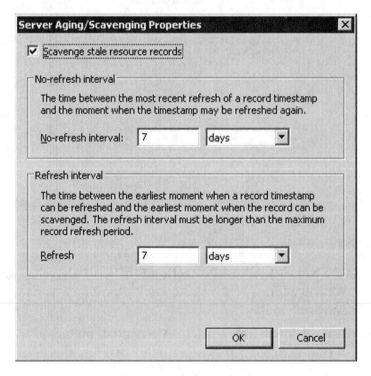

Figure 5-11
 DNS Server Aging/Scavenging Properties set at 7 days.

In your Windows SBS Native Tools Management console:

1. Double click on **DNS** at the bottom of the left column.

2. Click on **SS-SBS**.

3. Right click on **SS-SBS** and click **Set Aging/Scavenging for All Zones** on the context menu.

4. Tick **Scavenge stale resource records**.

5. Click **OK**.

6. On the **Server Aging/Scavenging Confirmation** page, tick **Apply these settings to the existing Active Directory-integrated zones.**

7. Click **OK**.

You can close the Windows SBS Native Tools Management console.

You now have all of the necessary SBS OS tweaks and adjustments in place in preparation for setting up the storage locations for SPRINGERS' data.

Default Company Shared Folder

There will be two primary data storage locations for all of SPRINGERS' data. One will be a folder called "Company" that will be shared and network-drive-mapped via the SBS SYSVOL script. The other storage location will be the built-in SBS CompanyWeb SharePoint site.

You will need the Windows SBS Console to carry out the creation of the Company shared folder (assume you click the **Next** button after each step):

1. On the Windows SBS Console (if it's not open, launch from the desktop), click on the **Shared Folders and Web Sites Tab**.

2. Click on **Add a new shared folder** under the Tasks column. The **Provision a Shared Folder Wizard** launches.

3. At **Shared Folder Location,** click the **Browse** button.

4. In the **Browse For Folder** area, click **L$**.

5. Click the **Make New Folder** button.

6. Name the folder **Company** and click **OK**. Figure 5-12 shows the completed step.

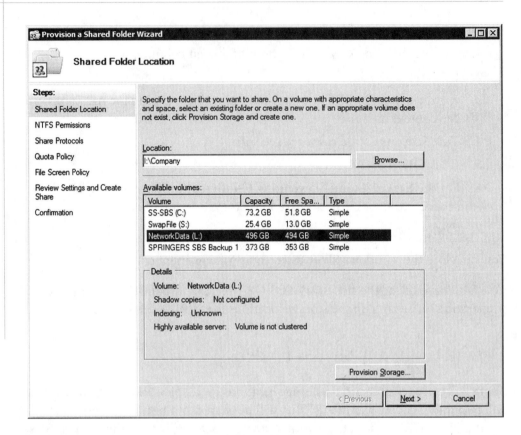

Figure 5-12
The Provision a Shared Folder Wizard with the Company folder location chosen.

7. Click **Next** to go to **NTFS Permissions** under **Steps**: Click the **Yes, Change NTFS permissions** radio button then the **Edit Permissions** button.

8. Under the Groups or user names list, click on **Users (SPRINGERSLTD\ Users),** and under the **Allow** column, check **Modify**.

9. Click **Apply** and **OK**.

10. Click **Next** for the **Share Protocols** page to appear: Leave the default **SMB** share name of **Company**.

11. Click **Next** for the **SMB Settings** page: Set the description to something like **Springer Spaniels Ltd default company shared folder**.

12. Click the **Advanced** button.

13. Tick **Enable access-based enumeration** and click **OK**.

14. Click **Next** for the **SMB Permissions** page. Click the last radio button for **Users and groups have custom share permissions,** then click the **Permissions** button.

> **TIP:** The default share permission will be **Everyone** with Read Only access. At the least, we want to have **Authenticated Users** with Read Only permissions. Setting the minimum access to users who have been authenticated will at the least prevent an unauthorized individual whose laptop is plugged into the network from gaining access to share's data.

15. Click on **Everyone** then click on the **Remove** button.

16. Click the **Add** button.

17. Type: **Authenticated Users; Domain Users; Domain Admins**. Don't forget the semicolon in between each user group.

18. Click the **Check Names** button to verify that there are no typos.

19. Click **OK**.

20. For share permissions, set **Authenticated Users** to **Read**, **Domain Users** to **Full Control**, and **Domain Admins** to **Full Control**.

21. Click **Apply** and **OK**.

22. Click **Next** to display the **Quota Policy** page: Check the **Apply quote** box and click the down arrow beside **Derive properties from this quota template** and choose the **5GB Soft Quota** we created earlier.

23. Click **Next** to display the **File Screen Policy** page: Leave the default for now.

24. Click **Next** to display the **DFS Namespace Publishing** page: Leave the default for now.

25. Click **Next** to display the **Review Settings and Create Share** page, shown in Figure 5-13, which gives you a last glimpse at the settings before you commit. Make sure they look correct before clicking the **Create** button.

26. You will receive a success message once the share and permissions have been set. Click the **Close** button to end the wizard.

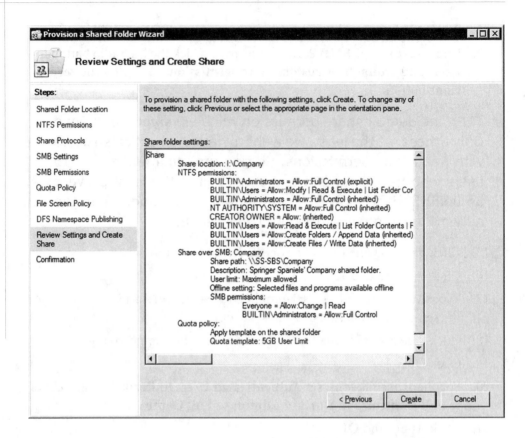

Figure 5-13
The Review Settings and Create Share window showing the settings to be applied when the Company shared folder is created.

Mapped Network Drive

Your SBS users will be used to the idea of getting access to shared folder resources via a drive letter or drive letters. So, you will be setting up a script to make sure that all users get connected to the share.

SBS 2008 handles start-up scripts a lot differently than SBS 2003 did out of the box. With SBS 2003, you had the start-up script embedded in the user's properties on the Profile tab. In SBS 2008, you will need to set up a Group Policy Object attached to the SBSUsers OU that will have the designated script setting in it.

Keep in mind that only after creating the GPO will you be able to place the script into the proper network location.

> **TIP:** When choosing a drive letter to assign to the folder share, keep in mind that there are any number of factors that may influence what letters to assign. Some workstations may have a USB-based card reader installed that will have anywhere from one to five or more drive letters assigned to it. Thus, the system drive plus an optical drive can secure drive letters C: through I:!
>
> If a physical drive in a workstation already has a drive letter assigned that the mapped drive will try to use, the mapping will fail. Many times that failure will happen with no indication that anything is amiss.

There will be a number of steps to get the drive letter mapped to the share. The first is the creation of the Group Policy Object (GPO):

1. Open the **Windows SBS Native Tools Management** console (Advanced Management MMC).
2. Click on **Group Policy Management**.
3. Double click on **Forest:springersltd.local** in the middle pane.
4. Double click on **Domains**.
5. Double click on **springers.local**.
6. In the left pane, click the + to expand **springersltd.local**.
7. Click the + to expand the **MyBusiness** OU.
8. Click the + to expand the **Users** OU.
9. Right click on **SBSUsers** and click on **Create a GPO in this domain, and Link it here...**
10. Name the new GPO **Windows SBSUsers Policy** and click **OK**.
11. Right click on the new **Windows SBSUsers Policy** GPO (nested under MyBusiness, Users, SBSUsers) and click **Edit**.
12. In the **Group Policy Management Editor**, click **User Configuration, Policies, Windows Settings**, to **Scripts (Logon/Logoff)** as shown in Figure 5-14.

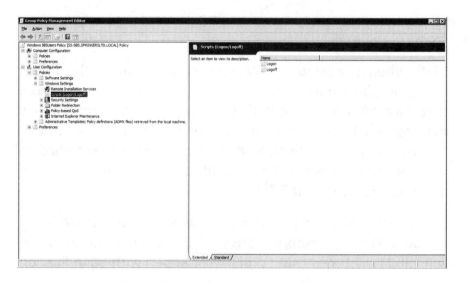

Figure 5-14
The new SBS Logon Group Policy Scripts location.

13. Double click on **Logon** in the right pane.

14. Click the **Add** button.

15. Select **Add a Script**. Click the **Browse** button. Note that the location opened is the default location for any logon scripts associated with this particular GPO.

16. Right click anywhere under **This folder is empty.** Select **New**.

17. Click on **Text Document** in the right flyout context menu.

18. Name the file **SBS_Logon_Script.bat**. Make sure to delete the **.txt** extension from the name before you hit [**Enter**]!

19. Answer **Yes** to the file name extension warning.

20. Right click on your new **SBS_Logon_Script.bat** file and click on **Edit**.

21. Click the **Run** button on the **Open File - Security Warning** pop-up.

22. Type: **net use m: \\ss-sbs\company.**

23. Click on **File** and **Exit** and the **Save** button when asked to save changes. The **0KB** file size should change to **1KB** once the save finishes.

24. Make sure the new script file is highlighted and shown in the **File name,** then click the **Open** button.

25. Click the **OK** button when you see **SBS_Logon_Script.bat** listed as the **Script Name** as shown in Figure 5-15.

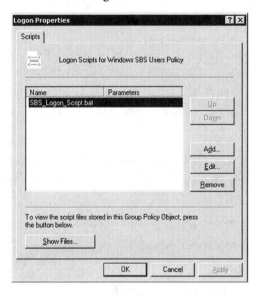

Figure 5-15
The new SBS_Logon_Script.bat file is now loaded and ready to apply.

26. Click **Apply** and **OK**.

27. Close the **Group Policy Management Editor** with our **Windows SBS Users Policy** in it.

Log off the server, then log on again and open Windows Explorer. You will now see **company (\\ss-sbs) (M:)** under **Network Location** in the drive list. Note that once you have logged back onto the server and opened Windows Explorer, you may see a **Red X** on the new M: drive. Double click on the drive to show the share's contents and the **Red X** will clear.

> **TIP:** One of the first folders that will be created on the new M: drive will be the Network Admin folder. It is in this folder that subfolders such as Drivers, Downloads, Utilities, Install Apps, and the like will be stored. Having this one-stop location for anything related to network management makes an SBSer or SBS Consultant's job a lot easier across any number of client installations.

So, here we are. We are now very close to where the SPRINGERS SBS setup is ready for the SBS Getting Started Tasks wizards which will be the final steps before the SPRINGERS SBS network goes live!

WSUS Sync Schedule

One of the final tweaks that will need to be accomplished is how frequently SBS checks for updates as well as dropping one class of updates so as to limit hardware and driver problems in the future.

In the **Windows SBS Native Tools Management** console (remember you can launch this from **Start** and type **SBS** in the search field and the console will be listed):

1. Click on the + to expand **Update Services**.
2. Click on the + to expand **SS-SBS**.
3. Click on **Options**.
4. Click on **Synchronization Schedule**.
5. Change the number of **Synchronizations per day** to **8**.
6. Click **Apply** and **OK**.
7. Click on **Products and Classifications**.
8. Click the **Classifications** tab.

Notes:

9. Enable all classifications except **Drivers**. Figure 5-16 shows the proper Classification settings.

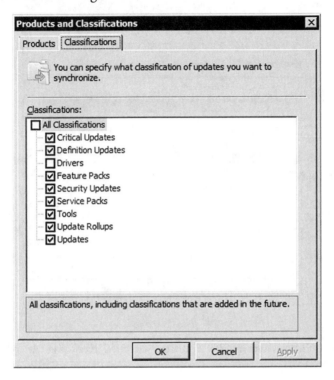

Figure 5-16
WSUS is set to check all classifications except drivers.

10. Click **Apply** and **OK**.

Definition Updates in WSUS

Since you already have the Update Services snap-in open in the SBS Native Tools Management console, there is one more modification that is needed: Add an automatic approval for definition updates.

Why do you need to do that? Well, if you decided to install Forefront Server Security during the initial SBS OS setup then you will be seeing a lot of the following:

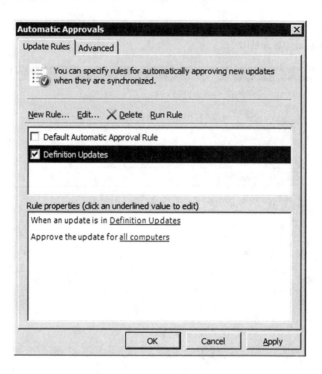

Figure 5-17
Definition updates required for Forefront-enabled Exchange Anti-Spam and Block List Updates.

If you licensed Forefront Server Security on SBS 2008, you receive a little bonus in the way of the reception of the Exchange 2007 Enterprise malware updates. These updates can be issued a number of times in one day. The key is to have Forefront licensed, though. If Forefront is not installed, or the trial period has expired then Exchange 2007 will receive the default Exchange 2007 Standard Edition Anti-Spam updates bi-monthly via WSUS.

Just as you could do with SBS 2003, you need to set up a definition approval in the WSUS console leaving the default WSUS SBS rules so things do not get broken.

To do this:

1. Open the **Windows SBS Native Tools Management** console and **Continue** at the UAC prompt if you closed it after the previous process.

2. Click the + beside **Update Services**.

3. Click the + beside **SS-SBS**.

4. Click on **Options** at the bottom of the list.

5. Click on **Automatic Approvals** in the middle pane.

6. Click the **New Rule...** button.

7. In the **Add Rule** window under **Step 1,** put a checkmark beside **When an update is in a specific classification**.

8. In the **Add Rule** window under **Step 2,** click on the **any classification** link.

9. In the **Choose Update Classifications** pop-up, uncheck **All Classifications** to deselect them all.

10. Put a tick beside **Definition Updates** and click **OK**.

11. In **Step 3 Specify a name,** call the rule **Definition Updates** and click **OK**.

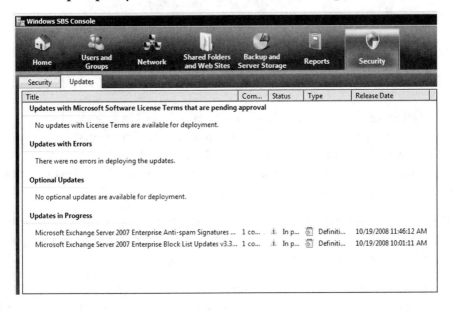

Figure 5-18
Automatic Approvals now include all definition updates for the server and workstations.

12. Back at the **Automatic Approvals** window, click **Apply** and **OK**.

The automatic approvals will also catch any Windows Defender definition updates for your Windows XP Professional workstations that have it installed and your Windows Vista workstations that have Windows Defender installed by default.

Server Updates

By now you will certainly have noticed that there are a number of things competing for your attention, including Windows Live OneCare for Server as well as server updates via the information balloons from the system tray. We will have a look at the Windows Live OneCare for Server setup later in this chapter under the **Getting Started Tasks** section.

Figure 5-19 shows one of the icons that you will see on a somewhat regular basis:

Figure 5-19
The Windows Update "New updates are available" icon in the system tray is the leftmost one.

Double clicking on this icon brings up the **Windows Update** window (alternatively, you can open Windows Update from **Start**, **All Programs**). You can click the **View available updates** link under the **Install Updates** button to have a look at the updates that are sitting in the install queue. For now, hit the **Install updates** button and restart the server when requested to do so.

Once the install routine starts, the **Windows Update** window will minimize back to the system tray. If you want to see how the update install routine is progressing, just double click on the minimized icon for a progress update.

Note that there may be a few updates that show up after each update install routine reboot. If that is the case, install those updates and send the server into a reboot if requested to do so until all of the updates have been installed.

> **TIP:** When it comes to updates, it is always a good idea to test them in a lab environment before deploying them to production environments. For the most part, updates will install without any hiccups, but some updates may cause conflicts with line of business applications, drivers, or other server components.

One thing to watch out for is a major service pack release for the SBS OS, the Windows Sever 2008 OS, or the desktop OSs on the SBS network. Pay attention to the Release Notes as well as the many prominent SBS blogs and resources for any conflicts that may come to light with a service pack.

Now that you have finished any required updating to the server, it is time to take a look at the various new SBS consoles a little more in depth.

Getting Started Tasks: In Order

Here we go, off to finish our SBS configuration with the thought of moving our newly minted SPRINGERS SBS box into production!

As discussed during the introduction to the Windows SBS Console, each of the Getting Started Tasks is grouped with like tasks, Internet-specific tasks are under the **Connect to the Internet** header, and so on.

Finish Installation

The one task under this section is a good read of the Windows SBS Help. While all of us are truly pressed for time, it is important to take at least 15 or 30 minutes in a day to read up on the products we are working with. Click **View installation issues** and check **Completed**.

Using the Windows SBS Console

You will find the **Using the Windows SBS Console** link to the SBS help useful. Besides the big picture view we are giving you here in this chapter, the SBS help will delve deeper into the inner workings of SBS and its consoles. Please have a look through the various help topics. Check **Completed**.

Connect to the Internet

This series of tasks will establish our SPRINGERS SBS connection to the Internet and allow connections to the server from the Internet.

Connect to the Internet Wizard

Our first task to accomplish on our Getting Started Tasks list is the **Connect to the Internet Wizard**. Shown working in figure 5-20, the wizard will run a routine to detect an existing router and its IP address. Once detected, the wizard will configure SBS to communicate with the Internet via the router.

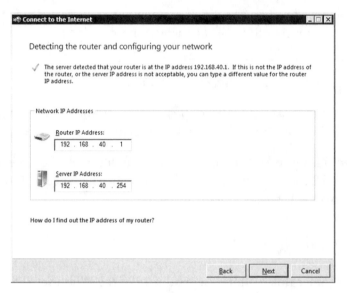

Figure 5-20
Once the router's IP address is discovered, the wizard will configure SBS to communicate with the Internet.

Note that this particular wizard is actually a part of the SBS 2008 setup routine. If the server was installed without an answer file, then just to be safe, run this wizard again. If the server was set up using the answer file, then you can check off this wizard if the server can freely connect to the Internet.

The steps:

1. Click on the **Connect to the Internet** link.

2. The **Before you begin** page appears. Every wizard starts with a greeting screen that explains just what the wizard will be doing. Click **Next**.

3. The **Detecting the existing network** page appears. The server will run a detect routine on all IP subnets 192.168.0.0/24 through 192.168.255.255/24 looking for the local IP subnet and a router.

4. The **Detecting the router and configuring your network** page appears. The wizard will show you which IPs it has picked up for the server and the router. Make sure they are correct before clicking **Next**.

5. The **Your network is now connected to the Internet!** page appears. A successful message indicates you are good to go. Click **Finish**, open Internet Explorer, and navigate to a Web site to confirm that the server is indeed connected to the Internet.

TIP: It is important to note that if the SBS answer file is not used to set up SBS, then the setup routine will set the SBS IP to the next one after the router. So, say you set up the router with the IP address 192.168.20.1. Once the SBS setup routine was finished, you would find the SBS IP at 192.168.20.2.

If you complete the setup without the SBS answer file and NO router/firewall device, then the default SBS 2008 server IP address will be 192.168.0.2.

Customer Feedback Options

Pretty much all of Microsoft's products offer the ability to send information back to them on the usage of those products called the Microsoft Customer Experience Improvement Program (CEIP). The information sent to them is used to refine the products themselves based on their actual usage. No identifiable information is sent to Microsoft at all.

In the case of our SPRINGERS SBS, the CEIP will send information on the use of SBS 2008, Windows Server 2008, and Windows SharePoint Services, which is the underlying technology behind the CompanyWeb SharePoint site.

TIP: It is a good idea to opt in if at all possible. The more information Microsoft receives on product usage, the better that product can be. For the SBS consultant, the question on whether to join would need to be posed to the client prior to enabling the CEIP.

For more information, see Microsoft's Web site: http://www.microsoft.com/products/ceip/en-us/default.mspx.

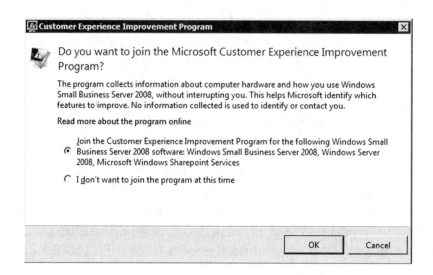

Figure 5-21
Do you want to join the Microsoft Customer Experience Improvement Program? Yes!

Once you have clicked on the **Customer feedback options** link, you will be presented with the question window shown in Figure 5-21. However, nothing will be chosen for you, of course! Click the radio button beside the option you prefer and click **OK**.

Set Up Your Internet Address Wizard

The **Set up your Internet address Wizard** is one of the most critical SBS wizards. This wizard will enable users to connect to the server's Internet- and Intranet-facing services such as the Remote Web Workplace and Outlook Web Access.

This wizard can take two directions:

1. **Already have a domain name**: In the case of our SPRINGERS company setup, we already have the domain springersltd.com registered and eager to go. Therefore, we will follow the wizard steps that take us in this direction.

2. **Register a new domain name**: If you do not have a domain name yet, you can use this direction to purchase and configure a domain name all from within the SBS wizard! A visit to one of the qualified registrars' Web sites would be required for the actual domain purchase. The wizard will take care of the required settings from there for you.

TIP: When using the domain registration method of the **Set up your Internet address Wizard**, make sure to do your due diligence on the registrar options offered to you in the SBS wizard.

Also, note that once the domain name purchase has been made, the username and password setup you choose would be typed into the wizard to set up the Internet DNS for your new domain to point to your SBS server.

So, we have our springersltd.com domain name registered. Some items related to Internet hosting need to be addressed before heading right into the wizard:

1. **RWW**: remote.springersltd.com needs a DNS A record that points to the IP address that is assigned to the WAN port on the router. In the case of SPRINGERS, that IP is 207.202.238.215, so the DNS entry would look like:

    - remote.springersltd.com. 3600 IN A 207.202.238.215

2. **SMTP**: mail.springersltd.com needs a DNS A record that points to the IP address that is assigned to the WAN port on the router. Its entry would look like:

    - mail.springersltd.com. 3600 IN A 207.202.238.215

3. **SMTP**: mail.springersltd.com needs an MX record with the highest priority so that e-mail will come to SPRINGERS SBS before the ISP's e-mail servers. Note that the lower the priority number, the higher the priority:

    - springersltd.com. 3600 IN MX 10 mail.springersltd.com

4. **SPF**: The DNS hosting company will need to create an SPF record that has the SPRINGERS ISP domain in it. An SPF record tells other e-mail servers on the Internet that it is okay for e-mail stamped with a User@springersltd.com e-mail address to come from the ISP's network which would normally be stamped user@ISPDomain.com.

    - springersltd.com. 3600 IN TXT "v=spf1 a mx ptr include:ISP1domain.com ~all" "v=spf1 a mx ptr include:ISP2domain.com ~all"

Figure 5-22 shows the **Before you begin** window that you will see once you start the wizard.

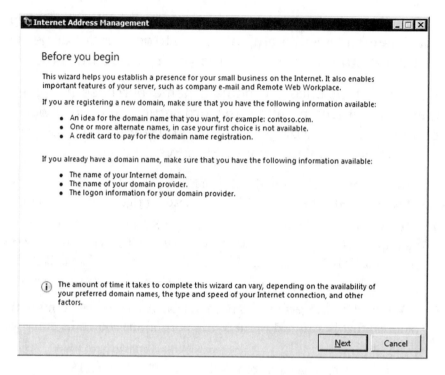

Figure 5-22
You can either think of and purchase a domain name or use an already existing domain name when running the wizard.

The **Set up your Internet address Wizard** has the title **Internet Address Management** during the wizard steps:

1. Click on the **Set up your Internet address** link.

2. Have a read through the information presented in the **Before you begin** step, then click **Next**.

3. Click the **I already have a domain name that I want to use** radio button then click **Next**.

4. Click the **I want to manage the domain name myself** radio button and click **Next**.

    a. The note under this radio button is telling us to have the above hosting-related items addressed prior to heading in this direction.

5. The **Domain name and extension** page appears. Type **springersltd.com** and click **Next**.

a. Note the **Advanced settings** link under the domain name and extension field gives you the option to change the prefix you will use to connect to the Remote Web Workplace: **remote.springersltd. com**. Keep in mind that your DNS A record will need to properly reflect whatever value you choose.

6. The **Configuring your server** page appears. A series of green checks will show up as the RWW, Exchange e-mail, and Internet router configuration steps are completed.

7. The **Congratulations!** page appears. You will receive a message that all of the steps are completed.

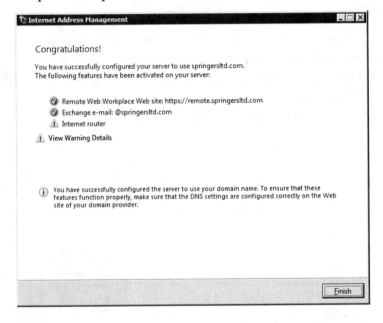

Figure 5-23
Internet Router shows a warning during the final wizard configuration steps.

Now, as a rule, Universal Plug and Play (UPnP) is turned off in the router. As a result, when the wizard goes to try to configure the port forwarding via UPnP, it will fail to do so as noted in Figure 5-23. Click on the **View Warning Details** link and you will be presented with a message about not being able to port forward 25, 80, 443, and 987.

TIP: Something to keep in mind as far as the security of your SBS network: The lower the number of ports open to the Internet, the less exposed your SBS network is. Port 80 is the Web standard HTTP protocol. When someone types **http://remote.springersltd.com** in their Web browser, when the browser hits SBS it will automatically be redirected to the SSL-secured Remote Web Workplace.

Close port 80, and SBS users will need to keep in mind that they must type or shortcut the SSL version **https://remote.springersltd.com** of the site instead.

Need a practical example? Try opening this Web site in your browser: **http://eopen.microsoft.com**. You should get nothing in reply. Try **https://eopen.microsoft.com**, and you will hit Microsoft's eOpen licensing Web site logon page. Microsoft has no automatic forward to the SSL based eOpen site.

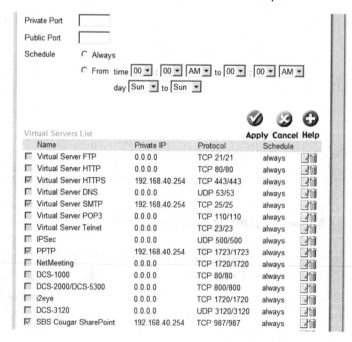

Figure 5-24
Router rules forwarding to the SPRINGERS SBS box.

Because UPnP is disabled, now would be a good time to verify that the appropriate ports are forwarded to the SBS server's IP address of 192.168.40.254:

- Port 25: SMTP – E-mail inbound.

- Port 443: HTTPS SSL – Remote Web Workplace, Outlook Web Access, Outlook Mobile Access.

- Port 987: HTTPS SSL for the CompanyWeb SharePoint site.

- Port 1723: PPTP VPN – Used for VPN connections if you enable them.

Configure a Smart Host for Internet E-Mail

A **smart host** is a dedicated e-mail server through which Exchange will send all outgoing e-mail. In most cases, the smart host server will be the ISP's e-mail servers that provide the Internet services to the company that owns the SBS server.

TIP: Depending on the Internet setup with the ISP, this wizard is optional. Some ISPs will not allow any SMTP communications to leave their networks outside of their own e-mail servers to reduce spam. If that is the case, then this wizard will be mandatory.

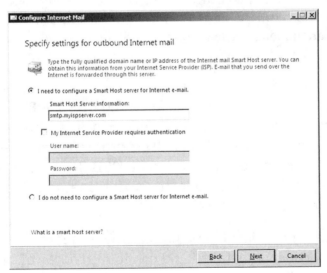

Figure 5-25
The smart host settings allow for the ISP's e-mail server and logon information.

Running the wizard is pretty quick:

1. Click on the **Configure a Smart Host for Internet e-mail** link.

2. The **Before you begin** page describes what the wizard will be doing. Click **Next** once you have read through.

3. You will need either the IP or the Fully Qualified Domain Name for the ISP's e-mail server in this step. Enter either one in the **Smart Host Server information** field. If the ISP e-mail server requires authentication prior to the SBS server sending e-mail through it, you will need to check the **My Internet Service Provider requires authentication** and input the e-mail **user name** and **password**. Click **Next**.

4. If successful, click **Finish**.

This wizard can be used to both set up the smart host or to remove it if something changes down the line. If the ISP changes, run the wizard to remove the old ISP's smart host e-mail server setting, then run the wizard again to set up the new ISP's smart host e-mail server.

Add a Trusted Certificate

SBS 2008 brings significant changes to the certificates setup especially when it comes to the SSL certificate for the Remote Web Workplace. It is important to note that we are no longer able to install the SBS self-issued SSL certificate into Internet Explorer while visiting the RWW as we could with SBS 2003.

> **TIP:** With the advent of relatively inexpensive SSL trusted certificates, there is little need to keep the SBS 2008 self-issued certificate as the default. The default self-issued certificate requires you to run a little install program that the user would need to bring home with them on a USB flash drive. You can no longer import the certificate via Internet Explorer on on-domain joined computers.

> This wizard provides a very simple way to get the third-party trusted certificate installed and configured for all of the Internet-facing SSL secured services. Note that if you already have an existing third-party trusted certificate for the URL you will be using for your SBS Internet services, you can import that

one instead of generating a new certificate request and subsequently importing the newly generated certificate. Keep in mind that some third-party trusted certificate providers will charge for every reissue of the certificate.

Once we have started the **Add a trusted certificate Wizard** and chose the option to buy a certificate, you will be greeted with the window shown in Figure 5-26:

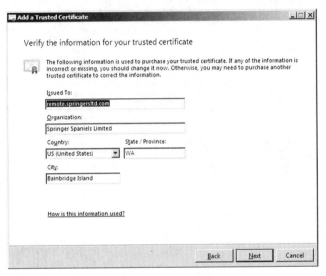

Figure 5-26
*Verify that the information is correct, especially the **Issued To:** field.*

The **Issued To:** field is set to the URL of your Remote Web Workplace. You set this URL during the **Setup up your Internet Address Wizard** in the above steps.

To complete the wizard:

1. Click the **Add a trusted certificate** link.

2. Note that there are two links in the **Before you begin** welcome screen. One explains what a trusted certificate is and the other explains how to import an existing trusted certificate. Click **Next** once you have read through them.

3. Click **I want to buy a certificate from a certificate provider** radio button and click **Next**.

4. The information fields should populate automatically. Verify them, especially the **Issued To:** field and click **Next**.

5. When the **Generate a certificate request** page appears, the request itself will be in the **Generate Trusted Certificate Request**. You can copy the text by clicking on the **Copy** button and pasting it into your certificate provider's Certificate Signing Request (CSR) box on its Web site if you have it open. Or, you can save the text to a text file and upload it to the CSR on your certificate provider's Web site at another time. Click **Next** to continue.

Figure 5-27
Our SPRINGERS certificate request pasted into Comodo's CSR.

6. The **A request is in progress** window gives you three options:

   a. **My certificate provider needs more time to process the request**. If you saved the certificate request to a text file to upload to your trusted certificate provider at a later time, choose this one. Click **Next** and then **Finish** on the **Importing the certificate request is postponed** window.

   b. **I have a certificate from my certificate provider**. If you were connected to your trusted certificate provider's Web site and it generated the certificate once you pasted the CSR, then choose this option. Click the radio button for this option and click **Next**.

   c. **I want to cancel my request**. Perhaps a mistake was made, or due diligence on a trusted certificate provider needs to occur. If so, then choose this option and restart the wizard at a later date.

7. Similar to Step 5, you have two options to **Import the trusted certificate**.

    a. If your trusted certificate provider issues the certificate in text format, you can copy and paste the new certificate into the **Paste the encoded text from your certificate provider** field. Click the **Next** button to begin the trusted certificate installation process.

    b. If the trusted certificate provider has issued the certificate in a zipped file, then extract the certificate files into a folder on the server and click on the **Browse** button in the wizard and navigate to the **remote_sprintersltd_com.crt** file, click on it, and click the **Open** button. Click the **Next** button to begin the trusted certificate installation process.

8. Notice that the **Trusted certificate is imported successfully** page appears. The trusted certificate is now imported and set up to use with the Remote Web Workplace. Click the **Finish** button.

Figure 5-28
The trusted certificate has been installed successfully!

9. Open **Internet Explorer** on the server and type **https://remote.spring-ersltd.com** in the address bar. Hit **[Enter]** key or the **Green Arrow** to the right of the URL.

10. In IE, click on the **Lock** at the right of the **Address Bar**.

11. Click on **View certificates** on the pop-up menu.

12. You should see the third-party trusted certificate information.

13. Steps **9** through **12** should be done on a remote workstation to also verify the certificate is installed correctly.

To set up ISA 2006 with the newly acquired trusted certificate, we will address this in the advanced SBS book.

Protect Your Data

Backing up your server is probably one of the most critical tasks that need to be accomplished for any business. Having the backup media rotated once a week or every couple of weeks along with the media being taken off-site also plays a critical role in a good Disaster Recovery Plan.

Second to backing up the server is protecting it from virus infections as well as malware threats. If you choose to install Microsoft Forefront Server Security as well as Windows Live OneCare for Server during the SBS OS install, then you are protected out of the box. You can choose not to install the security products if you plan to install a third-party security product or products.

Configure Server Backup

At the least, you will need a couple of USB hard drives to create your backup regimen. In the case of SPRINGERS SBS server, there is a total of 640GB of storage available. Ideally, the USB hard drive backup storage capacity would be calculated this way:

- 640GB full backup #1.
- 640GB full backup #2.
- 320GB incremental backup storage.
- 1.5TB total backup storage required.

Now, obviously SPRINGERS is not going to start out with a full server. So, depending on the amount of data the company has on all of its existing systems, you could choose either a 750GB or 1TB capacity to begin with. The drive does not need to be formatted prior to plugging it into the server.

To configure the server backup:

1. Plug in and power on your USB hard drive following the TIP advice below.

2. Click on the **Configure server backup** link. You see a small pop-up window indicating that data is being loaded.

3. At the **Getting started** window, read over the explanation and click **Next**.

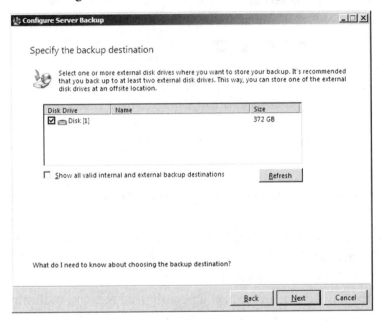

Figure 5-29
The USB hard drive should be shown as a backup destination. If not, cancel the wizard and check the drive connections, then run the wizard again.

4. The **Specify the backup destination** window will show your USB hard drive. By default, it should be checked as a destination. You can check **Show all valid internal and external backup destinations** then click the **Refresh** button to see any other possible locations to store backups. Click **Next**.

5. Label the **Disk 1 label**: SPRINGERS SBS Backup 1 and click **Next**.

6. On the **Select the drives to backup** page, it should have all three of the SPRINGERS SBS partitions selected by default. You can choose to deselect any of the partitions, but SBS will not allow you to deselect partitions that have critical data. Click **Next** once you have your selections.

7. By default, the **Backup Schedule** will be twice a day—at 5:00 PM and 11:00 PM. You can change this to any schedule you prefer. We changed ours to **Custom** and set the backup to run at **12:00 PM, 5:30 PM,** and **11:00 PM** to catch any late workers' changes. Click **Next** once you have made your choice.

8. A **Confirm backup details** window will show you your choices, have a look to make sure everything looks correct then click the **Configure** button.

Figure 5-30
Keep in mind that the Configure Server Backup Wizard will format any USB hard drive!

9. A warning pop-up will indicate that **You are about to format the selected disk drives!** Click **Yes** to continue or **No** to cancel if the USB hard drive has the family pictures on it!

10. Once you see the **Server backup configured** message indicating that the backup was setup successfully, you can click the **Finish** button.

TIP: The safest process for plugging a USB hard drive into the server is to:

1. Plug in the USB cable into the server.

2. Plug in the USB cable into the USB hard drive.

3. Plug in the USB hard drive power cable.

4. Power up the USB hard drive by flipping the power switch.

5. Reverse the process for removing the USB hard drive.

This process will best protect the server from any possible power spikes passed through to the server by the USB hard drive.

Help Protect Your Server with Windows Live OneCare for Server

To set up Windows Live OneCare for Server:

1. Click on the **Help protect your server with Windows Live OneCare for Server** link.

2. Click the **Update OneCare** button to begin the process. OneCare will check for updates.

3. The **Select your language and then click Next** page appears. Many languages are available for you to choose from.

4. Read through the Terms of Use and the Privacy Statement. Click the **I accept the terms of use** radio button if you do so and then click **Next**.

5. A status window shown in Figure 5-31 will show the approximate time needed to complete the downloading of the required OneCare updates.

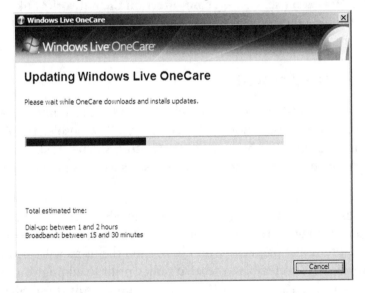

Figure 5-31
Windows Live OneCare downloading updates.

6. Once the downloads are completed, click the **Finish** button.

7. The Windows Live OneCare status window will come up, then a subscription window will pop up requesting that you subscribe to the OneCare service. For now you will click **I don't want to subscribe to OneCare yet.**

8. You may get a second request to sign in with your Live ID, which you will not be doing right now. Click **No thanks**.

Windows Live OneCare for Server should show a green status symbol in the system tray indicating that the server was up to date and scanning for threats.

Add Users, Computers, and Devices

We are now very close to having our SPRINGERS SBS set up and ready to go into production! We have the addition of our users, the connection of our client computers, and the setup of the Microsoft Office Live Small Business Web sites wizards left. The balance of the Getting Started Tasks are informational in nature.

How Can Users Access Computers on the Network?

Click on the **How can users access computers on the network?** link and an SBS Help topic **Understanding users and their computers**. A user's permission to access a computer or multiple computers is explained in the Help topic.

Add a New User Account

There are two methods for adding user accounts to the SBS domain as was mentioned in the above introduction to the Windows SBS Console: The **Add a new user account Wizard** found both under the **Getting Started Tasks** and the **Users and Groups** tab and then the **Add multiple user accounts** under the **Users and Groups** tab.

Something to keep in mind prior to adding your SBS users is the SBS domain password policy: That policy sets the number of characters, whether there needs to be complexity in the passwords, and how often the users will need to change their passwords. It is preferable to set that policy prior to adding your SBS users. Head on over to the **Password Policies** section under **Advanced SBS Security Topics** in Chapter 5 to dive deeper into this discussion.

In order to complete the Getting Started Tasks step, you will be running the wizard from the **Getting Started Tasks** list:

1. Click on the **Add a new user account** link.

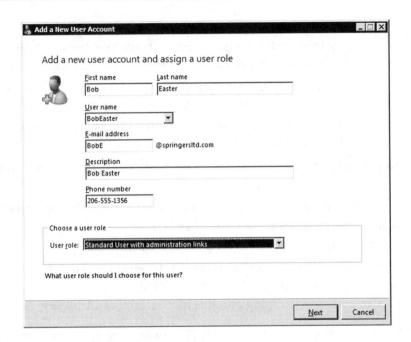

Figure 5-32

Bob Easter's user account information filled out.

2. Fill out the fields on the **Add a new user account and assign a user role** page, in this case Bob Easter's information as follows, then click **Next**:

   1. First Name: **Bob**

   2. Last Name: **Easter**

   3. User name: **BobEaster**

   4. E-mail address: **BobE**

   5. Description: **Dog Trainer and Manager Bob Easter**

   6. Phone number: **206-555-1356**

   7. User role: **Standard User with administration links**

3. Set a password for Bob: **Lots to eat!** Then click the **Add user account** button. Note that the **Complexity** green check will not appear until that exclamation mark is typed!

4. You will see the **User account Bob Easter has been successfully added to the network** window once the wizard completes. At the bottom of that window are two options:

1. **Assign an existing computer to Bob**: When clicked this brings up a list of workstations on the SBS domain. Since we are starting fresh and have not yet added any computers, that list will be empty.

2. **Add a new computer for Bob**: When this is clicked, you are given the option to use the http://connect internal Web site or to copy the Connect Computer program to a USB flash drive or CD along with instructions on the use of either method.

5. As part of the SPRINGERS methodology, select the **Add a New computer for Bob** link on the lower right.

6. Carefully read the **Add user accounts before connecting computers to your network account** page and click **Next**.

7. The **Run the Connect Computer program** page appears. There are two options and you will select the **Access the program through a web browser** option as part of the SPRINGERS methodology. But please carefully read this page as a new option using portable media (such as a USB key) now exists.

TIP: The portable media option (**Copy the program to portable media**) to connect a computer workstation reintroduces a concept not witnessed since the Networking Setup Disk—last seen in the SBS 2000 time frame (February 2001-October 2003). This procedure created one floppy disk that the SBSer took around to each workstation and ran the setup.exe file that gathered information for the Netparam.ini file on the diskette to attach the workstation to the SBS 2000 network. Funny what goes around comes around.

The real old-timer SBSers will recall that in the SBS 4.x era, you had to create a Networking Setup Disk for each workstation, so you ran around with a stack of diskettes! (Big Grin!)

The purpose of the portable media option in the SBS 2008 time frame is to support mobile workers (a concept that wasn't fully developed in the SBS 2000 legacy era). Brilliant!

8. The **Run the Connect Computer Program through a web browser** page appears. Carefully read the three-step procedure and perform the actions

on the workstation. Essentially, you will go to the client computer and type **http://connect in a web browser**. Click **Finish**.

Once you have finished creating the Bob Easter user account, you can then head on over to the **Users and Groups** tab and start the **Add multiple user accounts Wizard** by clicking on its link under **Tasks**.

Note that you will actually complete the computer connection process, where you add a workstation to the SBS 2008 Network (for real) in about two pages with the Connect computers to your network procedure.

Observe that Figure 5-33 shows a grid layout for the users and workstations that was done in Microsoft Excel:

	A	B	C	D	E	F	G
1	First Name	Last Name	Username	Password	User Role	E-mail Address	PC Name
2	Norm	Hasborn	NormHasborn	Sunny days!	User with Admin Links	NormH@springersltd.com	SS-President
3	Barry	McKechnie	BarryMcKechnie	Numbers fun?	User	BarryM@springersltd.com	SS-Accounting
4	Melinda	Overlaking	MelindaOverlaking	Working the desk.	User	MelindaO@springersltd.com	SS-OfficeAdmin
5	Linda	Briggs	LindaBriggs	Summer is here!	User	LindaB@springersltd.com	SS-Registration
6	Bob	Bountiful	BobBountiful	Lots of dogs!	User	BobB@springersltd.com	SS-Breeding
7	Tom	Benkert	TomBenkert	Time for fun.	User	TomB@springersltd.com	SS-Schedules
8	Norm	Hasborn Jr.	NormHasbornJr	Managing numbers.	User	NormHJr@springersltd.com	SS-Sales
9	David	Halberson	DavidHalberson	Making them count.	User	DavidH@springersltd.com	SS-Marketing
10	Elvis	Haskins	ElvisHaskins	Looking for genes!	User	ElvisH@springersltd.com	SS-Genealogy
11	Bob	Easter	BobEaster	Lots to eat!	User with Admin Links	BobE@springersltd.com	SS-CareFeeding
12	Bob	McKenzie	BobMcKenzie	Back bacon eh!	User	BobMcK@springersltd.com	SS-RemoteDesktp

Figure 5-33
  SPRINGERS user and workstation Excel spreadsheet grid.

The grid will make the multiple user additions and subsequently adding the workstations to the SBS domain a lot simpler. Just check off the user that has been set up, or run a ruler or straightedge down the list as each user is added to the network. Figure Z-05 in Appendix Z offers a full page of the above diagram.

TIP: For the SBSer and SBS consultant, having a checklist at the ready when it comes to more complicated tasks, such as setting up multiple users and/or workstations on the network, can help keep the tasks neatly organized. Checking off each item as it is accomplished can reduce confusion about what is next, especially if the tasks are interrupted, and keep a history of everything done.

To add multiple users at the same time, complete the following procedure. You will complete the procedure to add the ten users at Springer Spaniels Limited (listed in Chapter 2). You will run the **Add Multiple New User Accounts Wizard** twice to account for adding users with different roles (once for the **Standard User** role and once for the **Standard User with Administrative links** role).

1. Click on the **Users and Groups** tab.

2. Click on **Add multiple user accounts**.

3. Choose the **Standard User** role if it is not already chosen for you. If you are adding users to another role, then choose that role.

4. Click the **Add** button and fill out the information fields.

a. The user's **First name**.

b. The user's **Last name**.

5. The **User name** will automatically populate with **FirstLast**. If you require a different username format, this is the place to change it.

6. The **E-mail address** will also automatically populate with **FirstLast**. If you require a different format as we did for SPRINGERS first name and last initial **FirstL** (First name Last initial), then make the necessary change here.

7. The **Description** field is arbitrary. For SPRINGERS you set this to the job title on the table of users in Chapter 2.

8. The **Phone number** is the user's phone number—and extension if there is one—or direct line number. By default, the telephone number to use for Springer Spaniels Limited is 206-555-1356.

9. The **User password** must follow the SBS domain password policy as described in the requirements.

10. Repeat Steps 4 through 11 until all users have been added to the **Add user accounts** list as shown in Figure 5-34.

Notes:

Figure 5-34
All of SPRINGERS' Standard User role users.

11. Click the **Add user accounts** button to start the process. A progress indicator window will show you each user creation step as it happens. A green checkmark indicating success appears before each user when the step completes successfully.

12. Once the process completes, you will see the **All new user accounts have been successfully added to the network** message window. A link at the bottom of the window will generate and allow you to print a **Getting Started** page for each user that was created using this process.

13. Repeat this procedure for each user role.

TIP: You can now distribute the Getting Started page to your new users.

Connect Computers to Your Network

As mentioned above, there are two methods for connecting computers to the SBS network:

1. Use the Web-based method to run the Connect Computer program by starting **Internet Explorer** on the new workstation and opening the **URL http://connect**.

2. Copy the **Connect Computer** program to a USB flash key or burn it to CD to run on the new workstation.

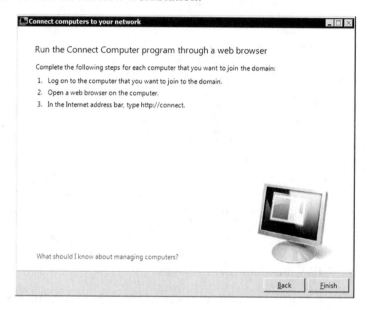

Figure 5-35
Using the http://connect Web page enables you to set up a new workstation via Web browser.

The overall best method of connecting any workstation to the SBS domain is via the Connect Web page. There are no USB keys to carry around that way.

Add a Computer with One User Using the Connect Computer Web Page

1. On the new workstation, open **Internet Explorer**.

2. Open the **URL http://connect**.

3. When the Internet Explorer security warning indicating Intranet settings are off by default comes up, click on it and then **Enable Intranet Settings** on the menu.

4. Click **Yes** on the **Are you sure?** security prompt.

5. Click on the **Start Connect Computer Program** link on the Welcome to Windows Small Business Server 2008 Web page.

6. When the **File Download – Security Warning** pop-up appears, click the **Run** button to start the process.

7. Click **Continue** for Vista's User Account Control (UAC).

8. On the **Choose how to set up this computer** you will be configuring it for the Norm Hasborn user account, so only one user will be added to this machine. Click the **Set up this computer for myself** link as shown in Figure 5-36.

9. A short verification of the computer system setup will run. If the system meets the necessary requirements, you will be able to move on. Click **Next** when the **Computer requirements are verified** window appears.

    a. Type your new user name and password: Enter the user name **NormHasborn** with the password **Sunny days!** and click **Next**.

    b. Verify computer description: The Name of the computer is **SS-President** and the Description is **Norm Hasborn**. Click **Next**.

10. **Move existing user data and settings**: For the SPRINGERS methodology, you are working with an existing workstation, so select the local profile <**NormH**> and click **Next**.

TIP: A neat new feature introduced with SBS 2008 is the ability to migrate a workstation that is already domain joined. Any local profile—whether it is strictly attached to the local machine or a domain-joined local profile on the workstation—can be chosen during the **Move existing user data and settings** step.

For SBS 2003, there were a number of user profile and registry hacks that could be done to migrate the original domain profile over, but there was no guarantee it would work.

11. **Confirm your user data and settings selection**: A confirmation request to verify that you are sure you do not want to use any existing user data. Click **Next**.

12. **Restart the computer**: To continue with the setup, click the **Restart** button. An option at the bottom of the window is given to log on the user automatically. It is not recommended to choose this option unless the user will be sitting in front of the workstation when the wizard completes.

13. Once the setup routine has completed, the system will log on, then automatically lock itself with the **Norm Hasborn** username and password. **Unlock** the workstation.

14. Click the **Finish** button on the **Connect Computer complete** window.

15. The system will finish some additional user profile specific setup tasks, then present the operating system's desktop. In the case of Windows Vista, you will see the **Windows Vista Welcome** screen.

Once the workstation is added to the SBS domain, depending on their update status you can expect your WSUS to require attention as it looks for updates on the newly added workstation. Since Windows XP Professional SP2 or higher and Windows Vista Business and Ultimate Editions are the supported desktop operating systems, you may see a large number of updates for each.

Add a Computer with One User Using the USB Device

1. Alternatively, in the **Connect computer to your network** page, you can select **Copy the program to portable media**.

2. On the **Specify a location to copy the Connect Computer program**, select **Browse** and select your USB drive you have placed in the SBS server machine. Click **OK** and **Next**.

3. The **Copying Connect Computer** program page briefly appears.

4. On the **Run the Connect Computer program** page, read the information and click **Finish**.

5. Place the USB key in the PC and run **Launcher.exe**. Note that we performed this on a Windows XP Pro machine and received an error message that declared: Need to install .NET framework 2.0 required (plus make sure that Windows XP Pro is SP2 or higher). This application was downloaded from Microsoft's download site (www.microsoft.com/downloads) and then we ran Launcher.exe again.

6. The **Connect Computer Wizard** launches and the **Choose how to set up this computer** page is displayed. Carefully review this page and then select **Set up this computer for myself**.

7. The **Verifying computer requirements** page is displayed with a progress bar.

8. The **Computer requirements are verified** page is displayed. Click **Next**.

9. On the **Type our user name and password** page, type **BobEaster** and **Lots to eat!** in the **User name (for your computer network)** and **Password (for your computer network)** fields. Click **Next**.

10. On the **Verify computer description** page, type **SS-FEEDINGCARE** in the **Name of this computer** field. In the **Description of this computer** field, type **Care, Feeding and Breeding**. Click **Next**.

11. The **Move existing data and settings** page appears. You can leave this set to **None** and click **Next**.

12. On the **Confirm your user data and settings selection** page, select **Next**.

13. On the **Restart the computer** screen, select Restart. The **Connecting to the Windows SBS network** screen will appear and then the computer will reboot.

14. After your logon to the computer again, the Connect Computer complete page is displayed. Click **Finish**.

TIP: Be advised that during the above procedure(s) to connect a computer to the SBS 2008 network, the authors encountered a problem where one of workstations WOULD NOT CONNECT! This problem was resolved by reading TechNet Article #957708 titled **Windows XP/Vista Workstations Fail To Connect To SBS 2008 When Using** Http://connect. This article had us make a DNS suffix entry at the workstation

Add a Computer with Multiple Users

Now, one of our SPRINGERS workstations may have any number of different SPRINGERS users sit at it. That workstation is at the Office Administrator's position. Therefore, we need to use the **Set up this computer for other users** setup procedure in the Connect Computer process.

We will be adding the following users along with Melinda Overlaking:

- Norm Hasborn
- Bob Easter
- Tom Benkert
- Norm Hasborn Jr.

Keep in mind that one of the steps will request a network administrator user name and password! In the case of our SPRINGERS methodology, that will be our handy JonathanPaul SBS Admin account.

Note that if you wanted to add multiple users to a computer, you would have a completely different response to Step 6 above and your actions would look like this:

> On the **Choose how to set up this computer** page you will be configuring the Office Administrator's system for some key SPRINGERS users, so click the **Set up this computer for other users** link as shown in Figure 5-36.

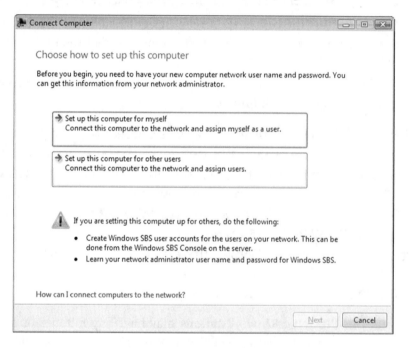

Figure 5-36
Choose how to setup this computer.

16. A short verification of the computer system setup will run. If the system meets the necessary requirements, you will be able to move on. Click **Next** when the **Computer requirements are verified** window appears.

17. You will now need your SBS Administrator account user name and password. Enter them into the **User name** and **Password** fields. In the case of our SPRINGERS methodology, that account is the JonathanPaul one. Click **Next** once you are done.

18. On the **Verify the name and description of this computer** window you will name the computer **SS-OfficeAdmin** and put the description of **Melinda Overlaking** since she is the primary user of the workstation.

19. At **Assign users to this computer,** you will add **Melinda, Bob, Norm Sr., Norm Jr.,** and **Tom** as users assigned to this computer and click **Next.**

TIP: As mentioned above, the ability to migrate domain joined local profiles is now a part of the SBS 2008 workstation setup routine. However, there may be times where migrating the existing user's local profile may not be beneficial. For the SBSer or SBS Consultant, part of the preparatory work for implementing an SBS based solution is having a discussion with each of the existing network's users. If they are experiencing problems with their current setup, then this very well could be the best time to start them with a fresh local profile.

Another consideration is whether the existing network setup has some form of **Roaming Profiles** or **Redirected Folders** to an existing server on the network. If Roaming Profiles are setup, then you can disable them prior to implementing the new SBS setup. If folders are redirected to a server, you can disable the Group Policy setting and the folders should automatically come back to the local machine depending on how the Group Policy setup was implemented in the first place.

20. Now, since this workstation has already had those users sit at it, they should have their own local profiles on the machine. So, on the **Move existing user data and settings** window make sure to click the **Down Arrow** beside each domain user name and select the user's local profile name. In the case of our SPRINGERS methodology, our existing profile names were **FirstL** (First name Last initial) which was their local username on the workstation. Once you have made your choices, click **Next.**

Figure 5-37
You can choose what access level each user will have when adding multiple users to a workstation in the Connect Computer Wizard.

TIP: For the SBSer and SBS Consultant when it comes to assigning access levels to a workstation, with the advent of Windows Vista with User Account Control, you now have a better chance of having your SBS users configured as a Standard User.

Even for the software applications that require elevated privileges, it is now possible to setup a structure so that a Standard user can be authenticated as a local administrator. All you need to do is create a local user account that is in the **Local Administrators Group** that the Standard User knows. They can then authenticate in the Vista UAC as the local admin to run that software application. Thankfully, software is more and more being written with the Windows Vista security model in mind.

For a tighter security ship, the Standard User does not need to know any local admin account information. The SBS Administrator can then log on to the workstation to make any necessary software changes or modifications to allow those errant applications to run on Windows Vista.

21. In our SPRINGERS methodology, **Jonathan Paul**, **Bob Easter**, and **Norm Hasborn** will have local admin rights. Click **Next** when you have made the choices.

22. Your last chance to make sure all of the settings are correct happen in the **Confirm user data and settings selections** window that comes up now. Click **Next** once you have done so.

23. You will be prompted to **Restart the computer** now. Click on the **Restart** button to begin the workstation setup process.

24. Once the setup routine does its final reboot, the workstation will logon and then lock using the SBS Administrator's account. In the SPRINGERS case that is the **Jonathan Paul** account. **Unlock** the workstation.

25. Click the **Finish** button on the Connect Computer complete window.

26. The system will finish some additional user profile specific setup tasks then present the operating system's desktop. In the case of Windows Vista, you will see the **Windows Vista Welcome** screen.

27. You can then log off the workstation and log on as one of the users to test it.

Now, if you go back to the **Proposed Network Diagram** in Chapter 2, you will see that we just added the two Windows Vista workstations.

TIP: Something to keep in mind when it comes to migrating existing networks to SBS is the state of the workstations. An SBSer or an SBS Consultant will need to verify the patch level of the workstations on the existing network.

In the case of Windows XP Professional, there is a need to have .NET 2.0 installed prior to running the Connect Computer Wizard. So, if Automatic Updates were not enabled on any of the Windows XP Professional workstations by default, it is very possible that those workstations will not have .NET 2.0 installed!

And, one more thing with regards to Windows XP Professional: Once the workstation has been added to the SBS domain, run the WSUSReset.bat file you created earlier to accelerate the workstation's check for updates. There are two critical updates that need to be installed first including the Windows Installer 3.1 version which will facilitate the subsequent automatic update installations. Note that the updates will require a reboot.

One of the neat new features of SBS 2008 is the ability to have an SBS Vista Gadget in your Sidebar to gain access to SBS resources anywhere you have an Internet connection.

Figure 5-38
The Windows SBS Desktop Links Vista Gadget.

It can be added to your Windows Vista Sidebar by clicking the + at the top of the Sidebar and double clicking on the Windows SBS Desktop Links gadget.

We will address the Windows SBS Desktop Links Vista Gadget and other more advanced SBS topics in our SBS 2008 Advanced Blueprint book.

How Can I add a Shared Printer to the Network?

Click on the Help link and you will get a set of instructions on the various methods to share a printer on the SBS network. The Help shows you how to share a printer from a Windows XP Professional or Windows Vista desktop, as well as from the SBS server itself when the printer is connected directly to the machines.

Given the way setting up a printer on the new SBS network has changed so much, we have a dedicated section in Chapter 10: Fax and Print.

Grow Your Business

Everyone wants to grow his or her business. Whether a one man or woman shop, or a small company with 3 or 4 employees, one of the business owner's goals is to grow the business.

To do so in today's Internet connected world means that the company needs to have an Internet presence.

Set Up Your Microsoft Office Live Small Business Web Sites

The Office Live Small Business is a new online toolset to facilitate an online presence for small businesses. We will address the setup of the Office Live service in Chapter 11: Internet and the Web.

Summary

Well, here we are! Our SPRINGERS SBS hardware has all of the needed setup steps completed, our SBS OS has been tweaked to your liking, the SPRINGERS SBS domain is setup, and the users are connected to their workstations and network resources. This was a chapter for big eaters and with its closure, you have reached a milestone in the successful deployment of your SBS 2008 network.

Specifically – the following topics were addressed.

- GUI Customizations – this included the Windows Explorer, Desktop toolbar, Start menu, notification area, and Internet Explorer.

- Partitioning – this included creating a NetworkData partition and moving the swap file

- Console customizations – this included adding the Group Policy Management Console (GMPC) to the Windows SBS Native Tools Console.

- Quota Templates – we discussed and you configured!

- DHCP IPv4, DNS – ditto!

- More and more topics presented to you - Company Shared Folder, Mapped Network Drive, WSUS synch schedule, updates (server, WSUS).

- The importance of completing the Getting Started Tasks in order – very important!

- Adding users and computers – very important!

Moving forward, consider the following. Once you complete the setup steps needed to setup the fax and print services in Chapter 10 and then the Office Live Small Business setup steps in Chapter 11 you will have a well designed and smooth running SBS infrastructure based on the SPRINGERS methodology! Way to go! Now on to Chapter 6 for a security conversation.

SMB and SBS 2008
Photo Essay

This section is dedicated to telling the SBS 2008 story with a look back to the SBS 2000 and SBS 2003 launches. The SMB Nation events in 2008, which featured SBS 2008, are then presented. You will find hundreds of more photos at www.smbnation.com and www.smbphoto.com.

Note: We acknowledge and extend a heartfelt thank you to SMB Photo for the use of the SMB Nation 2008 fall conference photos.

History

This section presents the SBS 2000 and SBS 2003 launches. The original SMB Nation fall conference from October 2003 is also displayed.

SBS 2000 Launch, February 2001, West Atlantic City, New Jersey

SBS 2003 Launch,
October 2003, New Orleans, Louisiana

SMB NATION 2003
September 2003, Indianapolis, Indiana

This is the original SMB Nation fall conference that celebrated the launch of SBS 2003.

Present

This section presents events in the SBS 2008 time frame including the SMB Nation 2008 fall conference (where a large SBS 2008 launch party was held).

SMB Nation East 2008, March 2008, New York City-area

SMB Nation Toronto 2008,
May 2008, Toronto, Ontario, Canada

SMB Nation 2008 Fall Conference,
October 2008, Seattle, Washington

A SBS 2008 "launch party" was held on the Seattle waterfront to celebrate SBS 2008. Over 600 attendees were present.

Visit www.smbnation.com for book updates.

SMB Nation London 2008,
December 2008, London, Great Britain, United Kingdom

User Group Visit,
December 2008, Dublin, Ireland

SECTION TWO

Extending Small Business Server 2008

Chapter 6
Standard Security in SBS 2008

Chapter 7
Messaging with Exchange 2007 and Outlook 2007

Chapter 8
Collaboration with Windows SharePoint Service

Chapter 9
Mobility and Remote Connectivity

Chapter 10
Fax and Print

Chapter 11
Internet and the Web

CHAPTER 6

Standard Security in SBS 2008

Blue oceans of opportunity! That is how we would summarize the security situation in SBS 2008. Microsoft has created an opportunity for the robust SMB ISV ecosystem to support the SBS 2008 product with third-party security solutions. Of course, you can still work with Microsoft's own Internet Security and Acceleration Server product (ISA).

This chapter is also unique in that the two authors implemented a well-known business strategy called "divide and conquer." Philip wrote about Untangle and ISA while Harry wrote about Calyptix, SonicWALL, and WatchGuard. We denote which author wrote which section to guide you.

SPRINGERS Network

First, a foundation comment. It is important to look at the SPRINGERS network, as it stands currently, so you can integrate the security concepts to the application of the firewall. This is shown in Figure 6-1.

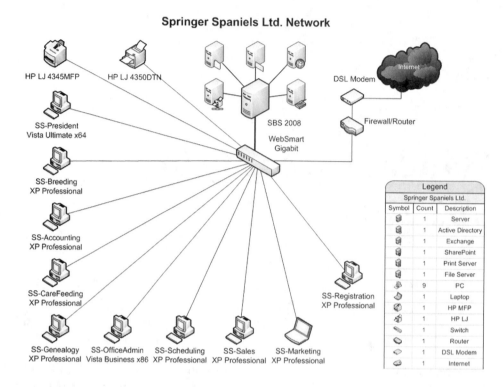

Figure 6-1
SPRINGERS network.

Calyptix (Harry)

Who would have thought that international relations would find a role in this chapter? Well it's true. When we were given the opportunity to review AccessEnforcer from Calyptix in an SBS 2008 environment, our first thought was to have Philip conduct the review. Philip lives in Alberta, Canada, and is very keen on the security conversation. But there was one hitch. As of this writing, Calyptix does not have export authority to ship its product to Canada. That is something that the CEO has assured me is being worked on and will be in place in the future.

So that meant I would review the AccessEnforcer product, the AE500, out at my house on Bainbridge Island. No problem because I had heard much about the Calyptix product from leading community members, including Amy Babinchak, an ISA MVP.

Setup

The first step in unpacking the AE500 was to review the Quick Start Guide. As it turned out, that was the only documentation I needed to get up and running. I followed the steps shown in Table 6-1, and I note where I made exceptions.

Table 6-1
   AE500 Setup

Step	Description	Comments
One	Open the box, verified shipment	Completed – all contents were shipped.
Two	Collect information about Internet connection	This included gathering the information from the ISP, which in my case was Comcast. Comcast assigns the IP address, Network Mask (also known as Subnet Mask), Gateway IP, and DNS information automatically. This information was easily gathered.
Three	Plug in the power cable Attach the crossover cable to the computer	In my case, I attached the crossover cable to an older laptop not on the SPRINGERS network. I did this so the AE500 could assign the IP address to the laptop automatically. NOTE: The AE500 is set up to act as a DHCP server on the LAN automatically.
Four	Log on to the AE500 using a browser	I pointed to https://192.168.51.1:9443/ and logged on as **admin** with the password provided in my packaging (your password will be unique). Clicked **I Agree** at the license page.
Five	Configure the AE500 to talk to your ISP	I used Comcast to dynamically assign the IP address to the WAN port of the AE500, so on the Internet page, I selected the following: IP address configuration: **DHCP** DNS Servers: **DHCP** Clicked **Apply Changes**.

Step	Description	Comments
Six	Configure your LAN settings	On the LAN 1 page, I made the following configuration changes to conform to the SPRINGERS methodology. IP address configuration IP address: **192.168.40.1** Network mask: **255.255.255.0** Network Address Translation (NAT) Checked **Enable NAT** DHCP Server Deselected (unchecked) **Enable DHCP server on this interface**. See the TIP below to explain this. Clicked **Apply Changes**. NOTE: The Calyptix Quick Start Guide has a very important note at this point to complete Step Seven (next) that attaches your firewall/router device to the Internet BEFORE you restart the firewall/router device.
Seven	Use the RED Ethernet cable to attach your Internet connection to the port labeled ETH0 on the back of the AE500	I attached the cable as instructed. Because I also changed the IP address scheme from the out-of-the-box 192.168.51.x LAN 1 scheme to the SPRINGERS methodology (192.168.40. x), I connected an Ethernet cable from ETH1 to the SBS 008 network switch. The LAN adapter card on the SBS 2008 server machine is also connected to this switch. See Figure 6-2.
Eight	Restart the AE500	Clicked **Restart**. After restarting, the AE500 worked as expected and I was able to connect to and use the Internet from my SBS 2008 network.

Figure 6-2
The AE500 connected the switch on Harry's SBS 2008 network using the SPRINGERS methodology.

In Figure 6-3, I show you a scanned Deployment Examples page from the Calyptix Quick Start Guide.

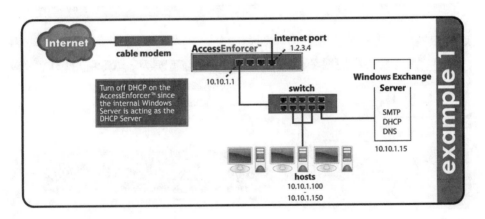

Figure 6-3
The SRINGERS network topology approximates the Calyptix Example 1 network.

TIP: It is essential you know that the SBS 2008 server machine must be the only DHCP server source (to assign IP addresses to network nodes) on LAN 1. Therefore, you must disable the firewall/router as a LAN 1 DHCP server.

Management

The management tool is the Web interface shown in Figure 6-4.

You can manage the following areas (and each of these areas goes very deep):

- System Status
- Network Alerts
- E-mail Quarantine
- Rejected Spam
- Web Traffic
- Traffic Graphs
- Live Connections
- DHCP Clients

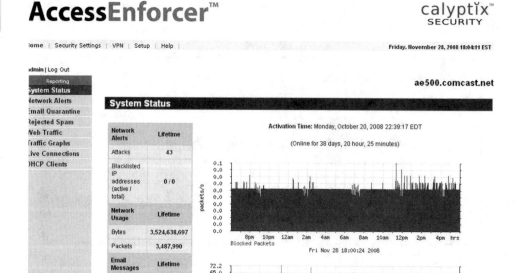

Figure 6-4
AccessEnforcer management.

Overall I had a very positive experience with the AE500. As you might imagine, it has rich configuration options that are well documented in its manual and beyond the scope of this text. I really liked the easy-to-follow, quick-setup guide.

SonicWALL (Harry)

The box from SonicWALL arrived FedEx on a Thursday, and I set up this firewall device on the weekend (which is when I typically get my best writing done and the telephone isn't ringing, etc.). I wanted to use my methodology of "what would it be like" to be an SMB consultant receiving the firewall device from any of the manufacturers I am reviewing in this chapter and undergo the "out-of-the-box" experience.

Setup

Here is my story for configuring the SonicWALL NSA 240. I immediately found that the Getting Started Guide required some study before proceeding, as it is over 80 pages in length. I then completed these basic steps for SPRINGERS, as seen in Table 6-2.

Table 6-2: NSA 240 Setup

Step	Description	Comments
One	Open the box, verified shipment	Completed – all contents were shipped.
Two	Read basic information pages and review scenarios	Completed the **Obtain Configuration Information** page with registration and networking information (pages 3-4) and selected Scenario A (Figure 6-5).
Three	Unpack and set up SonicWALL NSA 240 device. Turn on power. Attach LAN cable from the XX0 LAN port to the management laptop	Completed
Four	Power on and configure management laptop to configure and manage NSA 240. Attach WAN port	I had to configure the laptop to accept the default IP network for the SonicWALL at 192.168.168.x. I selected the laptop's IP address to be 192.168.168.20. I attached the WAN port (X1) to the live Internet connection.

Step	Description	Comments
Five	Connect to and perform configurations on the NSA 240	I connected to the NSA 240 by typing http://192.168.168.168 and logging on with the default admin settings. The user name was **admin** and the password was **password**. The **Network Security Appliance Web** page was displayed.
		Under **System, Administration**, I changed the admin name to **JonathanPaul** and the password to **L0ts and lots of fun!**
		Under **Network, Interface settings**, I configured the LAN port (XO) to conform to the SPRINGERS network (Figure 6-1) with the IP address 192.168.40.1.
		Under **Network, Interface settings**, I configured the WAN Port (X1) to acquire its information from a DHCP source. It is set to static by default. It acquired a 101.10.55 address from my ISP (Comcast). See Figure 6-6.

Notes

Step	Description	Comments
Six	Restart NSA240, register device at My SonicWALL, and attach to active Internet Connection	The NSA240 restarted and I had safe Internet connectivity. I registered my NSA 240 from **System, Status, Security Services, Click here to Register your SonicWALL**. This conformed my Internet connection and allowed me to use the My SonicWALL site. After providing basic name, company, street, city, state, zip code, telephone, and e-mail address information, I was e-mailed a MySonicWALL subscription code that needed to be activated within 72 hours. I performed this task immediately so as not to forget. Note I was required to provide the NSA 240 serial number and authentication code found from **System, Security, Security Services**.

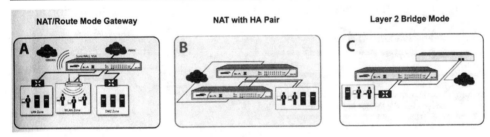

Figure 6-5
I selected Scenario A for the SBS 2008 network at SPRINGERS!

N otes

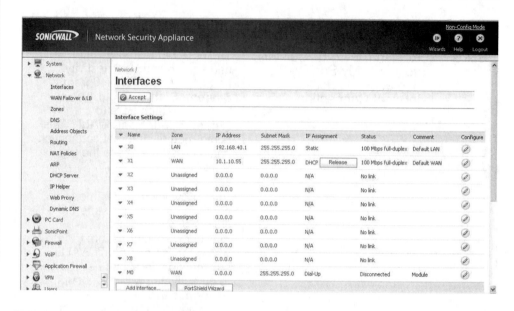

Figure 6-6
NSA 240 network configuration.

The Network Security Application Web page, used for NSA 240 management, is very robust with the following categories (each has a very rich configuration area).

- System
- Network
- PC Card
- SonicPoint
- Firewall
- VoIP
- Application Firewall
- VPN
- Users
- High Availability
- Security Services
- Log

At the MySonicWALL Web site, after you have registered and logged on, you can purchase additional services such as antivirus protection, etc. I can attest the entire setup process, from unpacking to configuring my secure, firewall-based Internet connection, took under one hour. I really liked the fact that the NSA 240 was configured with the static IP setting for the LAN port because, as you know now, SBS 2008 must be the only DCHP server source on LAN 1 or it gets fussy.

Figure 6-7
The NSA 240 powering the SPRINGERS SBS 2008 network.

WatchGuard (Harry)

When you watch Wall Street analysts on TV, they typically issue a disclaimer that they don't own stock in the company being discussed, etc. I can safely state that I do not own stock in the companies being discussed in this chapter, but I do live in the Seattle area, the hometown of WatchGuard. But I attest that my geographic proximity has not in any way impacted my review of this product. So let's get going.

Setup

On the SPRINGERS network, we are setting up the Firebox X Edge device. It is shown in Figure 6-8 on the SPRINGERS network.

Figure 6-8
WatchGuard's Firebox X Edge. Note the WiFi antennas.

Upon opening the Firebox X Edge packaging, I attached the antennas and read the six-step Quick Start Guide. Here is my experience as outlined in Table 6-3.

Table 6-3: Firebox X Edge Setup

Step	Description	Comments
One	Register with LiveSecurity Service	I completed the sign-up form and registered my device. I had to respond to two verification e-mails to validate my profile. These e-mails had a 72-hour limit, which meant I had to respond within 72 hours.
Two	Download software	Even though I was actually provided the latest software on a USB key (you will receive a USB key in your packaging as well), I downloaded the latest software as instructed in Step Two of the Quick Start Guide to conform to the WatchGuard methodology.

Step	Description	Comments
Three	Gather network information	This step includes gathering WAN information from your ISP such as IP address, DNS, etc. Because I use Comcast as my ISP and it assigns the IP address dynamically, I followed the sub-instruction in Step Three to proceed immediately to Step Four.
Four	Check before connecting	There are a couple of points worth noting. The LAN 1 PC that will manage the Firebox X Edge device had to be set to receive its IP address automatically. The Firebox X Edge device is set to act as a DHCP server automatically.
Five	Connect the cables and the power cord	Here you connect the Ethernet cable for LAN 1 to internal SBS 2008 network (SPRINGERS) and the WAN 1 cable to the "outside" connection to the Internet.
Six	Run the Quick Setup Wizard	I launched a Web browser and typed in https://192.168.111.1 in the address bar and logged on with the default user name (**admin**) and password (**password**). Under **Network**, I changed the **Trusted Network** (click **Configure**) to get an IP address of 192.168.40.1 and disable the DHCP Server. A reboot followed and the Firebox X Edge device immediately started working on the SPRINGERS network.

Management

The WatchGuard Firebox X Edge Web Manager, shown in Figure 6-9, is where the management functions are performed. The following management areas are accessible.

- System Status
- Network
- Firebox Users
- Administration
- Firewall

- Logging
- WebBlocker
- SpamBlocker
- Gateway AV/IPS
- VPN
- Wizards
- Authenticate User

As you might imagine, each of these categories has several sub-menus for more granular configurations.

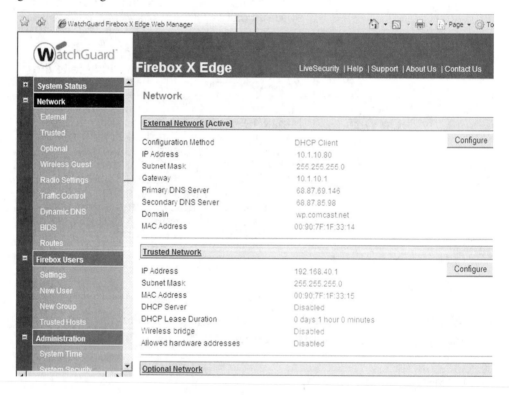

Figure 6-9
WatchGuard Firebox X Edge Web Manager.

One positive was the easy-to-run wizards beneath wizards. These wizard options are shown in Figure 6-10.

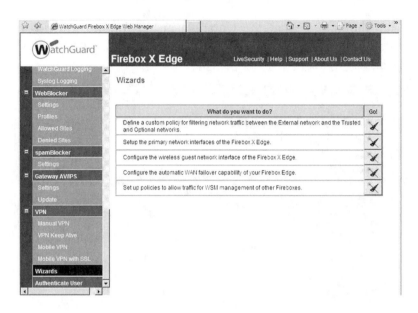

Figure 6-10
Default configuration wizards that are easy to understand.

I really enjoyed the easy-to-follow, quick-start guide. One observation is that changing the default password from **password** to a more complex passphrase occurs under the **Authenticate User** option but that was not apparent to me at first blush.

Untangle (Philip)

I first encountered the Untangle product in the late summer 2008 as I was preparing for a Webinar about SBS 2008 security with Harry. One of the reasons I am writing this section instead of Harry is that I do not have a personal relationship with Untangle, and the goal of this book it to provide you unbiased advice in critical areas such as security. Harry, on the other hand, has struck up a friendship with one member of the Untangle staff who is an avid cyclist, and so he excused himself from this chapter section.

It was very interesting to work with an open source product that was downloadable and runs on literally any system you might have as a remainder or lying around the shop. The Untangle product does not ship as a self-contained hardware device.

Figure 6-11 shows you what the Untangle install routine will do when the machine does not meet the minimum hardware requirements. The install routine will stall.

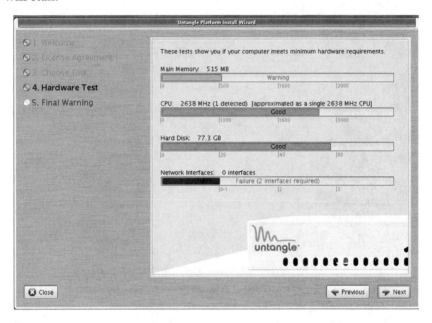

Figure 6-11
Untangle hardware requirements are pretty straightforward.

Our suggested hardware minimums:

- 1GB of RAM
- 1.6GHz CPU
- 40GB Hard Disk
- 2 Network Interface Cards

Once we have a system that will meet the hardware minimums, we can begin the install routine.

TIP: When it comes to the hardware configuration on which the Untangle product will run, keep in mind that Untangle is built upon the Debian Linux distro. Check with Untangle's Web site to verify that the hardware you have will meet the necessary requirements.

Setup

The Untangle product is available from Untangle's Web site at http://www.untangle.com.

Assuming we have our hardware in place with NIC Number 1 connected to our SPRINGERS network and NIC Number 2 connected to the Internet, the setup will proceed as follows:

1. Download the ISO file from Untangle's Web site.

2. Use a utility like CDBurnerXP (freeware) to burn the ISO to a CD.

3. After placing the CD in the system's optical drive, boot from the CD.

4. Once the CD has booted, you will be greeted with the Untangle Welcome screen shown in Figure 6-12. Click the **Next** button.

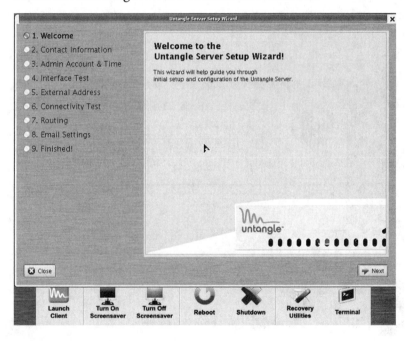

Figure 6-12
The initial Untangle setup welcome screen.

5. Read the license terms; if you agree with them, click the **Next** button.

6. A list of boot disks (hard drives) will show up in the next screen. Choose the disk you want Untangle to install into and click **Next**.

7. If your hardware meets the necessary requirements you will receive a **Results** pop-up. Click the **Close** button.

8. Click **Next**.

9. A **Final Warning** that all data will be wiped from the hard disk on which Untangle will be installed will pop up next. Click the **Finish** button.

10. You will receive another **Warning** about disk erasure. Click the **Continue** button.

11. The setup routine will continue until successfully completed. Click the **OK** button to conclude the setup procedure. Note that the system will power off after the OK button is clicked on.

Once you power it up, your Untangle machine will run right into the configuration wizard shown in Figure 6-13.

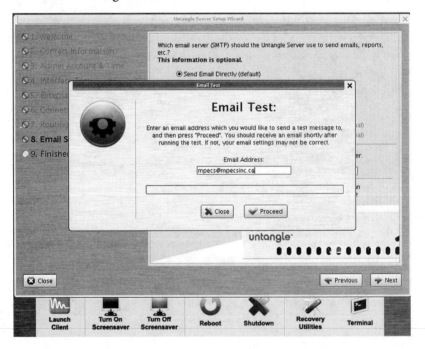

Figure 6-13
The Untangle Server Setup Wizard will run after the newly installed Untangle box is powered up.

1. On the **Welcome to the Untangle Server Setup Wizard,** click the **Next** button.

2. Fill out the appropriate information for the contact information and click **Next**:

   - Company Name: **Springer Spaniels Limited**
   - First Name: **Bob**
   - Last Name: **Easter**
   - E-mail: **BobE@springersltd.com**
   - Number of computers protected: **10**

3. Set the administrator's password and time zone for the Untangle box and click **Next**:

   - Domain admin's password: **L0ts and lots of fun!**
   - Time Zone: **Pacific**

4. The Interface Test will show whether or not the NICs are properly connected. Verify their connectivity and click **Next**.

TIP: Keep in mind that the Untangle setup routine may not pick the right NIC for the Internal/External network. Unplug one of the network cables to verify that the setup routine has chosen the right NIC. If it has not, reverse the network cables and make note of their new locations.

5. Set the host name for the box and whether the Internet connection will receive an IP via DHCP or static. Click **Next**.

   - Hostname: **SS-Untangle**.
   - External Network: **Automatically through DHCP**.

6. You can now perform a Connectivity Test by clicking the button. Click the **Close** button after the test and then **Next** once you have run the test.

7. Choose the **Router** option, set the IP and Netmask, then click **Next**.

   - IP: **192.168.40.1**
   - Netmask: **255.255.255.0**

TIP: Note that this option will enable the DHCP server on the Untangle Server. It is important to disable this option once the server has completed its server setup routine.

8. You can pass e-mail messages directly to the Internet or via the SS-SBS server. Choose to **Send E-mail Directly (default)** and set the **From Address** to **untangle@springersltd.com**. Click **Next**. You can send a test message to an e-mail address of your choosing if you want to test e-mail connectivity as shown in Figure 6-14.

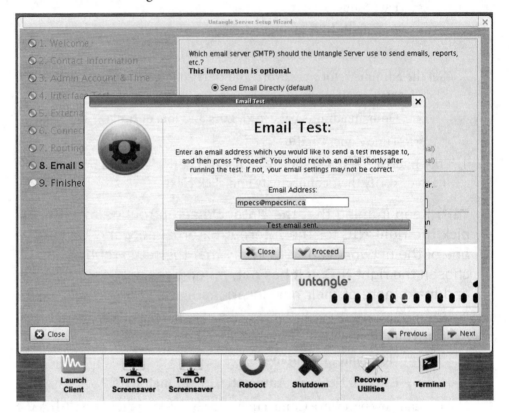

Figure 6-14
You can test the Untangle Server's ability to send e-mail directly to the Internet during the Untangle Server Setup Wizard.

9. Once you get the **Congratulations!** screen, you will be able to click **Finish** and the wizard will now be complete.

10. You will get the management console logon screen. Input the password you set in the above steps and click the **Logon** button.

Management

Out of the box, the Untangle server will come with no features installed. Figure 6-15 shows you the newly installed Untangle Server's management console which is arranged like a rack mount enclosure.

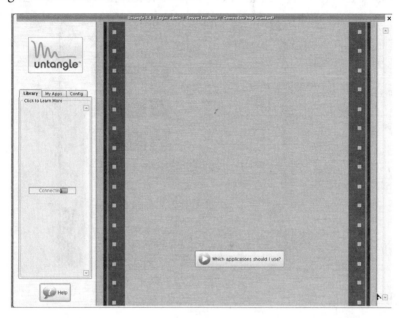

Figure 6-15
The newly installed Untangle Server has no features configured yet.

You manage the networking specifics by clicking on the **Config** tab and then the **Networking** button. Once the management Web page opens up, you can manage the server's underlying network settings via their respective tabs in the browser. Determine the role of the network interface cards and whether they are associated with the Internal or External networks. Relate the network adapter card's IP addresses of the Untangle Server, so that you are able to make any necessary changes. This is also the place to disable the DHCP service in the Untangle Server and to set the SS-SBS server as the DNS server.

Click on any button in the **Library** tab to download the respective component from Untangle's Web site. Once downloaded, it will install automatically. Any feature that has a subscription fee associated with it can be downloaded and installed for a trial period.

By default, the Untangle Professional Package subscription comes with the following:

- **Live Technical Support**. Available Monday to Friday from 6:00AM to 5:00PM Pacific Time. You can get in touch with Untangle for questions that seemingly can't be answered via their forums or online help.

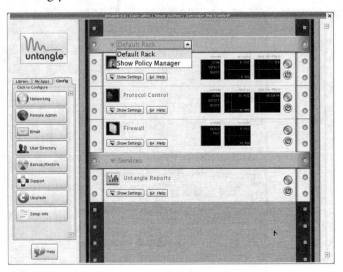

Figure 6-16
The Untangle Rack loaded up with features.

- **Policy Manager**. The Policy Manager enables you to create rules for users and groups based on schedules, sites, and more.

- **Active Directory Integration**. You can integrate the Untangle security product with your existing Active Directory to fine-tune user permissions. Tied into the Policy Manager, you are able to fine-tune those rules according to your Active Directory Users and Groups.

- **Custom Branding**. For the SBS Consultant, you can brand the Untangle interface with your own company's logos as well as customize product messages.

- **Hosted Config Backup**. You can backup your Untangle server's settings to Untangle's data center for access later if there is a need to restore the Untangle server.

- **Remote Access Portal**. Is a clientless VPN to allow you to securely access your network resources from anywhere.

Figure 6-17 gives you an idea of what Untangle's subscription rates are like. They are actually quite reasonable for the level of product you are receiving.

Figure 6-17
Untangle's pricing structure as of this writing.

Microsoft Internet Acceleration and Security Server (ISA) (Philip)

ISA Server, and its previous iteration in Proxy Server 2.0 on SBS 2000, has been around the SBS product for several historic release cycles. However, starting with this release cycle, SBS 2008 Premium excludes the ISA product from the SBS SKU. As far as I understand it, there are at least two reasons for the exclusion. I have been told that SBS Premium had a relatively low install base and most people were already using a third-party firewall. There was also a long-winded and spirited debate in the SBS community about having ISA on the SBS domain controller server machine. Security-minded leaders passionately felt that ISA should be located on a separate server machine on the perimeter. So this might be a case of "be careful what you ask for, you might just get it." That is, ISA is no longer part of the SBS product and, ergo, isn't assumed to run on the domain controller.

Another viewpoint concerns the complexity of the ISA product itself. ISA can be quite intimidating to those unfamiliar with its abilities and management features. Just check out the rule set in Figure 6-18.

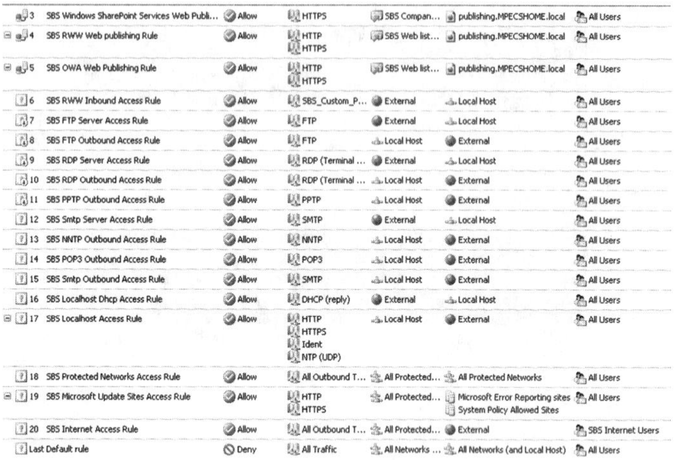

Figure 6-18
The default out-of-the-box SBS 2003 R2 Premium ISA 2004 Rule Set.

Given ISA is no longer included with SBS 2008 Premium, there's no ISA for you as part of the SBS out-of-the-box experience. That is why we are having this discussion about several third-party security products available to you for Internet and network security purposes.

Now for some bad news. I am unable to recommend an ISA for a SBS 2008 network at this time. As I write these words. I have not quite ironed out all of the hiccups with getting ISA 2006 completely configured on an SBS 2008 network. At a minimum, this would suggest the ISA implementation in an SBS 2008 network is not easy. I will leave the detailed setup discussion for our SBS 2008 advanced book.

The Final Words

This section has two interesting conversations to bring the basic SBS 2008 security conversation to a close. The first is a blog post in late November 2008 from the SBS Diva, Susan Bradley. The second topic reiterates both authors' belief that you should be a smart customer when seeking your SBS 2008 solution.

Windows Firewall

"...the firewall on the Internal NIC is NOT (let me repeat that) NOT to be seen/ used/or thought of as an external facing firewall."

Susan Bradley, SBS Diva (www.sbsdiva.com), November 2008

Caveat Emptor

Maybe you skipped studying Latin in school, but "caveat emptor" means "buyer beware" (see http://en.wikipedia.org/wiki/Caveat_emptor). Obviously, security is an important area for everyone working with SBS 2008. We encourage you to use this chapter as a starting point for learning more about protecting your SBS 2008 network. What is important to understand is that we presented a basic overview of a several solutions available to you. Please understand that each of these solutions have much richer configuration possibilities than displayed herein. We simply did not want to reprint each vendor's respective user manual. Once you have made your firewall choice, you will have the opportunity to do a deep dive into that solution as per the vendor's instructions.

Summary

So what's the best firewall for SBS 2008? This chapter does not answer that question. Rather, this chapter provides you with enough information to understand what possible solutions might work for you.

In this chapter, Harry and Philip took a unique approach for this book and wrote in the first person, sharing the play-by-play of setting up the separate solutions. Topics discussed included:

- Defining the context of SBS 2008 security needs
- Setup and management of Calyptix
- Setup and management of SonicWALL
- Setup and management of WatchGuard
- Setup and management of Untangle
- Overview of ISA Server for SBS 2003 RTM/R2 Premium Software Assurance

In the next chapter, we tackle Microsoft Exchange and Outlook!

CHAPTER 7

Messaging with Exchange 2007 and Outlook 2007

Take a bow. Why? Because even before you start reading this chapter on Exchange Server 2007 ("Exchange") and Outlook 2007 ("Outlook"), you really know more about these two messaging applications than you might admit in public. As the first part of the chapter will show, you've darn near completed the configuration of Exchange and Outlook just by deploying SBS 2008 over the past several chapters. So accordingly, we start with what you should likely already know up to this point. And after you finish the chapter and work more with Exchange in the real world, you'll really know these products inside and out from an SBS 2008 viewpoint.

By the way, this chapter isn't as SPRINGERS-centric as our other chapters are. This is in part because the SPRINGERS storyline doesn't need a lot of direct inter-action with Exchange Server 2007 for proper SBS 2008 network deployment to occur. So bear with us as we provide you a Texas-size buffet of Exchange and Outlook matters you're like to lasso up in the real world.

Another quick note: This is the introductory textbook for SBS 2008 to get you up and running FAST! There are many fine, thick books on Exchange that go to the next level and could be your next step to learn more about Exchange. Our advanced SBS 2008 book will also dig deeper into Exchange (mid-2009).

What You May Already Know About Exchange Server 2007!

This section of the chapter should inspire confidence as you'll likely comment "I already knew that" about certain Exchange matters. Let's get started.

- Core SBS component installation. Exchange is essentially completely set up for you when you install SBS 2008, such as what you did in Chapter 3 of this book. It's really that simple, and we liken it to a varied 80/20 rule (see www.wikipedia.org to learn more about the 80/20 rule in business). Basically the most popular 80 percent of the Exchange functionality you will need, encounter, and use is set up in about 20 percent of the core setup time. Nearly everything you will do with Exchange on a day-to-day basis has been magically set up for you.

- Global Address List. The Exchange Global Address List (GAL) is built when you input users into SBS 2008. Figure 7-1 shows the GAL for SPRINGERS in the SBS 2008 product.

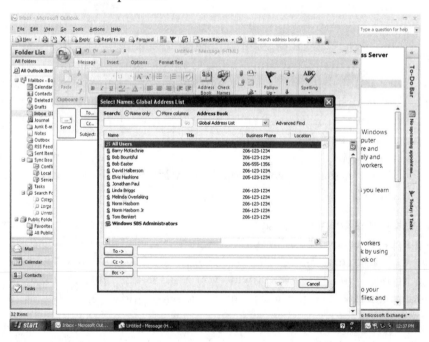

Figure 7-1
Viewing the Global Address List entries in SBS 2008.

- Active Directory-integration. Exchange does not live on its own! Exchange is very much integrated with Active Directory and one of the easiest ways to observe this is the properties for a user, as seen in Figure 7-2.

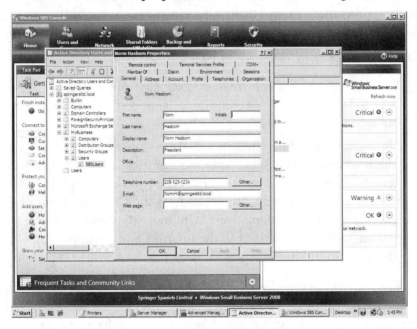

Figure 7-2

Viewing the e-mail address information in Active Directory for a user on the General tab.

TIP: Call it a missed opportunity, but this company information would have been great for creating an Outlook contact record for each user that is added to the SBS 2008 network. Said Outlook contact record could then be used by fellow workers to list your home and cellular telephones, making it possible to reach you with ease! Heck—such an Outlook contact record could be synchronized to your personal digital assistant (PDA), such as a sassy HP iPAQ, allowing you to find coworkers when you're out of the office. Other integration points for Outlook contacts—but not the GAL—include populating the Speed Dial feature in Windows 6.0 or later and important contacts in the super-cool Microsoft Response Point telephone system.

To be honest, small business people are much more likely to relate to Outlook contacts instead of AD user objects and GAL entries. You might consider creating an Outlook contact for each employee at the client site running SBS 2008. More on Outlook later in this chapter where you will create Outlook contacts for everybody at SPRINGERS!

- SBS application setup information. Exchange information is recorded and reported in the Event Logs of the underlying Windows Server 2008 operating system. 'Nough said.

- No more Configure E-mail and Internet Connection Wizard (CEICW). The infamous ICW (SBS 2000 time frame) and CEICW (SBS 2003) is gone in form but lives on in spirit! When you complete the Connect to the Internet, Set up your Internet address and Configure a Smart Host for Internet e-mail selections from Windows SBS Console, Home, Getting Started Tasks, and Connect to the Internet, you are impacting Exchange. These tasks were described in Chapter 4. More on these tasks later.

Always use antivirus and malware protection to create a safe Exchange environment! The Exchange store can be protected by the 120-day version of Forefront Server Security for Exchange that is included with SBS 2008 out of the box, or you can install your favorite third-party protection package.

What You May Already Know About Outlook 2007

You probably know more about Outlook, including the 2007 version, than you give yourself credit for. Consider the following:

- Pervasive usage. Perhaps the question to ask here is "Who hasn't used Outlook?" A show of hands would yield a very small data set. Just about everyone on Planet Earth has in some way or somehow used Outlook. In fact, for that reason, a change from Harry's past books on SBS is that we'll not show you how to send an e-mail message, as we'll assume you already know this basic function.

- Must buy to fly! In past SBS releases, the Outlook application was included in the SBS product. Such is no longer the case in the SBS 2008 timeframe.

In part, based on the point above about "pervasive usage," it wasn't lost on the SBS team in Redmond that everybody in the world ALREADY OWNS OUTLOOK and it's not necessary to include this feature in SBS 2008. Academically speaking, you could argue that in past SBS releases, you were overpaying for Outlook because you likely acquired it via the Microsoft Office application suite. In early 2004, best-selling author Brian Livingston reviewed SBS 2003 and addressed this exact issue (along with other topics). Search the archives at www.windowssecrets.com to learn more. But the point we are making here and now, is that the Outlook application must now be acquired outside of the SBS 2008 product (typically via the Office application suite).

- Automatic setup. The first time you launch Outlook on your computer in an SBS 2008 network, it will guide you through an automatic setup to connect you to the Exchanger server and set up cached mode to keep a local copy of your e-mail independent of the server. We really like this feature.

- Welcome notice. Imagine a certification exam focused on SBS 2008 (e.g., 71-635) and the exam writers wanted to write a trick question. If you were quizzed about whether or not a welcome message awaits you when you start Outlook, the message is "Welcome to Windows Small Business Server 2008" and speaks towards e-mail usage, Remote Web Workplace, the internal Web site, shared documents, mobile devices, and a cool "desktop links gadget."

Exchange Under the Hood

Before you trot off believing you know everything there is to know about Exchange, pull up for a moment and read this section on peeking and poking around under the hood. Granted, you'll likely know some of what is presented below, but perhaps you'll find a gold nugget along the way that you hadn't seen in prior sluicing runs.

Okay—What Is Exchange Server 2007?

A good instructor will always encourage even the most basic of questions by promoting a learning culture of "No question is stupid; the only stupid question is the one you don't ask." So it's fair game to ask, "Exactly what is Exchange Server 2007?"

Back in time, when SBS 4.0 was released in late 1997, the Exchange application was considered to be an e-mail program. It quickly became a popular e-mail program in an era where folks were relatively new to e-mail and all of its wonder. Fast forward a few years—and running around getting excited about e-mail is not only "legacy," it's so yesterday! Later on, the marketing message and positioning for Exchange was altered to reflect more noble goals, such as messaging, communications, and collaboration. A contemporary view of Exchange is that it's a robust message application with collaboration being better handled by SharePoint technologies (which you meet in the next chapter). To some extent, even the communications tag line is now deemphasized with the introduction of the Microsoft Office Communications Server (OCS) product.

But this section isn't placed here to reiterate what you likely know about Exchange production positioning. Rather, we wanted to weave in a neo-Exchange viewpoint served up by a fellow instructor on an SBS hands-on lab tour in late 2002. This gentleman proposed the thesis that Exchange is really nothing more than a set of messaging tools and functionality that resides atop Active Directory. Huh? We'll tease you with this hypothesis until the next section, where, what appears to be a ridiculous riddle is solved.

Really Managing Exchange

Exchange is even older than SBS (which in the 2008 release is over 11 years old), and it received a deep restructuring and management refresh in this release. Witness the strikingly different setup in the new Exchange Management Console shown in Figure 7-3.

Notes

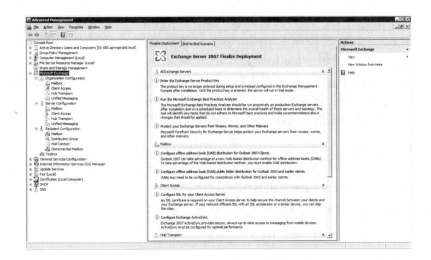

Figure 7-3
Things have changed significantly in the way we manage Exchange 2007.

When nature calls and you simply have to perform some heavy server-side configuration procedures in Exchange Server 2007, you'll use Microsoft Exchange snap-in in the Windows SBS Native Tools console, plain and simple. But it's not likely that you'll interact with this cool tool on a day-to-day basis.

> **TIP:** In this introductory textbook, your assignment is to do a "daze and amaze" tour on your sample SPRINGERS SBS setup by opening the Windows SBS Native Tools Console and clicking your way through the various hyperlinks and Help files contained in the Exchange 2007 snap-in. Go ahead and dig deep. Drill down into the countless child objects layered in this surprisingly powerful management tool.

Active Directory Users and Computers

Time to solve the riddle from a few minutes ago. The solution set is this: Exchange is tightly integrated with the core Windows Server 2008 operating system in places such as Active Directory.

The Active Directory Users and Computers MMC snap-in has added these two components in the "2008 time frame":

- Microsoft Exchange Security Groups. This contains different administrative groups that set permissions a user may or may not have for managing the various Exchange features and abilities, as seen in Figure 7-4.

- Microsoft Exchange System Objects. This includes the Exchange Install Domain Servers security group and the System Mailbox GUID (Globally Unique Identifier), as seen in Figure 7-5.

A couple of capabilities were removed from Active Directory Users and Computers-based Exchange management in the SBS 2008 product, including these tabs on the User Properties page. Oh well!

- Exchange General. Gone!

- E-mail Addresses. Gone!

- Exchange Features. Gone!

- Exchange Advanced. Gone!

All of those management features are to be found in the Microsoft Exchange snap-in.

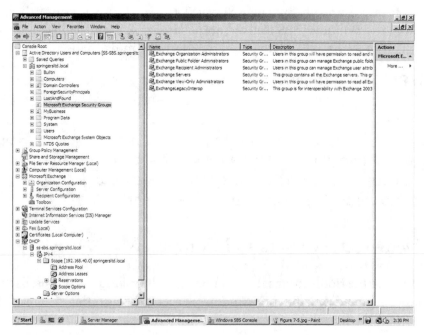

Figure 7-4
Microsoft Exchange Security Groups.

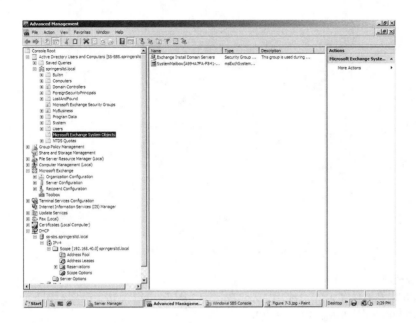

Figure 7-5
Microsoft Exchange System Objects.

While we're talking about Active Directory, let's add a little fuel to the fire. Remember that it's Active Directory providing several forms of critical support to Exchange Server 2007, including:

- Active Directory provides a storage location for all Exchange objects.

- Exchange uses Active Directory for all authentication and access control.

- Active Directory provides replication and the Global Catalog (GC). Exchange clients depend on the GC.

- Exchange makes irreversible Active Directory schema changes when installed into a new or existing Windows domain that had no Exchange server before.

Internet Information Server 7

Exchange is deeply integrated into Internet Information Server (IIS). Under the well-worn guise of a "picture is worth a thousand words," you can easily spot the integration points in Figure 7-6. You will find them in the Windows SBS Native Tools Management Console in the IIS snap-in.

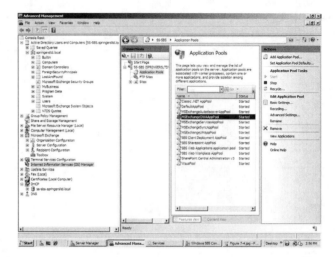

Figure 7-6
While the MSExchangeOWAAppPool is highlighted, you can see at least five Exchange IIS integration points.

TIP: Wanna test Exchange's dependence on IIS? A trick we've played in past Microsoft hands-on labs to confound the Doubting Thomases who can't draw out an Exchange/IIS relationship is the following: Simply turn off the World Wide Web Publishing Service in Services (from SBS Native Tools Console, Computer Management (Local), Services and Applications, Services, World Wide Web Publishing Service). Launch a Web browser (e.g., IE) and try to access Outlook remote via the Web (Outlook Web Access). You'll error out every time with the World Wide Web Publishing Server turned off. Turn this service back on and Outlook Web Access will work just fine.

Core Windows Server 2008 Services

We are honor-bound to show you how the Exchange services depend on the Underlying Windows Server 2008 operating system. Figure 7-7 shows the related services. The bulk of these are set to automatically start, and when Exchange is not working, a first troubleshooting step is to verify the appropriate services are started and running.

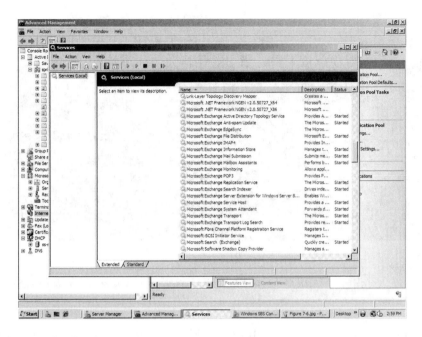

Figure 7-7
Microsoft Exchange services in the Services snap-in.

Blocking Attachments, E-mails, and Content

Without taking any third-party products, including Forefront Server Security for Exchange, into consideration, Exchange 2007 has a fairly robust set of protection measures built into it. You can filter out certain e-mail attachments, or even filter out an e-mail based on whom it was sent from, where it was sent from, or figure out whether the sender's IP address was on an RBL (Realtime Blackhole List).

For the sake of this introductory tome, we will look at some of the basic features.

Attachment Blocking

Should you choose not to run with Microsoft Forefront Server Security for Microsoft Exchange, or a third-party Exchange malware protection package, Exchange 2007 does indeed have the ability to filter out any e-mail attachments. If this is the road you decide to travel, keep in mind that you will need to get to know the new Exchange Management Shell as shown in Figure 7-8.

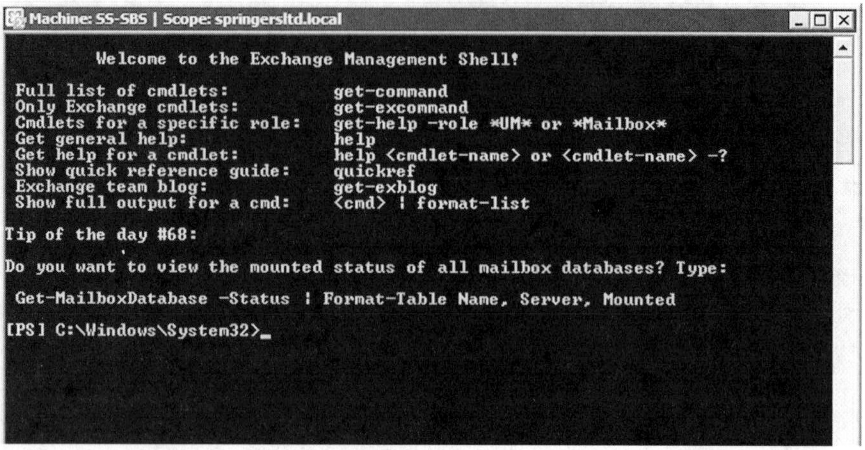

```
Machine: SS-SBS | Scope: springersltd.local                    _ □ X

           Welcome to the Exchange Management Shell!
Full list of cmdlets:           get-command
Only Exchange cmdlets:          get-excommand
Cmdlets for a specific role:    get-help -role *UM* or *Mailbox*
Get general help:               help
Get help for a cmdlet:          help <cmdlet-name> or <cmdlet-name> -?
Show quick reference guide:     quickref
Exchange team blog:             get-exblog
Show full output for a cmd:     <cmd> | format-list

Tip of the day #68:

Do you want to view the mounted status of all mailbox databases? Type:

Get-MailboxDatabase -Status | Format-Table Name, Server, Mounted

[PS] C:\Windows\System32>_
```

Figure 7-8
*The Exchange Management Shell is based on Microsoft's PowerShell
command line.*

Using the new shell, you will be able to enable, configure attachment types, or disable the built-in Exchange attachment filter.

Spam Filtering

There are a number of different filters in Exchange 2007 that can help filter out all of the spam e-mails that try to work their way into your Inbox.

- **Connection Filtering:** Allows you to set up IP addresses that are allowed to connect to the Exchange 2007 server or are blocked from connecting. You can manage the IP list or set up a subscription service to a Realtime Block List provider for a more up-to-date list of IP addresses. You can configure it in the Exchange Management Console or the Exchange Management Shell.

TIP: When it comes to implementing IP blocking, keep an eye on the IP addresses being blocked, as some businesses' ISPs provide their IP address on a consumer grade network which may cause their server's IP address to be on an RBL somewhere.

- **Content Filtering:** This is the next generation Intelligent Message Filter that was included with SBS 2003 and Exchange 2003 Service Pack 2. This filter assigns a Spam Confidence Level (SCL) that has a range of 0 through 9 to all incoming e-mail being processed by Exchange 2007. The higher the SCL, the more likely the message is spam. You can set what happens to an e-mail based on that rating. You can have it deleted, rejected, or quarantined. You can configure it in the Exchange Management Console or the Exchange Management Shell.

- **Recipient Filtering:** This filters e-mail based on the recipient's e-mail address. If the e-mail address does not exist, or a user is not permitted to receive e-mail from the Internet, or the recipient is on a restricted distribution list, Exchange 2007 will respond with a "550 5.1.1 User unknown" SMTP message. You can configure it in the Exchange Management Console or the Exchange Management Shell.

- **Sender Filtering:** This filters e-mail based on the sender's e-mail address. Since the FROM field can be spoofed, this methodology does not provide very much protection. You can configure it in the Exchange Management Console or the Exchange Management Shell.

There are a number of other spam features built into Exchange 2007 that go well beyond our introductory text. Suffice it to say, Exchange 2007's filtering capabilities are a huge step over the ones in Exchange 2003.

POP3 Connector

The POP3 Connector is still with us—although in its SBS 2008 form, in a deeply restructured way. It allows you to set up your SBS external e-mail, such as our springersltd.com e-mail domain, to be pulled from the Internet e-mail hosting company that hosts springersltd.com. The POP3 Connector then routes e-mail retrieved from the ISP's POP3 mailbox into the local user's mailbox.

Two new key features that are a part of the POP3 Connector:

1. The POP3 Connector now uses Exchange 2007's SMTP delivery mechanism for any e-mail it retrieves from the e-mail hosting company. Essentially, this means that the e-mail will now be run through all of the relevant spam filtering mechanisms *before* being deposited into the user's Inbox.

The previous POP3 Connector on SBS 2003 did not do this, so spam was a problem for those mailboxes.

2. The POP3 Connector now has the ability to retrieve e-mail from the e-mail hosting company every five minutes instead of every 15 minutes. This is good, as it decreases the turnaround time in an e-mail conversation for users. But, it is also bad, because many ISPs do not like their POP3 servers to be polled for e-mail more often than 15 minutes. Check with your ISP before setting the POP3 Connector to pull e-mail more frequently than 15 minutes.

You will find the POP3 Connector in the SBS Console under the Network tab and then the Connectivity tab as shown in Figure 7-9.

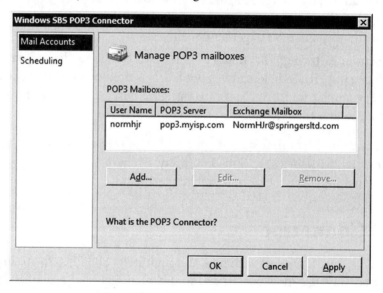

Figure 7-9
The SBS POP3 Connector management window.

Advanced Topics

As SBSers increasingly work with SBS 2008, the discussion will necessarily become more advanced. We believe this conversation can be handled at least three ways.

- Search engines. You should use the Web to stay current with Exchange topics. Keyword search, forums, and newsgroups are your friends!

- Content below. We teased you, in the introductory text, with a few advanced topics we think are cool.

- Future content. We like to write at least two books during any SBS release cycle so that we get an introductory text (this book) to the market right away and then follow up with a more thoughtful advanced text at a future date. Stick with us!

External Junk Mail Filtering

A long-time and upstanding SBS community member, Reflexion Networks (www. reflexion.net), provides external e-mail filtering for junk and spam for one of the authors and deserves your consideration as part of your SBS 2008 ecosystem. Reflexion is shown, from the channel partner view point, in Figure 7-10.

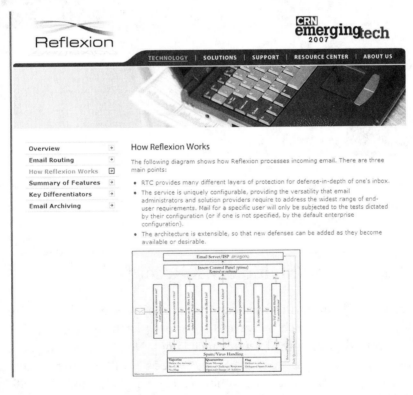

Figure 7-10
It is likely you will consider external solutions as part of your SBS 2008 world to embrace and extend the core SBS 2008 goodness.

M&M's Site

Two SBS MVPs, Mariette Knap and Marina Roos, host an amazing technical forum called SmallBizServer (www.smallbizserver.net). There are many advanced Exchange conversations, and we wanted to highlight one in Figure 7-11 on adding a disclaimer to your Exchange 2007 e-mail.

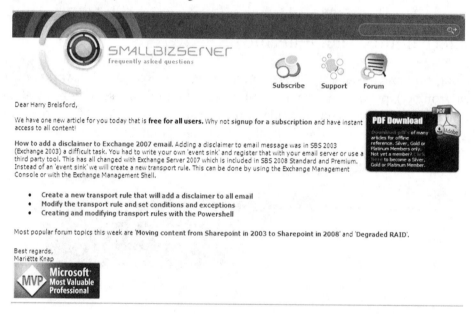

Figure 7-11
Use the online world of the M&M's site to go to the next level using the advanced features of Exchange 2007.

Mail Bagging and Multiple MX Records

Mail bagging is about having a backup location for your e-mail to flow to when your SBS 2008 server machine (properly running Exchange for SMTP e-mail) is offline. Instead of an e-mail sender receiving a Non-Delivery Report (NDR) or a bounced e-mail message if the SBS 2008 box is offline, these incoming e-mails can temporarily reside on another mail server. Later on, when SBS 2008 restarts and connects to your Internet Service Provider (ISP), the stored mail would be retrieved via the POP3 Connector and deposited into the respective user's mailbox.

TIP: If you think you might like to have this form of messaging redundancy, consult with your ISP to arrange it. Your ISP, whom we assume is holding your DNS records, will need to enter a second MX record with a lower priority that points to a backup mail server (typically maintained by the ISP).

Some ISPs do not agree with this type of setup, so keep that in mind when thinking about implementing it.

Before utilizing a Reputation Services Provider for our clients over at MPECS Inc., we used this method exclusively for all of our clients' e-mail domains. It provided an extra level of protection for those "just in case" moments.

Instant Messaging—NOT!

It's unfortunate but true. The internal instant messaging capabilities in the SBS product ended with the 2000 release many years ago. Such is still the case today. You will utilize an external IM program such as Windows Live Messenger. This is shown in Figure 7-12.

Figure 7-12
Instant Messaging, shown here, is popular with worker bees, teenagers, and many other demographic groups. It is an opportunity to extend the SBS 2008 experience using an external service.

Exchange Migrations

We're not even touching the topic in this introductory book! Best practice? Run, don't walk, over to SBS MPV Jeff Middleton's site at www.sbsmigration.com and immerse yourself in this advanced topic. You say the authors are a cop out? Perhaps, but the SPRINGERS methodology does not involve an Exchange migration.

Extending Exchange

Some topics fit better under a heading about extending Exchange rather than peeking under the hood, as the last section did. In this section, we share two thoughts about extending Exchange in SBS 2008: multiple servers and hosted.

Multiple Exchange Servers

In a recent US presidential election, there was a chant about "Yes We Can!" and this chant applies to the question of having multiple Exchange servers in a small business running SBS 2008. Admittedly, this strategy isn't likely for most small businesses and a business needing such a solution might really be a candidate for the Big Brother product called "Essential Business Server." But this is the type of paragraph we like to insert in a book such as this, for the SBS gurus out there who aren't happy with a text until they find something they don't know. Then these same gurus are your friends for life. So here is such an opportunity. You CAN have multiple Exchange servers on the same SBS 2008 network. There is going to be a reality that you will have to purchase another copy of the Exchange application, but then it's duck soup.

Why would you do this? Perhaps for performance gains. Perhaps for messaging store redundancy.

Hosted Exchange

Nearly a century ago, some of the great intellectuals debated the societal topics of the day on the Left Bank in Paris. We have a similar situation today as great minds question the need for on-premise e-mail and even a server box. Why, as a small business owner, wouldn't you simply use hosted services such as the Exchange? We covered this debate in a Software as a Service (SaaS) article in the February\

March 2008 issue of *SMB PC* magazine. This cover story featured Ken Uchikura, who owns and operates PSP, Inc. His business model includes hosted Exchange, and he's doing great business. It exposes a far larger argument (OK, conversation) than we can have here, but meet us at our blogs (see Appendix A) and we'll discuss the merits of hosted Exchange.

Outlook 2007

Now for the good stuff. Whereas we touted you might not confront server-side Exchange management issues daily, you will likely use Outlook each and every day (and perhaps all day!). This section starts by revisiting the SPRINGERS methodology where you will send an e-mail, enter contact records, and perform other such tasks.

Sending an E-mail

Time for some step-by-step, to have NormHasborn send an e-mail to all employees at SPRINGERS.

1. Have **NormHasborn** log on to **PRESIDENT** with his password **Sunny Days!**

2. Click **Start, E-mail**. This will launch Outlook. If this is the first time that you've launched Outlook 2007, you'll see a dialog box, Configuring Outlook, that automatically completes the configuration of Outlook accounts and generates the Welcome message.

TIP: You will also see a notice in the lower right that Outlook is setting up a local copy of your mailbox. Why is this occurring? Because back in Chapter 4 you might recall a TIP that displayed the advanced client computer settings, one of which related to the Outlook profile creation. This profile also configured local caching so you can use Outlook offline when you're not attached to the network.

3. You should have e-mails in your Inbox. Open and review.

4. Click the **New Mail Message** button on the **Outlook** toolbar to create a new message.

5. In the **To:** field, type **Springers** (in a moment, this entry will automatically resolve to the Springer Spaniels Limited distribution list entry which is basically sending out a message to everyone in the company). In the **Subject:** field, type **Ideas for forthcoming Dog Shows!**

6. Click in the text body portion of the message and type the following message: **G'day folks! I need your input on which dog shows we should attend this year with which dogs. Thanks!** This is shown in Figure 7-13.

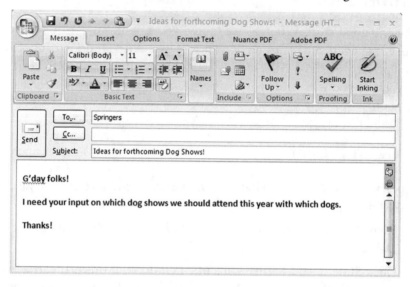

Figure 7-13
Your sample e-mail should look similar to this figure.

7. Click **Send** on the message toolbar to send the message. The message should now appear in your Inbox.

Congratulations! You've sent your first e-mail message as part of the SPRINGERS methodology.

Creating an Appointment

Now you will create an appointment in Norm Hasborn's calendar. It concerns the very important matter of Astro's mental health.

1. Assuming you are logged on as Norm Hasborn on PRESIDENT with Outlook open, select **Calendar** in the left pane.

2. Click the **New Appointment** button on the left of the upper toolbar.

3. An **Untitled – Appointment** window appears. Type **Take Astro to Thera-pist** in the **Subject:** line. Type **Dog Psychiatrist** in the **Location** field. Select a **Start time** of **October 9, 2010 1:00pm** and an **End time** of **October 9, 2010 3:00pm**. In the text field, type **Report on Astro's hypnosis progress**. You screen should appear similar to Figure 7-14.

4. Click **Save** and **Close**.

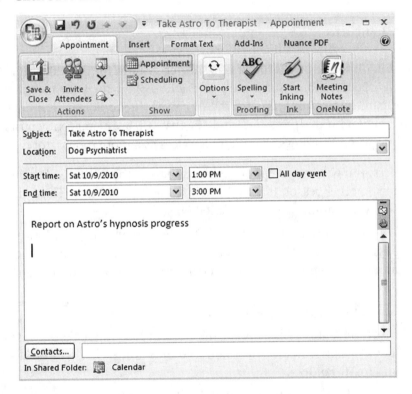

Figure 7-14
Again – congratulations! You've created your first appointment.

Creating Contacts

Let's start the procedure to enter yourself (that's "you") as an Outlook contact record.

1. It is assumed you are logged on as Norm Hasborn at the PRESIDENT workstation and that Outlook is open.

2. Click **Contacts** in the left pane.

3. Click **New** in the upper left corner on the left of the upper toolbar.

4. Complete the **Untitled – Contact** screen that appears with your full contact information (name, e-mail address, telephone information, address information, etc.) and click **Save & Close**.

You have now created a Contact in Outlook!

Public Folders

This section discusses public folders—a shorter story in the SBS 2008 time frame (versus SBS 2003). Gone is the built-in Public Folder for your company (e.g., SpringerSpanielsLtd Contacts) and the "archive" Public Folder. The contemporary explanation for this omission would be that you are being gently pushed and cajoled into using Windows SharePoint Services as a more robust store.

Nonetheless, you will create a public folder as part of the SPRINGERS methodology—if for no other reason than to be able to say you did that! This will be performed at a workstation with Outlook 2007 installed.

1. Log on as **Jonathan Paul** with the user name of **JonathanPaul** and password of **L0ts and lots of fun!** (His core user information can be found in Chapter 2.) After entering this in the Windows Logon dialog box, click **OK**.

2. Click **Start**, **E-mail** to launch Outlook 2007.

3. Click the **Folder List** icon at the bottom left under Folder List (looks like a yellow folder. The Public Folders folder list will be displayed under All Folders.

4. Expand **Public Folders;** expand **All Public Folders**.

5. Right click on **All Public Folders** and select **New Folder** from the context menu.

6. Type **Subscribers** in the **Name** field of the **Create New Folder** dialog box that appears and click **OK**.

7. Observe the new public folder titled **Subscribers**. Note that mere mortals at SPRINGERS do not have sufficient rights to create a public folder (that is why you logged on as Jonathan Paul).

TIP: Be aware that the public folder will have a SMTP-based e-mail address of subscribers@sprintersltd.com to receive e-mails from internal and external senders. This approach is handy when you have generic e-mail address like "jobs" or "info" and you want multiple people in the company to be able to see e-mails in a Public Folder.

Attachment Blocking and Warnings

Something folks love and curse is the native attachment blocking in Outlook 2007. They love it because it protects them from harmful e-mail attachments. They curse it because, in the heat of business battle, you can't get to your darn tootin' attachment that is mission-critical. But let's fight fire with facts here.

Outlook 2007 blocks the attachments identified in Table 7-1 by default.

Table 7-1
Blocked Attachments in Outlook

File name extension	File type
.ade	Access Project Extension (Microsoft)
.adp	Access Project (Microsoft)
.app	Executable Application
.asp	Active Server Page
.bas	BASIC Source Code
.bat	Batch Processing
.cer	Internet Security Certificate File
.chm	Compiled HTML Help
.cmd	DOS CP/M Command File, Command File for Windows NT
.com	Command
.cpl	Windows Control Panel Extension (Microsoft)
.crt	Certificate File

File name extension	File type
.csh	csh Script
.der	DER Encoded X509 Certificate File
.exe	Executable File
.fxp	FoxPro Compiled Source (Microsoft)
.gadget	Windows Vista gadget
.hlp	Windows Help File
.hta	Hypertext Application
.inf	Information or Setup File
.ins	IIS Internet Communications Settings (Microsoft)
.isp	IIS Internet Service Provider Settings (Microsoft)
.its	Internet Document Set, Internet Translation
.js	JavaScript Source Code
.jse	JScript Encoded Script File
.ksh	UNIX Shell Script
.lnk	Windows Shortcut File
.mad	Access Module Shortcut (Microsoft)
.maf	Access (Microsoft)
.mag	Access Diagram Shortcut (Microsoft)
.mam	Access Macro Shortcut (Microsoft)
.maq	Access Query Shortcut (Microsoft)
.mar	Access Report Shortcut (Microsoft)
.mas	Access Stored Procedures (Microsoft)
.mat	Access Table Shortcut (Microsoft)
.mau	Media Attachment Unit
.mav	Access View Shortcut (Microsoft)
.maw	Access Data Access Page (Microsoft)

File name extension	File type
.mda	Access Add-in (Microsoft), MDA Access 2 Workgroup (Microsoft)
.mdb	Access Application (Microsoft), MDB Access Database (Microsoft)
.mde	Access MDE Database File (Microsoft)
.mdt	Access Add-in Data (Microsoft)
.mdw	Access Workgroup Information (Microsoft)
.mdz	Access Wizard Template (Microsoft)
.msc	Microsoft Management Console Snap-in Control File (Microsoft)
.msh	Microsoft Shell
.msh1	Microsoft Shell
.msh2	Microsoft Shell
.mshxml	Microsoft Shell
.msh1xml	Microsoft Shell
.msh2xml	Microsoft Shell
.msi	Windows Installer File (Microsoft)
.msp	Windows Installer Update
.mst	Windows SDK Setup Transform Script
.ops	Office Profile Settings File
.pcd	Visual Test (Microsoft)
.pif	Windows Program Information File (Microsoft)
.plg	Developer Studio Build Log
.prf	Windows System File
.prg	Program File
.pst	MS Exchange Address Book File, Outlook Personal Folder File (Microsoft)

File name extension	File type
.reg	Registration Information/Key for W95/98, Registry Data File
.scf	Windows Explorer Command
.scr	Windows Screen Saver
.sct	Windows Script Component, Foxpro Screen (Microsoft)
.shb	Windows Shortcut into a Document
.shs	Shell Scrap Object File
.ps1	Windows PowerShell
.ps1xml	Windows PowerShell
.ps2	Windows PowerShell
.ps2xml	Windows PowerShell
.psc1	Windows PowerShell
.psc2	Windows PowerShell
.tmp	Temporary File/Folder
.url	Internet Location
.vb	VBScript File or Any VisualBasic Source
.vbe	VBScript Encoded Script File
.vbs	VBScript Script File, Visual Basic for Applications Script
.vsmacros	Visual Studio .NET Binary-based Macro Project (Microsoft)
.vsw	Visio Workspace File (Microsoft)
.ws	Windows Script File
.wsc	Windows Script Component
.wsf	Windows Script File
.wsh	Windows Script Host Settings File
.xnk	Exchange Public Folder Shortcut

TIP: You can learn more about the attachment-blocking ability in Outlook 2007 via Help, Microsoft Office Outlook Help.

TIP: You can get an offending attachment around the blockade by simply renaming it to an acceptable file format, such as *.doc (for a Word document). Then rename the file type back to its original name once you've saved it to your C: drive. This is commonly done with file attachments ending in *.exe because this attachment type might be legitimate business program that needs to be received.

Junk E-mail

Microsoft has one of the largest research and development (R&D) budgets in the corporate world. Sometimes, shareholders get a little fussy with billions being spent on R&D because they want to see things that immediately contribute to current earnings. One such R&D payoff is the sophisticated junk e-mail management approach built into Outlook 2007 (this actually started in the Outlook 2003 time frame). Since we won't sit here and retype the online help system in Outlook 2007, if you'd like to learn more about the Junk E-mail capability at a deep level, simply open Microsoft Office Outlook Help and select the Junk E-mail link.

Back to the real world. You're probably interested in knowing how to configure the Junk E-mail capabilities in Outlook 2007. It's simple. Just select **Tools, Options, Preferences**, and click the **Junk E-mail** button under **E-mail** in Outlook 2007. The **Junk E-mail Options** dialog box will appear, as seen in Figure 7-15. You can then change the default setting (Low) to a different level.

N otes

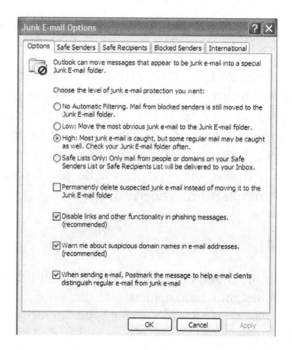

Figure 7-15
This figure shows all of the settings on Junk E-mail Options. Junk mail is moved to the Junk E-mail folder under All Folders in Outlook 2007.

So if you're a Microsoft shareholder, now you know how your R&D dollars are being spent!

Junk Users

Maybe you can relate to the following situation. Say you're on an e-mail list that has some annoying and verbose members. For business purposes, you can't leave the list, but you often become frustrated with the quantity of e-mails (often of a soap opera nature) that clog your Inbox. Because you're committed to staying focused on core business operations, and you'd rather review these distracting e-mails at a future decade (meaning date), you use a rule to move them to a folder titled "Much Later."

To do this you select **Rules and Alerts** from the **Tools** menu in Outlook 2007. Then select **New Rule** and click **Move messages from someone to a folder** under **Stay Organized**.

You then click **Next** and complete the **Rules Wizard** where you'll configure e-mails from certain people to be moved to a folder and out of your Inbox (for example, you'll enter the e-mail address of folks whose e-mail you want moved). This is an approach that might appeal to your SBS users as well.

> **TIP:** Perhaps you're just discovering this cool capability later in life and you've got an Inbox full of distracting e-mails you want to move. On the final page of the Rules Wizard, you have an option called Run this rule now on messages already in "Inbox" so that, post-hoc, you can improve the quality of your Inbox life.

Recovery Movement

No, this isn't about a battle with the bottle. Rather, this is how to recover deleted e-mail and move it back into the Inbox or the folder of your choice. To learn this capability using Exchange's delete item recovery capability, set to retain e-mails for 30 days by default in SBS 2008, complete the following procedure:

1. If necessary, have **BobEaster** log on to **SS-FeedingCare** with the password **Lots to eat!**

2. In Outlook 2007, delete the e-mail from Norm Hasborn created earlier in the chapter by dragging it to the **Deleted Items** folder.

3. Right click the **Deleted Items** folder and select **Empty "Deleted Items" Folder** from the context menu. Select **Yes** when asked in the **Microsoft Office Outlook** dialog box if you really want to delete the item. Observe the Deleted Items folder is now empty; it would appear you've lost this e-mail forever.

4. Now you will recover the deleted e-mail by selecting the **Deleted Items** folder and then selecting the **Recover Deleted Items** option under the **Tools** menu.

5. Norm Hasborn's e-mail appears in the **Recover Deleted Items** list from the **Deleted Items** dialog box that appears. Make sure this e-mail is highlighted and click the **Recover Selected Items** button. The e-mail will be returned to the **Deleted Items** folder.

6. Move the e-mail from **Deleted Items** back to **Inbox**.

Note that you can see the Exchange Server-side Deletion settings from Advanced Console, Console Root, Microsoft Exchange, Server Configuration, Mailbox. Right click **Mailbox Database** under **First Storage Group** and select **Properties**. See Figure 7-16.

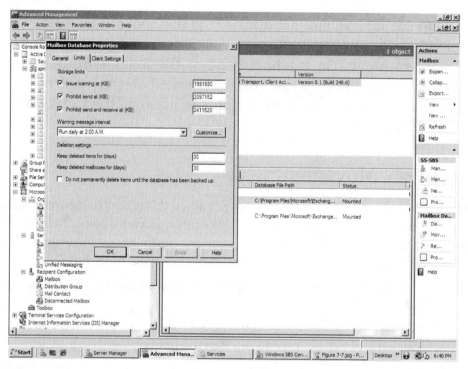

Figure 7-16
Default deletion settings in SBS 2008.

TIP: Time for a bit of BusinessSpeak, an SMB Nation tradition. Our books and events try to merge GeekSpeak and BusinessSpeak at every turn. It's our hallmark. The one time that one of the authors had to use the ability to recover deleted e-mails was when a terminated employee returned to her office and started deleting e-mails. The technical tool was recovering the deleted e-mails. The business scenario was human resources management and the termination of an employee. It was a real world business purpose application of the ability to recover deleted items.

Forwarding E-mail to Your Mobile Telephone

Something that is increasingly popular is the ability to forward e-mails to your telephone. That's because numerous technologies are converging and breaking down functional and feature barriers. Heck—many brands of mobile telephones now include cameras, so why not e-mail too?

The key step in this section is to forward the e-mails to your telephone. Of course, you'd want to keep a copy of the e-mail it in your server-based mailbox, because telephones aren't a good permanent repository and reading a large attachment on a telephone is darn near impossible! So here are the steps you'd take to forward e-mails to your mobile telephone (using the SPRINGERS methodology, of course).

1. In Outlook 2007, select **Rules and Alerts** from the **Tools** menu.

2. Select **New Rule**.

3. Select **Send an alert to my mobile device when I get a message from someone** and click **Next**.

4. Under the **Step 1: Select conditions list**, deselect the default selection of **"from people or distribution list,"** select **"where my name is in the To or Cc box,"** and then click **Next**. This will effectively forward all e-mail sent to you.

5. On the following **Select actions** page, keep the default selection of **"forward it to people or distribution list."** On the lower part of this page, click the people or distribution list hyperlink.

6. The **Rule Address** dialog box appears. Type the e-mail address of your mobile telephone in the **To** field. For example, you might type something like: 2065551212@tmobile.com. Click **OK**.

7. Click **Finish** followed by **OK** to close **Rules and Alerts**.

TIP: Related to the forwarding concept, note that we've used the Active Directory contact object forwarding capability when a customer has a remote office that uses (and will continue to use) POP3 e-mail. The good folks at the home office, seeking to create a uniform e-mail organization/image, will create an Active Directory user for the employee at the remote site. That allows the internal employees to e-mail the remote employee directly from the GAL in Exchange and so on. But this remote employee also has an associated Active Directory contact object that is really the e-mail address for their POP3 account. And voila! The forwarding occurs from the Active Directory user to the Active Directory contact object. How? On the property sheet for an Active Directory user (let's say Norm), click the **Exchange General** tab, click the **Delivery Options** button, and complete the **Forwarding** address box. Be sure to leave a copy on the server!

Cached Exchange Mode

All we want to do is work. So something you'll readily appreciate in Outlook 2007 will be Cached Exchange Mode that is set by default for all SBS 2008 users. This allows you to work offline with Outlook 2007 when Exchange is down for maintenance, you are traveling, or you have a slow link (56K modem) connection back to the server. What's cool is that this is implemented by default and removes a task that you and we likely performed manually at each user machine in the past: configuring offline storage (OST files). Bottom line: You can work with Outlook 2007 very effectively while on a plane, train, automobile, or "no-tell" motel room full of swimsuit models!

It's Client, Not Server!

It is not permissible to run Outlook 2007 on the actual SBS 2008 server machine. There are many reasons for this, the least of which is that a server machine is not to be used as a functional workstation.

Extending Outlook

In this section, you will learn two ways to further extend your use of Outlook in an SBS 2008 environment. These approaches are taken directly from the real world and reflect the reality you're likely to confront and embrace! Let's start with Outlook PDA synchronization and end with a totally cool add-on called "Outlook Business Contact Manager."

Outlook Mobile Access (OMA)

In the last book of this series (in the SBS 2003 time frame), a great amount of time was spent driving home the point (the procedure) for synchronizing your PDA with Outlook via a COM1 or USB "cradle." Guess what in the SBS 2008 world changed? Today, this synchronization largely occurs over the airwaves between Exchange on SBS 2008 and your Windows Mobile device (or BlackBerry for that matter – but we will stick with Windows Mobile). This is a VERY POPULAR SOLUTION with business people who want to carry Outlook information with them, such as e-mail, contacts, and appointments on their PDA. This is how people work in the real world and demand that this type of information be at their fingertips at any time.

> **TIP:** This is one area where making sure you have a good third-party certificate in place is a requirement. Windows Mobile 5 on some providers' phones will not import the SBS self-issued certificate, due to the provider locking out those areas of the phone. While Windows Mobile 6 phones may not be locked out in this manner, there are no guarantees. Also, getting the SBS self-issued certificate imported into every Windows Mobile device once SBS has been deployed is a bit of a hassle.

Mobile-side

The mobile device side (PDA, mobile telephone), for implementing Outlook synchronization is easy. The only real decision point is whether you have a certificate in the mix. The simple steps below were used to configure one of the author's mobile devices (an HP iPaq 6945). The steps should be similar for you regardless of your mobile device because you are really configuring Windows Mobile.

1. Turn on your Windows Mobile device (e.g., HP iPaq 6945).

2. Provide your four-digit password if necessary.

3. Enter your four-digit PIN if necessary to turn on your mobile telephone service (e.g., AT&T).

4. On your mobile device running Windows Mobile, click **Start**, **Programs**, **ActiveSync**.

5. Select **Menu**, **Configure Server**.

6. Type the server address (a public-facing URL such as server1.sprintersltd. com that is supported by an (A) record on public facing DNS servers). This address is typed in the **Server address** field. You will need to determine whether it is necessary to select the checkbox **This server requires an encrypted (SSL) connections**. This is the certification question alluded to above and this will depend on your situation. You can always try it both ways (non-certificate, certificate) if you are unsure. Click **Next**.

7. Complete the **Edit Server Settings** screen with the **User name**, **Password**, and **Domain,** then select the **Save Password** checkbox. Click **Next**.

8. Choose the data you want to synchronize on the next screen. Select **Contacts**, **Calendar**, and **E-mail** (the Settings button allows you to select additional items).

9. Click **Finish**.

Select **Sync** from **ActiveSync** and like MAGIC, the information from Exchange is synchronized to your PDA—and it is really cool. This magic is really known as "Direct Push Technology" because it is pushing the information out to the mobile device. The critical link to also make this magic happen is the availability of a data plan with your mobile telephone carrier. In the case of AT&T Wireless in the US, this data plan is known as the EDGE network and essentially uses a radio signal on the unused portion of the GSM mobile telephone spectrum. Plan highlights include:

- AT&T's EDGE network is the largest national high-speed wireless data network in the U.S.

- The network covers over 13,000 cities and along almost 40,000 miles of U.S. highways covering over 250 million people

- Average download speeds are 70-135 kilobits per second.

- User benefit from an unlimited data access plan with no domestic data roaming charges coast to coast—expanding coverage to 270 million people in the U.S.

This specific information is being shared as a representative example to what you might encounter in this area.

TIP: To learn more about these steps, search on terms like "Outlook 2007 OMA Exchange Windows Mobile" and you will be directed to Microsoft and third-party references with even greater detail on these configurations.

Outlook Business Contact Manager

Business Contact Manager is known in some circles as customer relationship management (CRM) for "da little guy," whereas Microsoft's full CRM product is positioned for the firms with between 25 and 500 employees and at least $5 million in sales. Other CRM competitors in the SBS space include Results (www.results-software.com)and NetSuite. One of the authors (who shall remain nameless) uses NetSuite. But we are here to talk about Business Contact Manager.

Outlook Business Contact Manager is an Outlook 2007 add-on to help small business people improve sales management. It is a way to add value to the SBS 2008 experience.

You acquire Business Contact Manager from Office 2007 (ultimate, professional, and small business editions). We're not going to delve much deeper into the definition of Business Contract Manager but rather encourage you to take a short pause here and ask you to read more at www.microsoft.com/outlook. When you return, we'll start the step-by-step procedure to install Business Contact Manager and make a couple of entries as part of the SPRINGERS methodology.

We're assuming you've already installed Office 2007 and Business Contact Manager on the SS-PRESIDENT workstation. If not, do so now with the normal or most common components installed.

1. Log on as **NormHasborn** with the password **Sunny days!** on **SS-PRESIDENT**.

2. Launch Outlook from **Start, E-mail**.

3. Observe and read the **Welcome to Microsoft Outlook with Business Contact Manager** e-mail. We're counting on you to read this to learn more about the product as we won't repeat it here.

4. Select **Business Contacts** from the **Business Tools** menu. Complete the screen, similar to Figure 7-17, for a fictional customer (e.g., Mrs. Jones). Click **Save and Close** to close the record.

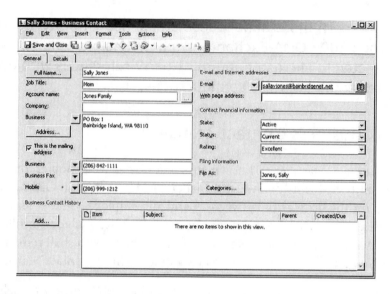

Figure 7-17
Adding a business contact.

5. Select **Accounts** from **Business Tools** and complete the screen similar to Figure 7-18 with fictitious information. Be sure to add a business note and link Sally Jones. Click **Save and Close**.

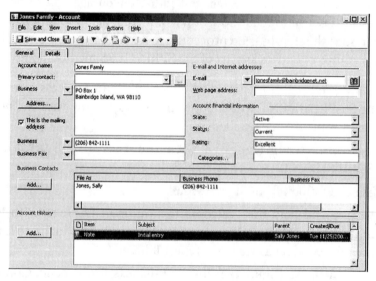

Figure 7-18
Creating an account in BCM. You're putting the pieces in place for a CRM system.

6. Next up, explore the other Business Tools menu options and create an **Opportunity**, **Product List** and, if connected to the Internet to launch a Web browser, select the **Business Tools** link that will take you to the BCM page at Microsoft for the latest updates.

7. Finally, play around with the **Reports** option under the **Business Tools** menu. One such report is shown in Figure 7-19.

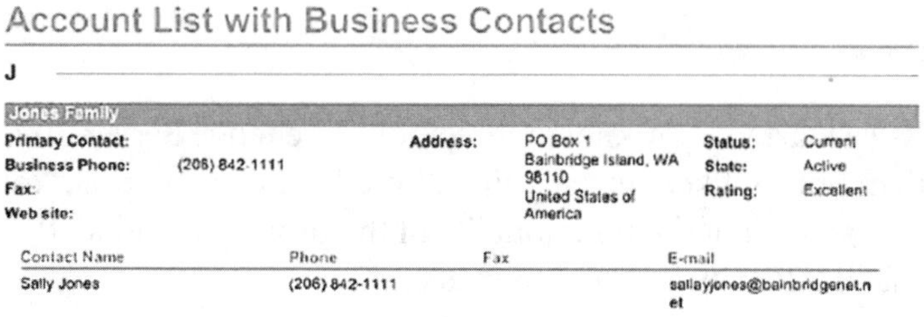

Figure 7-19
The fictitious information is shown in the Account List with Business Contact report.

Note that our intent isn't to teach mastery of BCM but rather to turn you on to this cool tool. Perhaps a full chapter in a future book will be dedicated to this tool for your reading pleasure.

Next Steps!

There are some next steps you can take that go above and beyond this chapter on Exchange and Outlook.

- Visit Microsoft Web Sites: Exchange and Outlook. Your very next step is to visit the sites at Microsoft for Exchange (www.microsoft.com/exchange) and Outlook (www.microsoft.com/office and select the Outlook link). Microsoft posts much of its technical resources to its sites and has created this treasure chest of current information on their products that this book can't hope to keep up with!

- Read Exchange and Outlook Books. While this book covers the full suite of products in SBS 2008, there are many excellent (and thick) books dedicated to Outlook and Exchange.

- Sign up for Sue Mosher's RSS feed for Exchange and Outlook issues: http://www.slipstick.com/rssnews/rssnews.aspx.

- Learn more cool Outlook features. This chapter is only the start, not the end of your time with Outlook. Please go forward and educate yourself on the vCard capability to mail your contact record to others, the mail merge capability, and the automatic meeting planning tool.

Summary

We end how we started. You know more about Exchange Server 2007 and Outlook 2007 than you've likely given yourself credit for in the past. You probably know about 80 percent of the functionality of the programs and it's the remaining 20 percent that'll take much longer to master.

Topics discussed in this chapter include:

- Reviewed what you might already know about Exchange Server 2007.
- Reviewed what you might already know about Outlook 2007.
- Took a tour of Exchange "under the hood."
- Talked about "really managing" Exchange with a look at Active Directory, Internet Information Server, and Core Windows Server 2008 services.
- Discussed server-side attachment blocking, junk e-mailing blocking. and content filter.
- Spoke towards how Exchange is backed up in an SBS 2008 environment.
- Provided details on the Smart Host for Internet E-mail.
- Presented the POP3 Connector
- Discussed numerous advanced topics including External junk mail filtering, the M&Ms, mailing bagging and multiple MX records, and the lack of Instant Messaging and Exchange migrations.
- A conversation about extending Exchange, included multiple Exchange servers and hosted Exchange alternatives.
- Outlook 2007 was presented procedurally and you sent an e-mail and created an appointment and a contact. You also created a public folder.
- Outlook 2007 attachment blocking was discussed followed by the Junk E-mail folder in Outlook and Deleted Item Retention. You also read about

sending an e-mail to a mobile device using a rule and Cached Exchange Mode.

- The chapter ended with two ways to extend Outlook including Outlook Mobile Access and Business Contact Manager.

Forward!

CHAPTER 8

Collaboration with Windows SharePoint Services

The term "Windows SharePoint Services (WSS)" means different things to different SBSers. For some, WSS is the fantastic Companyweb solution ready out of the box when SBS 2008 is installed. For others, WSS is also a brilliant development platform allowing infinite customization possibilities. The authors even know of SBSers who have niched on WSS, creating new career opportunities to serve small businesses. It's that powerful, and you will meet WSS right here, right now. Let's get started!

What's New

Since the SBS 2003 days, you have had the ability to build a robust collaborative foundation using the Companyweb Internal Web site based on Windows SharePoint Services (WSS) Version 2.0 technologies. In SBS 2008, you get WSS Version 3.0, which includes a number of key new features:

- **A Recycle Bin!** SBS consultants and gurus who support SBS 2003 installations where the Companyweb Internal Web site was used quite a bit understand the amount of labor involved in recovering that lost file or the lost folder and files. Users can now recover any documents they have deleted—whether purposely or accidentally—from the Recycle Bin.

- **Another Recycle Bin!** Well, at least one that is hidden from the users. You now have the ability to recover items that users have deleted from the user Recycle Bin!

- **Blogs**. Yes! Now you can set up a blog for the people at your firm! Even outside the company partners can share their knowledge and/or experiences using the blog feature. Alternatively, the company owner or CEO can use it to send out regular messages.

- **Wikis**. Do you see that stack of binders sitting on the shelves gathering dust with all of the company's knowledge, practices, and procedures in them? Well, a wiki would be the perfect place for all of those bits of information. And, because a wiki can be edited by anyone who has permission to do so, things like company procedures can be edited in real time by the folks actually performing the procedures to reflect what really happens when completing a procedure!

- **RSS**. Really Simple Syndication. If you have not heard of it yet, then now is the time to see what RSS is about! Essentially, it allows you to have Outlook or another RSS Feed Reader check for updates to content on Companyweb on a regular basis.

- **Two-Way Communication with Outlook 2007**. Out of all of the new Companyweb features, this one is probably the most important ! You can connect and make changes to Companyweb Calendars, Contacts, Discussion Boards, and Tasks. While Outlook is online, you can also see changes made to any other Companyweb SharePoint Library you add into Outlook, via the Action menu.

Notes

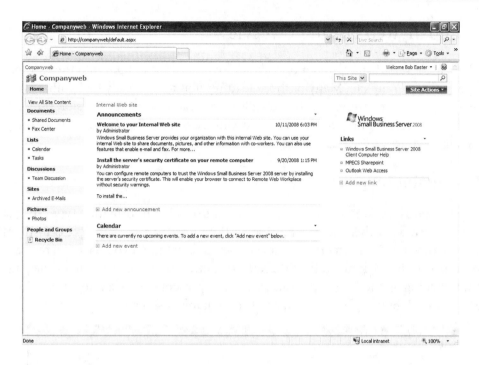

Figure 8-1
Here you see the new Companyweb Internal Web site. Note that we have already added a couple of links under the SBS logo.

Because of the amazing amount of depth in the Companyweb Internal Web site's features and abilities for both SBS Users and the SBS Companyweb SharePoint Administrator, we are going to give you some big-picture views for both. In some cases though, you will get detailed instructions on either how to use a Companyweb feature or how to administer it.

If anything, two of the best actions you can take to augment our introductory info are:

1. Delve into the Companyweb Internal Web site as one of the SPRINGERS users. Have a look at the various components and what they do by browsing the site. Click on the various links and drop-down menus to see what is contained behind them or under them.

2. Check our blogs. They will have up-to-date content on the various SBS 2008 server services. There will also be links to further resources you can click through to.

Companyweb Feature Overview

There are a surprising number of collaborative capabilities built into the Companyweb SharePoint site. Many of those features you may already be familiar with, due to their being present in the SBS 2003 timeframe. This new version provides such a robust structure, that it may be very likely you would consider the Companyweb as your primary data storage location.

SharePoint Libraries

Libraries are locations for you to store files and/or other information types so that you can work on them with others, keep them for later, or gain access to them via the Internet. You can create a new library at any time if you have the relevant permissions by clicking on the **Site Actions** button near the top right of the page then clicking on the **Create** button. You will be presented with a categorized list of SharePoint Libraries that you can create and name as shown in Figure 8-2.

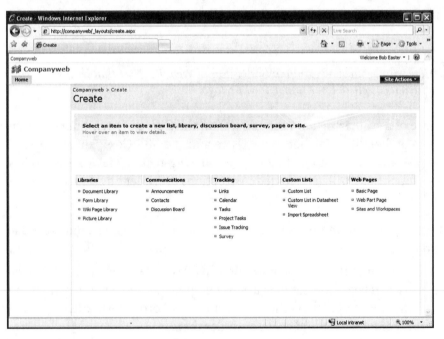

Figure 8-2
After clicking on the Create button, you will be able to create a wide variety of SharePoint libraries, lists, or even customized lists.

Document Library

You are able to store and work with pretty much all manners of document-related files in a document library. For example, you could have a document library that holds Microsoft Word, Excel, and PowerPoint files. You could have another one in which you store ZIP files for archival purposes.

When you store and work with Microsoft Office 2007 documents on the Companyweb site, you can enable Versioning of the documents by using the Check Out and Check In features. They are accessible by hovering over the document and clicking on the drop-down arrow to the right of the file name as shown in Figure 8-2. You can also use the Check Out and Check In menu items under Server in the Office Jewel (File) menu from within the Microsoft Office 2007 application.

Figure 8-3
*If you click just to the right of a file name, you will get a drop-down menu with
a number of different options for you to work with the file.*

If you intend to make modifications to a Word file, for example, you would not want anyone else who may also need to update the file to try and do so while you are working on it. So, before opening the file, you would click on the **Check Out** menu item as shown in Figure 8-3. Once the file is checked out, you can click on it to open it in its respective Office 2007 application.

RSS

When we started this chapter, we mentioned a bunch of new features that Windows SharePoint Services v3 brings to the SBS Companyweb Internal Web site. One of them was the Really Simple Syndication or RSS ability for SharePoint libraries. Since we are talking about one of the largest SharePoint features—Document Libraries—that utilize RSS, let us have a look at how RSS can help you keep track of what is going on in a library.

> **TIP:** Just like any methodology, there are a number of ways to do similar things. In the case of the Companyweb Internal Web site, another method of being alerted to an event in a given SharePoint Library is through the Alerts feature. An Alert is an e-mail that you receive indicating the changes in the library you specified when you set up the Alert.
>
> In virtually every SharePoint Library where you can click an Actions button, you will find the Alert Me link in the drop-down menu. Alerts are different from an RSS feed in that they are an indication that something has changed in the monitored SharePoint Library. They are highly customizable, since you can set them to occur in various ways: as soon as something changes on the site, in a daily change digest e-mail, or even in a weekly change digest. Digests are good for busy libraries, as your Inbox may fill up just with Alerts from the Companyweb libraries you are monitoring!
>
> From there you get added flexibility as to what types of events will cause an alert, such as content being added to the library, a change to the library other than an addition or deletion, or who made a change.

Open your Internet Explorer and the Companyweb site will come up by default. Click on the **Shared Documents** link in the Quick Launch column that is always on the left-hand side of the page. When the Shared Documents library comes up, it will probably be empty.

Have a look at Figure 8-4.

Figure 8-4
When you see this icon, an RSS feed is available. All blogs support some form of
RSS to let you know when they have been updated. The same is true with any
RSS-enabled Companyweb library.

In Internet Explorer, near the top right of the browser window you will see the
icon in Figure 8-4 and it will have a little black downward facing arrow just to the
right of it.

1. Click on the **RSS** icon down arrow in Internet Explorer.

2. The drop-down option will be **Shared Documents**. Click on that item.

3. A new Web page will come up with a description for the feed. Near the bot-
    tom of the description will be the **Subscribe to this feed** link. Click on it.

4. The IE Subscribe to this Feed dialogue box will pop up. You can change the
    name of the Feed and choose the default location for the Feed or create a
    folder for it, then click the **Subscribe** button.

5. If the Feed was successfully subscribed to, you will get a confirmation mes-
    sage. You can click the **View my feeds** link to see a list of your RSS feeds
    in Internet Explorer.

6. Click the **Companyweb: Shared Documents** link at the top of the Web
    page to be taken to the Shared Documents document library. If the Feeds
    list column in Internet Explorer is open, click the **X** to the right of the
    History button to close it.

7. Leave Internet Explorer open, as you are going to need it after the
    Outlook steps.

If you have Outlook 2007 installed on your workstation, when you subscribe to
a site's RSS feed in Internet Explorer, the feed will show up in your Outlook too.
The catch to that, however, is that you must have answered **Yes** to the RSS Enable

question Outlook asks you when you first opened it up. Not to worry, though, if you answered **No** to the original question; you can still enable RSS in Outlook:

1. Open Outlook from Start.
2. Click on the **Tools** menu then **Options**.
3. Click on the **Mail Setup** tab.
4. Click the **Send/Receive** button.
5. Make sure that All Accounts is highlighted and click the **Edit** button.
6. Click the **RSS** option in the Accounts list.
7. Check **Include RSS Feeds in this Send/Receive group**.
8. Click **OK**, **Close**, and **OK**.

Have a look at Figure 8-5, which displays the above dialogue box in Outlook. It shows you what the RSS settings should be and the fact that you have already subscribed to the Shared Documents RSS feed!

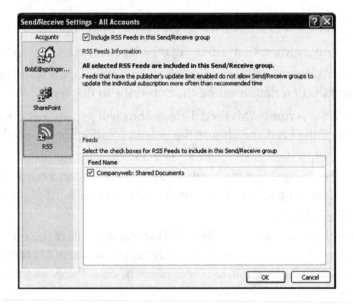

Figure 8-5
Once you have added the Shared Documents RSS and enabled RSS feeds in Outlook's Send/Receive group, you will see the feed listed in the Feeds window at the bottom.

Now, the next step is to add something to the library.

1. If you've already opened Internet Explorer, you will be at the Share Documents library. Click the **New** button, then click on **New Document** in the drop-down list.

2. Assuming Microsoft Office 2007 is installed along with Outlook 2007, Word 2007 will open up. Click the **Jewel** to display the drop-down menu and click on the **Save As** button.

3. The directory list window should be showing the Shared Documents library. Name the document **Test Document** and set the Save as type to **Word Document**.

4. Click the **Save** button.

5. Type a test sentence along the lines of: **This is an RSS feed test document.**

6. Close Microsoft Word 2007 and answer **Yes** if you are asked about saving the document.

7. You should now see your new document in the Companyweb Shared Documents library. Press **ALT+TAB** to bring Outlook back up or click on its button on the Task Bar.

8. In Outlook, under the Mailbox – Bob Easter folders list, you will see that RSS icon again. Click the + beside it to bring up your RSS feeds list.

9. You will eventually see the Companyweb: Shared Documents item go bold when new items have been added or existing items have been changed.

Depending on the RSS polling frequency set in Internet Explorer, your RSS folder in Outlook may take anywhere from a few minutes to 24 hours to recognize new content on the site. You can check the polling frequency in IE as follows:

1. In IE, click on the **Gold Star**.

2. Click on the **Feeds** button.

3. Right click on the **Companyweb: Shared Documents** feed and click on **Properties**.

4. Note the Update Schedule setting. If the default setting takes too long, then click the **Use custom schedule** radio button.

5. Click the **Frequency** down arrow to bring up the drop-down list and select the **Feed Minimum (Time Unit)**.

6. Click **OK**.

7.   Close the Feeds column by clicking on the **X**.

Different RSS-enabled sites will have different settings for the allowed polling frequency. For busier sites, expect that the allowed frequency may actually be less frequent than other not-so-busy sites. In the case of the various Companyweb libraries, the default polling rate is one hour.

Now, one last thing with regards to the connection between Internet Explorer and the Outlook 2007 RSS Reader function: While adding RSS feeds via Internet Explorer will also tie that feed into Outlook, they are mutually exclusive when it comes to removing that feed. So, if you delete a feed in one, you will need to manually delete the feed in the other.

Form Library

If you utilize Microsoft Office InfoPath as part of your business form workflow structure, then you will keep your forms in a Form Library. Examples of forms would be status reports or purchase orders that need to be filled out.

Wiki Page Library

Have a look at Figure 8-6 to see what a wiki can look like.

Figure 8-6
The various SPRINGERS employees will keep the Springer Spaniels' Procedure Manual wiki up to date in their respective areas.

Essentially, a wiki is a place to store knowledge. Since a wiki is set up in such a way that everyone will be able to edit it, you can assign different employees various areas within the business build-up, giving each employee the responsibility for maintaining a set of wiki pages relating to his or her area of expertise.

Whenever you are on a wiki page, there will be three buttons available for you to click on near the top right of that page.

- **Edit**. Click on this button to edit the page. You can add or delete content on the page.

- **History**. Click on the History button to see all of the additions or deletions that were made to a page. You can also Check Out a page if you want to lock it from being edited further, check the Version History that tells you who made what changes, and set up an Alert to let you know when any changes are made to the page.

- **Incoming Links**. You will be able to see any other wiki pages that link to the current page you are on by clicking the Incoming Links button.

Editing the wiki is actually quite easy. When there is a need to create a new wiki subject page that is under the current page that you are editing, you can do the following:

1. Bulleted list: [[Electric Clippers]], [[Electric Shears]], [[Scissors]]

    - Any new wiki page that is required on the fly needs to be encased in the double brackets as shown in Figure 8-7. Note the three new wiki category pages.

Figure 8-7
*When you need new wiki pages, encase the new page's title in double brackets, then click **OK**.*

2. Once you've finished making your edits to the page, click the **OK** button. You will see the three new category pages with a dotted line under each one on the now edited page.

3. Click on the **Electric Clippers** link.

4. You will get the New Wiki Page dialogue page. The Name will already be filled out for you with "Electric Clippers." Make the necessary edits in the editor, then click the **Create** button.

5. Click the **Incoming Links** button near the top right of the page.

6. You will find the page we were originally editing. Click on the link to go back to that page. In our example, as shown in Figure 8-8, that page is **Trimming**.

7. The Electric Clippers link will no longer have a dotted underline. Repeat the above steps to create the wiki pages for Electric Shears and Scissors.

While in the Companyweb wiki, a navigation list of the five most recently edited wiki pages will show up under the Quick Launch column on the left-hand side of the page.

You will also find a link to View All Pages under the edited pages list. When you click through to the list of wiki pages, you can see who created the pages, who modified them and when, and the date the pages were created.

Out of the box, Microsoft provides a wiki page called "How To Use This Wiki Library." It is linked on the default wiki Home page. Have a read through this page, as it is both straightforward and extremely helpful about how to build up the wiki.

Picture Library

Using the SPRINGERS methodology, a really good use for a picture library would be for pictures of the various Springer Spaniel dogs and their attributes. One library could be for the various colors, another for the various sizes, and yet another for dogs in their various life stages with a subfolder for each stage.

You can manage your picture libraries just as you would any other folder and file set up on your own computer, on a network share, or on an external hard drive. You have the ability to create a folder hierarchy that suits your needs and to sort images into their respective folders with relative ease using the Explorer View under the View menu near the top right of the images.

You can run a slide show using the images in a folder. Just click the **Actions** drop-down menu and click on the **View Slide Show** item. You will see a new browser window or tab open up with the Slide Show page shown in Figure 8-8. You can start the slide show by clicking on the **Play** button and stop it by clicking on the **Stop** button. If you want to advance the slide show, there is a Fast Forward button to do so. Alternatively, if you want to step back one image, you can do that too, by clicking the **Rewind** button.

Figure 8-8
The Slide Show gives you the opportunity to sit back and relax while enjoying the photos.

Back in the Picture Gallery, you can upload an image using the Upload link found under the Upload drop-down menu. To see an Upload Multiple Pictures menu item on the Upload drop-down menu as well, you will need to have the Microsoft Office 2007 Microsoft Office Picture Manager installed, as that is the intermediary that would be used.

If Office 2007 is not installed, you can click on the **Open with Windows Explorer** link under Actions to bring up a Windows Explorer window with the Picture Gallery opened. You can then use Cut and Paste or Copy and Paste to move large quantities of pictures into the library.

One of the neat features the Picture Library has built into it, is the ability to use a download dialogue to change the size of an image. If the images you have in your library are quite large, then this feature may come in handy. To do so:

1. Click on the checkbox under any one of the images you want to download and resize.

2. Click on the **Actions** drop-down menu, then click on the **Download** link.

3. You will see Figure 8-9. Click the radio button for the picture size you need and click the **Download** button.

Figure 8-9
You can take a large image and downsize it during the download process.

4. When the Download dialogue box comes up, your local My Pictures folder will be chosen by default. You may not be able to save to a network share. Choose your save location and click the **Save** button.

If you choose multiple picture files to download, you can also run the resize on them too.

SharePoint Communications

SharePoint Communications tools are features to facilitate communication with SBS domain users and others, along with the ability to centrally store and manage Contacts lists.

Announcements

When you first open up the Companyweb page, you will see the Announcements right there in the middle of the page. You can use announcements to communicate all manner of things, such as thoughts from the business owner or an employee's birthday or the arrival of a new baby in the company family.

When it comes to managing the SBS domain, you may want to use the announcements to let the folks know about important events—for example, that there will be an upcoming server reboot over lunch this coming Friday. Doing so would help the employees plan their time efficiently, knowing there would be no server and Internet access during that time.

You can add an announcement by clicking the **Add new announcement** link under the announcements list. If you click the **Announcements** header link, you will end up looking at a list of all of the current announcements. You can click the **New** button to create a new announcement from there.

When you create an announcement, you give it a title and type up the body of the announcement that will contain the bulk of your information. You can then set an optional expiration date for it. So, if you create a birthday announcement for Bob Easter, for example, you might do it like Figure 8-10:

- Title: Bob Easter's Birthday on Friday December 5.
- Body: We will have cake at lunch. Please be there!
- Expires: Saturday, December 6.

Figure 8-10
 *After you've created the announcement and filled in the particulars, click **OK**.*

Once you have completed the announcement, it will appear on the Companyweb front page either until it expires or another couple of announcements are made and it gets bumped off.

Contacts

You can create a contacts list to share specific contacts for a project. On the other hand, you can set up a contacts list that is integrated into Outlook 2007 to manage mailing lists for the company's e-mail newsletter.

For the longest time, SPRINGERS has sent out a paper newsletter to the dog owners. The newsletter had various features on the dogs—breeding, care, and more. With the cost of publishing that newsletter rising due to printing and postage cost increases, the question was put to their newsletter subscribers about having the newsletter go entirely electronic via a PDF document. The response was overwhelmingly positive.

Given the fact that we just implemented a nice, new SBS 2008-based network solution for SPRINGERS, one of the things we can do is to take advantage of the Companyweb Contacts Library. For example, you could move the contacts out of Melinda Overlaking's Outlook (to Companyweb Contacts), where she would run Mail Merges using Word to print up the newsletter mailing labels.

By centralizing the newsletter contacts on the Companyweb site, everyone at SPRINGERS would be able to connect their own Outlook into the list, providing a more streamlined subscriber management process. Prior to this level of integration, everyone would leave their notes at Melinda's desk about address updates, new owners opting in, or owners opting out of receiving the newsletter.

The first thing you need to do is to create a contacts list on the Companyweb site:

1. Click the **Site Actions** button near the top right corner of the Companyweb site.
2. Click the **Create** link in the drop-down list.
3. Click **Contacts** under the Communications column.
4. Give the new list the following settings and click the **Create** button:
   - Name: **Springer Spaniels E-Newsletter Contacts**
   - Description: **All contracts that receive our e-mail newsletter**
   - Display on Quick Launch? **Yes**

TIP: You do not need to put every newly created list on the Quick Launch bar. If you run into a need for multiple lists of the same type, create a new Links page that will contain hyperlinks to all of the necessary Companyweb Lists. You may need to aggregate a Links list page full of the various Companyweb Contacts list\, or, you may have a need to place a Projects link on the Quick Launch that is a Links list filled with hyperlinks that link to all of the company's projects.

Ultimately, how things are organized on the Quick Launch bar is up to you and the company owners. We do recommend, however, keeping the Quick Launch bar as simple as possible to eliminate the possibility that it may become something less than quick.

Once you have created the Contacts list, you will end up at the Springer Spaniels E-Newsletter Contacts (E-Newsletter) page on the Companyweb site. The contacts list will be empty. Since Melinda had all of the needed contacts in her Outlook, the simplest way to get those contacts into the new E-Newsletter Contacts list is to connect the list into her Outlook and then copy them over to the new list.

While in the Companyweb E-Newsletter Contacts list:

1. Click the **Actions** button to display the drop-down list and click the **Connect to Outlook** link.

2. Answer **Yes** to the Connect this SharePoint Contacts List to Outlook? question.

3. Outlook will open to the newly connected contacts list.

4. Click on the Outlook Contacts list that has the contacts you want to transfer into the new SharePoint Contacts list.

5. In Outlook, click on the **View** menu, **Current View, Phone List**.

6. Select all of the contacts by hitting **CTRL+A** or by clicking the **Edit** menu and **Select All**.

7. You can right click on the highlighted contacts and click on **Copy** or click on the **Edit** menu again and click on **Copy**.

8. Click on the newly created E-Newsletter Contacts folder, then click the Edit menu, and finally click on **Paste**.

TIP: Something important to keep in mind when it comes to some of the key features in the Companyweb SharePoint Web site, is that without Microsoft Office 2007 installed, many SharePoint and Outlook integrated features will not work.

Once you have transferred all of the contacts from Melinda's Outlook into the E-Newsletter Contacts list, you need to consider what to do with the original contacts folder. Keeping two lists of contacts would not be a good idea from an administrative point of view. The original list could be kept as a backup list with the E-Newsletter contacts list copied back into Melinda's Outlook once every week or two weeks. Or, the contacts could be deleted altogether since they will not be needed anymore.

You now have a fairly real-world experience on how the Contacts List can facilitate a greater efficiency in a company.

Discussion Board

When you open the Companyweb for the first time, the default setup includes a discussion board via the Team Discussion link found on the Quick Launch. If you have participated in an online forum, newsgroup, or e-mail list, then you will be familiar with the subject-driven conversations that are involved.

Once a discussion is started, it is at the root of the thread. The image that best describes a lively discussion list and the discussion is that of an inverted or upside-down tree. The initial post is the root thread, with the discussion around that post being the trunk. The main branches are produced when subtopic threads branch off of the original thread. Then smaller branch threads are created from the main branch threads, and so on, as the discussion takes on many different flavors.

Discussions in a team project setting may not be so lively with many different threads, but they will serve the purpose of providing team members with an easy way to stay in touch and work on different ideas and structures for the project.

For example, someone—in this case Bob Easter—with a question about a particular Springer Spaniel subject will initiate the discussion by creating a new discussion when he clicks on the **New** button in Team Discussion. When Bob creates the new discussion, he will set up a subject and structure the question in the body of the discussion post as shown in Figure 8-11.

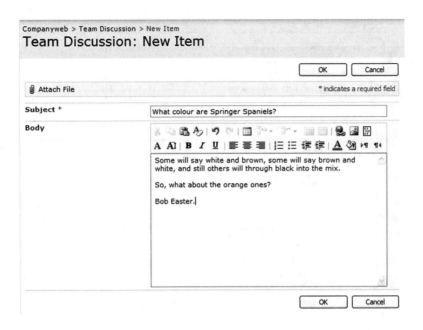

Figure 8-11
You can set the topic and fill out the details on what information is being sought when creating a new discussion thread.

Now, once the OK button is clicked on and the new discussion topic "What colour are Springer Spaniels?" will show up in the Team Discussion list. Anyone with a thought on the matter can click on the discussion heading link **What colour are Springer Spaniels?** and post a reply by clicking on the **Reply** button.

Discussion lists can be integrated into Outlook 2007. Not only that, you can actually carry on the discussion from within Outlook. So, if one of the SPRINGERS crew had the entire Team Discussion list connected to his or her Outlook and had a quick response to Bob's initial query, that person would be able to do so from within Outlook as shown in Figure 8-12.

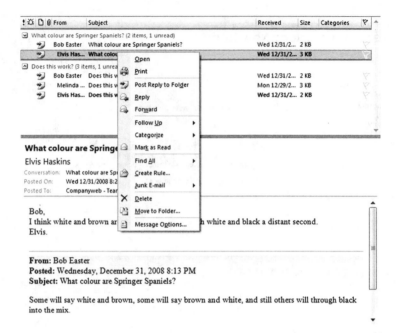

Figure 8-12

When you right click on a discussion item in Outlook, you can reply directly to the person that posted the item, post a reply in the discussion site, or forward the discussion post on.

Click on a discussion topic in the Team Discussion page and you will see the original post on the top and any replies under it. Look to the top right of the posts and you will see that you have a View option menu. Click on it, and there will be another option besides Flat, which is each post stacked from the oldest on top to the newest on the bottom. That option is to view the posts in the Threaded format.

Remember the image of the inverted tree? Well, when you switch the discussion view to Threaded on a busy discussion, you will see that there are indeed many discussion subtopics branching off from the original discussion topic. It can be pretty neat to see the various conversations flowing from the original question or topic.

SharePoint Tracking

Once you get your libraries in place and the necessary communication structures set up, you need to keep track of it all! With a Links library to handle Web site hyperlinks, Calendars for tracking the many appointments and meetings, Tasks to keep everyone on track, a new Project Tasks list with a Gantt chart structure just like Microsoft Project, Issues Tracking and even Surveys, you can keep a close eye on pretty much every aspect of a projects progress.

Links

A Links list is a group of Web page hyperlinks you and your team can build and use to connect to Web pages on a specific topic or relevant to a project.

Once you have used the **Site Actions** button to create a new Links list page—in our case we created one called "Springer Spaniels Sites"—you can populate the new links list by doing the following:

1. If on the Companyweb Home Page, click the new Links list **Springer Spaniels Sites** link.
2. Click on the **New** button.
3. Type or paste the URL into the Web address field: **http://blog.mpecsinc.ca**.
4. Click the **Click here to test** link above the Web address field to verify your URL.
5. The Type a description field will be the URL link: **MPECS Inc Blog**.
6. Type a brief description for the new link.
7. Click **OK**.

When there are links in the list, you can hover over one to display a drop-down arrow. When you see the arrow, click anywhere to the right of the link to bring up a menu. Don't click on the link itself as you will be taken to the respective Web site. These are the items you will see in that menu:

- **View Item.** Click on this link and you will be directed to the linked Web page.
- **Edit Item.** Click on this link and you will be able to edit the URL, description, and notes for it. Note that, if you do not have permissions to edit links created by other users, then you will not be able to edit a link created by another user.

- **Delete Item**. If you want to remove the item from the list, you can click this link. Again, if you do not have permission to modify links created by another user, you will not be able to delete the item.

- **Alert Me**. This is a neat menu item. Click on it, and you can have an alert sent to your Inbox if you, someone else, or anyone changes or deletes the link! These alerts can come to you immediately or in a daily or weekly digest form.

Calendar

On the Companyweb calendar list, shown in Figure 8-13, you will have the ability to configure a dedicated calendar for any number of appointment-tracking needs. One example would be a centrally located Vacation Calendar so that employees can keep track of who is going to be available or not available.

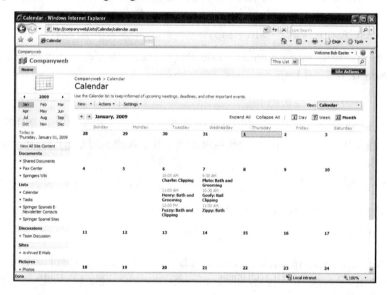

Figure 8-13
With a Calendar List, you can manage any number of different types of appointments.

When you first see the default calendar that comes with the Companyweb Internal Web site, the default view is the current month. Just as you can in Outlook, you are able to change the view of the calendar to show not only the current month but also the current week or day.

Depending on the view you are looking at, you will see the date, such as Thursday, January 01, 2009, for the day view; December 28, 2008 – January 03, 2009 for the week view; or January 2009 for the month view. You can use the left arrow to move back in time or the right arrow to move forward in time within the calendar, based on your current view.

Whether in Month or Week view, you will be able to click on the header for any day to bring up that day's appointments. There is a small month calendar just under the Companyweb Home tab above the Quick Launch, that highlights the currently selected day in your calendar view. Under that small calendar will be a Hyperlink indicating today's date so you can always click back to the appointments of the day with ease.

The Companyweb Calendar List, and any other calendar list you create, can be integrated into your Outlook 2007. As a result, you can copy appointments between any of your Outlook Calendars as shown in Figure 8-14.

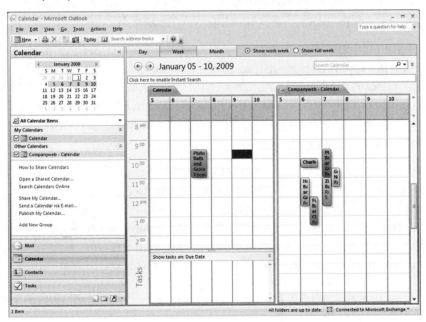

Figure 8-14

With Outlook integration, keeping on top of appointments between project team members is that much easier.

So, in our SPRINGERS calendar example shown in both Figure 8-14 and Figure 8-15, you can see that the appointments show up as hyperlinks in the Companyweb Calendar. But in the Outlook integrated Companyweb Calendar they show up "color–coded" due to each appointment having a category set.

> **TIP:** Specific to Outlook 2007, is the ability to customize the category names and the colors associated with them, which helps give you an at-a-glance view of your upcoming appointments. In the case of the various appointments for the dogs shown in Figure 8-14, each color represents the room where the procedure was to be carried out. Those category names and color associates can be used in any area of Outlook too.

If you click on one of the appointments in the Companyweb Calendar, you will be able to see the item's specific properties. You will be given the option to create a new calendar item, edit or delete the item you are looking at, set an alert for any changes to the appointment, or export the event to an .ICS file.

If you have Outlook 2007 installed, and you click the **Export Event** option and then click the **Open** button instead of the Save button, you will actually see an Outlook appointment window open up with the appointment's details. You can make changes to the appointment details and save them into Outlook. Note that when you do this, the exported appointment will be saved in your own calendar and not the Companyweb Calendar.

One more thing based on our current example of keeping track of the various appointments for the dogs, is to keep in mind that if a calendar is quite busy with all five work rooms being full, then it might be a good idea to have five calendars. You would be able to keep track of each room's appointments in one calendar. If you break up the calendar appointments in this manner, you could use the category color codes for the individual who would be working in that room.

If you do split things off, then initially one small sacrifice will be what you see in Figure 8-15.

Notes

Figure 8-15
Any appointments that are in the default Companyweb Calendar will appear on the Home Page.

While discussion of this particular point ventures beyond the scope of this introductory book, you can go ahead and click the **Edit Page** link in the Site Actions drop-down list to add the other four calendar appointment events to the page! It really is not that difficult, although a little investigation into how the appointment list on the Home Page is tied into the actual Companyweb Calendar Web part would be in order.

As you can see, there is a lot of flexibility in the way things can be set up for calendar appointments in the SharePoint calendar lists. On top of that, bringing Outlook 2007 into the picture really augments the way your users can streamline their workflows.

Tasks

Tasks are those actions—large or small—that must be tracked so that they do not fall through the cracks. They are the To Dos for almost any aspect of running a business—or even a family!

In Companyweb, you have an out-of-the-box Tasks list. When you click on it, you can then click the **New** button to create a new Task. So, let's say that SPRINGERS was running out of dog shampoo, we would set a task as follows:

1. Click on the **New** button.

2. When the Tasks: New Item page comes up, set the following info and click **OK**:

   - Title: **Pick up dog shampoo**
   - Priority: **High**
   - Status: **Not Started**
   - % Complete: Leave empty
   - Assigned to: **Bob Easter**
   - Description: **Bob, we need you to run to our supplier and pick up shampoo, please. Norm H**

Now, there are a couple of neat aspects to the Assign to field. First, the Check Name icon to the right of the field will do just that. It will tie into your Active Directory and check the name typed there. The second benefit is that if you type only the person's first name, such as "Bob," and click the **Check Name** icon, and there are multiple possibilities, you will get an error back as shown in Figure 8-16.

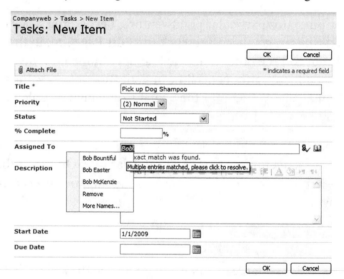

Figure 8-16

When you type a first name, and a number of people have that same name, you will be able to choose the correct name by clicking on the name with the red squiggly underline.

Tasks lists can also be integrated into Outlook 2007. With that integration comes the ability to manage task lists in Outlook and on the Companyweb site, giving your users a lot of flexibility.

Project Tasks

When you take everything you have seen in the above section on the SharePoint Tasks Lists and add a Gantt Chart to the task assignments to view of how things are progressing, you get the Project Tasks List. Have a look at Figure 8-17 to see what we mean.

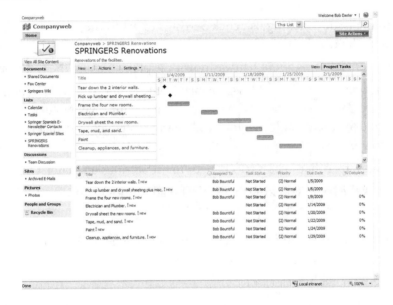

Figure 8-17
You can now create a set of project tasks along with their progress displayed using a Gantt chart not unlike Microsoft Project.

Management and Outlook integration for Project Tasks are identical to the standard Tasks Lists. We will now move right into the next SharePoint list type!

Issue Tracking

Any company that develops software or hardware or offers any type of product or service will be able to make use of an Issue Tracking list. Unfortunately, out of the box, the Companyweb site does not have an issue tracking list installed.

Just as you have for the other lists, you would use the Site Actions button to **Create** a new issue tracking list. Just as you can with the other lists, you can have the new issue tracking list linked to the Quick Launch.

Once you have created the list, you can set up any issues that need to be tracked. Creating an issue is as simple as clicking the **New** button, naming it, assigning it to one or more people, and setting its parameters.

However, you will need to set the Categories setting prior to going live with issue tracking. Once you have decided what types of categories you need for the issues to be tracked, follow these steps:

1. In the Issue Tracking list, click **Settings** to get to the drop-down list, then click the **List Settings** button.

2. Under Columns about halfway down the page, click on the **Category** link.

3. You will see the default (1) Category 1, etc., under Additional Column Settings. You can delete the defaults and enter your own. Note that the initial value for the default category will change to whichever one is first in the category list.

4. Make any other necessary changes to the settings and click **OK**.

5. Click the **Issue Tracking** link in the breadcrumbs just above the Customize Issue Tracking title to get back to the list.

Once you start creating different issues, you will be able to tie them together—if they are related—using categories and the Related Issues selection, which is actually a list of any ongoing issues.

Go ahead and create an Issue Tracking list. Once you start to play around with it, you will see how it can be utilized in the various SBS environments you encounter.

Survey

If you need to take a poll of everyone using the SBS environment to ask how they like or don't like the experience, you would create a survey.

To do so:

1. Click on **Site Actions** to get to the drop-down list, then click the **Create** button.

2. Select **Survey** from under the SharePoint Tracking section.

3. Give the survey a name and a description, note whether it appears on the Quick Launch, offer a couple of options, then click **Next**.

   - Survey: **Springer's Survey**
   - Description: **SBS Satisfaction Survey**
   - Quick Launch: **Yes**
   - Show user names: **No**
   - Allow multiple responses: **No**

4. On the next page:

   - Question: **Are you happy with the new SBS setup?**
   - The type of answer: **Choice (menu to choose from)**
   - Require a response: **Yes**
   - Type each choice on a separate line: **Yes, No**
   - Display choices using: **Radio Buttons**
   - Allow fill-in choices: **No**
   - Default value: **Yes**

5. You can repeat the above steps again to add another question, by clicking the **Next Question** button. If you are done, then click the **Finish** button.

Once you have created your survey, you can copy and paste the Companyweb URL into an e-mail to be sent out to the people or groups you want to respond to it. Once people have started to respond, you will be able to click on the **Show a graphical summary of responses** link or the **Show all responses** link to see how they respond.

Notes

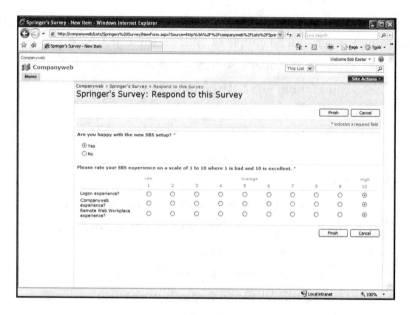

Figure 8-18
We built a two-question survey for the SPRINGERS crew to let us know what they think!

SharePoint Custom Lists

Given the nature of this introductory tome, we will not put too much time into the customizable lists. Needless to say, by using a little creativity and time or hiring someone who works with SharePoint professionally, you can get some pretty customized SharePoint solutions that are data-driven. That means that you can work with the list's data to extract any type of report or information that you need.

SharePoint Web Pages

You have the flexibility to add bits and pieces or highly customized pages to your Companyweb libraries and lists. When you click on **Site Actions** and then **Create**, you will see that you have the option to create a Basic Web Page, a Web Part Page, and additional Sites and Workspaces.

Basic Web Page

A basic Web page is just that: A plain-vanilla Web page, that you can customize with images, text, and tables. A basic Web page needs to be attached to a Document Library, so keep that in mind when you need to create one or more pages. You may need to create a dedicated document library for them.

Web Part Page

When you look at the Companyweb Home Page, you are looking at a Web Part Page. It takes bits and pieces of the various libraries and lists and displays them for you. You can create some highly customized pages using the various SharePoint Web Parts.

Sites and Workspaces

Depending on your permissions, you may be able to create a whole new site dedicated to a project or a new product focus, for a team to collaborate on. The site will reside within the Companyweb top-level site.

You use the Sites and Workspaces dialogue to add a new Team Site, Blank Site Document Workspace, Wiki Site, or Blog. You can also create Meeting Workspaces.

Ultimately, you are given a tremendous amount of flexibility to create a Companyweb SharePoint structure around your business or your client's businesses.

Fax Center

The Fax Center is a document library you can use to manage and sending faxes. You can store your fax templates and cover pages to easily access when sending out a fax. As we discussed in the SBS deployment chapter, you can have all of your incoming faxes stored in the Incoming Faxes folder. If you have a high volume of junk faxes, then not only will this save you paper and toner usage in a fax machine, it will save time for the person who needs to leaf through the pieces of paper.

Idle Timeout

One of the new features to come to the Companyweb Internal Web site is an idle time out. As shown in Figure 8-20, if you have a browser window opened to the

Companyweb site and left it idle for 30 minutes, you will be prompted to close the browser window or tab.

Figure 8-19
After 30 minutes of idle time, the Companyweb Internal Web site will prompt you to close the page!

Answer **Yes**, and the tab or browser window will close. Answer **No**, and you can click on the **Go back to site** link just above the words "Sign Out."

Summary

So much SharePoint, so little time! Both authors feel strongly that Windows SharePoint Services, as manifested via Companyweb in SBS 2008, is a killer application, although somewhat hidden. Folks who properly meet and greet the WSS "solution" tend to become big users of it and huge fans, and they often extend it beyond its out-of-the-box Companyweb functionality. This chapter was intended to be such an introduction and is only the start of your WSS journey. The following topics, presented in an overview fashion, were introduced in this chapter:

- New features, such as the Wiki, RSS, and two-way Outlook 2007 communication were highlighted at the start of the chapter and discussed in more detail as we moved through the text.
- The Companyweb features overview discussed:
  - SharePoint libraries where the document check-in, check-out capabilities were highlighted

- o   Communications, such as the Contacts
- o   Tracking, such as the Calendar and Tasks
- o   Custom lists
- o   Web pages
- o   Fax Center

Take it from the two authors. If you want to distinguish yourself as a superior SBSer, use this chapter as your WSS foundation and go out and learn more!

CHAPTER 9

Mobility and Remote Connectivity

Small Business Server has been about mobility and remote connectivity since SBS 2003. The "killer app" for SBS was and is the Remote Web Workplace. The Remote Web Workplace portal gives users the ability to connect to Outlook Web Access, remotely connect to their computer, connect to the Companyweb SharePoint site, and connect to various Web sites via a links list.

Outlook Web Access in SBS 2008 and Exchange 2007 Service Pack 1 is simply amazing. The Web interface has taken such a huge step forward, with it looking very similar to Outlook 2007's. The real bonus is that the functionality in Outlook Web Access is actually very similar to Outlook 2007! Previous versions of Outlook Web Access could not brag about that at all.

SBS and Outlook Mobile Access gives you the ability to quickly and efficiently connect a Windows Mobile 5 and 6.x phone to the Exchange e-mail server. This process is greatly simplified if you use a third-party trusted certificate.

In the SBS 2003 days, when you needed to connect a laptop user's Outlook to the Exchange 2003 e-mail server, you would set up the Exchange Proxy settings. Essentially that meant configuring Outlook to use RPC/HTTPS to connect whenever the user was connected to the Internet from outside of the office. Microsoft has given that ability a new name now: Outlook Anywhere.

And finally, you will, in some cases, need to create a VPN connection back to the SBS server to get access to data that may be needed.

Remote Web Workplace

The Remote Web Workplace (RWW) is probably one of the best remote access portals available anywhere, bar none. Why do we say that? Because, as folks in the Small to Medium Enterprise (SME) and Enterprise environments became aware of the RWW back in the SBS 2003 days, they wanted it. But, RWW was built right into SBS 2003 with no ability to extract it out!

The desire for RWW and SBS-like features was so strong in SME, Microsoft answered that need in the form of Essential Business Server 2008, which was formally released to market on the same day as Small Business Server 2008. While it shares RWW, EBS 2008 relies more heavily on the native tools snap-ins for management.

Figure 9-1
The new Remote Web Workplace portal logon page.

You will find a large-size image of Figure 9-1 in Appendix Z.

The Remote Web Workplace in SBS 2008 has been greatly improved over its predecessor for both the user and the SBS administrator. From the easier to navigate portal buttons and links, to the administrator's ability to fine-tune which portal resources a user can access, the new RWW makes a strong case for stepping into SBS 2008!

Remote Web Workplace Access

During the initial SBS setup, you got to configure the URL you and users will use to access the Remote Web Workplace: **https://remote.springersltd.com/ remote**. Now, since we do not recommend that you allow the HTTP port 80 to be opened in our deployment and configuration chapters, having the "S" in the HTTPS is important.

If you did not "port forward" port 80 to the SBS server on your Internet Gateway appliance, users will not get any response when they type in the following address: http://remote.springersltd.com/remote. For those SBS installations that had Software Assurance and have their SBS 2008 protected by ISA 2006, you will see the error shown in Figure 9-2.

Figure 9-2
   When SBS 2008 is protected by ISA and the HTTP port 80 is blocked, users will get an error about needing to use SSL (HTTPS).

TIP: When it comes to securing a server, the more doors you close, the better the security. While you could leave the HTTP port 80 open and forwarded to your SBS server, allowing it to redirect the request to an SSL-secured session, this is leaving an unnecessary door open to the server.

It is preferable to have port 80 closed and users trained to make sure they are using HTTPS when accessing the Remote Web Workplace or other SBS Web-facing services.

As pointed out in Figure 9-1, users will be greeted by a logon page when they navigate to the Remote Web Workplace. The RWW logon will be formatted using the same format to log on to a workstation on the SBS domain:

- Username: **BobEaster** (Note that names are not case sensitive).

- Password: **Lots to eat!**

After a momentary pause—which may take a little longer for the first user of the day—you will be greeted by the new portal. Figure 9-3 shows us the new Remote Web Workplace.

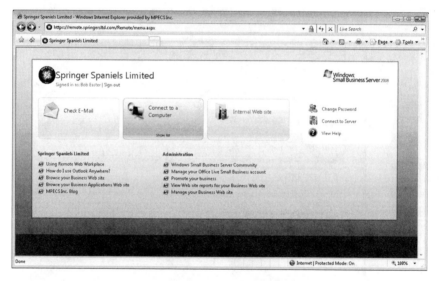

Figure 9-3
The new Remote Web Workplace portal page for a Standard User with Admin Links.

Portal Contents

It is important to note that while Figure 9-3 is showing you content that a user with Admin Links permissions would see, Figure 9-4 shows you the RWW portal for a user with Standard User permissions.

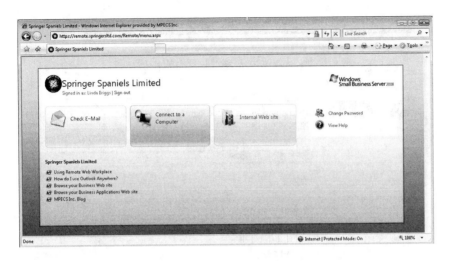

Figure 9-4
The new Remote Web Workplace portal page for a Standard User.

The Standard User with Admin Links has all of the same portal links with the addition of the Connect to Server link on the right side of the portal along with the addition of the Administration Links column in the list of various Web hyperlinks under the portal buttons.

The new RWW layout is very easy to use. The three primary feature access buttons are both color-coded and large to make it easy for the user to figure out which button to click.

Portal Header

As shown in Figure 9-5, you can set up a company logo across the top of the RWW title bar, along with RWW logo properties, the company name, the name of the user who logged on to the portal, a **Sign Out** link, and the Windows Small Business Server 2008 logo.

Notes

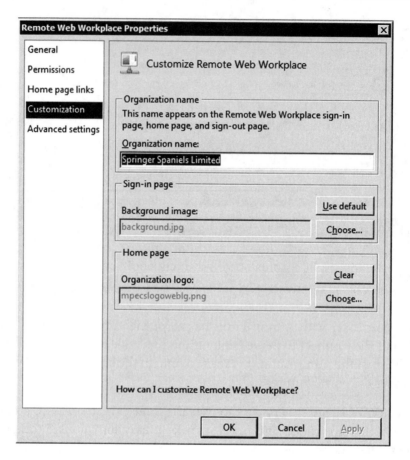

Figure 9-5
> *In the Remote Web Workplace Properties, you can add a company logo to be shown in the portal header under the Home page setting.*

The **Sign Out** link is very important, as it is probably one of the most important links on the entire Remote Web Workplace portal. Why? Because a user needs to sign out when she is finished using the portal. A user that gets up from a shared computer, say in an Internet café, leaving the browser still open, has left the next computer user a doorway into private company information!

While the Remote Desktop session and the Companyweb Internal Web site are protected by an extra level of authentication, Outlook Web Access is not. Fortunately the RWW portal and Outlook Web Access change password dialog boxes request the old password before allowing a user to change it to a new one.

Portal Buttons

The buttons are:

- **Check E-mail**. When you click on this button, you will have a new browser tab or a new browser window open depending on your browser configuration settings to the Outlook Web Access page.

- **Connect to a Computer**. Depending on a user's permissions, he may actually not have access to any computer on the SBS domain via remote connection. If this is the case, then the link will not be active. However, if the user has permission to access one computer he will be able to click on the button and will then be directed to log on to that particular workstation. If the user has permission to log on to more than one workstation remotely, then he will see a secondary **Show List** link at the bottom of the button. Click on that link to see a list of available workstations that the user can remotely connect to. Figure 9-6 shows you the pop-up that a user would see. Click on any one of the computers listed, then click on the **Make this my default computer**, and the Connect to a Computer button will be set to connect to that computer when clicked on.

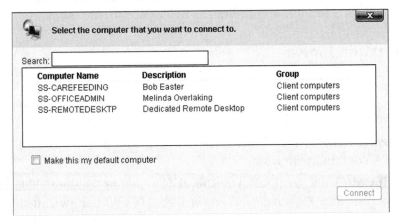

Figure 9-6
You can click on any computer that is available to you by clicking on the Show List link in the RWW.

- **Internal Web site**. Click on this link and a new tab or browser window will open with the Companyweb Internal site in it. But first, the user will be prompted for their network credentials. The username format will be just that: **BobEaster** with the user's password: **Lots to eat!**

Management Links

To the right of the buttons is an area with at least two links. One will be the Change Password link and the View Help link. If the user has Standard User with Admin links permissions, the **Connect to Server** link will be available, although the user will not be able to connect unless he has been given specific permission to the server itself.

- **Change Password**. The link is a new feature in the RWW portal. Click on it to get to a page that will ask you for your old password and to type your new one along with a confirmation of that password.

- **Connect to Server**. Click on this link to initiate a Remote Desktop session with the SBS server. Again, the user will need specific permissions set at the server to enable them to complete a connection.

- **View Help**. This link brings up the Windows Small Business Server 2008 Client Computer Help page. The page talks about SBS 2008 features, e-mail usage via Outlook Web Access information, how to work with the Companyweb Internal site, and more. While not an in-depth document by any means, this Help document does give a thorough overview of most of the SBS features and abilities as well as how to use them.

Organization Links

The list of links on the left-hand side of the portal under the buttons is the Organization Links. They contain some Help-related items along with links to your Office Live sites.

- **Using Remote Web Workplace**. You can find help items on the use of RWW and its features.

- **How do I use Outlook Anywhere?** Connecting Outlook 2003 or 2007 to your SBS Exchange server via RPC/HTTPS is now called Outlook Anywhere. This Help item contains the necessary information for configuring your Outlook 2003/7 to Exchange while outside of the SBS network. Keep in mind that the Outlook Anywhere username format is SpringersLTD\BobEaster.

- **Browse your Business Web site**. This link takes you to the Springer Spaniels' Office Live Web site.

- **Browse your Business Applications Web site**. You can connect to the Office Live SharePoint collaboration site using this link.

Administration Links

Users with Administration Links permissions will see the Administration Links to the right of the Organization links.

- **Windows Small Business Server Community**. When you click on this link, you will be taken to a Microsoft TechNet Web site that is solely focused on SBS. You will find links to blogs by Microsoft employees and click through to a list of the SBS MVPs, some Related Communities links that includes a link to the SMB Nation Web site, and pointers to other Microsoft communities, such as TechNet Edge.

- **Manage your Office Live Small Business account**. You click on this link and you will be taken to the Office Live Small Business management portal's home page. After logging on with Bob Easter's Live ID, you will be able to manage and configure all aspects of the Office Live sites.

- **Promote your business**. Click this link and you will be taken directly to the marketing portal on the Office Live Small Business management portal. You will need to log on to the site with Bob Easter's Live ID to gain access.

- **View Web site reports for your Business Web site**. You gain direct access to the Office Live Web site's analytics by clicking on this link. You will need to log on to the site with Bob Easter's Live ID to gain access.

- **Manage your Business Web site**. The Page Manager will be the first thing you see after logging on to the Office Live Small Business management portal via this link. You can then go on to edit the various Web pages on the Web site.

There you go! You now have an overview of the Remote Web Workplace and all of its available features.

Remote Web Workplace Idle Time

There is a difference in the way the new RWW handles idle time—that is the amount of time a session is not used. With RWW in SBS 2003, you could control how much time was needed before a session automatically closed itself by leaving the **I'm using a public or shared computer** option enabled for 20 minutes or disabled for 120 minutes of idle time.

The new RWW does not have this option to enable or disable. By default, the RWW session on SBS 2008 will close itself after 30 minutes of idle time. The time-out setting, from what we can tell as of this writing, is in the IIS manager under SBS Web Applications. Click on the Remote virtual directory then on Session State under ASP.NET. The time-out setting is near the bottom of the Session State pane.

Remote Web Workplace Advanced Features

There are a number of advanced features that can be tied into the Remote Web Workplace. While they are well beyond the scope of this introductory tome, one worth mentioning is Terminal Services Remote Applications or TS RemoteApps for short.

TS RemoteApps gives you the ability to publish a link in the Remote Web Workplace to an application that is resident on the Terminal Server. You click on the link to download an RDP file you will subsequently run. You end up with a window on your workstation with the application open and the ability to work with data on the local workstation and the remote network where the Terminal Server is.

The Terminal Server is the one doing all of the work. All the user sees is essentially a screenshot of the application running on the Terminal Server.

So, why is this important to mention? Well, think about the possibilities this gives you. You can publish all needed applications for the company in one spot. Internal users will run their applications via the Terminal Server. Users who have an Internet connection will be able to use the applications from virtually anywhere an Internet connection can be had!

The key to this feature working is the fact that SBS 2008 is running as a Terminal Services Gateway. Figure 9-7 shows you what the configuration looks like in the Windows Server 2008 Server Manager.

Notes

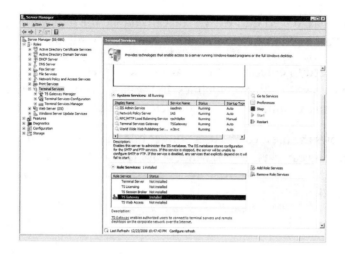

Figure 9-7
The TS Gateway role allows a direct Terminal Services session between a client system and a Terminal Server residing within the SBS network.

As of this writing, there are folks out there who have managed to get this feature working via the Remote Web Workplace, but none has published any kind of instruction on the Web yet. We will be including a chapter on configuring TS RemoteApps to be published via RWW in our Advanced Book, due in the second half of 2009.

User Password Expiry

One of the neat new features in the Remote Web Workplace is the notification that a user's password is soon to expire. Depending on how many days the SBS domain's Group Policy settings are configured to warn the user ahead of time, she will see Figure 9-8.

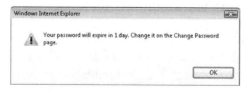

Figure 9-8
Whenever a user whose password will soon expire logs onto the Remote Web Workplace, she will be requested to change that password.

Once the user has logged into RWW, she can change the password by clicking on the **Change Password** link near the top right corner of the portal.

The user will need to enter her old password then enter a new one that meets the SBS domain password policy guidelines. In the case of our SPRINGERS methodology, that means a minimum of 10 characters including complex characters.

Figure 9-9 shows the message the user will see once her password has been successfully changed. She can close the IE window or tab once the process has completed.

Figure 9-9
Once the user has changed her password, she will see a confirmation message.

> **TIP:** This little feature is new to SBS 2008 and will provide organizations with mobile workers an opportunity to reduce support calls when the mobile worker's Outlook Anywhere no longer works, direct access to the Companyweb site seemingly stops working, or direct connection to a desktop via the SBS TS Gateway stops working.

With this overview of the Remote Web Workplace portal page now complete, we will delve into Outlook Web Access and its features along with how to connect to a workstation using the Connect to a Computer feature.

Since you have already delved into the Companyweb Internal Web site in Chapter 8, we will give a quick overview of the slight differences you will experience when connected to the Companyweb site via the Internet.

Outlook Web Access

Outlook Web Access (OWA) is now based on Exchange 2007 and is a vast improvement over its predecessor based on Exchange 2003. And by "vast," we mean "positively huge"! Check out the new Outlook Web Access interface in Figure 9-10.

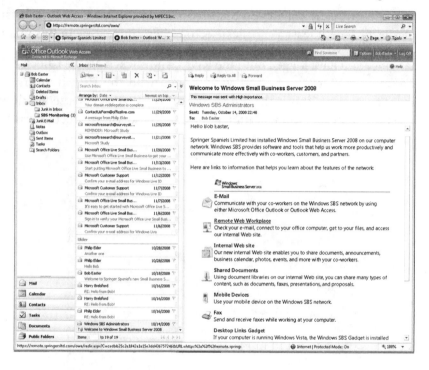

Figure 9-10
The new Outlook Web Access interface is so close to Outlook 2007 that it makes switching between the two a breeze!

Given the fact that OWA is much like Outlook 2007, we will not spend too much time delving into its usage. We will instead give you an overview, then delve into some of the features more unique to OWA. Suffice it to say, the right mouse button is much more your friend in SBS 2008 OWA than it ever was in SBS 2003 OWA!

There are a number of ways for you to gain access to Outlook Web Access.

- Connect via the Remote Web Workplace **Check E-Mail** link.
- Connect directly via https://remote.springersltd.com/owa on the Internet.

- Connect directly via https://remote.springersltd.com/owa from a SPRING-ERS workstation. When you connect directly you have the option to specify a longer idle time-out for your session, and/or to use Outlook Web Access Light that supports accessibility features for users who are blind or have poor vision.

- Connect directly via https://ss-sbs/owa from a SPRINGERS workstation. Expect to see at least a certificate error when connecting in this manner.

Note that, once you have logged onto the RWW and clicked on the **Check E-Mail** button, a new browser tab or window will open with the URL https://remote. springersltd.com/owa/. This is the direct access URL that can be used both internally or via the Internet. You will find all of the SBS services direct access URLs gathered into one spot in Appendix Z.

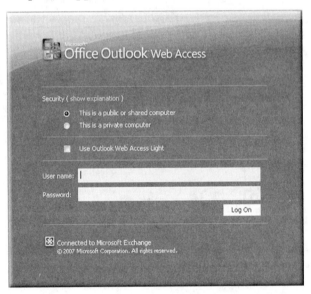

Figure 9-11
When you connect to Outlook Web Access directly, you will need to authenticate via Exchange.

Given the way the RWW is set up, you could potentially open Outlook Web Access, a Remote Desktop session to your workstation at the office, and a browser tab or window opened to the Companyweb Internal Web site. This would give you the ability to send and receive e-mail, shift data back and forth via the Companyweb site, and work with data directly on the SBS network.

Outlook Web Access GUI

As already mentioned and shown in Figure 9-10, the new OWA Graphical User Interface (GUI) is new and improved. Your ability to navigate around the interface is very close to being on par with the full version of Outlook 2007. What this means for your users is an ability to shift between using Outlook Web Access and the full version of Outlook with very little retraining.

OWA Header

The OWA Header has changed quite a bit! You now have an address book search available. Check it out in Figure 9-12.

Figure 9-12
You can now search every address book under the sun!

This is especially advantageous if you have a number of contact names across the various address books available to you at your desk. You no longer need to juggle contacts between your various other contacts lists.

Options

You can set your **Options** for the various features in OWA which we will outline for you here. Your best bet beyond our overview is to take a deep dive and click in and through the various options available to you. The options are numerous and give you a lot more control over your Outlook Web Access experience:

- **Regional Settings**. You can set your language, date, and time format options.

- **Messaging**. You can: set message options, such as the number to display or play a sound when a new e-mail arrives; set your e-mail signature for outgoing messages; select either HTML or plain text format along with the font to use; decide whether to track outgoing e-mail; and choose how the Reading Pane will behave.

TIP: Something to keep in mind when it comes to Read Receipts is that some users have set their e-mail client, whether Outlook, OWA, or others, to never send a response by default. In fact, that is one of the options available to you in this Options Area of OWA too. While this feature can have its uses in, say, troubleshooting e-mail delivery problems, in many cases it can be an annoyance. Most users will respond to an e-mail if they deem there is a need to, thus the "Never send a response" to Read Receipts.

The following option has to do with spelling. Since spellcheckers are essentially ubiquitous, there is no reason why an e-mail should leave a professional business with misspelled words. Grammatical issues such as "their" and "there" or "alot" (sic) instead of "a lot" are another issue altogether!

- **Spelling**. You can have OWA check the spelling in an e-mail prior to being sent. You can choose the default language setting for OWA to use. Note that Canadians spell some words slightly differently—for example, "labour" instead of "labor." So the appropriate dictionary should be chosen for your locale and audience.

- **Calendar Options**. You can enable capabilities like week numbers and set when the first day of the week starts. If you work Sunday through Thursday, you can set OWA to that work week along with your typical working hours. Default Reminders can be added to all appointments if you desire, and you can set how OWA handles shared meeting appointments, updates, and meeting requests.

- **Out of Office Assistant**. You have at your hands a very robust feature to set OOF (Out of Office) replies. You can set OOF to send replies only during a specified period, such as when you are off-site. You can also set it to send an OOF only to internal SBS domain contacts, to external senders if they are in your Contacts list, or to all external senders. Pretty neat, eh?

- **Rules**. The e-mail-sorting rules are virtually identical to your sorting rules available in Outlook 2003/7. You can create a rule by right clicking on an e-mail, or by creating them via this option. You can use this option to edit or delete existing rules as well.

- **E-mail Security**. You can set up S/MIME to enable e-mail encryption as well as digital signatures. A digital ID, as in certificate, along with a download to the connected workstation are required to enable this feature.

- **Junk E-mail**. You can manage your built-in spam filter's Safe Senders List (White List), Blocked Senders List (Black List) and Safe Recipients List to which you add mailing list e-mail addresses and the like so Exchange does not block them.

- **Change Password**. If there is a need to change your SBS domain password, you can use this option to do so with ease. This option accomplishes the same thing as the Change Password link in the Remote Web Workplace.

- **General Settings**. You can choose which address list Exchange will look through first, either the Global Address List or Contacts folder, when addressing a new e-mail. You can change the OWA Appearance, or "skin," from the default Seattle Sky to Carbon Black, Xbox 360, or Zune. Figure 9-13 shows you the Xbox 360 theme. You can also enable or disable Accessibility features.

Figure 9-13
Need a change of pace for your Outlook Web Access look? Then change its appearance!

- **Deleted Items**. You can enable an automatic emptying of the Deleted Items folder when you log off or gain access to already deleted items to recover them just as you would in the full version of Outlook 2007.

- **Mobile Devices**. You now have the ability to manage your Windows Mobile devices that are connected to your SBS Exchange. You can remove an old device, remotely wipe the device if it was lost or stolen, display the recovery password, and view the connectivity log.

- **About**. This is not so much an option but an overview of all of the relevant OWA connectivity information: OWA version, installed options, server and mailbox addresses, and more.

When you are done looking through the Options, you can click on the **Mail** button to get back to your Inbox.

Mailbox Connection

A new feature to OWA is the ability to connect to another user's Mailbox. Figure 9-14 shows you the pop-up dialogue box.

Figure 9-14
 If you have full access permissions to another user's mailbox, you can connect to it!

And, as the caption states, you need to have full use permissions to the user's mailbox to get access to it in OWA.

TIP: The one situation where a user will need access would be in the case of an executive assistant who needs full access to the executive's mailbox. Sometimes, just sharing Outlook calendars—or setting them up via the Companyweb or Public Folders—does not work for keeping things efficient and may not be the best way to meet compliance requirements.

Once you have entered the name of the user's mailbox you want to open, click the **Open** button. If you are on your SPRINGERS lab setup, you can type **Norm**, then the **Open** button, and you will be prompted by Exchange with both Norm Senior's and Norm Junior's mailboxes. Hover over either name and you will see a **Properties** link that you can click on to verify that you have the right user along with his current Free/Busy status.

You can cancel the request by clicking on the "X" in the top right-hand corner of the dialogue box.

Log Off

One of the most important buttons or links in any SBS remote session is **Log Off**. We cannot emphasize enough that when a user is finished working with her OWA session, she should click that button before walking away from the workstation or laptop.

After clicking the button, you will be greeted with a successful logoff message from Exchange. You can click the **Close Window** button to close the browser tab or window.

Since much of your OWA experience while working with e-mail, calendaring, etc., is similar to your Outlook 2003/7 experiences, we will mention some of the new OWA features for the next sections. Keep in mind that you may see these features in the Outlook application, but they are new to OWA on Exchange 2007. Some features have actually been added with Exchange 2007 Service Pack 1.

Help

Just below the Log Off button is a **Help** button. The Help resource in Exchange is awesome. If you have any questions while working in the various areas of OWA, you will more than likely find the answer you are looking for in the Help.

The blue Help button or a blue button just showing the white question mark in it—this might be the case if you are in one of the various dialogue windows such as when you create an appointment—are always available.

Check it out, as it will fill in all of the blanks!

Categories

You can assign Categories to your E-mail, Calendar appointments, Contacts, Tasks, and items in Public Folders. This is just as straightforward as it is in Outlook 2007. While in OWA, you can change the view for Mail, Contacts, and Tasks to List View (Single Line icon) to see the category colors along with the ability to click on an item to add, remove, or change its category.

Using categories can greatly improve your ability to find and sort items in Outlook 2007. And that is the key. Using Outlook 2007 in tandem with OWA can greatly improve your user's ability to communicate and keep track of things.

Mail

The default view once you have logged into OWA is the Mail view. The Inbox will be selected, and the top-most e-mail in your e-mail list will be the e-mail of choice in your Reading Pane.

Have a look at Figure 9-15. As you can see, you have a number of choices for sorting your e-mail.

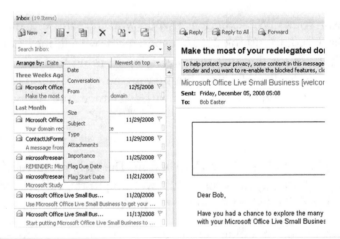

Figure 9-15
You can sort your e-mail almost any way possible in OWA.

Click on the **Arrange by:** header and you will see the options available to you in Figure 9-15. And, just as you have options for sorting your e-mail, you will find buttons with options for your Reading Pane—whether your e-mails are listed in a single line or multiple lines, as seen in Figure 9-15—and to move or copy the selected e-mail(s) to another folder. The rest of the buttons in the line under the header are your standard fair: delete an e-mail, check for new e-mail, and message-specific.

Right click on an e-mail and you will see your options to reply, mark as unread, create a sorting rule, set the Junk E-mail status for it or the sender, delete, move, or copy the e-mail to another folder.

You have the ability to create subfolders and sort your e-mail automatically into those folders. An example sort would be having a folder for a client with a sorting rule based on his e-mail domain or domains being moved into that folder. Any new e-mail that lands in that folder will cause the folder's appearance to **bold**. This gives you the ability to quickly ascertain your e-mail answering priorities. Check out Figure 9-16, as it shows you what a folder looks like with new e-mail in it.

Figure 9-16
  All of Bob Easter's SBS Daily and Weekly reports are automatically sorted to the SBS Monitoring folder.

Calendar

Using the calendar to manage your appointments and meetings can help to keep things under control when there are a lot of things that need to be done! You can manage your appointments and create or modify meetings.

As already mentioned, you can set the OWA calendar to your work week. One of the view options is to show the current work week or any work week of your choosing in the past or future. Other view options are for the day, full week, or by the month.

When scheduling a meeting, you can choose those attendees who are required and those who are optional, and you can use the Scheduling Assistant tab to see other SPRINGERS users' calendar status to help with scheduling. Click on any of the attendee links, such as Required, and you will get a pop-up window containing the Global Address List and other internal address books, along with your Outlook Contacts list.

Contacts

As was mentioned earlier, Categories can greatly improve a user's efficiency. One of the things you will notice, at least as of this writing, is the inability to sort your contacts by category while in List View.

One of the new OWA features is the ability to add, remove, and manage e-mail Distribution Lists.

Distribution Lists

The Distribution List feature is quite robust. You have the ability to add and remove members; click on the list to get a quick view of list membership; and click on any member in the List View to bring up his or her contact properties so you can edit, categorize the list, and more.

Distribution Lists can be used to send company newsletters, broadcast e-mail specials for those who opt in to receive them, or perform other creative tasks that do not involve sending out unsolicited commercial e-mail (SPAM).

Tasks

Tasks are the To Dos that you set up for yourself. You can use them to track a task from start to finish, establish a timeline along with a progress indicator, or even insert a reminder to pop up in OWA, Outlook, or your Windows Mobile device if you have one connected.

The Tasks list is also used when you flag a Contact for a follow-up at a later time or when you flag an e-mail to follow up on. To flag an e-mail, at the right hand side of the e-mail, click on the flag to get a list of follow-up options. Once a task is complete, you can right click on its flag to Mark Complete.

You can enable or disable a default reminder to be attached to any task in the Calendar Options section in the OWA Options list mentioned earlier in this chapter.

Documents

A new feature, and a welcome one at that, is the ability to gain access to files located on an SBS file share such as the Company shared folder we created in Chapter 5 or on the Companyweb Internal Web site.

Getting OWA file share access set up is beyond the scope of this introductory book, so look for the proper configuration procedure in our upcoming SBS 2008 Advanced book. Also, check our blogs to see if we have posted any configuration steps and caveats there too.

Figure 9-17
Once you have connected to a file share, such as the Company shared folder, you can gain Read-Only access to any documents stored there.

As you can see in Figure 9-17, access to a folder share is relatively straightforward. Once you have established the connection, you can right click on the share you need and click on **Add to Favorites**. From there on in, you will have quick access to that share via the Favorite.

If you need a file locally, you can double click on the file to open it, then use the Save As dialogue to place a copy on your workstation. You can then modify the local file and move it back to the network when you get back in the office. A file pulled from the Companyweb Internal Web site could be uploaded back to the site after modification via the Remote Web Workplace link or via direct link.

Public Folders

Public folders is a centrally located folder set that you can access via Outlook 2003/7 or OWA. Out of the box, there are no folders set up on SBS 2008. So, you will need to run through the setup process to establish the following folder types:

- **Mail-Enabled Folder**. An e-mail-enabled folder allows you to connect a number of users to work with e-mail located in that folder.

- **Calendar Folder**. You may need to manage a number of users' schedules or have a companywide calendar for vacation schedules. If there is such a need, you can use a Calendar folder to locate all of the relevant appointments and meetings.

- **Contact Folder**. You can centralize your company Contacts so that everyone's Outlook or OWA has access to the same Contacts list.

- **Task Folder**. You can set up a central Tasks folder to assign Tasks to users, monitor the ongoing status of Tasks, and perform other Task-related central management.

- **Notes Folder**. You can share company notes with useful information in them.

Public folders can be set up in such a way as to limit who has access to what folder. The permissions structure is tiered too. That means you can have a group of users who have Read-Only access while others can create and edit only their own items. Still other users may have the ability to add, edit, and delete all items in a folder.

Keep in mind that the Companyweb Internal Web site also has much of the same functionality with the ability to tie into Outlook as well. How the similarities between the Public Folders and SharePoint Web sites features set has yet to play itself out in the SMB community. As of this writing, the Exchange team has professed full support for the Public Folders feature built into Exchange 2007. But only time will tell what wins the data store war: SharePoint or Exchange-based public folders.

Remote Desktop Web Access

Many of the SPRINGERS users are using a workstation as opposed to a laptop. This means that they can gain access to their workstation from the Internet using the Internet Explorer browser as the starting point.

Once connected to the Remote Web Workplace, any user who has permission to access a workstation remotely will be able to either click on the **Connect to a Computer** button to see a list of available workstations or connect directly to her workstation if she is permitted to connect to only one.

For Bob Easter, who can access a number of different workstations remotely, you will see that he has an additional **Show list** link inside of the Connect to a

Computer button. When you click on this link, you will see a pop-up window showing the available workstations as shown in Figure 9-18.

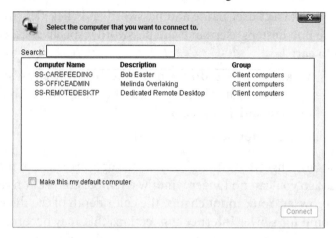

Figure 9-18
Bob can access three different workstations remotely.

TIP: For you SBS consultants and SBSers, having the ability to limit the workstation list to only those computers users who have permission to access will greatly reduce some of the initial struggles they may have experienced in the SBS 2003 days when they saw the entire list of workstations. This was especially true for clients who named their workstations in relatively generic ways. That situation would almost always lead to the question, "Which one was mine again?" Sometimes, that question would be followed by a support call.

Notice in Figure 9-18 that there is an ability to set the default computer from those presented in the list. The default computer is the one you will connect to directly if you click on the **Connect to a Computer** button in the RWW.

The process of connecting to the computer is quite simple:

1. Click on the **Connect to a Computer** button.

2. If presented with a list, select one and click the **Connect** button.

3. If warned about wanting to start a remote connection, verify that the correct local resources are selected and click the **Connect** button. Your local

resources can be things like printers connected to your computer and/or the clipboard that stores copied content such as text or an image.

4. Enter the correct user name and password and click **OK**. In this case we will use Bob Easter's username and password respectively: **BobEaster** and **Lots to eat!**

   - Make sure the domain at the bottom says springersltd. If it does not, then append the domain to the username: **springersltd\BobEaster**.

5. The Remote Desktop session should start.

Note that you no longer have the ability to set options such as the size of the remote display, so you can no longer window a remote connection in your Internet Explorer browser. You cannot change the color depth of the display either, so keep this in mind for slower Internet connections that may become congested if more than a few users are going to be connected at the same time.

Once finished with the remote session, log off the workstation just as you normally would. If the RWW portal is still open and there is nothing left to do, then click the **Sign Out** link near the username at the top left of the portal.

Companyweb Internal Web Site

Since we spent a good deal of time going through the various Companyweb Internal Web site in the previous chapter, you can rest assured that you have full access to all of the Companyweb goodness via the Remote Web Workplace **Internal Web site** button.

But first, you will be asked for your SBS domain credentials. The username is the same as it would be at any workstation: **BobEaster** along with the password: **Lots to eat!**

When the Companyweb page comes up in a new browser tab or browser window, you will notice that the URL being used to connect to the site is:

- https://remote.springersltd.com:987

You can use this URL to connect directly to the Companyweb Internal Web site via the Internet using pretty much any Web browser.

Once you are finished with the Companyweb Internal Web site, click on the **Welcome Bob Easter** link near the top right corner of the page and then click on the **Sign Out** link.

Outlook Anywhere

A detailed Help link, **How do I use Outlook Anywhere?**, is available in the RWW for getting Outlook Anywhere up and running.

Assuming that you are using a third-party trusted certificate, the process is actually quite simple:

1. Click **Start**, and then click **Control Panel**.
   - If you are viewing Control Panel in the default Category view, switch to Classic view, and then double click **Mail**.
   - If you are viewing Control Panel in Classic view, double click **Mail**

2. In the Mail Setup dialog box, click **E-mail accounts**.

3. Click **View or change existing e-mail accounts** then click **Next**. You may not get this dialogue box depending on your Office and OS versions or if you are setting up a workstation that is outside of the SBS domain.

4. In the E-mail accounts dialog box, click **Microsoft Exchange Server**, and then click **Change**. If there are no accounts on the computer, click the **New** button.

5. In the Microsoft Exchange Server box, type the local name of the Exchange server: **SS-SBS.springersltd.local**.

6. In the User Name box, type the user name that you use to log on to the Remote Web Workplace: **Bob Easter**. Do not click **Check Name**.

7. On the Exchange Server settings page, click the **More Settings** button.

8. On the Connection tab, under Outlook Anywhere (Outlook 2007), click the **Connect to Microsoft Exchange using HTTP** button.

9. Click the **Exchange Proxy Settings** button.

10. For the Exchange Proxy Settings, set the following then click **OK**:
    - Use this URL **remote.springersltd.com**.

- Check **Only connect to proxy servers that have this principal name in their certificate** then set it to: **msstd:remote.springersltd. com**.
- Leave **On fast networks…** unchecked.
- Leave **On slow networks…** checked.
- Proxy authentication settings: **Basic Authentication**.

11. Click **Apply** and **OK**.
12. Click the **Check Names** button.
13. Authenticate:
    - User name: **springersltd\BobEaster**
    - Password: **Lots to eat!**
    - Once authenticated, both the server name and the user name should be underlined, which indicates a successful logon.
14. Click the **Next** button. Note the location where e-mail will be stored.
15. Click the **Finish** button.

Now, for laptops that are set up on the SBS domain and have Office 2007 installed on them, Outlook 2007 should pick up the user's Outlook Anywhere proxy settings automatically. Outlook 2003 will still require the above setup procedure for domain joined workstations though.

When the user is outside the SBS network and has an Internet connection, he will need to use the following username and password:

- **Springersltd\BobEaster**
- **Lots to eat!**

Note the inclusion of the domain name prefix. You need to have the credentials formatted this way to have a successful Outlook to Exchange connection.

Outlook Mobile Access

Outlook Mobile Access setup is pretty much the same whether you are manually connecting a Windows Mobile 5, 6, or 6.1 Professional device.

Note that we are assuming you have a third-party trusted certificate installed on the SBS for your SSL needs. If you do not, then you will need to pull a copy of the certificate from the SBS Public share and place it on your device. From there, you must double click on the certificate on the device to import it into the local certificate store on the device.

On the Windows Mobile device (Ours is a WM 6.1 Pro):

1. Click the **Start** button and tap on **Programs**.
2. Click on **ActiveSync**.
3. Click on **Configure Server**.
4. On the Server Settings page, enter the following and tap **Next**:
   - Server address: **remote.springersltd.com**
   - SSL: **Required**.
5. For the User Information, enter the following and click **Next**.
   - User name: **BobEaster**
   - Password: **Lots to eat!**
   - Domain: **springersltd**
   - Save Password: **Checked**
6. Enable the following data sets:
   - **Contacts**
   - **Calendar**
   - **E-mail**
   - **Tasks**
7. Click **Finish**.

You can initiate a manual Sync with Exchange by tapping the **Sync** button near the bottom of your device's display. The layout for item locations will vary by device vendor and phone/data service provider.

Once your device has finished synchronizing your mailbox, you will be able to gain access to your E-mail Inbox, Contacts, Calendar appointments, and Tasks.

Now, if you have extensive E-mail sorting rules along with the requisite folders, you will need to take a couple of extra steps to get any e-mail folder beyond the Inbox to synchronize to the device.

1. Click your way into the Outlook Inbox.

2. Click **Menu**.

3. Click **Tools**.

4. Click **Manage Folders**.

5. There will be a + to the left of the Inbox; tap on that and put a check beside any folder you want to synchronize to the device. You can also sync your Sent Items and Outlook-based RSS Feeds.

6. Click **OK** when you are finished.

The device should automatically synchronize the newly selected folders to the device.

One final thing you may need is an e-mail signature for your device's outgoing e-mail.

1. While still in your Outlook Inbox, tap **Menu**.

2. Click **Tools**.

3. Click **Options**.

4. Click the **Signatures** button.

5. You can enable the following settings along with setting your signature, then tap **OK** twice:

   - Account: **Outlook E-mail**.

   - Use signature with this account: **Checked**.

   - Use when replying and forwarding: **Checked**.

   - Signature: Thanks, Bob. Sent from an SBS integrated Windows Mobile Phone.

From there, you are pretty much good to go!

Any changes you make on the device will show up in your OWA and your desktop Outlook.

One thing to keep in mind regarding some customized settings in Outlook at the workstation will not extend to your device. For example, the Outlook setting to save all replies to an e-mail in the folder the original e-mail was invoked at the workstation, the device will behave differently. If you reply to the e-mail on the device, the reply will remain in the Sent Items folder on the device and subsequently the Sent Items folder in your Outlook and OWA. It will not be otherwise processed according to your customized rule.

VPN Connectivity

If you need to have users connect to the network via the built-in SBS PPTP VPN, you need to run the **Configure a virtual private network** wizard you will find in the SBS Console Network tab Connectivity sub-tab.

Create a Connection

We will use Windows Vista to create a connection here. Windows XP will be somewhat similar in its set up procedure.

1. Click **Start, Connect To**.
2. Click the **Set up a connection or network** link near the bottom left of the Connect to a network window.
3. Click on the **Connect to a workplace** option and click **Next**.
4. Click the **Use my Internet connection (VPN)** option.
5. Click on the **I'll set up an Internet connection later** option.
6. Set your Internet address settings then click the **Next** button:
   - Internet address: **remote.springersltd.com**
   - Destination name: **Springer Spaniels VPN**.
7. You can set your username and password if needed, then click the **Create** button.

Once you receive a successful connection creation message, you will need to click back into the **Connect to window** to initiate the VPN connection.

Connect to SBS Resources via VPN

If you are connecting to the SBS network via a SPRINGERS domain-joined laptop or workstation, you will be able to connect to any mapped network drives just as you normally would.

If not, you will be able to find any shared resources on SBS by opening Windows Explorer and typing either of the following in the Address Bar:

- \\SS-SBS\
- \\SS-SBS.SpringersLtd.Local\

One of the above links should get you to the root of the SBS server.

While you will have access to all of your SBS-based resources, there are limitations to the VPN setup, such as the loss of bandwidth due to the PPTP tunnel session.

VPN Access Permissions

Now, out of the box, SBS will allow only SBS Domain Admins to VPN into the server. To verify this, in the SBS Console click on the **Users and Groups** tab and then the **User Roles** sub-tab. Double click on the **Network Administrator role** and click **Groups**. You will see Windows SBS Virtual Private Network Users in Group Membership.

The simplest way to give your existing users, and any additional users, access via VPN is to set up a User Role for VPN access and then use the Change group membership wizard.

1. Open the SBS Console and click **Continue** for the UAC.

2. Click the **Users and Groups** tab.

3. Right click on any Standard User, in this case **Barry McKechnie**, and click on **Add a new user role based on this user account's properties**.

4. When the User Role wizard window comes up, name it: **Standard User with VPN Access**.

5. Give the User Role the following description: **Users can VPN into the server.**

6. Leave the defaults checked and click the **OK** button. Figure 9-19 shows you this dialogue box filled out.

Notes

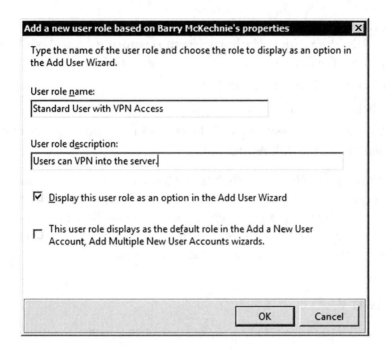

Figure 9-19
Once you have created the VPN-based User Role, you will still need to add the necessary permissions group.

7. Now, click on the **User Roles** tab in the SBS Console.

8. Double click on the new **Standard User - VPN Access** user role.

9. Click on the **Groups** category.

10. Click the **Add** button.

11. Click on **Windows SBS Virtual Private Network Users** and click the **Add** button.

12. Click **Apply** and **OK** twice.

13. Repeat Steps 3 through 12 using Bob Easter's (a Standard User with Admin Links) account to have a VPN user role for Standard User with Admin Links. Name it **Standard User - Admin Links and VPN**.

14. Click on the **Users** tab.

15. Click the **Change user role for user accounts** task under User Tasks.

16. Select the new **Standard User - VPN Access** user role, **Replace user permissions or settings** radio button, and click **Next**.

17. Select the user accounts that need their user role changed. In the case of SPRINGERS, **Norm Hasborn**, **Norm Hasborn Jr.**, and **David Halberson** will be added to the list.

18. Click the **Change user role** button.

19. Click the **Finish** button.

20. You can then repeat Steps 15 through 19 to change the user role for any Standard User with Admin Links.

You now have users who can VPN into the SBS domain, and you have provided yourself a quick and painless way of setting up any new users who will require VPN access. Having to manage VPN access by manually adding the Windows SBS Virtual Private Network Users security group to the user's properties can be painful and leaves lots of room for mistakes to happen.

Summary

You now have a pretty good big-picture view of SBS 2008's mobility and remote connectivity features.

You discovered that the Remote Web Workplace portal is a very robust remote connectivity solution for your SBS users. You have the ability to provide your users with access to the following SBS services through RWW:

- Outlook Web Access, whose feature set is more in line with Outlook 2007.

- Remote Desktop access to any computer a user may have permission to access on the SBS domain.

- Companyweb Internal Web site access can be used to work with documents directly, upload or download content, or work with other Companyweb SharePoint features.

- Hyperlinks to various SBS-related and other online resources.

From the Remote Web Workplace portal, you were introduced to some of the key new features in Outlook Web Access, such as the ability to connect to other users' mailboxes, fine-tune your OWA experience via the OWA Options, work with appointments and meeting requests, create and manage Distribution Lists, and gain access to SBS-shared folders.

The newly named Outlook Anywhere and Outlook Mobile Access setup steps were outlined for you along with some added customizations that can work on your Windows Mobile device.

The SBS 2008 PPTP VPN structure is available out of the box, but you now know that you need to tweak things a little to get your SBS Standard Users and SBS Standard Users with Admin Links to gain access to the server via VPN.

CHAPTER 10

Fax and Print

Introduction

Two critical forms of communication within and outside of an office are sent via fax and print. Having incoming faxes being routed via e-mail or sent directly to the CompanyWeb site can save a company time and paper.

In the case of the SPRINGERS methodology, there are 10 users. Therefore, when it comes to printing documentation in the SPRINGERS office, having one printer capable of handling the office printing volume at low cost is critical. That is why we chose the HP LaserJet 4345MFP. The printer is easy to operate, fits into an SBS network with ease, and does not require any messy toner bottles or changes like a photocopier. Changing toners is the same as changing a toner on a regular HP LaserJet printer.

To set up the SBS fax service, there are two sides to work with: The SBS server and the user's workstation.

> **TIP:** When it comes to consulting on a multi-function printer setup versus a photocopier setup, take great care to get all of the relevant information on the units being considered.

Competition is fierce in this particular market, so it is especially important to make sure the products are going to perform as expected. Keep an eye on your *overall* cost per copy. That includes *all* costs, including maintenance contracts if they are being offered.

Keep in mind that compatibility with the SBS network is important. Make sure drivers for the products being considered will work on both 32bit and 64bit Windows XP Professional, Windows Vista, and Windows Server 2008 systems. Verify that they will be able to print via a network connection using TCP/IP, have a Web management interface, have a scan to a network folder feature that will work with the SBS security setup, and offer users the ability to manage their print/fax/scan jobs via the console, their workstation, and a Web console.

SBS Fax

Since you have completed the deployment steps in Chapter 5, you now need to set up the SBS Fax service.

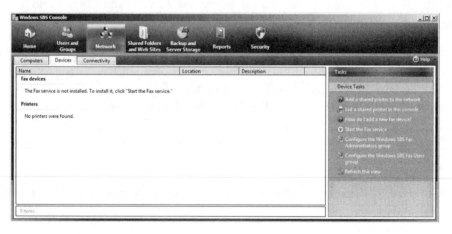

Figure 10-1
*You need to click on the **Start the Fax service** link under **Device Tasks** to set up the SBS Fax.*

SBS Fax Modem

Now, before you configure the fax service, make sure that your 56K fax modem has been installed. Follow your fax modem's manual for installation and to configure the correct driver for a Windows Server 2008 64bit operating system. If no specific instructions exist, connect the modem and have the **Found New Hardware** wizard search the driver CD for the best driver to use.

In the case of our trusty SPRINGERS SBS Intel Server, we connected a U.S. Robotics 56K Faxmodem USB to a USB port on the server and had the driver CD handy. Once the modem was installed, we were good to go!

SBS Fax Service Setup

Begin the fax service setup:

1. Open the **Windows SBS Console** if it is not already open. Click **Continue** for the UAC prompt.

2. Click on the **Network** tab.

3. Click on the **Devices** tab.

4. Click on the **Start the Fax service** link.

5. At the **Do you want to install the Fax service?** pop-up, click on the **Yes** button to start the installation. An installation status window will come up once the install routine starts.

6. You will get a **The Fax service has started successfully** window. Click the **OK** button.

7. Click the **Yes** button when you are prompted to run the **Configure Fax Service Wizard**. You will get a **"Please wait..."** message while the Fax Component is installed and configured.

8. When you are prompted to specify information for the fax cover page, click **Next**:

   a. Organization: **Springer Spaniels Limited**

   b. Phone number: **206-555-1356**

   c. Fax number: **206-555-1599**

d. Address: **3456 Beach Front Road, Bainbridge Island, WA 98110**.

9. You will need to type the fax header text **Springer Spaniels** and click **Next**. Note that the fax header is limited in the number of characters you can input.

10. The fax modem is the next item to choose. Put a checkmark beside your modem. In the case of our SPRINGERS methodology, it is the **U.S. Robotics 56K Faxmodem USB**, Click **Next**. Note that if the server had multiple modems installed, it is possible to have the fax delivery location to be set per modem.

11. Your next step is to designate the route all incoming faxes will take. You can choose all or one or a combination of the four destination options you are given:

   a. **Route through e-mail**: One or more e-mail destinations.

   b. **Store in a document library**: Internal Web site – Fax Center.

   c. **Print**: Choose a networked printer to print off the faxes.

   d. **Store in a folder**: Incoming faxes will be stored in the chosen folder as a TIF image file.

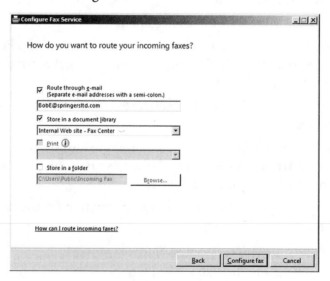

Figure 10-2
You can route your incoming faxes in one or more of the destination options given.

12. Once you have chosen your fax destinations, click the **Configure fax** button.

13. The **Configuring Fax service on your server** status window will show the fax setup progress. Once you see three green buttons with checkmarks in them, click the **Finish** button.

You will now see your fax modem listed under **Fax devices** in the Windows SBS Console.

For Windows XP and 2000 Professional boxes, the Group Policy Deployment automatically connect the clients to the SBS Fax service. We will discuss more, later in this chapter.

For Windows Vista, we need to run through a couple of configuration steps on the Windows Vista workstation. That will be discussed later in this chapter after we have deployed our printers, via Group Policy.

SBS Network Printing

Physically Connecting a Printer

Now, for those who may be running the SPRINGERS methodology in a virtual lab setup, we need to look at another option besides the network one.

So, for those of you in the classroom, or running on Hyper-V, here is another method to get a printer setup into your SBS server: Install one on the LPT port.

To do so:

1. Click on the **Start** button.

2. Type **Printers [Enter]**.

3. Right click anywhere under the list of printers and click on **Run as administrator.** Then click the **Add Printer** menu item. See Figure 10-3.

Notes:

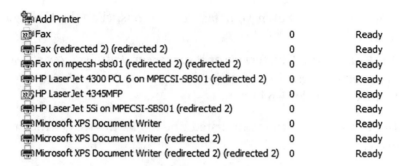

Add Printer		
Fax	0	Ready
Fax (redirected 2) (redirected 2)	0	Ready
Fax on mpecsh-sbs01 (redirected 2) (redirected 2)	0	Ready
HP LaserJet 4300 PCL 6 on MPECSI-SBS01 (redirected 2)	0	Ready
HP LaserJet 4345MFP	0	Ready
HP LaserJet 5Si on MPECSI-SBS01 (redirected 2)	0	Ready
Microsoft XPS Document Writer	0	Ready
Microsoft XPS Document Writer (redirected 2)	0	Ready
Microsoft XPS Document Writer (redirected 2) (redirected 2)	0	Ready

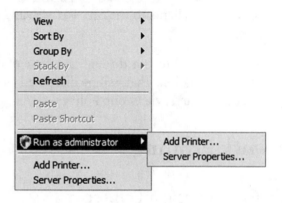

Figure 10-3
*You must right click under the list of printers and select the **Run as administrator** menu item to install a printer physically connected to the server.*

TIP: When the Add Printer menu comes up after clicking through the above steps, note that you must use this method to install a wireless or Bluetooth printer as well.

4. Click **Continue** for the UAC prompt.

5. Click on the **Add a local printer** button.

6. Choose **LPT1: (Printer Port)** for the **Use an existing port** radio button and click **Next**.

7. Choose **HP** for a manufacturer and **HP LaserJet 4345 MFP PCL 5** for your printer model and click **Next**.

8. Leave the default **HP LaserJet 4345 MFP PCL 5** printer name as well as the **Set as the default printer** checked. Click **Next**.

9. Once the printer is installed, fill out the following information and click **Next**:

    a. Share name: **HPLJ4345MFP**

    b. Location: **Front Office**

    c. Comment: **HP Multi-Function Fax and Printer**

10. Once successfully installed, click the **Finish** button.

You now have a printer that you will be able to use for Group Policy deployment later in the chapter and for any other network printing-related needs.

Connecting a Network Printer

The Help file indicates that if you are connecting a network-based printer, in our SPRINGERS methodology an HP LaserJet has been plugged into the Gigabit switch, it may or may not show up as an option under the **Network, Devices**.

TIP: When plugging a network based printer into the SBS network, the printer will likely be set up to get an IP address via DHCP. To make things easier to manage down the road, especially in the case of multiple network printers, we keep DHCP enabled on all network printers and assign an IP address to the printer by DHCP Reservation in the DHCP manager on the server.

As an example, a printer can then be moved from the main SBS office to another branch office that may have its own Windows Server 2008 Standard Edition serving Active Directory, DNS, and DHCP to the local branch office users. The local server can have a DHCP reservation created for the printer so that users can begin to use it as soon as it is plugged into the network and turned on.

Also, make sure to download the newest PCL driver, PostScript driver, and any firmware updates from the printer manufacturer's Web site! If the firmware update is available, please make sure to run it to update the printer, if the firmware on the printer is out of date. The new drivers and firmware will improve printer stability and printing speeds.

In the case of our SPRINGERS methodology, we have just plugged the HP Laser-Jet into the network and turned it on.

The first thing to do is give it a new IP address via DHCP reservation so that SBS and the workstations can always find it! SBS will give the printer a new address, but it will be from the regular IP address pool all workstations use.

> **TIP:** For SBSers and SBS consultants: When configuring our IP subnet for clients, we always use the 192.168.40.0/24 subnet. That is, any address between 192.168.40.1 and 192.168.40.254 can be used on the SBS network. We tend to put servers at the top end of the scale with all of our SBS boxes getting 192.168.40.254. Routers are assigned 192.168.40.1 and a DHCP exclusion is set up for IP addresses 192.168.40.1 through 192.168.40.10 and 192.168.40.245 through 192.168.40.254 depending on the size of SBS network.

> So, for our SPRINGERS HP LaserJet printer, we are going to assign the printer the IP address of **192.168.40.5** to leave a little room both above and below it for other devices that may be added to the network later, such as a Point of Sale payment terminal, networked receipt printer, and other such devices.

The first thing to do is to have a look at the DHCP snap-in, to see what IP the printer picked up:

1. Open the **Windows SBS Native Tools Management** console.
2. For the UAC, click **Continue**.
3. Expand **DHCP**.
4. Expand **ss-sbs.springersltd.local**.
5. Expand **IPv4**.
6. Expand **Scope [192.168.40.0] springersltd.local**.
7. Click on the **Address Leases** folder.

8. The printer will have a blank **Name** or some sort of garbled name versus the name of our workstations: SS-Marketing etc. Click on the printer and take note of the **Unique ID**. You will need this Unique ID (printer's MAC address) later. Figure 10-4 shows you the IP address of the printer. HP tends to name their printers NPIxxxxx out of the box.

Client IP Address	Name	Lease Expiration	Type	Unique ID	Description		Actions
192.168.40.32	SS-BREEDING.springersltd.local	11/2/2008 7:53:19 PM	DHCP	0003ff05b1df			**Address Leases** ▲
192.168.40.31	SS-REGISTRATION.springersltd.local	11/2/2008 7:53:25 PM	DHCP	0003ff04b1df			More Actions ▶
192.168.40.28	SS-Sales.springersltd.local	11/2/2008 8:01:12 PM	DHCP	0003ff04abea			
192.168.40.27	SS-Marketing.springersltd.local	11/2/2008 8:01:07 PM	DHCP	0003ff05abea			**192.168.40.23** ▲
192.168.40.26	SS-GENEALOGY.springersltd.local	11/2/2008 8:01:18 PM	DHCP	0003ff02abea			More Actions ▶
192.168.40.25	SS-SCHEDULES.springersltd.local	11/2/2008 8:01:15 PM	DHCP	0003ff07abea			
192.168.40.23	NPI0D7007.springersltd.local	11/2/2008 2:27:04 PM	DHCP	001b780d7007			
192.168.40.22	SS-ACCOUNTING.springersltd.local	11/2/2008 7:54:31 PM	DHCP	0003ff09b1df			
192.168.40.21	SS-CAREFEEDING.springersltd.local	11/2/2008 7:54:35 PM	DHCP	0003ff0bb1df			
192.168.40.20	SS-PRESIDENT.springersltd.local	11/2/2008 7:53:21 PM	DHCP	0003ff7cd921			
192.168.40.19	SpringersVista0.springersltd.local	10/26/2008 1:45:38 PM	DHCP	0003ff7fd921			
192.168.40.18	SS-OFFICEADMIN.springersltd.local	11/2/2008 7:58:54 PM	DHCP	0003ff7ed921			

Figure 10-4
The SPRINGERS HP LaserJet IP address is highlighted.

9. **Minimize** the **Windows SBS Native Tools Management** console.

10. Open **Internet Explorer** on the server.

11. Click **File** and **Open** and type **http://192.168.40.23** (the IP address shown in Figure 10-4).

12. You should be greeted by the printer's Web-based management page. From here you can change that NPIxxxxx to the printer's actual name, set a management password, and reset the printer after the following steps. We will change the printer **Host Name: HPLJ4345MFP**

13. **Minimize** Internet Explorer with the printer's Web management console for later.

14. **Restore** the **Windows SBS Native Tools Console**.

15. Under the DHCP snap-in, right click on the **Reservation** folder and click on **New Reservation**.

16. Move the **New Reservation** window over so that the top of the window resides just below the printer's **DHCP Unique ID** listing. Click on and hold the left mouse button on the blue title bar. Drag the window over to the **Unique ID** and let go of the mouse button.

17. Fill out the **New Reservation** fields as follows, then click the **Add** button:
    - Reservation Name: **HPLJ4345MFP**

- IP Address: **192.168.40.5**
- MAC address: **001B780D7007** (shown in Figure 5-97)
- Description: **HP LaserJet 4345MFP**

18. Click the **Close** button on the **New Reservation** window.

19. You will now see the **HPLJ4345MFP** reservation with a status of **Reservation (inactive)**.

20. Power cycle the printer or **release and renew the IP address** via the printer's Web console, to obtain the newly reserved 192.168.40.5 IP address. Note that you will lose your access to the printer's Web console when the IP address changes!

21. In the **Windows SBS Native Tools Console DHCP snap-in** again, make sure the **Address Leases** folder is highlighted or click on it to get it highlighted.

22. Click on the **Refresh** button on the Windows SBS Native Tools Console toolbar or click **Action** then click on **Refresh** to refresh the DHCP address list.

23. You should now see your **HPLJ4345MFP.springersltd.local** with a **Reservation (active)** status under **Lease Expiration**.

SBS Printer Setup

You now have the printer setup with a dedicated IP address. The next step is to get the printer set up on SBS and subsequently shared to all of the workstations. To set up the printer on SBS:

1. Click on the **Start** button.

2. Click on **Printers** in the right-hand column.

3. Right click on **Add Printer** and click on **Run as administrator**.

4. Click **Continue** at the UAC pop-up.

Notes:

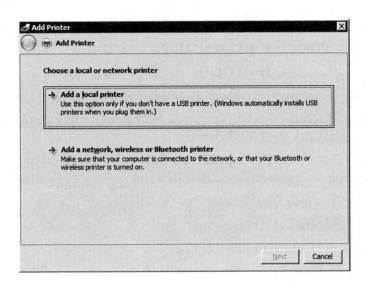

Figure 10-5
The proper window you will see when adding a printer with elevated privileges.

5. Click on the **Add a network, wireless or Bluetooth printer** link.

6. If the printer does not show up in the list, click **The printer that I want isn't listed** link.

7. Click the **Add a printer using a TCP/IP address or hostname** radio button and click **next**.

8. For the **Type a printer hostname or IP address** window, enter the following then click **Next**:

- Device type: **Autodetect** (default)

- Hostname or IP address: **192.168.40.5**

- Port name: **192.168.40.5**

- Leave the **Query the printer and automatically select the driver to use** option selected.

9. On **Install the printer driver,** click the **Browse** button and navigate to the folder or CD with the drivers, then double click on the **.inf** file.

10. Click **OK**.

11. Select your printer from the list presented and click **Next**.

12. You can leave the default on the **Type a printer name** window. Check the **Set as the default printer** if that is the case for the printer you are installing.

13. On the **Printer Sharing** window, type the following and click **Next**:
    - Share name: **HPLJ4345MFP**
    - Location: **Front Office**
    - Comment: **HP Multi Function Fax and Printer**

14. You will receive the **You've successfully added HP LaserJet 4345MFP** message. Click the **Finish** button.

15. Right click on the newly installed printer in the **Printers** window and run the printer's **Properties** as **Administrator**.

16. Click **Continue** for the UAC.

17. Click the **Sharing** tab.

18. Check the **List in the directory** option.

19. Click **Apply** and **OK**.

20. Open the **Windows SBS Console** if it is not already open.

21. Click **Continue** for the UAC.

22. Click on the **Network** tab.

23. Click on the **Devices** tab.

24. If the printer does not show when the console opens, click the **Refresh this view** button to bring it up.

You now have a printer that all users will be able to use, as shown in Figure 10-6!

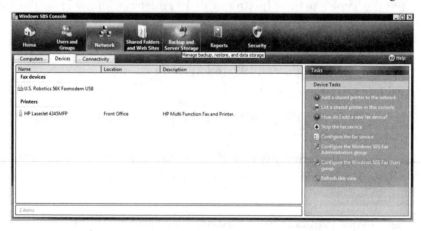

Figure 10-6
The HP LaserJet 4345MFP shows up in the SBS Console.

Deploy Printer via Group Policy

Windows Vista

Windows Vista makes printer deployment quite simple. We run the **Deploy with Group Policy** wizard in the Print Management console and the next time the Windows Vista workstations refresh their Group Policy settings, they will have the printer installed and ready to use.

We will address Windows XP Professional and Windows 2000 Professional after we set up for Windows Vista, since there are a number of extra steps to get a printer share connected to them via Group Policy.

> **TIP:** Group Policy printer deployment in Windows Server 2008—and thus SBS 2008—is pretty neat. No longer do we need to struggle with printer drivers for the various desktop operating systems that may be connected to the SBS network. On an SBS 2003 network, the moment we implemented Windows Vista, we ran into issues with the fact that the driver that was stored on the SBS server was primarily for x86 Windows XP operating systems.
>
> With the print management system we now have in Windows Server 2008, the drivers are stored independently of the print share host's operating system! So, when Windows 7 becomes official and we start implementing Windows 7 workstations in our existing SBS 2008 networks, we will be able to download and install the printer's Windows 7 drivers on the print share host without any compatibility issues. Our client's Windows 7 workstations will print as soon as they are connected to the SBS domain! Pretty neat, eh?

First, we set up the printer to deploy via Group Policy on the SBS server:

1. Click on **Start** and type **Printer [Enter]**. The **Print Management** console should be the highlighted item in the search results under **Programs**. If not, mouse over to it and click on it to open the console.

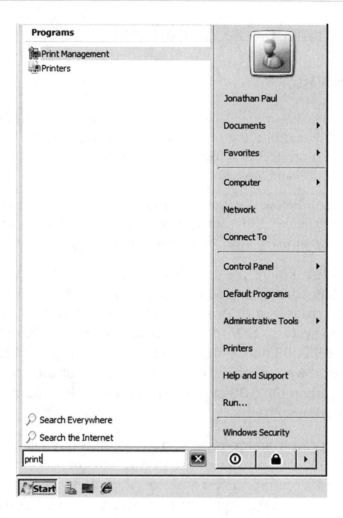

Figure 10-7
The Search feature in Windows Vista and Server 2008 makes things so accessible!

2. Click **Continue** when prompted by UAC.

3. Expand **Print Servers**.

4. Expand the server name **SS-SBS (local)**.

5. Expand **Printers** at the bottom of the list.

6. Right click on the printer you want to deploy. In the case of our SPRING-ERS SBS server, it is the **HP LaserJet 4345MFP**. Click on **Deploy with Group Policy**.

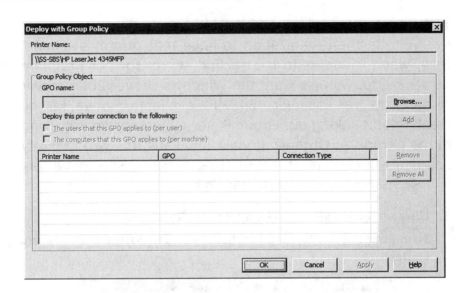

Figure 10-8
The Deploy with Group Policy window.

7. You will be greeted by the **Deploy with Group Policy** window shown in Figure 10-8. Click on the **Browse** button.

TIP: When it comes to Group Policy, we need to keep in mind the scope of the policy settings we are implementing. By that we mean, which users and/or computers need these settings? Is it just the sales people, their computers, or both?

In the case of printer deployment, only one department in larger organizations may use a particular printer. Designing your Group Policy and Organization Unit structures around this kind of scenario is beyond the scope of this book. Have a look at Philip's blog for some specific Group Policy guidance: http://blog.mpecsinc.ca.

8. You use the **Browse for a Group Policy Object** window much the same way as you do your **Save As** dialogue in Microsoft Word, Excel, or other Windows Applications.

9. Expand **MyBusiness.springersltd.local**.

10. Expand **Computers.MyBusiness.springers.local**.

TIP: In the case of our SPRINGERS methodology, we want everyone in the organization to have that printer available. Now, when it comes to the second server for our Premium server setup, we also want the Windows Server 2008 server to have the HP LaserJet 4345MFP available, so we will be creating and linking our Group Policy Object for print sharing to the Computer Organizational Unit. Thus, the Group Policy settings will cascade down to objects in the SBSComputers and SBSServers Organizational Units.

11. Click on the **Create New Group Policy Object** button.

12. Name the Policy Object **Default Printer Deployment Policy** and hit [**Enter**].

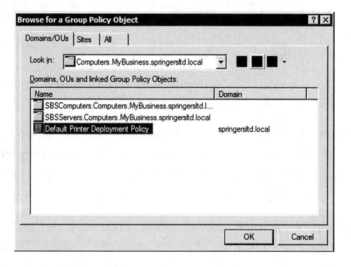

Figure 10-9
The new Default Printer Deployment Policy.

13. The new Default Printer Deployment Policy object should still be high-lighted. If it is not, click on it to highlight it.

14. Click the **OK** button in the **Browse for a Group Policy Object** window. Your new policy object **Default Printer Deployment Policy** should now be under **GPO name:** in the **Deploy with Group Policy** window.

15. Put a checkmark beside **The computers that this GPO applies to (per machine)**.

16. Click the **Add** button. The **HP LaserJet 4345MFP** should now appear in the window down below along with the **Default Printer Deployment Policy** with a Connection Type of **Per Machine**.

17. Click **Apply**.

18. You will get a **Printer deployment or removal operation succeeded** message. Click **OK**.

19. Click **OK** in the **Deploy with Group Policy** window to close it.

20. In the **Print Management** console, click on **Deployed Printers**. You will see the newly deployed HP LaserJet 4345MFP printer in the list.

21. Repeat the above steps for deploying the fax printer. You will select the **Default Printer Deployment Policy** and choose not to create another one when it comes time to **Browse for a Group Policy Object**.

If you open up the Windows SBS Native Tools Management console, and click on the **Group Policy Management** snap-in (keep in mind we customized the Windows SBS Native Tools Management console in Chapter 5), you can then drill down to the SBSComputers and SBSServers Organizational Units. You will find the Default Printer Deployment Policy Group Policy Object we created in the first run through the above steps linked to the Computers. Organizational Unit as shown in Figure 10-10.

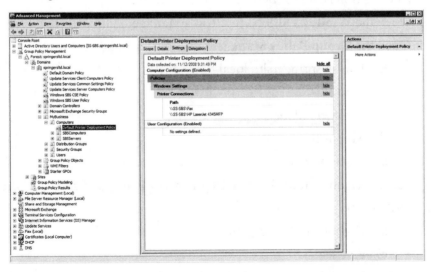

Figure 10-10
The Default Printer Deployment Policy showing our newly deployed printers.

Click on the policy object, then click on the **Settings** tab in the center pane. Click on **show all** near the top right, and you will see our newly deployed HP LaserJet 4345MFP and the Fax printers listed under **Printer Connections**.

Windows XP Professional, Windows 2000 Professional

Now, things take a bit of a twist when it comes to deploying to Windows XP Professional, Windows 2000 Professional, and Windows Server 2003. We need to use a startup script and an .EXE file to deploy.

It is important to note that as of this writing there is a gotcha to deploying printers to Windows XP Professional and Windows 2000 Professional 32bit clients. The PushPrinterConnections.exe utility that ships with SBS 2008 is an x64 or 64bit utility. You will need to find yourself a copy of the x86 or 32bit version of the PushPrinterConnections.exe utility. Check Philip's blog at http://blog.mpecsinc. ca for updated information on this situation.

Note that for Windows 2000 Professional you have to use per-user logon scripts to deploy printers via Group Policy to them.

To do so, we are going to need the Group Policy Management console we added to the Windows SBS Native Tools Management console.

1. Open the **Windows SBS Native Tools Management** console.

2. Open the **Group Policy Management** snap-in and drill down:

   a. Forest: springersltd.local

   b. Domains

   c. springersltd.local

   d. MyBusiness

   e. Computers

3. Right click on **Default Printer Deployment Policy** and click on **Edit**.

4. Drill down:

   a. Computer Configuration

   b. Policies

   c. Windows Settings

   d. Scripts (Startup/Shutdown)

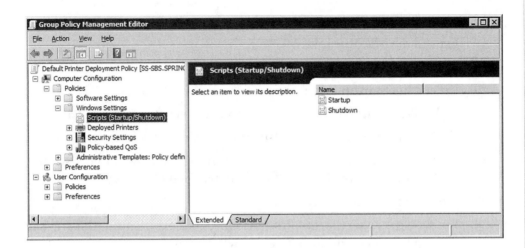

Figure 10-11
After finding the Startup container, you will setup the PushPrinterConnections executable.

5. Right click on **Startup** in the center pane and click on **Properties**.

6. In the **Startup Properties** window, click the **Show Files** button near the bottom left. Once the window has opened, take note of the policy's GUID. It will be a number set that looks like {0A92BD39-1338-4105-90AF-DB669BA0F689}. Leave the Window open.

7. Click on **Start** and type **%windir%\system32** and hit **[Enter]**. This will open a Windows Explorer window at the System32 folder in the Windows OS directory.

8. Click in the **Search** field at the top right of the Explorer window and type **push**. The PushPrinterConnections.exe file will show up in the results.

9. Right click on the **PushPrinterConnections.exe** file and click on **Copy**.

10. Click on the **Blue Button** with the white **X** to the right of your "push" search to close the search results.

11. In the **Address Bar**, click on **Windows** to the left of **System32**. You should now be in the Windows folder with the System32 folder highlighted.

12. Expand the **sysvol** folder down below the System32 folder.

13. Expand the **sysvol** folder (yes, again).

14. Expand the **springersltd.local** shortcut.

15. Expand the **Policies** folder. Note the list of GUIDs that comes up.

16. Expand the **GUID** that is identical to the one above.

17. Expand the **Machine** folder.

18. Expand the **Scripts** folder.

19. Expand the **Startup** folder.

20. Right click anywhere under the **This folder is empty** and select **Paste**.

21. Click the **Continue** button on the UAC warning.

22. Click **Continue** on the second UAC warning. You should now see the **PushPrinterConnections.exe** utility in that folder window.

23. Close the **Startup** Explorer window.

24. You should now see the PushPrinterConnections.exe utility in your *original* **Startup** Explorer window. Close that window too.

25. Click the **Add** button in the **Startup Properties** window.

26. Type **PushPrinterConnections.exe** in the **Script Name** field.

27. Type **-log** in the **Script Parameters** field. Your window should look like figure 10-12.

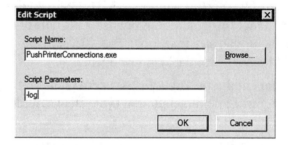

Figure 10-12
Adding the startup script for Windows XP Professional and others.

28. In the **Script Parameters** field put **-log** to enable logging on the client computers. The log can be found in **%windir%\Temp\ppcMachine.log** for per-computer connections or **%temp%\ppcUser.log** for per-user connections.

29. Click **OK** in the **Add a Script** window.

30. Click **Apply** and **OK** in the **Startup Properties** window.

31. Close the **Default Printer Deployment Policy** editor.

32. Click on the **Start** button and type **Run [Enter]**.

33. Type **GPUpdate /force [Enter]**. This will force the Group Policy changes to be updated on the server.

Configure the Vista Workstation Fax Service

The final step to getting the fax service up and running on the workstations is to configure **Windows Fax and Scan** on the Windows Vista workstations.

1. Click on the **Start** menu and type **Fax**.

2. Click on **Windows Fax and Scan** in the search results.

3. Click the **New Fax** button.

4. When the **Fax Setup** window pops up, click on the **Connect to a fax server on my network** option.

5. Type the name of the fax server on the network. In this case it is our SS-SBS server: **\\ss-sbs.** Click **Next**.

6. You can leave the default fax server name: **\\ss-sbs**. Or, you can change the name depending on your SBS setup. Click **Done**.

Figure 10-13
Once the fax service is configured, the Windows Vista Firewall will block its communications.

7. As shown in Figure 10-13, the Windows Vista Firewall will block the initial communication attempts made by the fax service. Click the **Unblock** button to allow the service through.

8. Click the **Continue** button for the UAC prompt in the case where the user has local admin rights, or enter a local (domain) admin user account if you are prompted for credentials.

9. Fill out a legitimate fax number in the **To:** field, type up a subject such as **Test Fax from User Name's Desk,** and put something like Test fax from User's desk today at 15:30hrs.

TIP: Before clicking on the **Send** button, click on the **Tools** menu and then the **Options** menu item. You can have the fax service issue a Delivery Receipt sent via e-mail that can also include a copy of the original fax. You can also prioritize the fax or schedule the fax to be sent at a later time.

10. Click the **Send** button.

11. Once the fax process has begun, you will be prompted to enter the **Location Information** for dialing rules. Enter your country/region, area code, carrier code, whether you dial a number such as "9" to gain access to an outside line, or whether the phone system uses tone or pulse dialing. Click **OK** once you have made your selections.

12. The **Phone and Modem Options** window will come up showing you the Location Information setting you just created. Click **OK**.

You will be brought back to the Windows Fax and Scan window. Traditionally, once the fax was sent on Windows XP Professional or Windows 2000 Professional, no indication of the fax being sent would be received until the e-mail notification.

Windows Vista Fax and Scan

In Windows Vista, that has changed. The **Windows Fax and Scan** console gives you direct access to all fax-related information from that workstation. The information includes the status of the fax being sent via the SBS server.

Notes:

Figure 10-14
The Windows Vista Fax and Scan console.

The console consists of the following:

- Any currently incoming faxes will end up in the Incoming folder. You can monitor the receive progress of the fax.

- Once a fax has been received, it will end up in the Inbox.

- The Drafts folder will hold any faxes that have been started but not sent yet.

- Whenever a fax is being sent, it will remain in the Outbox until the fax is successfully sent. If the fax send fails, said fax will remain in the Outbox.

- Click on the Sent Items folder to see a list of all faxes sent from the user.

- The Tools menu at the top of Windows Fax and Scan allows you to manage your Sender Information, Cover Pages, Fax Contacts, Fax Settings, Fax Accounts, and Options. You will find the Fax Status Monitor that indicates the current Receive Status.

Notes

Summary

This chapter addressed legacy topics that are still relevant today: printing and fax-ing. It was these two areas that scored major "wins" in local area networks (LAN) deployments. These are also two areas you will hear most often about if for some reason either is a point of failure.

In this chapter, we discussed the following topics.

- Fax modems were discussed.
- The SBS Fax Service was setup.
- SBS network printing was discussed two ways. First was a direct connection (LPT1) where the printer was shared. The other conversation was a shared network printer. .
- Significant discussion was held about e deployment of a printer via Group Policy. The discussion incorporated both Windows Vista and Windows XP.
- You read about configuring the Windows Vista Fax Service.
- You learned about implementing the Windows Vista Fax and Scan capabilities.

CHAPTER 11

Internet and the Web

Introduction

In this chapter we will focus in on the Office Live Small Business service that Microsoft has bundled into the SBS 2008 server.

For Windows Vista desktops on the SBS 2008, you can access the Office Live Small Business Web and Application sites by clicking on the Springer Spaniels Limited link in the Windows Small Business Server 2008 Desktop Gadget.

The setup link is in your SBS Console under the **Getting Started Tasks** as shown in Figure 11-1.

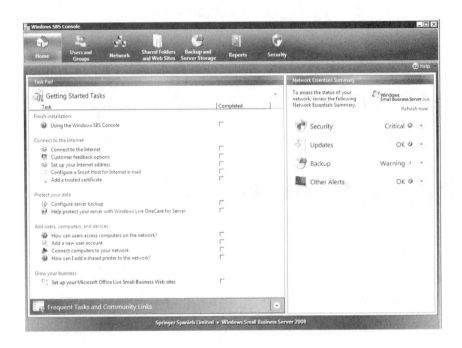

Figure 11-1
The last Getting Started Task is the setup of your Microsoft Office Live Small Business Web sites wizard.

Once you have gone through the setup steps later in this chapter, you will have both the Office Live Small Business (OLSB) Web site and the Office Live Small Business Application site, which is a SharePoint collaboration site configured for use by the SPRINGERS users.

In the case of our SPRINGERS methodology, we created a Live ID using Bob Easter's e-mail address since our SPRINGERS methodology is a "live" production network for the purposes of writing this book. You may need to get a little creative for your OLSB setup steps.

Once up and running, you can check the OLSB sites status in the SBS Console as shown in Figure 11-2.

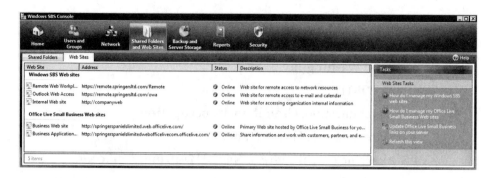

Figure 11-2
 Once the OLSB sites are configured, their status will show up in the SBS Console in the Web sites tab on the Share Folders and Web sites page.

Office Live Small Business Setup

Set Up Your Microsoft Office Live Small Business Web Sites

Once you run through the following setup steps, you will have two fully configured OLSB sites.

To begin the setup process, click on the **Set up your Microsoft Office Live Small Business Web sites** link in the **Getting Started Tasks**:

1. Click on the **Set up your Microsoft Office Live Small Business Web sites** link.

2. The explanation is pretty straightforward for the wizard. Once you have read it, click **Next**.

3. In the case of the SPRINGERS methodology, you are starting fresh, so you will click on the **Sign up for a new Office Live Small Business account** button.

4. A Web browser will open. If you are running this wizard on the server, click the **Close** button on any Security Configuration warnings.

5. Click the **Sign Up Free** button.

6. Type the following in the e-mail address field **BobE@springersltd.com** and click **Next**.

7. Fill out the form as follows and click the **Save and continue** button:

   - Choose a password for the account: **L0tsandlotsoffun!**
   - State: **Washington**
   - Zip: **98110**
   - Secret question: **Grandfather's occupation**.
   - Secret Answer: **Horse Trader**.
   - Alternate e-mail address: **NormH@springersltd.com**.

8. Enter your information as follows, then click the **Save and continue** button:

   - First name: **Bob**
   - Last name: **Easter**
   - Organization name: **Springer Spaniels Limited**
   - Type of organization: **Other**
   - Number of employees: **5-10**

9. Enter the security measures characters and click the **Save and continue** button.

10. Read over the **Microsoft Service Agreement** and **Privacy Statement** before clicking the **I Accept** button.

11. Again, if you are running this wizard from the server, you may get security warnings. Click the **Close** button to continue.

12. A **Check your Inbox to activate your account** page will show. Log on to Bob Easter's workstation and open Outlook to find the e-mail from Microsoft. The e-mail will look like Figure 11-3. Note that the next steps will be completed via the Bob Easter user account and that the **Set up your Office Live Small Business Web sites** wizard is still waiting for input during this process.

Notes

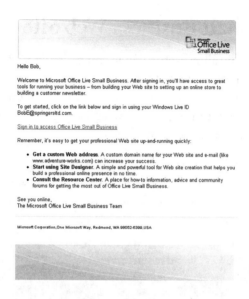

Figure 11-3
The confirmation e-mail sent to Bob Easter.

13. Click on the activation link. You will need to sign in with Bob Easter's new Live ID.

14. Once signed in you will be greeted by the Microsoft Office Live Small Business dashboard.

15. Once you have confirmed that the Live ID is functional by signing into the Office Live Small Business site, sign out and close the Web browser window. You will get a **You have signed out of Microsoft Office Live** when the sign-out completes.

16. Back to the **Set up your Office Live Small Business Web sites** wizard. Type in Bob Easter's Windows Live ID and password and click the **Sign In** button.

17. The process will complete and, if successful, you will be able to click a **How can I manage my Office Live Small Business Web sites?** link for Help on that topic. Click the **Finish** button to close the wizard.

Once you have finished setting up the Office Live Small Business Web sites, you will be able to use your Live ID—in this case Bob Easter's, to manage the look and feel of the Web site as well as set up the online collaborative features of the Office Live Small Business Applications site.

Office Live Small Business Web Site

Once you go through the above setup steps, you have the SPRINGERS OLSB Web site in the out-of-the-box template form. From there, you will need to customize the site for the company. We will give you a general overview of the management and editing you can do with the site, but deep diving into Web site development and content is beyond the scope of this book.

The SPRINGERS OLSB Web site is at http://springerspanielslimited.web.officelive.com. Figure 11-4 shows what the default site will look like.

Figure 11-4
The default Springer Spaniels Office Live Small Business Web site.

Office Live Small Business Management Portal

To manage the Web site, or make changes to it, you will need to log on to the OLSB Business Applications Web site at http://springerspanielslimitedweboffic-elivecom.officelive.com/default.aspx using the Live ID that was used to create the OLSB Web sites. In this case, Bob Easter's Live ID was used to create the sites, so we will log on using his Live ID.

Once you log on to the site, your navigation point will be one step down from the Home page at the Business Applications management portal. Click on the **Home** link in the breadcrumbs links near the top left of the Web page to get to the default Home page for your OLSB sites.

Figure 11-5 shows what the default Home page should look like.

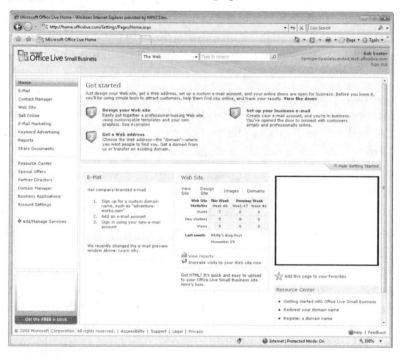

Figure 11-5
The Springer Spaniels default management portal Home page on OLSB.

Note that the Home page presents you with a list of links for you to manage the various aspects of both OLSB sites as well as some analytics capabilities for the

Web site itself. As you can see in the Figure 11-5 screenshot, our SPRINGERS Web site has already seen some traffic!

You will see in the top right corner of your Web browser the name of the user logged on as well as the URL of the site being managed. This will be helpful for those who may manage more than one OLSB site.

Here is a quick overview of the management links presented in the Home page:

- **Home**. This link is pretty self-explanatory. Click on it to be brought back to the Home page in the management portal.

- **E-mail**. You can manage any e-mail-related activities on this page. You can set up and take advantage of the Office Live E-mail using their domain—or in the case of SPRINGERS, it would be springersltd.com—or register and use your own domain name. Office Live Mail gives you 100 users that will use the domain OfficeLiveUsers.com out of the box. If you have registered and redirected the DNS for an existing domain name to Office Live E-mail, then you will be able to set up your e-mail domain too. Users can use their e-mail much like Hotmail or hook things into Microsoft Outlook.

- **Contact Manager**. The Office Live Contacts can be used as a central location for your company's contacts. You can even have anyone who has checked off the E-mail Subscription box on the OLSB Web site's contact form turned into a contact automatically!

- **Web Site**. Use this page to customize the OLSB Web page. You can edit the existing pages, add new pages, and add images, documents, and templates to the management portal. You can also configure Web site components such as the e-mail form and more. The OLSB analytics and reports for Web traffic on the site are to be found here too.

- **Sell Online**. You can set up an online store using OLSB. This is not a free service, although as of this writing, you can set it up and use it free for the first month. The store gives you up to 10,000 items to sell, integration with eBay, payments via credit card or PayPal, SSL security, simple design tools, and around-the-clock support. After the first free month, the next twelve months will cost $14.95 per month. After that twelve -month period, the fee increases to $39.95 per month.

- **E-mail Marketing**. Create and e-mail out customizable newsletters, promotions, and announcements that share the look of your OLSB Web site theme. There is a free trial month and then a set of fees based on the number of e-mails being sent out through the service.

- **Keyword Advertising**. You can advertise your business online using keywords that come up when people are using online search. In the case of SPRINGERS, keywords may include "Springer Spaniels," "Spaniel Breeding," and the like. You pay per click. That means you would pay the advertising provider only when users click through to your Web site via the keyword advertising.

- **Reports**. You can view traffic analytics on the number of visitors to your OLSB Web site. The analytics are pretty good and should provide a broad overview of the traffic along with the top five referrals to your OLSB Web site. You can set Events into the Web site usage graph to track things like initiating online advertising, making changes to the site, or registering the site with Web search engines. Having the Events set into your graph on the day they happened can be helpful for tracking which situations improved traffic to your site. You can also drill down into statistics for referrals, page usage, and keywords that allow you to query.

- **Share Documents**. This link clicks through to the Office Live Workspace Beta (as of this writing). This Workspace provides a similar experience to SharePoint for the sharing of Microsoft Office documents for Microsoft Word, Excel, and PowerPoint. The site can be set up with permissions to access various content.

- **Resource Center**. The Resource Center has a number of different Help subjects on the use of Office Live Small Business, articles on E-mail and Search Marketing, as well as help links for the OLSB Management portal and its features that include how-to articles, getting started information, and more.

- **Special Offers**. Current specials from various Microsoft Partners for their services.

- **Partner Directory**. Find a Microsoft Partner. The current page as of this writing has Microsoft Partners in the United States and the United Kingdom.

- **Domain Manager**. You can manage any domains that you have tied into the OLSB service or the default domain you were given when you set up the OLSB service. In the case of SPRINGERS, that domain is http://springers-panielslimited.web.officelive.com. You can actually change the OLSB URL, but this will impact the many services tied into it. So, if that is something you want to do, make sure to do it right after you set up the services. You can also redirect your existing URL to your OLSB Web site. In the case of SPRINGERS, this means you would change the DNS at the hosting provider for springersltd.com to the IP provided by the OLSB service when you set up springersltd.com in the Domain Manager.

- **Business Applications**. You manage the OLSB Applications site that you created when you set up the Office Live Small Business service. You can create a Team Workspace for sharing documents, calendars, announcements, and more. You can add collaboration features and a lot more. User access, invitations, user permissions, and more are available to you here.

- **Account Settings**. You are able to manage Users & Permissions, Alerts on the site, E-mail Accounts, the OLSB service owner's details, the business information such as address and e-mail, and any domains associated with the OLSB service.

- **Add/Manage Services**. You can add more storage for your OLSB Web or Application sites, add users for the Application site, use Premium E-mail with no banner ads, market your business online, and set up the online store.

Now, let's have a look at changing the default OLSB Web site.

Modify the Default Office Live Small Business Web Site

You can work with the design of the site via the Getting Started links presented near the top of the Home page or via the Web Site link in the management links list on the left-hand side of the page.

For simplicity's sake, we will start from the Home page:

1. Click on the **Web Site** link.

2. Scroll down to the Page Manager section and click on **Edit** beside the Home page. You will be greeted with the Web Page Editor shown in Figure 11-6.

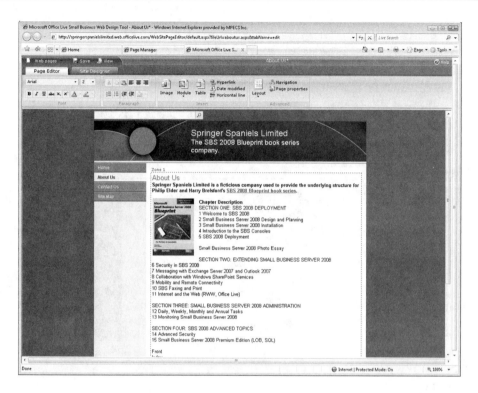

Figure 11-6
The Office Live Small Business Web site editor is fairly straightforward, making site changes a breeze.

You can click on any of the basic editing buttons to change the appearance of the text on the page. You can add bulleted or numbered lists, images, a site module (Contact Us form, Map & Directions, Slide Show, etc.), tables, Hyperlinks, and more.

While in the editor, you can navigate to the various Web site pages by clicking on the relevant Hyperlink. So, if you want to edit the About Us page, click on its respective link.

Click on the **Site Designer** tab while in the editor and you will see the page in Figure 11-7.

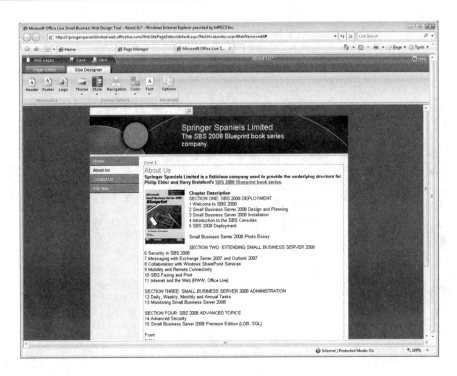

Figure 11-7
You can modify a number of global site elements such as the site's style, color, fonts, and more while in the Site Designer.

Go ahead and modify the site's header and footer and add a logo to it. From there, you can set the theme of the site according to a short list of various industries, how the site header will look, the placement of the navigation buttons, colors, and fonts for the site.

If you have the time, experiment with the various settings to get an idea as to how the overall appearance and feel of the OLSB Web site will be impacted by the changes you make.

Office Live Small Business Applications Web Site

Out of the box, the OLSB Applications site is a Windows SharePoint site. In the case of the SPRINGERS methodology, you can reach the OLSB Application site via the Windows Vista SBS 2008 Gadget or directly at:

- http://springerspanielslimitedwebofficelivecom.officelive.com/default.aspx

Now, the owner of the OLSB Applications site can manage its features using the methodology written about earlier in this chapter. The owner is also the one to issue an invitation for users to use the OLSB Application site.

Out of the box, the OLSB Application site comes with:

- 50MB of storage space for shared documents and the like.
- The ability to add up to 5 users for free.

TIP: In the case of our SPRINGERS methodology, we have 10 users in place for the company. Since Springer Spaniels Limited has its own SBS 2008 server on site, using the online OLSB Application site may not be expedient—especially since there are costs associated with stepping up the data storage and the number of users that can access the site.

The OLSB Application site would be a good solution for a small company that does not have its own SBS server on site.

A Live ID will be required for connecting to the OLSB Application site. The user that will connect to the OLSB Application site will need to have a Live ID. The Live ID will need to be the same as the one used in the e-mail invitation. The OLSB Application site owner, in this case Bob Easter, will send out the invitation e-mail.

After users sign into the OLSB Application site, they will be presented with the Web page shown in Figure 11-8.

Notes

Figure 11-8
After signing in, one of the authors who has been given OLSB editing permissions can work with both the OLSB Web site and the Application site.

The Office Live Small Business Application site has some of the following features:

- **Document Manager**. This has two tabs for a Document Library and Picture Library. You can upload and work with Microsoft Office documents and images here. Just as you can with the Companyweb SharePoint site, you can edit documents stored on the OLSB Applications site live without needing to copy them down to your local machine. A check-out and check-in system is available just as it is on the Companyweb SharePoint site.

- **Team Workspace**. When you click on the Team Workspace link you will be greeted with the Dashboard. It has any recent announcements, upcoming calendar events, and any links listed. Besides the dashboard tab, there are tabs for creating and managing Announcements, Calendar events, Web site Links, a Shared Documents library, Tasks, and a Team Discussion board. Figure 11-9 shows the Team Workspace Dashboard.

Figure 11-9
The Team Workspace Dashboard gives you an at-a-glance view of the user's workspace.

Management for the various SharePoint elements is much like it is for the Companyweb SharePoint site. You can customize the look and feel of each SharePoint feature, manage permissions for each feature, and a lot more.

The SharePoint discussion in Chapter 8 covers most aspects of managing the Companyweb SharePoint site, so check it out if you have not already done so!

Summary

In this chapter, we learned how SBS 2008 can impact the external world and realized this represents a shift in thinking. Much of the SBS 2008 magic is assumed to occur on the LAN or via authenticated workers using the mobility or remote capabilities. But this chapter showed you how the general public can interact with the small business running SBS 2008 that also uses Microsoft Office Live Small Business Web sites.

Specifically, in this chapter:

- We completed the final SBS Getting Started Task for setting up the Microsoft Office Live Small Business Web sites.
- We provided you an overview of the Management Portal and its features.
- You were shown how to modify the Office Live Small Business Web site using the Site Editor and Site Designer tabs in the Web site editor.
- Since the Office Live Small Business Application site is a SharePoint Services site, we gave you a brief of its features. (Note that Chapter 8 spends a bit more time with the Companyweb site.)

Forward to the next chapter!

SECTION THREE

Small Business Server 2008 Administration

Chapter 12
Daily, Weekly, Monthly, and Annual Tasks

Chapter 13
Monitoring Small Business Server 2008

CHAPTER 12

Daily, Weekly, Monthly, and Annual Tasks

This important chapter takes a very real-world view of SBS. You will find an assortment of tasks and duties you are likely to perform on your SBS network. Granted, the frequency with which you perform these tasks will depend on your unique situation. We are assuming the tasks outlined here would be performed daily, weekly, monthly, and annually. You will likely have your own tasks to add to this list—for example, performing some re-indexing job on a business accounting application.

It has been our observation that how and when SBS tasks are performed depends on the following factors. It might be that your skill level as an SBS administrator or consultant affects the tasks you perform. A newbie might perform minimal tasks and a guru might perform more tasks. The activity on your SBS network can determine which tasks you feel comfortable performing and when. Some tasks, such as those highlighted early in the chapter (backup, virus detection, spam blocking, spyware removal, etc.) are to be performed religiously, regardless of your SBS skill level.

Don't overlook how the computer knowledge of your users can determine what maintenance tasks are performed (especially the end-user support tasks). And believe it or not, physical stuff impacting the quality of your network—from wiring to server brand—can affect your task list too!

By this point, we assume that you've correctly set up a robust SBS network based on the SPRINGERS methodology used in this book. (Yes, it's the sample company Springer Spaniels Limited again.) When you get to this point for real (that is, with your real SBS implementations), we hope that your SBS network is stable and functional and allows the time you need to perform other important work. We understand that small businesses ask much of us, and we often have several jobs, not just those of a SBS guru.

So, now that we've had our fuss above, on with the SBS administration show using SPRINGERS! Note that as you read this, you will see the two authors offer individual opinions. This dialogue is healthy and reflects the real world, where there are many choices.

> **TIP:** Numerous studies confirm that data protection is the most important concern of a small business owner with respect to data networks. The authors have seen this confirmed with studies by Yankee Group, AMI, Jupiter, and others. As this chapter was being written, Connect IT News at Integrated mar.com sent this newsletter story out (reprinted here with permission):

> **Many SMBs' data protection practices risky**
> *(December 2, 2008, Vanessa Ho)*

> *When it comes to backing up their data, 92 per cent of small to midsized businesses (SMBs) have deployed some sort of solution, but 50 percent of those respondents have also lost data, according to a new Symantec Corp. study of IT decision-makers at several hundred small businesses of fewer than 250 employees in North America.*

> *"As businesses grow & their environment becomes more complex, the causes of data loss are more diverse for them. What that may indicate is what they were using as a smaller business is not working as they grow," said Anne O'Neill, senior manager of product marketing with Symantec.*

She added that manual processes that may have worked in the past become much more cumbersome for them to manage.

The reason why SMBs may not have updated their processes is a lack of time. "In a very busy small business, there is always something more important to do than focus on backup policies and solutions," O'Neill noted.

Of the companies that lost data, approximately a third have lost sales, 20 percent have lost customers, and a quarter claimed the data loss caused severe disruptions to the company.

According to survey results, causes of data loss were diverse. Although natural disasters were often cited as a risk, onsite disasters were the primary contributing factor of data loss. Sixty-three percent of respondents cited hardware failure as a cause of data loss incidents, 27 percent from deliberate sabotage by employees, and 27 percent from theft.

Also, Symantec noted that SMBs rated backup as their second-highest computing priority, after defense against viruses and other malware, and ahead of issues such as reducing costs and deploying new computers.

Examples of data backup technology that SMBs have deployed include USB drives, DVD burners, on-premise backup solutions, and attached tape drives or disk arrays.

However, according to Darren Niller, senior manager of product management with Symantec, 85 to 90 percent of respondents were not completely confident that they could recover their data using their current solution.

Additionally, many companies indicated they did not back up their computers fully. About a quarter of SMBs conducted no backup of their PCs, and another 13 percent did only informal backups where employees decide the frequency and which files were protected without corporate guidance. The situation is similar for servers; about 20 percent of SMBs conducted no server backup.

"SMBs are using risky backup practices and although they are doing something ... they are still exposed based on the practices they are following," said O'Neill.

Niller added that companies need to be backing up their data at least once a day in order to minimize potential downtime they would have in between backups and restore points.

When backups do occur, most backup files are not stored remotely. More than half of all backup files on PCs and servers were stored in the same location as the originals, which leave the company vulnerable to permanent data loss.

"[SMBs] are not as educated in terms of best practices, it is almost like, something like a theft or some sort of site disaster won't happen to me," commented Niller. "I think they downplay that event and they don't necessarily take every precaution they can with their data."

O'Neill added that getting data offsite is another process that takes time, is complex and not an easy process to manage for companies. Niller further explained that moving data offsite is a very manual process, even if an organization is using an automated backup solution. It requires a user to pull a tape out of the tape drive and have someone pick it up like a service provider.

However, an automated solution can help SMBs ensure their data is well protected and secure.

Solutions such as Symantec Online Backup can help SMBs centrally manage their backup practices and policies as well as automate it.

"The more automation they can put in place, the more they can ensure they are following company policies and not relying on employees to be using manual process," said O'Neill.

Niller added one of the advantages of an online solution is it continually protects a customer's environment.

Also, since respondents had low confidence in their current backup solutions, Niller said that the channel can play a role in protecting a customer's data. He explained that partners can go in and offer alternative solutions like an online backup product.

Backup Setup

This section discusses three backup scenarios: the built-in SBS solution, the on-premise third-party solution, and the off-premise backup solutions available to the SBSer in the SBS 2008 time frame.

SBS 2008 Backup

Having configured the initial server backup in Chapter 5 on deployment, you are familiar with how to set up the SBS 2008 backup system.

Once you have set up the SBS backup, you can make changes to the backup setup in the SBS Console under the **Backup and Server Storage** tab then the **Backup** tab.

The **Configure server backup** link you find when you first open the **Backup** tab is the same wizard you used to first set up the SBS backup in the **Getting Started Tasks**.

Notes

Click the **Restore server data from backup** link and you will be greeted by the Windows Server Backup console snap-in as shown in Figure 12-1.

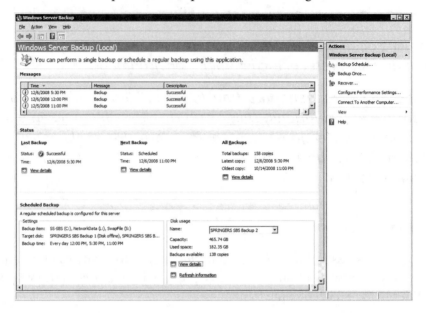

Figure 12-1
The Windows Server Backup console snap-in.

The Windows Server Backup console gives you the ability to fine tune the SBS backup settings, run a manual backup by clicking on the **Backup Once** link, or recover files, folders, applications, such as the SharePoint and Exchange databases or full disk volumes. However, you will not be able to restore the system C: volume while the server is online.

As an example, let's say that one of our SPRINGERS users has deleted a folder and needs it and the folder's contents recovered.

In the Windows SBS Console:

1. Click on the **Backup and Server Storage** tab.

2. Click on the **Restore server data from backup** link in the Backup Tasks column. Note that once the Windows Server Backup console comes up, the Windows SBS Console will be locked out until the Windows Server Backup console is closed.

3. Click the **Recover...** link under the Actions column.

4. Leave the SBS server as the server to recover from and click the **Next** button.

5. Choose the date and time you need to recover the folder from and click **Next**.

6. Leave the default **Files and Folders** radio button and click **Next**.

7. Choose the folder to restore in the list of Available items and click **Next**.

8. Click the **Another location** radio button and click the **Browse** button. Navigate to the folder you need to recover to and click the **Make New Folder** button and name it **Restore**. If restoring a folder, re-create it first, then click the **Make New Folder** button again and create the **Restore** subfolder. Click **OK**, then click **Next**. Leave the default settings unless it is necessary to change them.

TIP: As a rule, when we recover a folder, files, or an individual file, we will create a "Restore" folder under the original folder the data was located in and restore the data to the Restore folder. In the case where we may be searching for a particular data set and may need to recover multiple versions of the data, we will use the following naming convention to make it easy to figure out which data set we were working with:

- 08-11-15-1507hrs-DataName
  (Year-Month-Day-24hrTime-DataName)

- 08-11-15-1523hrs-DataName (Later time)

9. Make sure you have the correct data to restore in the Confirmation window and click the **Recover** button to initiate the data recovery.

10. Once the restore has completed, you can click the **Close** button.

11. Close the Windows Server Backup console.

SS-SBS Backup Tasks and Wizards

Click on the backup item in the backup list and you will see a list of specific SBS Backup Tasks shown in Figure 12-2.

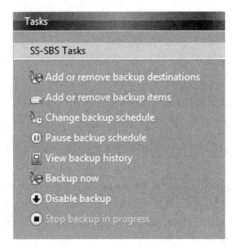

Figure 12-2
You can make changes to pretty much any aspect of the SBS 2008 backup in the SBS Console.

Some of those tasks contain wizards; others are specific to the backup service and its management.

The following wizards will help you to keep your backup setup in order:

- **Add or remove backup destinations**. When you click on this link, you will get the Server Backup Properties window opened to Backup Destinations. Click the **Add or remove drives** button and you will be able to add a new USB hard disk or several if the need arises. You can also take any drives that may have failed or are being used for compliance out of the rotation via this wizard. You can see the associated USB hard drive and the soon to be added USB hard drive in Figure 12-3.

Notes

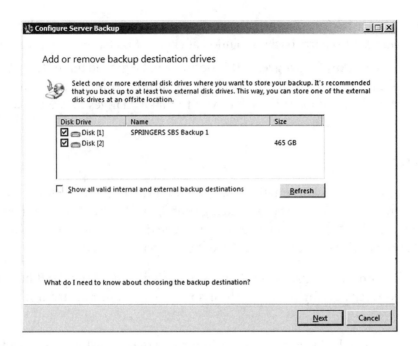

Figure 12-3
Disk [2] is soon to be added to the SBS 2008 backup rotation.

- **Add or remove backup items**. You can add a new partition to the backup setup or remove a partition from the current backup setup. Keep in mind that the SBS backup will not allow partitions that contain critical system data to be removed from the backup setup.

- **Change backup schedule**. When we first set up the SBS backup, we had three backup times set. If you need to add, subtract, or change any of the scheduled backup times, this is the wizard to use.

- **Pause backup schedule**. When you click this link you can permanently pause the backup schedule. If you do so, you will need to click the **Resume backup schedule** link in its place to get things going again.

- **View Backup History**. When you click on this link, you will get a window showing all of the previous backups and whether they were successful or failed.

- **Backup now**. When you click this link you are able to initiate an immediate backup of the server.

- **Disable backup**. You can disable the built-in SBS backup if you decide to go with a third party backup solution after your SBS has been in production.
- **Stop backup in progress**. This option will be grayed out unless a backup is currently running. If a backup is running, you can click this link to stop the backup. This enables you to make changes to the backup once it has stopped.

Rotations

When it comes to backup rotations, we provide a rotation service for our clients. We pop in every couple of weeks to change out the USB hard drives on their servers. Since the backup solution data is all encrypted, we do not need to worry too much about any of the data on the drives being compromised.

Depending on the industry the client is in, we will rotate two USB hard disks every two weeks giving us a month or so of backups to pull from if we need to restore.

For those clients that need a little more in the way of data history, we will add one or more USB hard drives to the rotation to deepen the backup history.

Compliance Considerations

In the case of client businesses that require some backup grandfathering, we will have a drive with a dedicated 6, 12, 18, 24, or longer backup sets on them. Having this style of backup storage gives us the ability to restore data from any possible time in the company's recent history.

On-Premise Third-Party Backup

Since the start of SBS well over a decade ago, the robust third-party ISV community has provided excellent backup solutions. In fact, ArcServ (before it was acquired by CA) and Backup Exec (before Veritas was acquired by Symantec) both integrated with SBS 4.0 at the management console level in the late 1990s!

Harry's View

At SMB Nation, we purchased and use ShadowProtect from StorageCraft. We have strong working relationships with MaxSP, Acronis, Symantec, and Highly Reliable. All readers are encouraged to wisely investigate each solution. StorageCraft is displayed in Figure 12-4. Interestingly, at the SMB Nation Europe workshop (London, December 5, 2008), speaker Jeff Middleton raved about Highly Reliable.

Figure 12-4
StorageCraft

Philip's View

With our SBS 2003 clients, we have had great success with the ShadowProtect product from StorageCraft. We have used it to facilitate SBS 2003 Swing Migrations (www.sbsmigration.com) to new hardware or to refresh the OS on existing hardware.

We have used the product to recover SBS boxes in a matter of hours after catastrophic failures. We have also had to tie in the ShadowProtect recovery process with a Swing Migration structure to fully recover a server that had some bad sectors on one of the OS RAID array members (the server also turned out to have some bad RAM) that did not show itself until a fateful reboot.

We had previously used other third-party products, but when we failed to restore a server after a catastrophic failure, we needed something that would work 100 percent of the time or at least give us options if things did not work as they should. ShadowProtect does that in spades.

Off-Premise Third-Party Backup

Several years ago, enterprising entrepreneurs started offering online backup solutions. Some of these solutions were offered ahead of marketplace acceptance. Here's an example. At the first SMB Nation conference in 2003, there were three sponsors. One sponsor was a dapper dude from Cincinnati who was trying to have the online backup conversation with a room full of SBSers. But he had an uphill battle as a pioneer in the field. Folks were worried about data security, HIPPA compliance in the medical field (US), etc. We truly felt sorry for him but appreciate his trail-blazing efforts. (Unfortunately, he was not financially successful.)

Today, in the latter part of the decade, the story is far different. There are numerous online storage solutions to select from.

Harry's View

At SMB Nation, we have a two-part backup strategy utilizing both on- and off-premise backups. Such "double coverage" allows me to sleep well at night. Our off-premise backup is provided by Divinsa. We have long-standing relationships with Vembu, eFolder, EMC Retrospect, Zenith, StorageGuardian, Backup Assist, CRU DataPort, and Symform (full disclosure here). Divinsa is shown in Figure 12-5.

Notes

Figure 12-5
Divinsa

Philip's View

Since we are the off-site backup secured storage for most of our clients, we have not looked to Internet-based backup strategies too deeply. For some of our clients, the idea is not feasible, since their data stores can grow by tens of Gigabytes a week during their peak seasons.

For us, our critical business-related data is encrypted and taken off-site on an Intel SS4000 series NAS box. A few of them take care of our rotation needs. Our data, too, grows quite quickly and until we have a fibre fully duplexed connection in our shop, we will keep the method we have now.

We here in Alberta are still quite far behind other parts of Canada as far as our ISP upload speeds are concerned. At best, we are looking at 1Mb of bandwidth. This is not a lot when it comes to changes in the magnitude of hundreds of Megabytes or even Gigabytes of data needing to be uploaded to an Internet-based storage facility.

AntiVirus and Malware

The great thing about writing a book as a team is that you get to engage in some spirited conversations and explore diverse opinions. Perhaps nowhere was this more evident than in the anti-virus and malware protection area. As you will see, we hold different opinions, which we will express here. But one thing we certainly agree on is the need for complete protection in this important area.

Harry's View

We currently use Trend Micro at SMB Nation and have for several SBS genera-tions. We have also used CA, AVG, and Symantec Norton on individual PCs and under different scenarios. Trend Micro is shown in Figure 12-6.

Figure 12-6
Trend Micro

Philip's View

AntiVirus has been a hit-or-miss situation for our business. For the last 10 years or so, Symantec Corporate AntiVirus products have been our primary choice. We've had pretty good success with the product itself and keeping our clients' sites virus-free. The Symantec management sites and phone support were a bit of a struggle, but we managed.

We did try out Trend Micro's product last spring but didn't have too much success with it. We had some problems when we installed their SMB product on a client's SBS, which resulted in a virus infection at the client's site. That particular client had previously been virus-free for 10 years using the Symantec product.

I was very happy to hear about the Forefront Server Security for Exchange SP1 being included with SBS 2008. Until late November 2008, Windows Live OneCare for Server was also a part of the package. I was really hoping that our company would be able to provide a 100 percent Microsoft server/client antivirus and malware protection suite to our clients as a result. As of this writing, however, there still was not a clear direction for the desktop.

Forefront Server Security for Exchange SP1 Reports

Essentially, once you have your SBS set up, you can then configure Forefront to fire off an e-mail to yourself and one of the company contacts whenever it encounters a virus or malware problem.

You do that by opening the Forefront Server Security for Exchange console, acknowledging the UAC, and connecting to SS-SBS when prompted for the server name.

Once the console has opened up, you click on the **Reports** button in the console and click on the **Notification** button. Each Administrator's setting has an e-mail TO field associated with it. You can put the necessary e-mail address in each Administrator's category.

Live OneCare for Server Status

Unfortuantely, Windows Live OneCare was removed from the SBS 2008 product shortly after its release. But it is still discussed here for modularity purposes. Windows Live OneCare for server provides a simple GUI interface. You can check the status of Windows Live OneCare at-a-glance by the color of the OneCare circle in the System Tray. Green is good, yellow means some items need your attention, and red signifies a critical situation. Figure 12-7 shows the OneCare GUI.

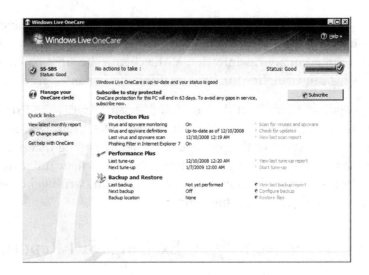

Figure 12-7
The Windows Live OneCare GUI.

Task Scheduler

The Task Scheduler has changed significantly in the new Windows Server 2008. Figure 12-8 shows just how much it has changed.

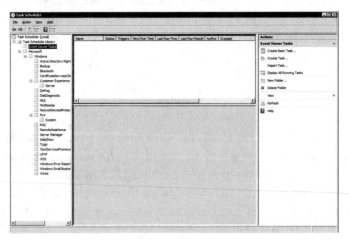

Figure 12-8
The new Windows Server 2008 Task Scheduler console.

There are two methods for scheduling a task in the Task Scheduler:

1. **Create Basic Task**. When you use the Create Task link, you will have a wizard-driven method to create a new task.

2. **Create Task**. When you click this link, you will be presented with a full set of Task property tabs that you can use to custom configure a Task. Figure 12-9 shows you the General tab.

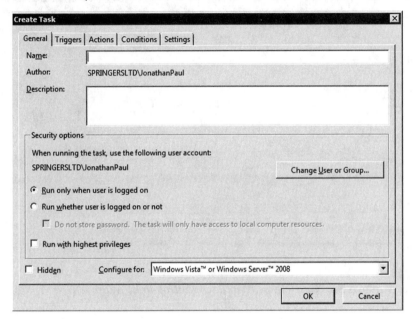

Figure 12-9
You can create a task using an advanced method in the Task Scheduler.

The Task Scheduler also provides a number of built-in tasks that you can go ahead and configure—from defragmenting the hard disks to managing the SBS backup schedule.

Take a deep dive into the various built-in tasks that may or may not have a pre-defined task in place.

Notes

WSUS Update Monitoring

Most of your update monitoring will take place in the SBS Console shown in figure 12-10.

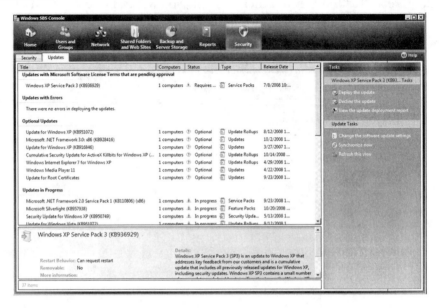

Figure 12-10
The Windows SBS Console with updates waiting to be approved.

Each update listed in the pending approval categories can be double clicked on to get a detailed description of the update, what it does, which product it applies to, and whether the update may need to request a reboot.

The update approval process is very simple:

1. Right click on the pending update and click **Deploy the update**.

2. Click the **OK** button when you receive the Deploy Updates pop-up.

3. Click **OK** for the deploy timing warning pop-up.

4. The update will move down into the **Updates in Progress** status.

You may need to adjust your WSUS settings for synchronization depending on how things go through the SBS product cycle.

Quick Hitters

This section is a list of quick hitters to consider as you interact with SBS 2008 (either as the consultant or small business).

Daily/Weekly

In this section, we speak towards the type of things you're likely to do on a daily or weekly basis. There are no hard and fast rules here, so please add to this list as you see fit. You are welcome to participate in the ongoing conversation at the author's blogs (See Appendix A for more information).

- **Sharing Files and Folders.** Configure server-side shared folders from Shares (Local) under Standard Management in Server Management. Shares allow data to be easily accessed over the network (files can't be shared in the SBS 2003/Windows Server 2003 time frame, something NetWare gurus notice as a difference immediately). Note that the Windows SharePoint Services (WSS) concept directly competes with the concept of sharing folders and files by placing shared data on the Companyweb SharePoint site.

- **Mapping drives.** We assume you're comfortable with the drive mapping and shared drive concepts. Typically you map a drive to a shared folder. In Windows XP, an easy way to map a drive is to right click on **My Computer** and select **Map Network Drive**. Vista performs a similar keystroke from Start, Network.

- **UPS power levels**. If you believe all the APC ads you see in computer trade journals and consumer magazines, you'd believe that protection from power matters is important with your computers. It is! Not only should you have bona fide UPS devices and surge protectors in place, but you should monitor power levels with the software tools like PowerChute. (This typically ships with an APC UPS.) Power to the people, baby!

- **End-user support.** Even pious and haughty SBSers have to engage in end-user support. It's a double-edged sword: technical support and customer service. (Harry's *SMB Consulting Best Practices* book goes much deeper into this!) The authors didn't have to look far for an example of end-user support. As this chapter was being written, Patti at SMB Nation e-mailed Harry with a concern about processor utilization (Patti wanted to roll back to Windows XP!) and Philip was called out to client site. You gotta love it.

- **Disk defragmentation.** Use Diskeeper. Enough said.

Monthly/Annual

With the generational evolution of the SBS 2008 product, the list of specific tasks to complete on a monthly or annual basis has actually gotten shorter. That is because Microsoft has either taken over the operation programmatically or the technology has evolved and there is no need to continue out-dated "best practices." An example of this is the referral to a set of prescriptive whitepapers in the SBS 2003 edition of this book. Those white papers are not even available anymore.

- **Test restore.** Regardless of the snake oil you might have purchased or the magic elixir you use that cures everything, you are hereby commanded to perform a TEST RESTORE both monthly and annually. A full-blown disaster recovery exercise performed annually isn't out of the question and should receive your serious consideration.

- **Google it.** The authors are the first to admit that much of the SBS knowledge has moved online in a Web 2.0 kinda way. Search engines, blogs, twits, and the like have changed the way we find information. Figure 12-11 shows a recent GoogleAnalytics report from the SMB Dude blog showing key search terms.

- **Watch it.** Both authors are committed to bringing Webinars to the readers during the shelf life of this book. This will make this book more active—as the authors discovered in two well-attended Webinars in the fall of 2008. The interaction afforded by Webinars really adds to your SBS experience and allows you to ascend to the next level.

- **Read it.** Books and magazines are still relevant. Both of these printed media provide more context than clicking on a Web banner or reading a truncated blog entry.

- **Plan it.** SBSers who serve small businesses are themselves small businesses. And one thing small businesses often do not have enough time for is strategic planning. That's too bad because there are many technology benefits for the small business that go underutilized in an SBS 2008 environment. For example, at SMB Nation, we honor and respect our SBS infrastructure but, truth be told, our ERP solution (NetSuite) is hosted. Another strategic conversation would be going GREEN! Did you know that you can optimize the SBS 2008 server's power consumption by selecting **Power Options** from Control Panel? Go ahead and go GREEN!

- **Attend it.** SBSers are professionals. And professionals should attend at least one conference per year. Not surprisingly, we recommend the SMB Convergence events put on by SMB Nation. ☺ See Figure 12-12.

Today

Search	Views
hp proliant server bundle sbs 2008	1
selling your small consulting practice	1
procedure how to set up computer?	1
windows 2003 business come with sharepoi	1

Yesterday

Search	Views
"large file" iis sharepoint –upload	4
70–282	3
small business server web email access h	3
how to set up windows sbs 2003	2
best sbs 2003 book ?	2
how do i setup sbs 2008	2
sbs2003 disk quota	2
firewall for sbs 2008	2
sbs2003 backup	2
sbs 2003 change share name user shared f	2

Figure 12-11
Important search terms used to find SBS information.

TIP: The next chapter on performance topics aligns well with the above quick hitter discussion. Much of the SBS 2008 reporting alerts you to performance, storage, and security issues.

Figure 12-12
SMB Convergence events bring together GeekSpeak and BusinessSpeak.

Role of Managed Services

Guess what? When the last version of SBS shipped (that was SBS 2003 in October 2003), the word "managed services" was not in common usage. Today, as the authors wrote this chapter on the traditional daily/weekly/monthly/annual tasks view of the world, it became apparent that what we're running around doing is now, to a large extent, called MANAGED SERVICES!

There are many opinions, books, blogs, and thought leaders in the managed services space. This section simply introduces a relevant conversation about managed services in the SBS 2008 time frame. So we have three conversations here: Harry, Philip, Karl (long-time SBSer Karl Palachuk was invited to share his thoughts).

Harry

Fad or here to stay? As a long-time industry observer, I have watched from afar the madness surrounding the managed services paradigm shift in the SMB sector in general and in the SBS community in particular. There are a lot of new players in the managed services game hoping to assist you in managing your SBS world. Here is a list of our SMB friends in this space, and I heartily encourage you to learn more about the solutions being offered up.

- Management
    - o   AutoTask
    - o   ConnectWise
    - o   TigerPaw

- Monitoring
    - o   Level Platforms
    - o   Kaseya
    - o   Zenith Infotech
    - o   HoundDog
    - o   N-able Technologies

- Miscellaneous
    - o   19thMarketPlace
    - o   Fieldpoint (alert software)

o   LabTech Software

o   NetEnrich

o   NTR Global

o   VirtualAdministrator

Philip

We decided that for our company we would take a hybrid approach to managed services. We did this because the primary client industry we support is accounting. When we broached the subject with our accounting clients about adopting a managed services model, they did not go for it. Since we were already providing them with a stable infrastructure, the value was not there for them.

We ended up with a compromise: We would bill monthly for all of the reporting and monitoring that we were doing, along with remote patch management (as we refreshed their server hardware we implemented Intel's Remote Management Module 2 for out-of-band and remote console access) and other small things such as that five-minute support call. We would provide a "living" audit of the client's network along with an up-to-date Visio network drawing. System serial numbers, age, warranty status, and the users who have a particular piece of equipment would be a part of the audit as well.

As we migrate our clients to SBS 2008 and have access to WSS V3, we will transition our extensive audits to a secured Wiki on the client's Companyweb site. Wiki access will be restricted to those who need to know.

Keeping the managed services model in mind, we set up a fee structure of other services we were providing on a regular basis such as backup management and off-site rotations. We started offering the backup rotation service when we had a client's server crash completely and the person who was responsible for changing the magazines in the tape libraries went sheet white when asked for the previous magazine sets. He had not been rotating them and the backup software did not fire off any e-mail events to that effect. We managed to recover all of their data with the exception of 24 files out of 650GB-worth of data using a combination of a number of data redundant systems we had in place, including the tapes. The partners were pretty happy with that.

We then added a quarterly recovery option, which close to 100 percent of our clients took. So, we amalgamated that extra service into the backup rotation service to provide more value. We then added an option for monthly recovery tests.

A recovery test is defined as taking the client's ShadowProtect image and restoring it to a server in our shop that may not necessarily share the same hardware configuration as our client's server setup. We could then take a laptop from that client, log on to the newly recovered SBS domain, and have full access to all of the user's data.

Karl

Managed computer systems take some time to set up. You have to decide what to monitor and which kind of alert will to generate. But once you've got it set up, the automated monitoring takes the place of manually checking up on every server every day (week, month).

It took me a long time to feel comfortable NOT doing a complete daily, weekly, and monthly checkup for all client servers. We whittled down the list slowly over time. We became comfortable with the fact that disc space, SMTP queues, and CPU time were monitored twenty-four hours a day, seven days a week. So were all the critical services.

Once we were comfortable that our system never missed a critical or important event, we stopped manually checking events every day. In the end, we found that only one item from daily/weekly/monthly checklists still needed to be done manually: verifying backups. As much as we tried to work with clients on this, we decided that a 100 percent reliable backup and recovery scenario still requires one of us to verify the backup every month.

When we do daily/weekly/monthly monitoring by a manual process, it can easily take several hours per machine over the course of a month. When we narrow it down to one item, it takes less than half an hour of labor per month. That's what managed services is all about!

Notes

Managed Services and the Daily/Weekly/Monthly checklist

For reference, my 68-point checklist has long been the basis for monthly maintenance. To get a copy, send email to checklist@kpenterprises.com. The list will bounce back.

- Monitoring:
    - o Is the machine online?
- Base Server Performance
    - o Memory % Committed Bytes In Use
    - o Memory Available MBytes
    - o Memory Page Faults/sec
    - o Memory Pages/sec
    - o Paging File % Usage
    - o Processor % Processor Time Total CPU
    - o Processor Queue Length
- Critical Services
    - o AntiVirus Service
    - o Blackberry Server
    - o DHCP Server
    - o DNS Service
    - o IISADMIN
    - o MSExchangeIS
    - o MSExchangeMGMT
    - o MSExchangeSA
    - o MSExchangeSRS
    - o MSSQL$SBSMONITORING
    - o MSSQL$SHAREPOINT Sharepoint
    - o MSSQL$xxx etc.
    - o Print Spooler
    - o Server Reboot (Check the Status of Server Uptime)
    - o SMTP Queues

o   SQL Server common threads

o   Terminal Services

o   WinVNC

o   w3svc

o   w32time

Patch Management

Normally, there is a schedule. Let's say Microsoft releases something on Tuesday. We at KP normally wait a day and watch the board to make sure there are no problems (or on rare occasions that a patch is recalled). We schedule updates to be pushed to our own servers on Thursday night. Again, assuming there are no issues, we schedule the updates to be pushed to clients on Sunday night.

Any time frame will work. We recommend a bit of a delay between a Microsoft release, the application in-house, and the application on client machines. Sunday is a good time for system work because we can address any unexpected issues first thing Monday morning.

Summary

When an author updates a book for a new product cycle, there is always the belief the chapter updates will be easy and essentially consist of minor date changes. In writing this chapter, it became apparent how much the world has changed between SBS 2003 and SBS 2008. Tasks performed daily, weekly, monthly, and annually just a few years ago have changed.

In this chapter, the following topics were discussed.

- The care and feeding of a SBS 2008 server was presented in the context of daily, weekly, monthly, and annual tasks.
- The importance of backup was stressed.
- Three backup methods where explored including the native SBS 2008 backup, on-premise third-party solutions, and off-premise hosted backup solutions.
- Antivirus and malware solutions were presented, primarily from a third-party point of view.

- Microsoft strategy concerning ForeFront and Live OneCare were presented.
- There was a discussion about a Task Scheduler and WSUS.
- Quick Hitters were presented for the daily, weekly, monthly, and annual time frame.
- The role of managed services in the SBS 2008 world was discussed.

We move forward into the next chapter on monitoring.

CHAPTER 13

Monitoring Small Business Server 2008

This chapter concludes the core SBS 2008 discussion in this text with a bang—namely the exciting area of performance monitoring. This is a special chapter to write as it brings back the thrill Harry felt sixteen (!) books ago when he wrote the initial chapter of his first book on network performance monitoring. Hopefully, you'll pick up on this excitement and not treat it as a task area with the drudgery of auditing! No offense to our friends in the wonderful accounting profession.

So why get excited about performance monitoring? One reason is that performance monitoring includes both the "bits" and "biz" of technology. It's the hardcore system statistics that MCSEs love. And it's trend-watching that the MBAs like. This mindset maps very closely to the SBS product position, as it's a product with both a technical and business dimension to it.

Past readers of the *SBS Best Practices* books from SMB Nation Press and real-world SBS gurus might be asking, "Just what are some of the "delta" changes in the performance monitoring area with SBS 2008?" We've compiled a short list:

- Improved and simplified reporting. The basic monitoring paradigm is essentially two reports: Summary Network Report and the Detailed Network Report.

- Turned ON by default. The performance reports are turned on by default and e-mailed to Windows SBS Administrators. This is different from SBS 2003.

- Emphasizing what's needed and deemphasizing what's not needed. You will no longer have direct access to the Health Monitor application. It is not shown in the Administrative Tools Program group.

- Snap-ins. You can open a MCC and select the Reliability and Performance Monitor and the Reliability Monitor if you want to do a deep dive into performance analytics.

- Monitoring workstations. The SBS 2008 monitoring process extends down to the workstation level. This is a huge improvement from prior SBS releases.

- The ability to receive the network reports via fax has been removed.

You Are Already Doing It!

Here's an SBS confidence booster. You are already engaged in performance monitoring whether you know it or not. Sure, you're waiting with bated breath to complete the procedures to configure and implement native SBS monitoring. But that telephone call you got from a client (or user) today to complain a network is running slow IS PERFORMANCE MONITORING! Folks using your network will always be your number one performance monitor on a network, plain and simple. Don't believe us? Well, what if the power went out and the fancy network monitoring tools in SBS 2008 couldn't fire? A user can easily reach you via your mobile telephone to report those infamous words "…the network is down." We rest our case.

As you work on an SBS network, you might be your own toughest critic (aka, performance monitor). You are going to be the one who knows that something just isn't right! It's running slow. It's not running at all. It's running intermittently, etc. Consciously or unconsciously, you're already engaging in performance monitoring. All this chapter will do is add more tools to your toolkit and more arrows to your quiver.

Configuring Monitoring

A few 50,000 foot-level comments before configuring the "good stuff," as a friend of ours in the Microsoft server clustering testing area would say. (That's you, Jimbo!) On a plus note, it's now VERY EASY to implement the important performance monitoring function in SBS 2008. You'll do so in just a few seconds by reviewing the Reports page in the Windows SBS Console.

So let's rock and roll and review performance monitoring:

1. Log on to the SBS 2008 server machine as **JonathanPaul** with the password **L0ts and lots of fun!**

2. Click **Reports** on the Windows SBS Console.

3. Select **Summary Network Report** and view the information on the screen You will review the information for Security, Updates, Backup, Other Alerts, E-Mail Usage and Mailbox Sizes, and Server Events Logs. Your screen should look similar to Figure 13-1.

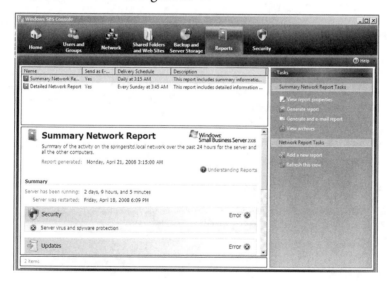

Figure 13-1
Core performance information is displayed on the Summary Network Report page.

TIP: Click the **Understanding Reports** link. You will be taken to the online Windows Small Business Server TechCenter at Microsoft TechNet. Read it now!

4. Select **View report properties** under the Summary Network Report Tasks. The Summary Network Report Properties dialog box will appear.

5. In the left column, click each option (**General, Content, E-mail Options, Schedule, Archives**) and click **OK**. You will get a quick view of the settings for the report.

6. Select **Detailed Network Report** and click **View report properties**.

7. Click the settings for **General, Content, E-Mail Options**, and **Schedule** and **Archives** in the left column and click **OK**.

TIP: Did you notice something on the Content page between the Summary Network Report and the Detailed Network Report? The Detailed Network Report had every content selected: Summary, Security, Updates, Backup, Other Alerts, E-Mail Usage, Server Event Logs. (See Figure 13-2.) The Summary Network Report had only the Summary selection. Makes sense to us!

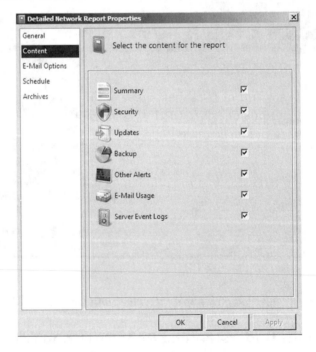

Figure 13-2
Content selections for the Detailed Network Report Properties.

8. With Detailed Network Report selected in the items list, scroll down to the center of the page and observe the high level of detail being reported. An example of this is Figure 13-3.

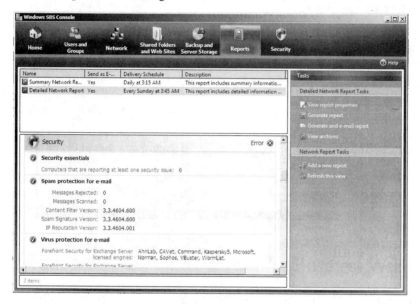

Figure 13-3
Viewing the security details.

9. Click **Generate Report** under Detailed Network Report Tasks under Tasks. Click **OK** when the Generating report dialog box completes the task. Observe the report content is updated in the center of the screen.

10. Click **Generate and e-mail report** under Detailed Network Report Tasks under Tasks. Click **OK** on the Generating report dialog box.

You have now completed your "learning lesson" about monitoring on the server-side, and we will have you move to the client side:

1. Log on to the workstation **SS-FeedingCare** as **BobEaster** with the password **Lots to eat!**

2. Launch Outlook from Start.

3. Observe the Inbox, which should look similar to Figure 13-4. The Summary Network Report was sent from the SBSMonAcct. The Detailed Network Report was sent from JonathanPaul (as a result of your actions above in the prior procedure).

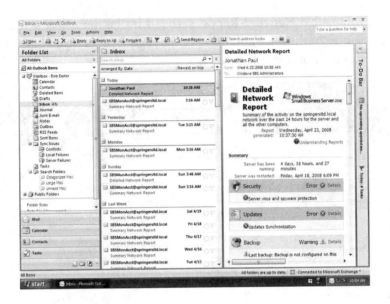

Figure 13-4
Receiving monitoring e-mails.

The question is, why did Bob Easter receive the reports? You would have noticed that Bob's name was actually enabled to receive the daily and weekly reports in the E-mail Options section of the report's properties.

The process of enabling an SBS user or an outside SBS consultant to receive the reports is fairly straightforward:

1. Log on to the SBS 2008 server machine as **JonathanPaul** with the password **L0ts and lots of fun!**

2. Click on the **Reports** tab in the Windows SBS Console.

3. Click on the **Summary Network Report** item in the list.

4. Click on the **View report properties** under the Tasks column.

5. Click the **E-mail Options** category.

6. Put a checkmark beside **Bob Easter**.

7. Click **Apply** and **OK**.

8. Repeat the process for the **Detailed Network Report**.

Bob Easter will now received the daily and weekly e-mailed SBS reports. The above reports e-mail properties for Bob Easter are shown in Figure 13-5.

Figure 13-5

Bob Easter, along with MPECS Inc., will receive the daily and weekly server monitoring reports.

TIP: This might be a good place to call it a night. Why you ask? Because by default both the detailed and summary reports are scheduled to send very early in the morning. Specifically, the Summary Network Report is scheduled by default to send at 3:15AM daily. The Detailed Network Report is scheduled to send every Sunday at 3:45AM. This once-a-week report is timed to arrive just before church so you can both pray for and be thankful for your SBS 2008 network.

The beauty of having the Summary Network Report sent at 3:15AM daily is several-fold. First, it's late enough that things like the backup will have been completed and an accurate backup log will have been generated. We also like the 3:15AM time frame because we're receiving the report shortly before the start of the business day. Therefore, we know that as of 3:15AM, the SBS server machine was up and running. We also know the site had power, an Internet connection, and about five other things going for it (e.g., several Exchange services were functioning).

Interpreting Monitoring Settings and Results

Simple is as simple does. Remember that we are working with small businesses, not the enterprise. So it is essential to remain rational and not become too obsessed with the deep object: counter reporting and trying to monitor stuff that really doesn't matter. Basically you should read the daily summary e-mail and the weekly detailed e-mail to monitor the primary areas outlined for you: Security, Updates, Backup, Other Alerts, E-Mail Usage and Statistics, and Server Event Logs.

For now, in this introductory text, let common sense be your guide (see our next TIP). In the advanced SBS 2008 text to follow this book, you will be treated to engineering-level analysis that takes monitoring to an entirely new level. You will also learn about intermediate monitoring topics later in this chapter.

> **TIP:** What to do with all this data? The answer is to use common sense. A few time-tested rules known by many administrators (going back to the early Novell CNE days) are:
>
> - Add for more disk space when you have less than 20 percent free space. Also make sure disks are healthy and not excessively fragmented.
>
> - A processor that exceeds 80 percent utilization over several days suggests a processor or hardware upgrade is in order.
>
> - RAM memory consumption should be monitored to make sure it doesn't grow excessively and you have sufficient free RAM memory (say, 25 percent free).
>
> - Network traffic. Watch for broadcast storms that could slow network traffic.

Okay—this is the point at which SBS readers ask, "What do I do with this stuff?" or "Why am I here?" The concern expressed is about adding more value for the customer from the performance-monitoring tool in SBS 2008. So here is your payoff. YOU REPLY BACK TO YOUR SBS 2008 CUSTOMERS THAT EVERYTHING IS FINE! The point we're trying to make here, on which Harry spends over 600 pages in his SMB Consulting Best Practices book, is that you need to reply back to your client each and every day to the Summary Network Report e-mail you receive as the SBS consultant. Over-communicate with your client and riches shall follow!

If you simply click **Reply**, it will revert to the sender's account. So add the appropriate customer name in the **To** field in the e-mail. When you add a few warm comments like "Good Morning" and "The backup reports were successful last night," you will be a bona fide hero. You've put the office manager at ease.

It shouldn't be lost on you that you've "touched" each of the key stakeholders at each of your SBS customer sites each day with the suggested monitoring scenario here. That's how you get referrals and additional business in the whacky world of SBS consulting and riches will follow!

By the way, it's also acceptable to report that things are not well, such as the backup failed. SBS customers can handle bad news. It's more important that they receive such information rapidly and straight up. Then you can go solve the problem.

SPRINGERS time: Go ahead and reply to the Summary Network Report e-mail you have in the Inbox for Bob Easter. Tell Norm Hasborn that all is well and life is good. Be the bearer of good news (a rarity for many technical professionals who only appear in public when trouble arrives).

We close this interpretation section with a final thought. You'll be the best judge of what values are valid, germane, and correct as you work with SBS 2008 over time. You'll learn to detect false alarms along the way, and you'll know a double-911 emergency when you see it. The point is to use these cool server monitoring tools in SBS 2008 and make 'em work for your individual situation.

More Monitoring Tools

Forward we move. Here are some intermediate tools for your consideration in the SBS 2008 monitoring area. First, let's highlight additional Windows SBS Console tabs that provide monitoring-like information. Then you will be exposed to some native Windows Server 2008 tools.

1. Log on to the SBS 2008 server machine as **JonathanPaul** with the password **L0ts and lots of fun!**

2. Click on the **Network** tab in the SBS Console, followed by the **Connectivity** tab. Observe the Status column, indicating Internet and network connectivity.

3. Click on the **Backup and Server Storage** button followed by the **Server Storage** tab. Observe the Status column.

You will recall the consoles were explored in Chapter 4 (we thought you might appreciate that cross-reference).

Snap-Ins

Now you need to add two snap-ins into an MMC as per the following procedure:

1. If necessary, log on to the SBS 2008 server machine as **JonathanPaul** with the password **L0ts and lots of fun!**

2. Click **Start**, **Run** and type **MMC** in the **Open** field.

3. Click **Continue** at the User Access Control dialog box. Console 1 appears.

4. Select **File, Add/Remove Snap-in**.

5. Select **Reliability and Performance** under Available Snap-ins and click **Add**.

6. Select **Reliability Monitor** under Available Snap-ins and click **Add**. Your efforts should look similar to Figure 13-6

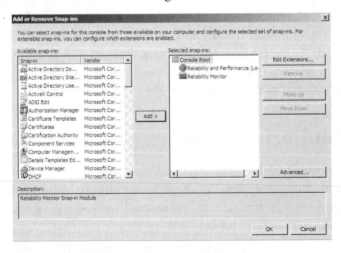

Figure 13-6
Adding performance monitoring tools to the SPRINGERS methodology.

7. Click **OK**.

8. Click **File, Save** and name the MMC as **SpringersPerformance.msc**. Note, this will now appear in the Administrative Tools program group.

9. Expand all categories under the Console Root until your screen appears similar to Figure 13-7.

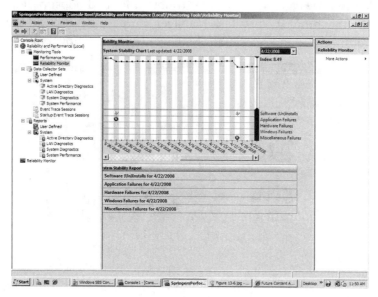

Figure 13-7
Here is where you find the hidden performance monitoring power in SBS 2008!

Baselining

There are many good network-performance monitoring white papers on the concept of baselining. This is the idea: You visit a client site and conduct a site survey (create an as-built drawing of the network layout, take initial baseline performance readings using a variety of tools, etc.). You then have a comprehensive baseline of the SBS 2008 network. At future dates, say quarterly, you revisit the SBS network and simply repeat the same performance measurements. Over time, you build up a pretty good-sized database, can track declines in performance with precision, and can lucidly plan for network enhancements based on solid performance data. If you're an SBS consultant, you can bill some great hours providing this valuable service for your customers.

Task Manager

In the business world, at least until the fallout from Wall Street, it was "understood" that a chief financial officer (CFO) always kept a few tricks in his hip pocket to boost quarterly earnings. On a technical note, we consider Task Manager to be a hip-pocket tool we can use to quickly troubleshoot and boost performance on an SBS server machine. To view Task Manager, simply right click on the Task Bar on the server machine and select Task Manager (which is shown in Figure 13-8).

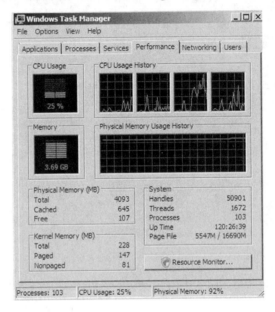

Figure 13-8
The Performance tab is perhaps the most useful part of Task Manager in glancing at processor utilization and memory consumption.

TIP: The Networking tab in Task Manager is an excellent way to glance at network traffic when a user complains that the "network is running SLOOOOW!"

Disk Defragmenter

While we discussed disk defragmentation in the last chapter, we're honor-bound (that's honour-bound in British Commonwealth countries) to repeat ourselves here. One of the fastest ways to boost SBS network performance is to run **Disk Defragmenter** from the **System Tools** program group (from **Start, All Programs, Accessories**). Note that the SPR doesn't provide information on the fragmentation of disks on the SBS 2003 server machine. You can get that information only by using Disk Defragmenter and clicking either the **Analyze** or **Defragment** buttons.

Performance Monitor

Talk about a tool that's stood the test of time! Performance Monitor (also known as System Monitor) has been around since the earliest versions of SBS! It's found from the SpringerPerformance MMC you created earlier.

1. Open the SpringersPerformance MMC (from your Administrative Tools program group).

2. Click **Reliability and Performance → Monitoring Tools → Performance Monitor**.

3. Click the **Add** button (green plus sign) to display the Add Counters dialog box.

4. Add these three counters from Available Counters by finding them, then clicking on them, choosing <**All instances**> and then the **Add** button under the instances list.

   - **% Usage** (from Paging File)
   - **Avg. Disk Queue Length** (from Physical Disk)
   - **% Processor Time** (from Processor)

5. Click **OK**. Your screen should appear with a graph showing you instant performance statistics.

Notes

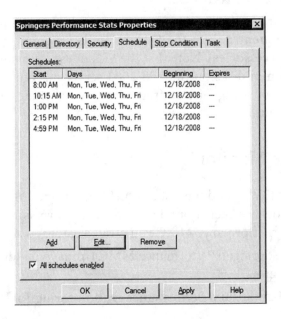

Figure 13-9

Like other cool monitoring tools, Performance Monitor is free in SBS 2008, so take it for a test drive. It's an excellent baselining tool with its ability to save data logs.

TIP: Two cool things you can do with Performance Monitor (amongst hundreds of cool things), are to view the data as a histogram (Ctrl-G keystroke) and save the chart as a dynamic Web page that's cooler than a childhood in Canada or Alaska. (Right click on the chart and select **Save As** from the secondary menu that appears.)

One more thing to check out before we move on to other monitoring tools and abilities in SBS: One way to establish the baseline to work from is to create a standard collector set in the Reliability and Performance node while in the SpringersPerformance MMC.

1. Click on the **Data Collector Sets** node.

2. Right click on **User Defined**, hover over **New**, and click on **Data Collector Set**.

3. Name the new set: **Springers Performance Stats** and click **Next**. Leave the "Create from a template" option for now.

4. Select **System Performance** for the template and click **Next**.

5. Leave the default location for storing the data and click **Next**.

6. Leave the default for Run as and click the **Finish** button.

You will now have a data collector set ready that you can use to understand how your SPRINGERS SBS box is performing throughout the day.

Right click on the Springers Performance Stats data collector set and click **Start**. A Play icon will appear on the Springers Performance Stats under the User Defined folder and you will see the directories appear where the data that is being collected will be stored.

Once the data collection has completed, you will find the report that has been created by right clicking on the Springers Performance Stats data collector set and clicking on **Latest Report**.

You will see a System Performance Report as shown in Figure 13-10.

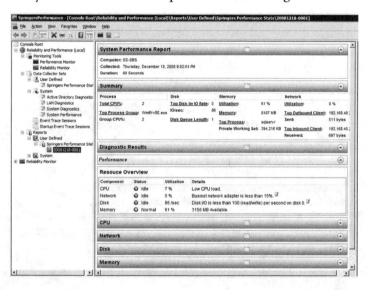

Figure 13-10
From establishing your baseline to keeping an eye on your SBS performance over time—you can do it.

Obviously, running the data collection once is not going to cut it when it comes to establishing and keeping an eye on the SBS box's performance metrics.

Head on up to the Springers Performance Stats data collector set and right click on it then click on **Properties**. Among the various tab options available to you there is a schedule tab. You can create a set of daily data collection times, such as 8AM when everyone is logging in for the morning, around 1PM when they are back from lunch, then a few sample times through the work day to see how things look during a regular work day.

The benefit of having the data collection scheduled over the process of the work day is the ability to discern patterns of behavior in the server. Your initial reports give you an idea of how the server behaved while fresh out of the box, while the reports 18 months or 30 months down the road can show how the various patches and updates have impacted the server's performance.

Command Line Stuff

Time to throw a bone to the SBS gurus again. Here's a bona fide command line-based performance monitor tool you can use to aid and assist your efforts to manage your SBS 2003 network. From the command line, simply type **netstat –o** and observe the port scanning activity in real time that affects your SBS 2008 server machine. This is shown in Figure 13-11 below.

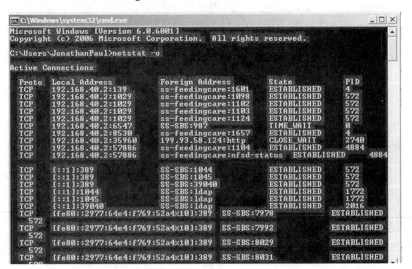

Figure 13-11
   A quick (and also free) way to observe traffic by port is the netstat –o command. Bon appetit!

One more little tidbit for you: PortQry V2.0. Go to http://support.microsoft.com/kb/832919 to check out the abilities of this powerful little utility. Along with the netstat command, PortQry will give you the ability to query the various ports on a server and workstation.

Event Log Structures

The Event Logs in SBS 2008 have been greatly improved beyond the passive event logging we had in Windows Server 2003 and SBS 2003.

The traditional Event Logs are present as shown in Figure 13-12.

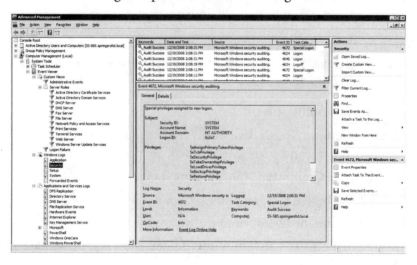

Figure 13-12
Along with the traditional server event logs, you can now set up filters, e-mail alerts, and more for most, if not all events on the server.

The Event Logs are to be found in the Windows SBS Native Tools Management console:

1. Open the Windows SBS Native Tools Management console.

2. Click **Continue** when prompted by the UAC.

3. Click on the **Computer Management (Local)** snap-in.

4. Double click on **System Tools** in the middle column.

5. Click on the **Event Viewer** node. You will see a summary list of the various event logs.

6. Click the + beside Event View to break out the various sub folders.

Have a look around the new Event Log setup. There are a number of new already-defined filters in place for you to use, as a quick way to narrow your troubleshooting or performance evaluation efforts.

Click on each of the custom filters under the Server Roles folder to see events specific to that server role.

When it comes to managing your SBS servers, it is important to know when there are failed attempts to log on to the SBS domain.

With the new Event Log setup, you can now set up an e-mail notification if a certain event happens. So, that means you can receive an e-mail every time an attempt to log on to the server fails.

To set up the e-mail notification:

1. If the Windows SBS Native Tools Management console is not already opened, open it and acknowledge the UAC prompt.

2. Click on the **Computer Management (Local)** snap-in.

3. Click the + beside System Tools.

4. Click the + beside Event Viewer.

5. Right click on the **Custom Views** folder and click on **Create Custom View...**

6. Set the following settings in place for the Filter and click **OK**:

    - Logged: **Any time**
    - By log: **Security**
    - Event ID: **4625** (note that the <All Event IDs> will disappear when you click in that field)
    - Computers: Remove the <All Computers>

7. Name the filter: **SBS Failed Logons**.

8. Give it a description: **Any failed logon events.**

9. Click **OK**. Do not close the Event Viewer node yet as you will need to work the filter a bit more.

Okay, so, now you have the custom filter for failed logons. However, go ahead and click on it and you will see a list of failed logons for a large number of different situations. In this case, you are looking only for failed user logons, so you will need to tweak the underlying XML code to narrow the filter's range:

1. Right click on your new custom filter **SBS Failed Logons**. Click on **Properties**.

2. Click the **Edit Filter** button.

3. Click the **XML** tab.

4. Click the **Edit query manually** option near the bottom left.

5. Click the **Yes** button when you receive the Event Viewer warning.

6. Place your cursor in the middle of the two]] to the left of </Select> shown below.

    • The line: <Select Path="Security">*[System[(EventID=4625)]**HE RE**]</Select>

7. Type the following: and EventData[Data[@Name="SubjectLogonId"] = "0x3e4"]

    • The exact line: <Select Path="Security">*[System[(EventID =4625)] and EventData[Data[@Name="SubjectLogonId"] = "0x3e4"]]</Select>

    • Note that there is a space in between the first] and the word "and".

    • Figure 13-13 shows you the exact syntax of the XML. Note that it is case- and space-sensitive!

8. Click **OK** twice. If you get an invalid code error, you will need to bring the filter's XML back up and look through it to see where the mistake is.

9. Leave the SBS Failed Logons highlighted for the next steps.

otes

Figure 13-13
The exact syntax for the custom filter.

The final step is to set up the filter to fire off an e-mail if an event fits the filter criteria:

1. Right click on the SBS Failed Logons filter and click on **Attach Task to This Custom View...**

2. Leave the default name and click the **Next** button.

3. Click **Next** at the Custom Event Filter step.

4. Click the **Send an e-mail** radio button and click **Next**.

5. Fill out the Send an E-mail form as follows, then click **Next**:
   - From: **SpringersSBS@springersltd.com**
   - To: **BobE@springersltd.com**
   - Subject: **Failed User Logon**
   - Text: **A failed attempt to log on to the server has been logged**
   - SMTP server: **SS-SBS**

6. Have a look at the summary and make sure all the settings are correct, then click the **Finish** button.

7. Click **OK** when you receive the editing information pop-up.

To test the configuration, connect to the Remote Web Workplace and try to log on as Bob Easter with an incorrect password. Once you have done that, log on as Bob Easter and click into his Outlook Web Access to view the resultant e-mail (Figure 13-14).

Figure 13-14
The e-mail shown was the one that arrived in the general MPECS Inc. e-mail box. If the need is high enough, a rule can be set up in Outlook to page us.

We have just touched the tip of the new Event Log's iceberg. There are so many new features and abilities, we can show you only these few. Dig deeper, read the Help files associated with the new Event Logs, browse the Internet, and, of course, keep an eye on our blogs for more!

Poor Man's Managed Services

Talk about a workshop just waiting to be developed. Taken as a whole, the monitoring and management tools in SBS 2008 are like a poor man's managed services (without the legal contracts and written proposal). Think about it. Managed services is made of up two components: technical and business. This chapter has shown you the technical-side SBS 2008 tools that make up this equation. Now the business discussion.

Back to Business!

At the end of the day, many SBSers ask how something in SBS 2008 improves their life and that of their customers. With respect to having a network that purrs and hums, the monitoring tools contribute greatly. With respect to SBS consultants, the gold standard is slightly different: It's based on gold. That is, how can you make money in the performance-monitoring area with your SBS customers? There are many different business models out there. We are aware of the following ways that SBS consultants are implementing the performance-monitoring area into their service model:

- Fixed fee. You could charge $100 per month to continuously monitor the SBS 2008 network.

- Maintenance contract. You could charge $500 per month to maintain the SBS 2008 network and those services would include performance monitoring.

- Day rate. How 'bout a dollar a day for network performance monitoring, eh?

- Give away the milk, get the cow. This is actually our favorite. Provide the performance-monitoring function free and make it all up in extra work (because your superior customer service leads to great billable hours) and/or billable time you book to resolve problems. Don't laugh, as this approach deserves a serious second look.

TIP: The road to SBS consulting profitability travels through the performance-monitoring area, irrespective of what your specific business model is. Why? Because performance monitoring will most assuredly result in better customer service. You'll be well aware of SBS 2008 maladies and performance-related matters before your customer will. You'll be "Johnny on the spot," already working on a solution when the customer calls with a problem. Better yet, you'll call the customer in advance of them discovering the problem. You read it here first!

Notes

Third Partyisms

This section discusses some cool third-party ecosystem participants and how they roll in the SBS 2008 performance monitoring space. God bless small businesses for the daily ingenious innovations that are created!

But those evangelical comments aside, what the third-party ecosystem really does is take you, the SBSer, to the next level. We like to think of the native SBS monitoring tools as akin to WordPad and the more advanced third-party resources as akin to Microsoft Word 2007. Hopefully you get our drift.

SBS Code Plex

A resource mentioned in Appendix A and other places in this text is Susan Bradley, the SBS Diva. Susan created a spot on the Code Plex site at www.codeplex.com/sbs/ for some XML code you can use to create Custom Alerts that will fire a Code Red in the SBS Console under Other Alerts! The site is shown in Figure 13-15.

Figure 13-15
The SBS Code Plex site has a number of Custom Alerts for you.

We will let the SBS Code Plex site explain the specifics to you. However, one example on the site is a contribution by one of the authors to fire an alert when there is a user logon failure.

Figure 13-16 shows you the result when you install the FailedLogon.XML file in the appropriate place on the SBS server.

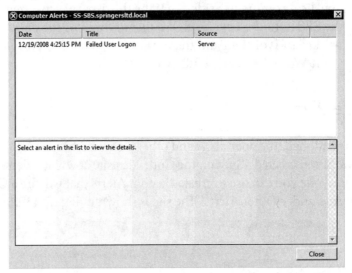

Figure 13-16
A failed logon attempt causes the Other Alerts to go red on the SBS Console Home Page. Click through to **Computers** *and click* **View computer alerts** *to see the alert content.*

As you can see, the new Event Log and monitoring setups are very robust. You can take their features and abilities and create some very robust monitoring setups.

Level Platforms (LPI)

The LPI story is amazing. This firm emerged on the scene shortly after the launch of SBS 2003 and successfully marketed monitoring to the SBSers. Its business model has changed over the years, starting with a fee per day per workstation and evolving into a mature managed services offering. This Canadian-based company is a long-time supporter of the SMB channel in general and SBS in particular, and it deserves your consideration. LPI is shown in Figure 13-17 and you can learn more at www.levelplatforms.com.

Figure 13-17
Meet LPI!

Kaseya

It is always interesting to see how loyal customers are to a particular firm or solution. When we have met SBsers using Kaseya, we hear that they LOVE IT! Compared to LPI, Kaseya is a relatively new entrant to the SBS crowd, but it has made great strides and built up significant good will in a short amount of time. You can learn more about Kaseya at www.kaseya.com and can contact one of its 20 offices worldwide. Kaseya is shown in Figure 13-18.

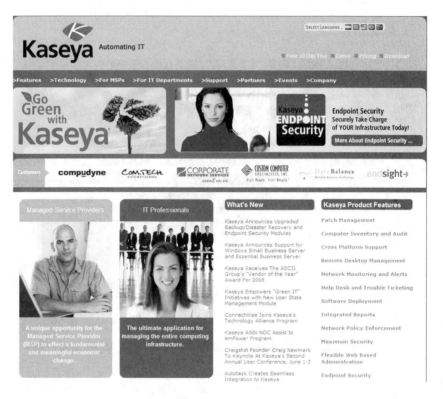

Figure 13-18
Kaseya has built a loyal following in the SBS crowd.

Summary

It goes without saying—but we'll say it anyway—that performance monitoring in SBS 2008 is one of the great opportunities to excel as an SBSer! Use the launch pad provided in this chapter to implement the native performance monitoring in SBS 2008 and then go forth and take it to the next level. This chapter covered the following topics:

- Delta differences from SBS 2003 to SBS 2008 were pointed out to you.
- We confirmed you are already monitoring performance.
- You learned how to configure basic performance monitoring.
- Guidance on interpreting performance monitoring settings and results was provided.

- You were introduced to additional monitoring tools in SBS 2008 and the underlying Windows Server 2008 operating system.

- A lively conversation on the "poor man's managed services" paradigm was presented.

- You were introduced to third-party ecosystem resources and partners.

Consider performance monitoring to have a high return on investment. The hours you invest herein are returned many times over with an optimally performing network or the financial rewards that accrue to the SBS consultant amongst us. Bravo!

SECTION FOUR

Small Business Server 2008 Advance Topics

Chapter 14
Small Business Server Advanced Security

Chapter 15
SBS 2008 Premium and SQL Server 2008

Chapter 14

Small Business Server Advanced Security

Welcome to THE chapter on advanced security. This is our view of the world on advanced security topics you should be aware of early in the life of SBS 2008. We are completely aware that security is a career path; there are several major certifications dedicated to security along with numerous books and conferences that focus on the technology security topic. We do not claim to upstage those discrete resources in this chapter. Rather, we are providing you with security knowledge you need right here, right now. But, your security journey is only starting; it never ends.

Thinking Security!

When it comes to advanced security on any Windows domain setup, you will see that Group Policy offers a way of tightening things up for both servers and desktops.

There are actually some very simple things that you can do to make things a bit more difficult for an outsider to gain access to the SBS domain.

Here are some things to train your users to do:

- Lock their workstation when they are going to walk away from it for more than a minute. If they are in a publically accessible location such as a reception desk, then they should be locking the computer just before getting up for any reason.
  - o **CTRL+ALT+DEL** then **Lock this computer**.
- Close and save any work, then log off their workstations at the end of the day. Remember, if an update is released, the workstation will automatically install it and reboot even if there are applications open on it.
- Use passphrases for their logons. They are easy to remember.
- Never keep a sticky note with their network password anywhere around their workstation or desk!
- Keep Internet use to company-related tasks only.

We will address user network use later in this chapter when we address the need for an Acceptable Use Policy.

Some of the things that you can do as an SBS domain administrator is to tighten up desktop access and usability to facilitate those "Oops, I forgot to lock my workstation" moments.

To do this, you will be using Group Policy Objects and enabling some settings to harden your SBS network.

You will also set up a software distribution share and configure Windows Defender to be distributed to all of your Windows XP Professional desktops and laptops. Windows Defender is included in Windows Vista by default. It provides a level of malware protection for the local desktops.

Desktop Security

Keeping things fairly secure on the SBS domain workstations can facilitate the establishment of some professional usage boundaries when it comes to the company's IT infrastructure.

If security on the workstations is too lax out of the box, a company may experience an inordinate amount of productivity time lost to things like online messengers, online social sites, and the like. The other side to this coin is the loss of productivity due to virus or Trojan infections on company workstations and/or servers. Lost time, in whatever form that loss takes, costs the company money.

Acceptable Use Policy

It is imperative from a management and a legal perspective for a company to have an Acceptable Use Policy (AUP) in place. The AUP will outline what a user can and cannot do with company property, such as workstations and laptops. It will also outline what can and cannot be done with the company's Internet connection at their one site,, or all sites for branch office scenarios.

Some of the specifics that an AUP will contain:

- The user's username and password.

- Any username and password for Line of Business Applications.

- Password (passphrase) policies including the number of characters and password change frequency. Sticky notes with passwords are grounds for dismissal!

- How network resources such as shares, the Companyweb site, and mapped network drives are to be used or not to be used. Restricting video files from being saved or other large image files are some examples.

TIP: Keep in mind that there are file-filtering capabilities built into the Windows Server 2008 operating system. that underlies SBS. If large video, image, or other files are a problem in user's shares, then filters can be set up to put a limit on them or even eliminate the ability to store them in company shares.

As the SBS consultant, you could provide a service to your clients by building out a lawyer-vetted AUP and subsequently providing a customized version to them for a fee. We do this in our IT practice at MPECS Inc., with the service providing a nice feathering of the nest.

- Internet Explorer as the company's Web browser of choice with no other browsers to be installed on company equipment.

- AntiVirus and AntiMalware products that are to be on at all times.

- Outlook as the default e-mail, calendaring, task management, and contact management application.

- Laptop specific policies for connecting to the Internet via open wireless Hot Spots. For example, at-home make it a requirement for a WPA secured wireless access point.

- A signature line for both the employee and a witness signed on two copies—one for the employee and one for the company's records.

Having the AUP in place provides a starting point if you need to have a chat with a user about browsing habits, storing personal data on the network, or other situations that may arise in a workplace.

The AUP also provides a legal standing to work from if things go beyond a chat and into full-blown confrontation mode. While this type of situation rarely occurs, it is good to have things in place for those just-in-case situations.

Group Policy Workstation Security Settings

The settings to tighten up workstation security will be set into a Group Policy Object (GPO) that you will create at the SBSComputers Organizational Unit (OU) level.

1. Open the Windows SBS Native Tools Management Console.

2. Click **Continue** when you are prompted by the UAC.

3. Click on **Group Policy Management**.

4. You will need to drill down to the SBSComputers OU: Forest: springersltd. local → Domains → springersltd.local → MyBusiness → Computers → **SBSComputers**.

5. Right click on the **SBSComputers OU** and click on **Create a GPO in this domain, and Link it here…** as shown in Figure 14-1.

Notes

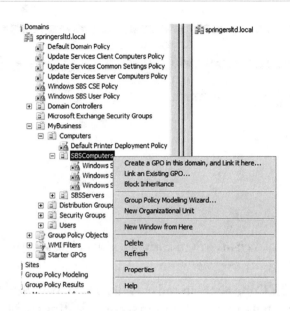

Figure 14-1
*To create a GPO that is OU-specific, right click first on that OU, then on **Create a GPO in this domain, and Link it here...***

6. Name the New GPO **Windows SBS Client - Default Security Policy** and click **OK**.

7. Leave the console open to the GPME snap-in for the next steps.

You now have a new GPO that you will use to establish a security structure for workstations and laptops on the SBS domain. You will change certain things, like how the user will log on to the workstation or unlock it, as well as setting the screen saver in place after a predetermined time are the next steps. However, before doing that, it is important to set a comment into the GPO itself so that others who may work with the SBS server will understand when the GPO was created and why.

Local Policies: User Rights Assignment

You will set some specific permissions for domain users.

1. Right click on the new GPO and click on **Edit**.

2. Right click on the GPO name at the top left and click on **Properties**. Figure 14-2 shows the right click menu.

Figure 14-2
When you right click on the GPO name you will be able to bring up its properties and set its scope as well as comments.

3. Click on the **Comment** tab and enter **08-11-15: New SBS Client Security Policy Created to set workstation security settings in place.** Click **Apply** and **OK**.

4. Under Computer Configuration click through to Policies → Windows Settings → Security Settings → Local Policies → **User Rights Assignment**.

5. To change the settings:

    • Double click on **Force shutdown from a remote system**.

    • Check **Define these policy settings:**

    • Click the **Add User or Group** button.

    • Click the **Browse** button.

    • Type **Domain Admins** and click the **Check Names** button. The name should be underlined if the group was found in Active Directory.

    • Click **OK** and **OK**. You should now see SPRINGERSLTD\Domain Admins in the policy setting window.

    • Click **Apply** and **OK**.

6. Click the **Start** button then **Run** and type: **GPUpdate /Force [Enter]**. If you are asked to log off after the update say **No** for now.

7. Do not close the GPO Editor as there is more to come.

TIP: You enable this setting for domain administrators because they need the ability to reboot servers and workstations remotely. You do not want your users to be able to reboot or shut down a workstation remotely because there may be a circumstance, such as a weekend, where no one will be available to turn that system back on!

Local Policies: Security Options

You will make some settings changes to tighten up workstation logon security, password security, and data protection.

8. Under Computer Configuration, click through to Policies → Windows Settings → Security Settings → Local Policies → **Security Options**.

9. Change the following settings:

- Interactive logon: Do not display last user name: **Enabled**. Note the Explain tab gives you a detailed explanation for the setting.

- Interactive logon: Do not require **CTRL+ALT+DEL: Disabled**. Note that some laptop manufacturer's security software may override this setting.

- Interactive logon: Number of previous logons to cache (in case domain controller is not available): **2 logons**.

- Network Security: Do not store LAN Manager hash value on next password change: **Enabled**.

- Shutdown: Allow system to be shut down without having to log on: **Disabled**.

10. Click the **Start** button, then **Run**, and type: **GPUpdate /Force [Enter]**. If you are asked to log off after the update say **No** for now.

11. Don't close the GPO editor as there are further changes afoot.

TIP: Interactive Logon: Okay, you now have the workstation set up so that users will need to type their username fully when they go to logon. This setting avoids a situation where just about anyone could walk up to the workstation and CTRL+ALT+DEL to see who last logged on to it.

By default, you want users to use that keystroke combination, as it is very difficult to mimic beyond the keyboard so you disabled the bypass for it. Keeping the last two credentials cached minimizes the possibility of having someone's credentials compromised when the workstation or laptop was not connected to the network.

Network Security: By not storing the LAN Manager hash value on the local workstation, you make it a lot more difficult for anyone to crack passwords on a stolen system. Windows Vista has this setting enabled by default.

Shutdown: It is always a good idea for the user to be logged on before shutting the system down. This gives any user-related services or applications the opportunity to be properly closed and/or shutdown prior to the system being turned off. If a shutdown is initiated from the logon screen, it is possible that services and/or applications may be corrupted by the inability to properly shut themselves down.

Shared Remote Connectivity Protection

One thing to keep in mind—besides the above shutdown protection for users who remotely connect to a computer—is to manage how users will interact with workstations while connected. You do not want users to be able to shut down the workstation when they are connected to it via the Remote Web Workplace.

However, you also do not want them to disconnect from the Remote Desktop session either. It is preferable to have users learn that they must close all work and log off.

In the case where multiple users may connect to one desktop, this consideration is very important. It is also a good idea to make sure users log off properly as a rule so to reduce the possibility of lost work due to applications being left open and not saved to disk or network.

So, we need to make a setting change in our Windows SBS Client – Default Security Group Policy Object.

Remove Disconnect from Start Menu

Again, in the Group Policy Management editor with the policy object opened for editing:

1. Under Computer Configuration, click through to Policies → Administrative Templates → Windows Components → Terminal Services → Terminal Server → **Remote Session Environment**.

TIP: This would be a good time to introduce Group Policy Filtering to you. This new feature, which is a part of the Windows Server 2008 Group Policy structure, allows you to find Group Policy settings under the Administrative Templates node for both the Computer and User Configuration nodes. It is a very powerful tool that will greatly simplify your Group Policy settings management.

You need to be in the Group Policy Object Editor to use the filtering feature. So, in the case of the editing you have been doing above, you could use the Windows SBS Client – Default Security Group Policy Object as an example. When you click on the **Administrative Templates** node for either Computer Configuration or User Configuration, you will find an **All Settings** node. Right click on that node, then click on **Filter Options**. You can set up your filters according to a wide variety of criteria as shown in Figure 14-3.

Notes

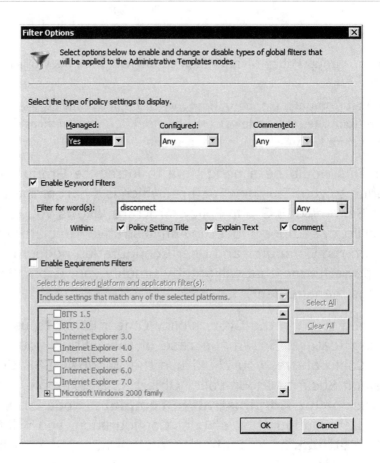

Figure 14-3
With the new and improved Group Policy setup in Windows Server 2008, you can find any Administrative Template setting with ease using Group Policy Filtering.

Once you have put your criteria in place and clicked **OK** in the Filter Options dialogue, you will be shown all of the GP settings locations your filter discovers. You will also see the filter symbol on the Administrative Templates note and any sub-folders indicating that only those folders that contain filter results will be shown.

Check out Figure 14-4. Talk about a totally cool feature in GP Filtering!

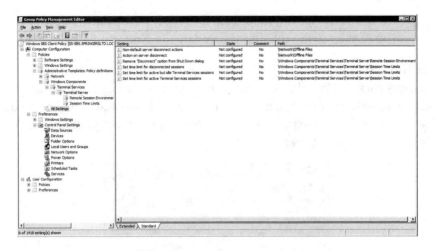

Figure 14-4
Once a filter has been set, only those settings that successfully meet the filter criteria will be seen!

For the SBS consultant, this will save you a lot of time over the course of supporting SBS 2008 installations.

2. Double click on the **Remove "Disconnect" option from Shut Down dialog** GP setting.

3. Click the **Enabled** radio button.

4. Click on the **Comment** tab and enter the following comment: **08-12-01: Enabled to prevent disconnections while remote.** Note the date format is Year-Month-Day for our file and folder structure.

5. Click the **Apply** button.

6. Click the **Next Setting** button to get to the Remove Windows Security item from Start menu GP setting.

7. Click the **Disabled** radio button.

8. Click on the **Comment** tab and enter the following comment: **08-12-01: Disabled to give users access while remote.** Note the date format is Year-Month-Day for our file and folder structures.

9. Click the **Apply** button.

10. Click **OK**.

11. Close the GPO Editor.

12. Click the **Start** button, then **Run**, and type: **GPUpdate /Force [Enter]**. If you are asked to log off after the update say **No** for now.

The second option makes sure the Windows Security item stays on the Start menu. When users click the Windows Security item, they will be presented with options to lock the computer, log off, change their password, and start the Task Manager. Figure 14-5 shows you what the Windows Security options look like on the SBS box while connected remotely.

Figure 14-5
After clicking on the Windows Security item, you have a number of security options to click on.

Even from home, a user should be in the habit of locking the workstation in a remote session. Whether little are hands about, or even paws and claws, there are any number of security and data loss risks to be considered when a remote session is left unattended.

Set GPO to Enforced

Finally, you will set the GPO to be enforced so that no other GP settings can override the ones in the GPO.

1. Right click on the **Windows SBS Client – Default Security Policy** and click on the **Enforced** option. You will notice a gold lock appear on the policy icon. This insures that the policy's settings will be applied to all workstations in the SBSComputers OU and override any upper-level GPO settings.

Figure 14-6 shows some of the impact of the above settings.

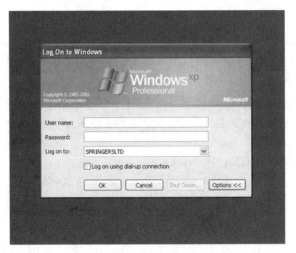

Figure 14-6
Once the policy settings have taken hold, users will now need to type in their full username and password. They will also no longer be able to shut down the system.

Now that the workstations and laptops have been further secured, the next steps are to tighten up things for the user's domain profile.

Group Policy User Security Settings

While it may be possible to completely lockdown users' profiles to the point where only those applications and company-related needs operate on their desktop, doing so tends to reduce a user's productivity!

So, you need to find a balance between security needs and users' needs to customize or tailor their local profiles to their tastes.

There are a few places where we can further configure settings in the user profile.

Screen Saver Management

Consider the following three tactics: limiting the amount of idle time before the workstation automatically locks, choosing the right type of screen saver used on the desktop, and enabling a password to get back into the desktop after the screen saver kicks in.

To implement these tactics, we will need to create a new Group Policy Object such that all SBS domain users will have the same settings applied to them.

1. Open the Windows SBS Native Tools Management console and click the **Continue** button for the UAC prompt.

2. Open the Group Policy Management snap-in by clicking on the plus sign to its right.

3. You will need to navigate to Forest:springersltd.local → Domains → springersltd.local → MyBusiness → Users → **SBSUsers**.

4. Right click on the Windows SBSUsers Policy you created in Chapter 5 and left click on **Edit**.

5. Navigate to User Configuration → Policies → Administrative Templates: Policy Definitions → Control Panel → **Display**.

6. Double click on the **Screen Saver** GP setting.

7. Click the **Enabled** radio button and then click the **Comment** tab.

8. Add the following comment: **08-12-20: Added Screen Saver Enabled.**

9. Click the **Next Setting** button.

10. Add the following comment: **08-12-20: Logon.scr set as default.**

11. Click the **Setting** tab, click the **Enabled** radio button, then type the following screen saver executable name: **Logon.scr.**

12. Click the **Next Setting** button.

13. Click the **Enabled** radio button for the password protect the screen saver setting.

14. Click the **Comment** tab and add the following comment: **08-12-20: Password enabled.**

15. Click the **Next Setting** button.

16. Enter the following comment: **08-12-20: Screen saver timeout set to 45 minutes.**

TIP: The timeout setting you decide on should be in consultation with the company's users. In the case of MPECS Inc.'s accounting firm clients, there are obvious times when users are working on paper-related tasks and calculations that can keep them away from their keyboard for a large chucks of time. We decided on 45 minutes as a reasonable length for the in-between computer times.

17. Click the **Setting** tab, click the **Enabled** radio button, and set the **Seconds** to: **2700**. Figure 14-7 shows this setting enabled.

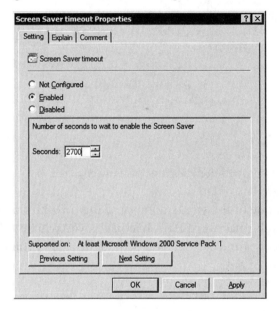

Figure 14-7
  Setting the screen saver timeout to 45 minutes means the workstation will at least lock!

18. Click the **Apply** and **OK** buttons.

19. You can close the GPO editor now.

20. Start → Run → **GPUpdate /force [Enter]**. If you are asked to log off after the update say **No** for now.

All right! You now have the desktop set up so that even if the user forgets to lock it before heading out for lunch or the end of the day, the computer desktop will lock after 45 minutes. The other very important element in this security policy is the locking of the session. By default, no password would be required if the screen saver kicked in. This is an unacceptable policy for any company that wants to keep its data safe from prying eyes.

Figure 14-8 shows you what the policy settings will look like once you have set them up!

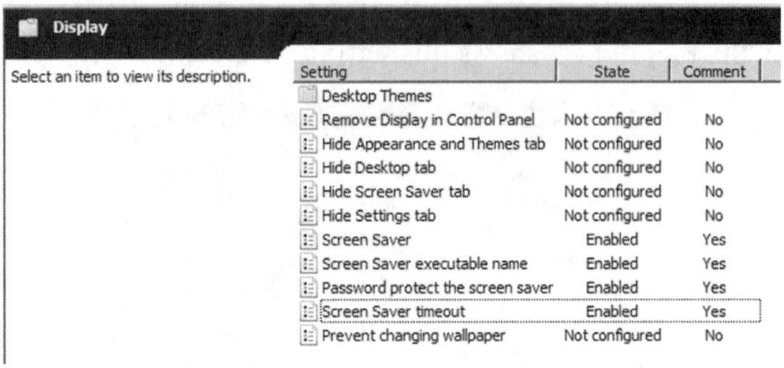

Figure 14-8
The screen saver Group Policy settings are now engaged.

Now, if you go to one of the workstations and log on with our test user account Bob McKenzie and his password **Back bacon eh!**, you will be able to bring up the screen saver properties and see that you will not be able to change the settings, as they have been grayed out.

While it is not so common anymore, screen saver files were once a very prominent way to infect a system with a virus. The .OCX extension that screen savers can use contain active code that would initiate a transaction via the Internet to download and install the virus or Trojan or, in some cases, hold the virus code within the .OCX file itself!

Deploy Windows Defender to XP Pro Clients

Out of the box, Windows XP Professional—in its various service pack levels—does not have Windows Defender or any form of malware protection set up on it. To maintain malware protection on the SBS domain, it is a good idea for you to work with similar products. In this case, Windows Vista has Windows Defender installed and working right out of the box, so to keep things similar across the organization we will deliver Windows Defender to the workstations via Group Policy.

Share Setup

Out of the box, SBS 2008 no longer delivers any applications, updates, service packs, or even browsers via Group Policy or startup scripts. So, we need to set up a share for this purpose.

In the SBS Console:

1. Click on the **Shared Folders** tab.
2. Click on **Add a new shared folder** under the Shared Folders Tasks column.
3. Click the **Browse** button and click on the **L$**.
4. Click the **Make New Folder** button and name the new folder **ClientApps**.
5. Click the **OK** button.
6. Click the **Next** button.
7. Click the **Yes, change NTFS permissions** radio button, then click the **Edit Permissions** button.

TIP: The NTFS and share permissions steps are critical to getting everything to work as it should. Why? Because the security groups Domain Computers and Domain Controllers need to be added to both NTFS and share permissions for any software package to be delivered to the workstations.

8. Click the **Add** button and enter the following groups exactly as written:
   - Domain Computers; Domain Controllers
9. Click the **Check Names** button to verify the names. An underline should appear under them indicating that things are as they should be.
10. Click the **OK** button.
11. Click on **Domain Computers** and give the group **Full Control** permissions. Do the same for **Domain Controllers**.
12. Click on the Users group and give that group **Full Control** too.
13. Click on **Apply** and **OK**.
14. Click the **Next** button in the NTFS Permissions window.

15. Leave the default SMB Share name and click **Next**. It should be ClientApps.

16. Set the following description: **Software Distribution Point.**

17. Click the **Advanced** button, then click **Enable access-based enumeration**.

18. Click **OK** and **Next**.

19. Click the **Users and groups have custom share permissions** and click the **Permissions** button.

20. Set the following permissions for the folder, then click **Apply** and **OK**.

    - Click on and remove the **Everyone** group.

    - Add: **Domain Users**; **Domain Admins**; **Domain Computers**; **Domain Controllers**

    - Give all four groups **Full Control** permissions.

21. Click **Next** for the SMB Permissions window.

22. Click **Next** for the Quota Policy window.

23. Click **Next** for the File Screen Policy window.

24. Click **Next** for the DFS Namespace publishing window.

25. Click the **Create** button after reviewing the settings shown.

26. Click the **Close** button once the share has been set up.

The new share will now be listed in the Shared Folders tab of the SBS Console. Besides Windows Defender for Windows XP Professional, you will also be able to use the ClientApps share to be a part of the Office 2007 installation via Group Policy, which we will write about in our advanced book due out sometime in the second half of 2009!

Download Package

Now, you need to head on over to the Microsoft Download site at http://www. microsoft.com/downloads and do a quick search for the Windows Defender download. Figure 14-9 shows you the results for the search.

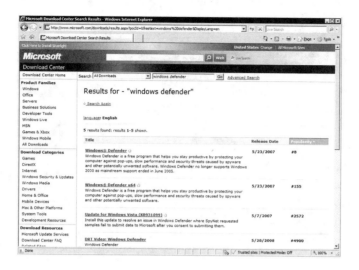

Figure 14-9

When you search for Windows Defender, you will need to validate your Windows install as genuine before the download will be available.

Once you have validated your Windows installation, you can go ahead and download Windows Defender. When you do, the simplest thing to do is to download it directly to the ClientApps share. Assuming a Windows Vista workstation:

1. Click on the **Windows Defender** download link in the search results.

2. Click the **Continue** button where it mentions validation is required.

3. Install the **Windows Genuine Advantage ActiveX** component via the IE Info Bar by clicking on the bar and clicking the **Install ActiveX Control** link.

4. Click on the **Continue** button for the UAC.

5. Click on the **Install** button for the IE Add-on Installer pop-up. The install routine will run, validate Windows, then move onto the download page.

6. Click the **Download** button.

7. Click the **Save** button.

8. Click the **Browse Folders** button on the bottom left corner of the Save As dialogue window if you do not already see the list.

9. If all you see is a list of Favorite Links, then click the **Folders** link at the bottom of the list. Figure 14-10 shows you what this window will look like before you click on the **Folders** link.

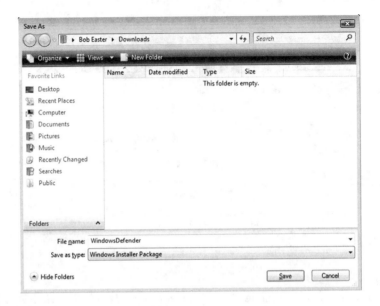

Figure 14-10
When you first use the Save As dialogue, you may not see any folders listed at all.
Click the folders link at the bottom of the Favorite Links list to bring them up.

10. Scroll down the folders list and click on **Network**. If you see a Windows Vista warning about network discovery, click the info bar to turn it on and continue on the UAC prompt.

11. Double click on **SS-SBS** in the list.

12. Double click on the **ClientApps** folder.

13. Click on the **New Folder** button and name the new folder **WindowsDefender**. The Save As dialogue should automatically open the new folder. If not, double click on it to open it.

14. Click the **Save** button.

15. Close the Thank You for Downloading Internet Explorer window.

The software package is now in the right spot for us to set up SBS to deliver it to the XP Professional workstations!

Setup Delivery

We now need to have our trusty Windows SBS Native Tools Management console open to the Group Policy Management console.

From there:

1. Navigate down to Forest:springersltd.local → Domains → springersltd. local → MyBusiness → Computers → **SBSComputers**.

2. Right click on the Windows SBS Client – Windows XP Policy GPO and click on **Edit**.

3. Navigate down to Computer Configuration → Policies → Software Settings → **Software installation**.

4. Right click on **Software installation** and hover over **New** then click on **Package…**

5. When the Open dialogue pops up, type the following in the File name box: **\\ss-sbs\clientapps\windowsdefender** and hit **[Enter]**.

6. Double click on the **WindowsDefender.msi file**.

7. Leave the default **Assigned** radio button and click **OK**.

8. Close the Windows SBS Client – Windows XP Policy GPO editor.

9. Click **Start** → **Run** → **GPUpdate /Force [Enter]**.

Figure 14-11 shows you what the GPO will look like once you have deployed Windows Defender.

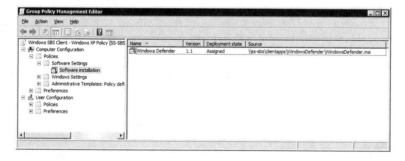

Figure 14-11
Windows Defender will now be installed on all Windows XP Professional workstations on the SBS domain!

We chose the Windows SBS Client – Windows XP Policy GPO because SBS has this GPO set up out of the box to focus only on XP Professional clients. How do we know this? After closing the GPO editor, you can click on the **Windows SBS Client – Windows XP Policy GPO** then click on the **Scope** tab if it did not come up by default.

Have a look at the bottom of the center column where you see WMI Filtering. Notice that a WMI filter is being used to set the limits on which clients can and cannot receive the settings in the GPO. Click the **Open** button to check out the syntax of the WMI filter. There is a lot there, and learning how to configure WMI filters is beyond the scope of this introductory tome!

Once you have deployed, your Windows XP Professional clients will pick up the software the next time the user logs onto the workstation.

One thing to keep an eye on with delivering Windows Defender to XP Pro workstations is shown in Figure 14-12.

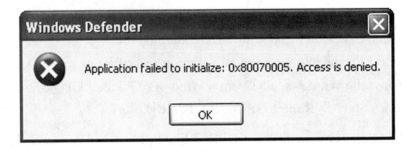

Figure 14-12
Until after Windows Defender takes all of its updates, you will see the Access Denied error. It is safe to ignore this error.

You now have your entire SBS domain protected from malware threats. Pretty neat, eh?

Summary

We have arrived at the end of a "must read" chapter that highlighted, discussed, and allowed you to explore the evergreen and all important advanced SBS security topic. We are sure you join us in agreement that security cannot be overlooked and ongoing attention to security is essential to SBS success. This chapter highlighted and/or discussed the following topics:

- User desktop security and the Acceptable Use Policy
- Setup Group Policy for workstation restrictions
- Setup Group Policy for user screen saver restrictions

- How to deliver Windows Defender to Windows XP Professional workstations via Group Policy

We now journey forth to the final chapter of this book. But before we go, we leave you with a "continuing education security secret." Get active in the SBS community (see Appendix A), follow blogs and postings from folks like Dana Epp, Amy B., and Thomas Shinder, and you'll be "right."

CHAPTER 15

SBS 2008 Premium and SQL Server 2008

This is the final chapter of this book and has a "premium" placed on it as you extend the SBS network to include an additional server and run SQL Server 2008. You could share the view of the authors that this is where SBS 2008 really shines. You have received an additional Windows Server 2008 operating system AND the SQL Server 2008 database with the SBS 2008 Premium edition. This is where business gets serious. This is how we roll!

You will first install Windows Server 2008 on a second machine and then install SQL Server 2008. When you install SBS Server 2008, you will create a database table for SPRINGERS. Simple stuff.

Meet the "Other Server"

Much like meeting the "other woman," meet the mistress of SBS 2008, the other server. For many years, leading SBSers, including SBS MVPs, have called for a second server role to be included in the SBS product line-up. Be careful what you ask for. A second copy of Windows Server 2008 is now included in the SBS 2008 Premium package. To be honest, you need to embrace this as an opportunity to have a second server in an SBS network that is fully endorsed and supported. We believe it also makes the economics of the SBS 2008 Premium product very compelling. Heck, you are getting the second server and the SQL Server 2008 product in the SBS 2008 Premium SKU.

And you know who else is happy with the second server support? Your friendly hardware manufacturers, including Intel, HP, Dell, and others. These firms are delighted about the second server software package for obvious reasons. They sell more servers!

Installing Windows Server 2008

You will now perform a Windows Server 2008 installation in "Full Installation" mode to create a server named SS-TWO for SPRINGERS.

1. Insert the Windows Server 2008 Disc in the server machine.

2. When the Auto-run dialog box appears, click **Install Now**.

3. Follow the instructions on the screen to complete Setup. This is similar to the first part of Chapter 3 with time zone selections, etc.

4. After Setup completes, press **CTRL+ALT+DELETE**, click **Other User**, type **Administrator** with a blank password, and then press **ENTER**. You will be prompted to set a password for the Administrator account.

5. You will then configure the server machine to join the SPRINGERSLTD domain as a member server.

TIP: You are strongly encouraged to complete this homework assignment. At the Microsoft TechNet site, read the article *Installing Windows Server 2008* at this location: http://technet. microsoft.com/en-us/library/cc755116.aspx.

Meet SQL Server 2008

Talk about a career path. Not only can you find very good (and large) texts dedicated to the SQL Server 2008 database application (a database application helps you gather, organize, and report information), but more than one Microsoft Certified Professional (MCP) has made a good living doing the SQL thing. Studying SQL Server introduces you to one of the largest bodies of knowledge and know-how contained within SBS 2003 (Premium Edition).

Given this overwhelming perspective, we've made the decision to keep the SQL Server discussion germane, practical, and relatively brief (and, as always, with the SPRINGERS point of view).

If we were to delve into the depths of SQL Server at the level of the dedicated SQL Server 2008 books, you would not only be here late into the night, but we'd be together for many days and nights forward. We can appreciate your interest in learning more about SQL Server, so bear with us and consider this a sampler.

On the one hand, you can say SQL Server 2008 is a very important part of SBS 2008 Premium. Call it the revenge of the good old "It's the data, stupid" crowd. When you really think about it, the whole reason any of us technology professionals are here is because the underlying data drives business computing. Get it? No? Then consider how we interact with our clients on any given day. The property management firm we serve calls when they can't run payroll, not because some SBS event log entry looks interesting. A true story: The payroll program at the property management firm needed Internet access to obtain updated tax tables and forms before it would cut the paychecks. The solution was to open a port in the firewall to allow the traffic through. But understand that the call we received from the client was much more about the "data" than asking one of the authors to come over and open up a firewall port. So it truly is "the data, stupid!"

On the other hand, we can't deny that, in its natural state, SQL Server is one of the least used components in SBS 2008 (which is indeed unfortunate). Part of that might be attributable to the fact that SQL Server 2008 is shipped only with the premium edition of SBS 2008, not the standard version. One interesting thought along these lines of SQL Server de-emphasis (and don't worry, we get to the "emphasis" argument in the next paragraph) relates to being an actual SQL language programmer. It's highly unlikely that, as an SBSer, you'll program inside of SQL Server (using the SQL programming language) at an SBS site. With respect to building custom applications and other SQL goodies (such as stored procedures), SQL Server is much more at home in development and enterprise environments. It's not our world, but we sure like the business applications that SQL Server developers create!

Now for some good news about SQL Server, starting with the old saying about having nothing to fear but fear itself (with all due respect to United States President Franklin Roosevelt). SQL Server has a very important role that we haven't even discussed yet: supporting business applications. To understand this supporting role, you'll learn the basics of SQL Server in this chapter. Such an understanding will aid greatly in supporting applications that run on top of SQL Server.

To understand SQL Server at an appropriate level for an SBS site, you'll spend the first part of the chapter creating a simple table to manage some information for SPRINGERS via SQL Server (yes, that never-ending SPRINGERS methodology is utilized yet again). Later in the chapter, the focus shifts to advanced SQL Server tidbits (such as publishing data as a Web page) that you need to know about to better manage SQL Server. We do want to manage your expectations: Today is not a day to master SQL Server; today is a day to meet and greet SQL Server.

> **TIP:** In all seriousness, we hope we've managed your expectations to this point about what SQL Server is and isn't. More important, we want to emphasize that in no way, shape, or form is this day anything more than a SQL Server sampler. As stated previously, several thick books dedicated to SQL Server await your reading pleasure.

SQL Server Defined

At its heart, SQL Server is a database, but you likely already knew that from the introductory discussion. Did you know, however, that it differs from other databases you might have worked with in the past, in that SQL Server is a client/server database? Perhaps you've worked with other databases that are relational databases (similar to SQL Server), but don't exploit the power of the network's server (the SBS server machine on an SBS network). Other databases are flat files and more akin to a spreadsheet.

Features and Functionality

On the SBS server machine, the data resides not only in tables, but also is manipulated by the SQL Server engine. These SQL Server server-side capabilities include the following functional areas:

- Analysis Services. SQL Server 2008 helps enable organizations to build comprehensive, enterprise-scale analytic solutions that deliver actionable insights through familiar tools.

- Data Mining. SQL Server 2008 empowers informed decisions with predictive analysis through complete and intuitive data mining, which is seamlessly integrated throughout the Microsoft BI platform and extensible into any application.

- High Availability—Always On. SQL Server 2008's Always On Technologies provides a full range of options to minimize downtime and maintain appropriate levels of application availability.

- Integration Services. SQL Server 2008 provides a scalable enterprise data integration platform with exceptional ETL and integration capabilities, enabling organizations to more easily manage data from a wide array of data sources.

- Manageability. Microsoft SQL Server provides a policy-based system for managing one or more instances of SQL Server, along with tools for performance monitoring, troubleshooting, and tuning that enable administrators to more efficiently manage their databases and SQL Server instances.

- Performance and Scalability. SQL Server 2008 provides a comprehensive data platform and includes technologies to scale-up individual servers and scale-out very large databases, along with tools to optimize performance.

- Programmability. Discover how SQL Server 2008 enables developers to build powerful, next-generation, database applications with the .NET Framework and Visual Studio Team System.

- Reporting Services. Learn how SQL Server 2008 Reporting Services provides a complete server-based platform designed to support a wide variety of reporting needs to deliver relevant information where needed across the entire enterprise.

- Security. Microsoft SQL Server 2008 offers security feature enhancements that help provide effective management of security feature configuration, strong authentication and access control, powerful encryption and key management capabilities, and enhanced auditing.

- Spatial Data. SQL Server 2008 delivers comprehensive spatial support that enables organizations to seamlessly consume, use, and extend location-based data through spatial-enabled applications, ultimately helping end users make better decisions.

Services and Databases

The main server-side services for SQL Server are found in the Service MMC. There are over a half-dozen services related to the operations of SQL Server 2008. This is where some of your early troubleshooting efforts will occur when SQL server 2008 fails to start properly.

The following SQL Server system databases are automatically constructed when SBS 2003 installs SQL Server 2000:

- Master. This is the mother of all tables in SQL Server. Lose it (with no back up) and you'll die. Simply stated, it controls SQL Server operations completely (including user databases, user accounts, environmental variables, system error message, and so on). It is critical that you back up this database on a regular basis.

- Model. A template provides basic information used when you create new databases for your own use. This is akin to the metainformation you entered when you installed SBS 2003 (company name, address, fax, and telephone numbers) that reappears each time you add a user, via one of the SBS consoles, to your SBS network. You might recall that meta-information is information that is used globally by the computer system, not just in one place.

- Msdb. The SQLServerAgent uses this for scheduling and job history.

- Tempdb. This is another database that's very important to the operation of SQL Server. It's a temporary storage area used by SQL Server for working storage. This is akin to the paging file used by Windows 2000 Server (the underlying operating system in SBS).

Note that Northwind and Pubs have been removed in the SBS 2008 time frame.

Installing SQL Server 2008

Complete the SQL Server 2008 with the following procedure.

1. On the server machine SS-TWO, log in as **JonathanPaul** with the password **PASSWORD**.

2. Insert the SQL Server 2008 Disc and the autorun.exe program will execute. Approve the UAE message if it is displayed.

3. If you receive the Microsoft SQL Server 2008 Setup dialog box regarding the Microsoft .NET Framework and an updated Windows Installer, click **OK**. A standard installation, not central to the SQL Server 2008 setup experience, occurs.

4. The SQL Server Installation Center will appear. Select **Installation** followed by **New SQL Server stand-alone installation or add features to an existing installation**.

5. You will witness the Setup Support Rules page. Click **OK** when the operations are completed.

6. On the Product Key page, enter your 25-character product key in the **Enter the product key** field and click **Next**.

7. On the License Terms page, select **I accept the license terms** and click **Next**.

8. On the Setup Support Files page, click **Install**.

9. Click **Next** when the operations are completed.

10. On the Feature Selection page, under Instance Features, select **Database Engine Services** and **Full-text Search**. Under Shared Features, select **Management Tools – Basic** and **Manage Tools – Complete**. Click **Next**.

11. Accept the default selections on the Instance Configuration and click **Next**.

12. Click **Next** on Disk Space Requirements.

13. On the Server Configuration page, on the Service Accounts tab, select **NT AUTHORITY\SYSTEM** for the SQL Server Agent and SQL Server Database Engine services. Click **Next**.

14. On the Database Engine Configuration page, select **Add Current User** and click **Next**. This will add JonathanPaul as the SQL administrator because that is the name you are logged on as currently.

15. Click **Next** on the Error and Usage Reporting page.

16. Click **Next** on the Installation Rules page.

17. Click **Install** on the Ready to Install page.

18. When the installation completes on the Installation Progress page and you have success, click **Next**.

19. On the Complete page, click **Close**.

Using SQL Server 2008

In this section, you will create a SQL Server 2008 database for SPRINGERS, then a tracking table and then add data.

Create a Database

You will now create a database in SQL Server 2008 for SPRINGERS.

1. Click **Start, All Programs, Microsoft SQL Server 2008,** then select **SQL Server Management Studio**.
2. Click **Connect** on the Connect To Server dialog box.
3. Right click **Databases** under the Object Explorer column and select **New Database** from the context menu.
4. The New Database page appears. Type **SSLDOG** in the **Database** name field. Click **Add**.
5. Click **OK**.

Create a Table

You will now create the tracking table.

1. Expand **SSLDOG** under Databases and right click **Tables**.
2. Select **New Table** from the context menu. The table will automatically be named.
3. Complete the column names based on the data in Table 15-1. This is a data dictionary that had the input for the SSL database.
4. Click **File, Save Table_1** and name the table **Tracking** in the Enter a name for the table field in the Choose Name dialog box. Click **OK**. Your table should look similar to Figure 15-1 once complete with the information in Table 15-1.

Notes

Table 15-1

SPRINGERS Data Dictionary

Item (Column Name)	Description
SSLDOG	Database name
Tracking	Table name for tracking SPRINGERS
DogName	Name of dog (column name, Data Type = char, Length = 30)
ShowName	Long name of dog for show purposes (column name, Data Type = char, Length = 50)
FatherDN	Father dog's name (column name, Data Type = char, Length = 30)
MotherDN	Mother dog's name (column name, Data Type = char, Length = 30)
DDOB	Dog's date of birth (column name, Data Type = date, Length = automatic)
AKCNum	American Kennel Club (AKC) registration number (column name, Data Type = char, Length = 15)

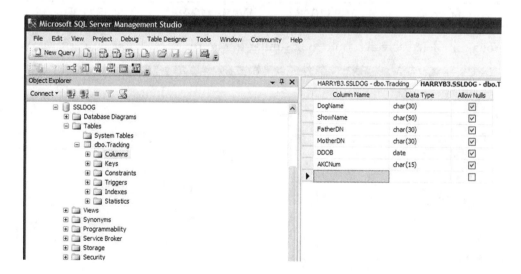

Figure 15-1

This is a SQL Server database table to track SPRINGERS information.

Add Data

You will now add data to the Tracking table.

1. Right click **dbo.Tracking** under Tables under SSLDOG, Databases in the Object Explorer column.

2. Select **Edit Top 200 Rows** in the context menu. A data-entry type screen appears in the center.

3. Complete the table rows with the information shown in Table 15-2.

Table 15-2
SSLDOG Data

Item	Dog1	Dog2	Dog3
DogName	Astro	Brisker	Jaeger
ShowName	Sir Astro Moonbeam	Sir David Brisker	Sir Jaeger Matthew
FatherDN	Pepper2	Pepper	Pepper
MotherDN	Maria2	Maria	Maria
DDOB	6-15-2004	8-15-1993	8-15-1993
AKCNum	WA98110A	WA98119A	WA98119B

Your completed screen should look similar to Figure 15-2.

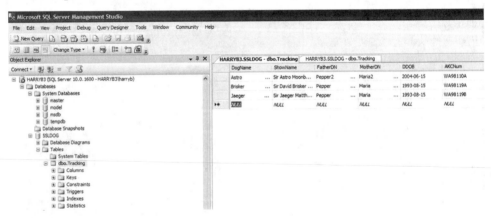

Figure 15-2
Congratulations! You have created a SQL Server 2008-based database and table and entered data.

Query the Data

You will now query the database.

1. Click **New Query** on the Standard toolbar in the Microsoft SQL Server Management Studio application.

2. Type **select * from tracking** in the center screen.

3. Click **Execute** on the SQL Editor toolbar. The results should appear similar to Figure 15-3.

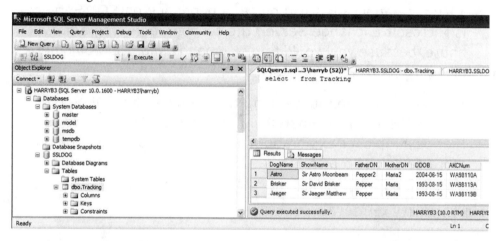

Figure 15-3
More success. You have actually used the database!

Line-of-Business Applications

While directly interacting with SQL Server 2008 is interesting and provides you with a richer SBS 2008 experience base, the real purpose for having this powerful relational database is really here, in our humble opinion, to support line-of-business applications.

There are at least four conversations you can have about line-of-business applications.

Microsoft Dynamics

Microsoft's venture into the land of business applications has largely been via mergers and acquisitions (M&A) including the purchase of Navision, Great Plains, and others. As they say, M&A is a quick way to get into a line of work. In this case, it allowed Microsoft to have its Dynamics applications in CRM, ERP, and accounting on the market very quickly. These applications have a dependency on SQL Server.

> **TIP:** One application without a dependency on SQL Server is Microsoft Exchange Server, the collaboration program. Go figure, because you would think Exchange and SQL would get along like peas and carrots.
>
> Another application just asking to play nice with SQL Server 2008 is the Windows SharePoint Services application. We see that as a topic for exploration in our next SBS 2008 book on more advanced topics.

Third-Party General

Simply "Google" terms related to important real-world business applications and you will make a startling discovery. Many applications in the real world use SQL Server as the background engine. Our research, using the terms "line-of-business applications sql server" revealed interesting third-party general business solutions in the document management area and more.

Third-Party Narrow Vertical Markets

Something everyone who has ever been a technology consultant knows is that every customer (past a certain size) in a specific industry will have a narrow vertical market application that must be supported. Both authors have seen this in the medical field (HIPPA compliance in the US) and manufacturing. There are hundreds of niche business applications, many of which are written to utilize SQL Server.

Custom

More than one techie has made a great living programming custom business applications using a database framework. We would like to wager a bet with you right here, right now. It is our belief that, at least once in your career as a techie, you will encounter a customer business program written for a specific customer. What say you?

Summary

This chapter focused on the SBS 2008 Premium edition and featured the second server running Windows Server 2008 and the SQL Server 2008 product. You enjoyed the following topics:

- We defined the SBS 2008 Premium SKU containing Windows Server 2008 and SQL Server 2008.

- You installed Windows Server 2008 on a second server and attached this second server machine to the SPRINGERSLTD domain.

- You learned about and defined SQL Server 2008 as a powerful client/server relational database to use with SBS 2008 Premium.

- We discussed SQL Server 2008 specific features, functionality, services, and native databases.

- You installed SQL Server 2008 on the second server machine.

- You created a database for SPRINGERS called SSLDOG, created a table, and populated the table with "dog data."

- You ran a query against the SSLDOG database.

- We discussed the types of line-of-business applications that depend on SQL Server in the real world.

This is the end of the book. Go forth and save the world with SBS 2008. The world can use your assistance right now. Thank you for reading!

Appendix A
Small Business Server 2008 Resources

Appendix B
Book Configurations

Index

Appendix A

Small Business Server 2008 Resources

This appendix is intended to provide you resources that will assist your SBS 2008 journey and participate in the community. Numerous passages in the book referred you to this, Appendix A, to find more information. You are encouraged to monitor the SMB Nation site for updated SBS 2008 resources at www.smbnation.com.

SBS Blogs

- Philip Elder: http://blog.mpecsinc.ca
- Harry Brelsford: http://blog.smbdude.com
- Susan Bradley: http://www.sbsdiva.com
- The Official SBS blog: http://blogs.technet.com/sbs
- Sean Daniel's site (MS SBS development team member; great list of SBs resources here): http://sbs.seandaniel.com/
- Windows Small Business Server and Essential Business Server documentation: http://blogs.msdn.com/sbsdocsteam
- Spanish SBS site: http://blogs.technet.com/sbs_esp

- Microsoft SMB Community Blog: http://blogs.msdn.com/mssmallbiz
- Microsoft TS2 blogs: http://ts2blogs.com/blogs
- SBS MVP blogs: http://www.msmvps.com
- Eriq Oliver Neale: http://simultaneouspancakes.com/Lessons
- Dana Epp: http://silverstr.ufies.org/blog
- Kevin Beares: http://blogs.technet.com/kevin_beares
- Charlie Anthe: http://blogs.msdn.com/canthe

TIP: Create your own blog and join the SBS community.

SBS Websites

- The SMB Nation site: http://www.smbnation.com (publications, events, SBS exam forums)
- Microsoft SMB Channel Community: http://www.mssmallbiz.com/
- Andy Goodman: http://www.sbs-rocks.com
- M&M's: http://www.smallbizserver.net
- Wayne Small: http://www.sbsfaq.com
- Jeff Middleton: http://www.sbsmigration.com
- Microsoft site: http://www.microsoft.com/sbs
- Daniel Petri: http://tinyurl.com/qq2l3
- Legacy SBS link site: http://www.sbslinks.com/

SBS Partner Sites

- Microsoft Partner Program: http://www.microsoft.com/partner
- Microsoft Small Business Specialist Community: http://www.sbscracing.com

SBS-related sites

- Microsoft TS2 events (includes system builder events, customer events, road shows and Microsoft Across America) http://www.ts2seminars.com/default.aspx

SBS User Groups and Partner Groups

- Here is the worldwide list of SBS user groups: http://www.sbsgroups.com/default.aspx

TIP: Be sure to search via Google and Live on keywords such "Small Business Server" and "SBS" to name two common searches. You can also subscribe to Google alerts to be advised when SBS-related news occurs.

Appendix Z

Tips, Tricks, Diagrams, and Grids

This particular appendix will give you an opportunity to see more detail in some of the key figures in our book. Things like the network diagrams and user grids are critical to putting together the SPRINGERS SBS setup.

SBS 2008 Direct Connect URLs

As with the previous version of SBS, you can connect to the desired resource directly rather than taking the extra step to log onto the Remote Web Workplace first.

Here is the list:

- Outlook Web Access: **https://remote.springersltd.com/owa**
    - o You will be greeted by the Outlook Web Access page to logon.
- Companyweb Internal Web site: **https://remote.springersltd.com:987**
    - o You will be prompted for your username and password just as you would if clicking through to the site via the Remote Web Workplace.
- Direct Desktop via SBS TS Gateway:

- o Desktop: **SS-RemoteDesktp**
- o Credentials: **SpringersLtd\BobEaster**
- o Advanced Tab TS Gateway Setting: **remote.springersltd.com**
- o Advanced Tab TS Gateway Setting: **Use my TS Gateway credentials for the remote computer** enabled.

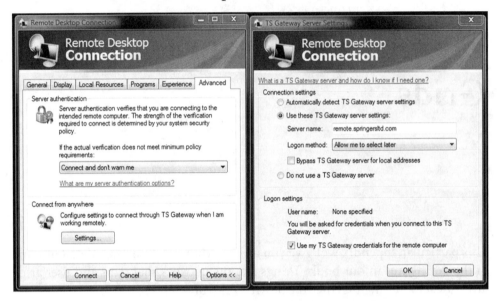

Figure Z-1
The Remote Desktop Client settings for the SBS TS Gateway.

As you can see by the above list, it is quite possible for mobile workers to totally bypass the Remote Web Workplace portal if they only need to use one Internet facing service such as the Companyweb Internal Web site.

Philip's Lab Setup

In my case, I set aside some space on the workbench at MPECS Inc. for the lab setup. Since I was looking at getting an SBS production ready lab environment together based on the SPRINGERS methodology, I wanted to make sure that everything was as close to "real life" as possible.

The Server Setup

Because of that, I had a server put together that would be more than powerful enough for 10 real users. The server was configured as follows:

- Intel 3000 Series Xeon S3000AHLX Server Board
- Intel 3070 Dual Core Xeon CPU clocked at 2.66GHz.
- 8GB Kingston ECC ValueRAM (4x 2GB)
- Intel SRCSASRB SAS/SATA PCI-E 4x RAID Controller
- 4x 320GB Seagate Enterprise Series SATA Hard Drives in RAID 1+0
- Intel SC5299DP Server Chassis Series
- 16x DVD-RW

The server configuration has been handling our SPRINGERS setup like a champion. No hiccups or hardware related problems have happened at all.

The Workstation Setup

Since SPRINGERS has three Windows Vista workstations and eight Windows XP Professional workstations I decided to use three systems dedicated to serving the SPRINGERS workstations as virtual machines.

The resource requirements for Windows Vista are quite a bit higher than Windows XP Professional. In a virtualized environment, you can get away with setting 512MB of RAM to the XP virtual machine (VM), while Windows Vista will run smoother with at least 1GB of RAM.

The three Windows Vista VMs ran on their own lab system. However, that system could have handled at least two more Vista VMs on it.

I split the Windows XP Professional VMs in two groups of four. The whole SPRINGERS environment can run on less hardware if need be, but one of the things I would be testing for is both load on the server and the workstations by having some friends log on through the Remote Web Workplace and run them through a series of tasks. This experience would help facilitate a better understanding of what will work in a real world SBS 2008 setup for 10 clients or more. The desktop OS VMs were served on the following setup:

- Intel DQ35JOE Executive Series Motherboard with vPro (AMT remote management).
- Intel Q6600 2.4GHz Core 2 Quad CPU or Intel Q9450 2.66GHz Core 2 Quad CPU.
- 8GB 800MHz DDR2 non-ECC Kingston ValueRAM.
- 2x 320GB Seagate Enterprise Storage SATA hard drives in RAID 1.
- Antec Minuet 350 for space savings.
- D-Link 4 Port USB KVM
- Windows Vista Ultimate x64 Edition (Retail)
- Virtual PC 2007 SP1 x64 Edition

An external USB DVD-RW drive was used whenever there was a need for it as the systems were not set up with an internal optical drive.

SPRINGERS User and Workstation Excel Spreadsheet

Figure Z-2

SPRINGERS user and workstation Excel spreadsheet.

	A	B	C	D	E	F	G
1	First Name	Last Name	Username	Password	User Role	E-mail Address	PC Name
2	Norm	Hasborn	NormHasborn	Sunny days!	User with Admin Links	NormH@springersltd.com	SS-President
3	Barry	McKechnie	BarryMcKechnie	Numbers fun?	User	BarryM@springersltd.com	SS-Accounting
4	Melinda	Overlaking	MelindaOverlaking	Working the desk.	User	MelindaO@springersltd.com	SS-OfficeAdmin
5	Linda	Briggs	LindaBriggs	Summer is here!	User	LindaB@springersltd.com	SS-Registration
6	Bob	Bountiful	BobBountiful	Lots of dogs!	User	BobB@springersltd.com	SS-Breeding
7	Tom	Benkert	TomBenkert	Time for fun.	User	TomB@springersltd.com	SS-Schedules
8	Norm	Hasborn Jr.	NormHasbornJr	Managing numbers.	User	NormHJr@springersltd.com	SS-Sales
9	David	Halberson	DavidHalberson	Making them count.	User	DavidH@springersltd.com	SS-Marketing
10	Elvis	Haskins	ElvisHaskins	Looking for genes!	User	ElvisH@springersltd.com	SS-Genealogy
11	Bob	Easter	BobEaster	Lots to eat!	User with Admin Links	BobE@springersltd.com	SS-CareFeeding

Sample SPRINGERS Virtual Machine Setup Grid

Figure Z-3
Sample SPRINGERS Virtual Machine setup grid.

Philip - Lab Map to User and Workstation Grid.xlsx

	A First Name	B Last Name	C Username	D Password	E Pwd Change Date	F PC Name	G Lab PC	H VM Name
1	First Name	Last Name	Username	Password	Pwd Change Date	PC Name	Lab PC	VM Name
2	Norm	Hasborn	NormHasborn	Sunny days!		SS-President	Vistax64-Lab02	NormHasborn-Vista01
3	Barry	McKechnie	BarryMcKechnie	Numbers fun?		SS-Accounting	Vistax64-Lab05	BarryMcK-XP01
4	Melinda	Overlaking	MelindaOverlaking	Working the desk.		SS-OfficeAdmin	Vistax64-Lab02	OfficeAdmin-VistaBiz
5	Linda	Briggs	LindaBriggs	Summer is here!		SS-Registration	Vistax64-Lab05	LindaBrigs-XP07
6	Bob	Bountiful	BobBountiful	Lots of dogs!		SS-Breeding	Vistax64-Lab05	BobBountiful-XP08
7	Tom	Benkert	TomBenkert	Time for fun.		SS-Schedules	Vistax64-Lab02	TomBenkert-XP03
8	Norm	Hasborn Jr.	NormHasbornJr	Managing numbers.		SS-Sales	Vistax64-Lab02	NormHJr-XP04
9	David	Halberson	DavidHalberson	Making them count.		SS-Marketing	Vistax64-Lab02	DavidHalberson-XP05
10	Elvis	Haskins	ElvisHaskins	Looking for genes!		SS-Genealogy	Vistax64-Lab02	ElvisHaskins-XP06
11	Bob	Easter	BobEaster	Lots to eat?	October 17, 2008	SS-CareFeeding	Vistax64-Lab05	BobEaster-XP02

SPRINGERS Summary Network Report

Figure Z-4

Sample SPRINGERS Summary Network Report.

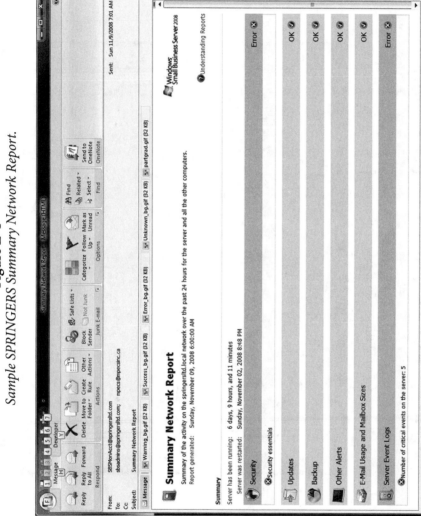

SPRINGERS Detailed Network Report

Figure Z-5

Sample SPRINGERS Detailed Network Report

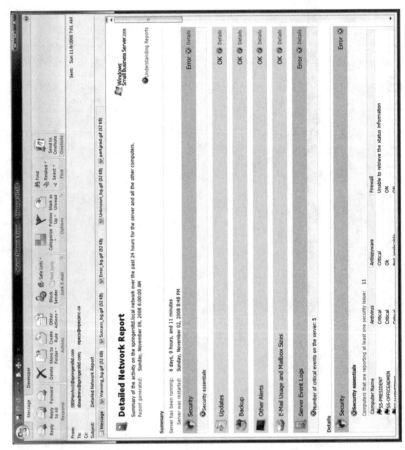

Springer Spaniels' Remote Web Workplace Portal

Figure Z-6

The new Remote Web Workplace portal page.

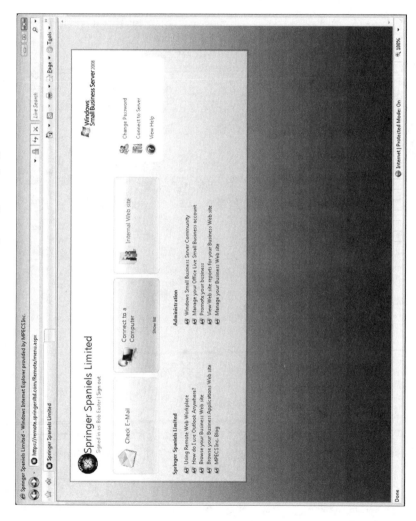

Index

A

B

G

H

S

V

Vembu, 3-12, 12-12
vCard (Outlook), 7-38
Vembu, 12-12
video card, 3-8, 7-38
Virtual Desktop, 1-39
virtualization rights, 3-30
Virtual Machine (VM), 1-34, 5-2
Virtual Memory, 5-14
Virtual Server, 5-2
virus
    desktop security, 14-3
    detection, 2-35
    scanning, 2-27
    screen saver, 14-16
Visio, 2-7, 12-23
Vista. *See also* Windows Vista
    fax service, 10-21 to 10-22
    Vista Gadget, 5-66, 11-12
Visual Studio Team System, 15-5
VPN (virtual private network) connection and access permissions, 4-11, 4-24, 9-31 to 9-34, 9-35

W

wall jacks, 2-8, 2-9
WatchGuard, 6-1, 6-11 to 6-15, 6-25
Web browser, 2-25, 5-54 to 5-55, 14-3
Webinars, 12-20
Web page(s), 8-31
    connection, 5-59
    development, 2-27
Web site, default, 110
Web Sites tab, 4-24, 4-27 to 4-29
Websmart features, 2-8
Welcome to Windows Small Business Server Web page, 5-58
WESTMATE, 1-35
wiki, 8-2, 8-11 to 8-12, 8-32, 12-23
WIM (Windows Imaging), 3-39
WiMAX urban wireless networks, 1-23
Windows
    drivers, 4-1
    Microsoft support for operating systems, 1-34
    networking environment, 2-26
    operating systems, 1-34, 3-10, 14-3
    setup screen, 3-27 to 3-28